McEWAN, Peter J. M., ed. Twentieth-century Africa. Oxford, 1968. 517p map tab bibl (Readings in African History) 68-105176. 8.00

CHOICE   SEPT. '69

History, Geography & Travel

Africa

The third volume of the series edited by McEwan (*Nineteenth-century Africa*, CHOICE, Apr. 1969, and, with Sutcliffe, *Modern Africa*, CHOICE, June 1966). In all there are 50 contributions, mostly from American and British scholars, but 11 are by white South Africans, three by Africans (if one includes President Nasser as an African), and three by French authors in translation. McEwan is the director of the family research unit at the Harvard Medical School and was previously with the Rhodes-Livingstone Institute. It is to be noted that a preponderance of the contributors are political scientists rather than historians, *pace* the title. All articles included were previously published in journals or symposia, such as *Historians in Tropical Africa*. All of the journals and books the excerpts are taken from should be readily available in the larger university and college libraries, but this is nevertheless a useful compilation for teaching at both the undergraduate and the graduate levels as the readings are well selected and representative of modern scholarship. A few of the sources of the

Continued

McEWAN

CHOICE   SEPT. '69

History, Geography & Travel

Africa

articles are not adequately identified and a more extensive bibliography would be welcome. Clear maps; useful chronological table; comprehensive index.

Dr McEwan is the author (with R. B. Sutcliffe) of *The Study of Africa* (Methuen). He is a former Research Fellow of the Rhodes-Livingstone Institute in Zambia, and Visiting Professor of African Studies at the State University of New York. He is now Director of the Family Research Unit at Harvard Medical School.

Readings in African History
Edited by P. J. M. McEwan

AFRICA FROM EARLY TIMES TO 1800
NINETEENTH-CENTURY AFRICA
TWENTIETH-CENTURY AFRICA

TWENTIETH-CENTURY AFRICA

EDITED BY
P. J. M. McEWAN

LONDON
OXFORD UNIVERSITY PRESS 1968
IBADAN NAIROBI

Oxford University Press, Ely House, London W.1

GLASGOW NEW YORK TORONTO MELBOURNE WELLINGTON
CAPE TOWN SALISBURY IBADAN NAIROBI LUSAKA ADDIS ABABA
BOMBAY CALCUTTA MADRAS KARACHI LAHORE DACCA
KUALA LUMPUR HONG KONG TOKYO

© in Preface, Introduction, Maps, Select Bibliography,
Chronological Table and Index, Oxford University Press 1968

Maps drawn by Regmarad

PRINTED IN GREAT BRITAIN BY
THE CAMELOT PRESS LTD, LONDON AND SOUTHAMPTON

Preface to
Readings in African History

FOR the past eighty years the continent of Africa has been steadily increasing its proportion of the limelight in world affairs. There have also occurred, during the same period, a general educational awakening and a dramatic refinement of the techniques available for the advancement of knowledge.

The coincidence of these developments has led to African studies, social, political and economic, past as well as present, becoming a recognized part of a balanced university curriculum.

The history of Africa holds a special position as a subject worthy of study. In the first place, it is that part of man's heritage which most strongly captures the interest of modern African men and women. The long-run contours of African history are rich in content and often revealing in their illumination of the present.

African history has, indeed, the same claims to be studied as British history or American history, and just as its role in Africa is much the same as the role of British history in British schools and universities, or American history in American schools and colleges, so is its role in these countries similar to that which the study of British and American history has to play in Africa.

But, in addition to the intrinsic importance of the subject, it has a further significance within Africa itself. It provides a context of man's development into which many of the problems and aspirations of the present can be meaningfully placed, thus stimulating a broader sense of tradition and a deeper pride of achievement which lend natural and legitimate support to the growth of nationhood.

In the second place, the rapid growth of African influence and importance in the world, together with previous neglect of its history, give to the study unusual significance. For too long, and with increasing incongruity, nations have studied and taught only the history of their own people. As the world shrinks and the extent of national inter-dependence expands, our knowledge of other civilizations and other continents becomes commensurately more necessary.

There is a third, more technical, reason for the importance of African history. This is the direct relevance to it of other disciplines, principally archaeology, ethnography and comparative linguistics, and the further problems raised by oral tradition. The nature of their respective associations, and the issues that each separately raises, brings the student of history in continuous contact with these other studies, making him more responsive to their application and value.

African historians have tended to fall into two groups. There are those who seek to identify common factors in disparate regions of space and differing periods of time, and who, perhaps mindful also of the practical need for comprehensive texts, write in unifying and comparative terms of tropical Africa as a whole. There are others who prefer to narrow the focus so that it embraces one selected area or a single nation. The former provide the condensation necessary for comparative study and for a more complete understanding of those developments, such as partition, which have been transcontinental in character and origin. The latter, on the other hand, provide the detail and depth necessary for detailed understanding. As time goes by and our knowledge extends so may the more intensive studies increasingly outnumber the continental histories. For the present, however, there is room for both.

In addition, there are a number of historians who concentrate still more intensively, writing only in learned journals.

Where, in this scheme of things, does the present work stand? The aims of the three volumes are several. First, their essential aim is to provide the student of African history with a comprehensive but detailed understanding, through writings by recognized authorities, of the major events and developments in their subject. Whether the readings are studied on their own or in conjunction with one of the several general histories now available, the reader will have at his disposal the most significant events and movements as recorded and interpreted by leading historians.

A second aim, and a corollary to the first, is to provide a necessary adjunct to general history texts. It is impossible to deal adequately with even the most influential sequences of events in Africa's past within the confines of a single volume. It is difficult to do so even in a regional history. The present volumes will allow the student to undertake a closer examination of the more important of these developments. It also offers a useful corrective against the bias of a single author when dealing with such discursive material as, for example, partition, or the rise of nationalism, making direct comparison possible between different points of view.

A third important objective has been to bring together definitive writings which are not generally available, either because of inadequate library facilities or because of their original appearance in a comparatively obscure publication, perhaps in a language other than English.

A book of readings is inevitably susceptible to the sins of omission and commission. Selections always invite criticism not only for the subjects chosen but for the writings chosen to cover them. The present work can be no exception. In determining what to include, the following criteria have been employed. With regard to design, three volumes were decided on as being the least possible number to allow adequate treatment of the major themes. In order to follow the flow of history and to draw appropriate comparisons, with due reference to regional and temporal interrelations, each volume deals with a different period of time. Volume I takes the reader to the end of the eighteenth century, Volume II is concerned with the nineteenth century, and Volume III with the twentieth century. Thus, while early times are by no means neglected, there is an emphasis on the history of the last two hundred years.

Within each volume the material is presented in sections. These follow the same geographical pattern throughout, in the order: West Africa, North Africa, Egypt, Ethiopia, East Africa, southern Africa. In the sections themselves, the readings are presented in the order approximating most closely to the connexion, logical and temporal, between the material they discuss. Thus, within a framework based on chronology, the readings are organized in accordance with geography as well as with time. In this way, it is hoped that convenient reference will be facilitated without sacrificing the occasional need for ignoring spatial boundaries in the interest of historical accuracy.

There are, however, a number of issues which do not fit neatly into any conventional category of either time or space. These include the spread and influence of the two great religious movements Islam and Christianity, partition, and the rise of nationalism and pan-Africanism. In accordance with their closest logical affinity, treatment of the religious questions is included in Volume I, partition in Volume II, and nationalism and pan-Africanism in Volume III. In each case, the subject is treated as a whole in its own specific section with the same geographical order of presentation, wherever this is appropriate.

There is a further subject amenable to study only in a single, continent-wide context. This is the study of pre-history, which comprises the opening section in Volume I.

As will have been observed from the geographical order of presentation, two countries have been singled out for specific reference, Egypt and Ethiopia. The long history of Egypt cannot, of course, be encompassed in a work of this nature and, in any case, until the nineteenth century Egypt was closer in her development to Asia Minor than to Africa. Since, however, our concern is with the whole continent of Africa and because the influence of Egypt had been felt to the south and west for many centuries, its inclusion was demanded. In order to account for Egypt's peculiar role in African affairs, as a nation at the crossroads of three continents, its individual role has been accordingly recognized in the text.

Ethiopia has been singled out in the same manner on account of her long history of independence and for the long periods of her isolation from outside influences. Where her development has been associated with other forces, as has occurred increasingly since the early part of the nineteenth century, these factors are discussed in the sections dealing with Ethiopia.

An examination of the section headings will indicate a slight bias towards political history and, in Volume III, towards political science. Although every effort has been made to give full attention to economic, religious and social developments, it is perhaps inevitable that the main emphasis has been on political change, on the fluctuating powers of government and on conflict. Detailed comparative studies of African economic and social history are still awaited.

There is another bias which should be mentioned. Movements and events that are discussed in the following pages have been chosen not only on account of their intrinsic importance but also because, in the majority of cases, they figure in one or more of the commoner examinations in the subject.

In spite of this consideration, it must not be thought that the readings have been stream-lined to fit probable examination questions. This would be a task not only impossible but contrary to our intention of providing a comprehensive selection. Thus, for example, considerable space has been given in the third volume to the question of *apartheid*. This subject, which seldom appears in any examination, has been analysed in detail because of its importance for the whole continent, not only as national policy but as a rallying point for international opposition.

Turning from design to detailed content, it was only when the choice seemed to lie equally between two or more readings that criteria other than pure merit were introduced. Length and accessibility were then considered, the less readily accessible and the more concise being preferred. Articles were generally more suitable than extracts from books, especially if the book had just been published and was in most libraries. Articles, apart from being less widely known and more difficult to find, have the advantages of being self-contained, of paying greater attention to the general historical context of their subject matter, and of bringing a sharper focus to bear on a narrower front—all important factors for our purpose. At the same time, where there has seemed no adequate alternative, rather than have no reference to an important question, an extract has occasionally been chosen from a book, however recent, and, if unavoidable, however derivative.

There are a number of works which, although strongly criticized in their main thesis, nevertheless contain, often as an introductory chapter, a summary of an important sequence of events which in accurate conciseness is not to be found elsewhere. Such books present a problem: should the extract be included, at the risk of inviting ready criticism, or should general suspicion be allowed to drown incidental quality? In a limited number of cases, which it would be invidious to identify, where the alternative has been less than satisfactory, the editor has therefore included what has seemed to him a sound extract from an otherwise doubtful source.

One final category of choice should be mentioned. In three cases, readings have been included because of their own historic quality as classical statements on important issues, in spite of more modern treatments of the same topic. These are Professor Schapera's paper on 'Economic changes in African urban life', first published in Volume I of *Africa* (1938), Dr Gann's paper on 'The significance and suppression of the slave trade in British Central Africa', which first appeared in the *Journal of the Rhodes-Livingstone Institute* (1954), and an extract from Sir Winston Churchill's *The River War*, first published in 1899. In their contrasting ways, each is a model of its kind.

Finally, a word about interpretation. History, once it passes beyond being a mere chronicle of events, becomes inevitably interpretative. Interpretation implies selection. The historian of an epoch or a movement or a personality selects his data and reaches a general conclusion. In many cases, more numerous than is sometimes appreciated, the conclusion is reached prior to the selection. The result may be accepted at once, in which event it will pass into the realm of historic fashion, or it may evoke alternative, perhaps contradictory, interpretations, firing a general dispute. Occasionally, when it is openly polemical or intentionally provoking, the bias is transparent and may therefore be easily countered. But it more often happens that the selectivity is hidden and the assumptions and personal prejudices of the historian are occluded by an aura of objectivity, and an apparently scrupulous concern with accuracy. Whether this obscuring is conscious or otherwise makes no difference to its effect, which is that the unprepared observer accepts as proven what is only hypothesis, and is left in ignorance of the existence of any solid grounds for an alternative explanation. It is true, of course, that certain subjects in history, as in other things, are more emotive than others. Subjects also vary in their degree of certitude. It is these two factors, emotion and doubt, which most often give rise to the hidden premiss and an un-hinted selectivity. Thus, to mention just two examples from the study of African history, one has to be particularly cautious when considering colonialism (particularly in southern Africa), and the factors leading to partition.

In the first (emotive) case, fashions have changed, and to be implicitly anti-colonial is to be as modish as was the almost unconditional praise of the colonist by white historians in the 1900s. Thus we find writers suppressing data that reflects badly on the colonized while concentrating on evidence that reflects adversely on the colonizer.

This is not intended as a general indictment of historians but as a warning against the common academic hypocrisy of believing that in one's own work the hidden value-judgement is not only hidden but non-existent.

Faced with this situation, the aim of the present volumes has been to give expression, as far as space permits, to alternative interpretations, exposing the critical reader to more than one point of view, leaving him, with the guidance of his teachers, to make up his own mind.

Similarly, in an area of doubt, such as the principal causes of partition, where opinions are no less biased for being openly divided, there have been included alternative explanations, Stengers as well as Robinson, Hyam as well as Gallagher. The same applies to other discussions, the comparative influence of Islam and Christianity for example, wherever space has allowed, and contentious selectivity demanded.

For myself, as editor, the selection of readings has been as objectively chosen as it is possible for one man to make it. My main regret is that there have not been many more African written texts from which to choose. One may be confident, however, that in twenty years time, if these volumes should be revised or others written, then the ratio of texts written by Africans to others would be about reversed. Such is the rate of change in all things African.

Contents

IX. NATIONALISM AND PAN-AFRICANISM

Acknowledgements

THESE volumes, prepared in three continents over a period of two years, would not have been possible without the co-operation of a very large number of people.

Although, of course, I am alone responsible for all the deficiences involved in the selection and exclusion of material, I wish to express my deep appreciation for the manner in which so many scholars allowed me to consult their wisdom and consume their time. Often this was done more intensively than anyone has the right to request, but always more willingly responded to than anyone has the right to expect.

Mention cannot be made of all the help I have received, but a special word is due to Professor J. D. Hargreaves, Professor J. F. Ade Ajayi, Professor George Shepperson and Mr Anthony E. Atmore. Their constant advocacy of alternatives proved invaluable. My greatest debt in this regard, however, is to Dr Robert I. Rotberg, whose patient criticisms and comments extended as fully in time as they did in detail. I am extremely grateful and I hope that the final result will not be too disappointing to him.

I would like to record my thanks to the many librarians who gave so freely of their time and who allowed me the use of their facilities, often from a distance, and to all the authors and publishers who kindly gave permission for me to include their material. The fact that only two readings have had to be excluded from a final list of 140 choices reflects the extent of their co-operation.

The maps on pages 480 and 481 are based on maps taken from *The Changing Map of Africa*, by R. D. Hodgson and E. A. Stoneman, by permission of the publisher, D. Van Nostrand and Company Inc.

Dr Ian Lockerbie, of the Department of French at Aberdeen University, did a magnificent job in rapidly organizing the translation of difficult material when he and his colleagues could ill afford the time. To him and his team I am deeply grateful.

My sincere thanks to Carol Stein and Ruth Spivack who hunted countless books through countless shelves, and to Madeleine Allen, Dorothy Roberts and Florence Zamchek, who spent many daunting hours establishing order out of chaos.

An immeasurable debt of appreciation is due to my wife. Without her long-term patience and encouragement through many vicissitudes these volumes could never have been completed.

P. J. M. McEwan

Boston, Massachusetts
January 1967

Introduction

I T is intended that the fifty readings included in this volume will provide students of African history, politics and sociology with a balanced and representative review of the most important developments that have occurred in the continent during the first sixty-six years of the present century.

The history of Africa in the twentieth century is the story of evolution and revolution, of rampant nationalism, abdicating colonialism, uncertain economic growth and rapidly changing social circumstances. If it is the most exciting period in the history of the continent it is also the most provocative. There are more nations with histories to record and more historians to record them. Events of the past sixty years have an immediacy that prevents the growth of impartiality which stems from the advantage of a long-range perspective; it is often difficult to disentangle the causal chain of developments and to identify the most significant events. Ephemeral solutions to transitional states appear as universal answers to permanent problems; historical fashion, tempered by social needs and the general climate of opinion, has only recently begun to enjoy the correction that is the gift of time. If the issues of the present become the assumptions of the future, the opposite is also true; present assumptions become future issues. For all these reasons the student of history should tread warily as he approaches the twentieth century.

There is, of course, no single focus for the study of African history that is better than any other, but many possible focuses depending on the nature of one's main interest. This may be, for example, political organization, economic and industrial development, or social change. The present volume endeavours to cover all these areas with, perhaps, a slight emphasis on the first.

There is another reason why the study of modern African history tends to differ from the history of earlier times. Apart from the lack of dependence on oral traditions and the greater volume of official and unofficial documents as written source material, the modern school of African history has itself evolved during this period. Attracted by an expanding field of learning and stimulated by popular demand for historical information modern historical scholarship has tended to concentrate on contemporary events and their preludes.

In accordance with the pattern followed in the two preceding volumes, the writings here presented have been separated into sections according to their subject and geographic area, with a progression within each that follows the course of events. Thus, the first section is concerned with the socio-political forces that were evolving in West Africa from the turn of the century to the present. This is followed by an examination of nationalist assertions in North Africa using the examples of Algeria, Libya and Tunisia. Moving eastward, Sections III and IV discuss the emergence of populist government in Egypt and critical aspects of the development of modern Ethiopia. East Africa, including for these purposes Malagasy, forms the subject of Section V.

These are followed by a section dealing with the South African dilemma, including the growth of industrialization and the coming of apartheid, and also the problem of South-West Africa. Lengthy treatment has been given to the case of South Africa on account of its atypical development, and because it has attracted widespread hostility as well as stimulating opposition from every other independent government in Africa, excepting only Rhodesia. The significance of South Africa's role in the future of the continent is likely to increase rather than to diminish, and it is clearly important that all evaluation should be well informed.

Four readings, comprising Section VII, outline the passage of events in Rhodesia, while a similar number in Section VIII deal with critical phases in the evolving nationhood of Zambia and Malawi. The final group of readings is intended to present an account of the most salient characteristics of the nature and growth of African nationalism, including its social and religious factors, its political antecedents and concomitants, the related development of pan-Africanism and the characteristic African foreign policy of non-alignment.

For the convenience of readers, a short bibliography and a list of major events with dates are provided at the end of the text.

I. FORCES IN MODERN WEST AFRICA

1. Social forces in West African political development

MARTIN L. KILSON *Journal of Human Relations* Vol. 8, Nos. 3/4, 1960; pages 576–80, 582–3, 586–8

Modern political development in West Africa has been rooted in certain social forces emanating from Western contact with African pre-industrial societies. . . .

In West Africa, no less than in India, capitalist colonial expansion generated conditions which eventually gave rise to new social forces and processes. Through the spread of Western education in government and mission schools, the establishment of Western political organizations and institutions, the rise of commercial and some industrial economic activity, among other things, the traditional social system so affected by these phenomena became a thing of the past, and new social forces emerged to replace it. As the quantity, and in time the quality, of these social forces developed apace, they of necessity gave rise to social and political conflict between themselves and the dominant colonial system. Viewed in terms of George Balandier's concept of *"la situation coloniale"*, the main characteristic of the colonial system in West Africa is the relationship of dependence between the dominant European minority (viz., entrepreneurs, managers, colonial administrators, etc.), and the indigenous African majority (including, especially, those Africans embraced by the modern sector of colonial society). This relationship of dependence both creates the conditions of socio-economic change in the colonial situation, as well as determines the tempo and character of this change. It comes into existence precisely to create situations of change— that is, capitalist economic and commercial development; while at the same time it seeks, through political control and military predominance, to regulate and control such change. Such a task, as history testifies, is difficult indeed, and tends to create situations which ultimately overturn the whole colonial system, especially the relationship of dependence. . . .

Some Factors of Social Change in West Africa

Basic among the factors of social change under Western influence in West Africa was *education*. Well before the more far-reaching influences of capitalist economic activity touched West African societies, Western education spread to the coastal areas through missionary channels. Ghana (then the Gold Coast) received a Dutch mission in 1722, followed by English mission schools in 1751 and 1756.[1] During this period, one Ghanaian youth was sent to Europe where he pursued studies at Halle in Saxony and at Wittenberg, with the latter institution conferring upon him the doctorate degree in 1734. Though certainly a very exceptional case at the time the work of other mission schools during the nineteenth century prepared the way for attainment of further professional degrees by Africans. By 1881 Ghana claimed 139 schools (3 government, 47 Basel mission, 84 Wesleyan mission, 4 Bremen mission, and 1 Catholic); and several years later, in 1887, its first citizen was admitted to the English Bar, with another following in 1896. From the turn of the present century, further advances in education in West Africa were registered.[2] Nigeria claimed in 1912 (for the Southern Provinces) about 313 primary schools (59 government schools, 91 government-assisted, and 163 unassisted) and 10 secondary schools; by 1926 there were in this area 3,828 primary schools (58 government, 192 government-assisted, and 3,578 unassisted), 18 secondary schools, and 12 teacher training institutions. Northern Nigeria also had, in 1926, some 125 primary schools, a large number of lesser quality Muslim schools, and one teacher training institution with 55 students. In Ghana (population around 1,600,000 in 1911, against 18,000,000 for Nigeria), there were some 377 schools as well as "special schools for artisans, in which the aim is to educate skilled workmen". Within ten years, Ghana had nearly 500

---

[1] C. P. Groves, *The Planting of Christianity in Africa*, 1948.

[2] Statistical Data from *African Education*, Nuffield Foundation, Oxford University Press, 1953; *Journal of African Society*, October 1912 and January 1913; *Nigerian Handbook*, 1926; Thomas J. Jones, *Education in Africa*, Phelps-Stokes Fund, 1922; *Handbook of Sierra Leone*, 1925; *The Gold Coast Handbook*, 1928.

schools enrolling about 19,000 pupils, as well as a government-assisted teacher training school, and an industrial and technical school. In Sierra Leone (population about 1,500,000 in 1920), there was a total of 250 schools with an enrolment of 18,000 pupils. These schools included 10 secondary schools in the Colony, 5 industrial schools, the N'Jala Agricultural College, and the Bo School in the Protectorate which enrolled sons and nominees of Chiefs. Mention should also be made of Fourah Bay College, founded by the Church Missionary Society in 1827 and affiliated with Durham University, England, in 1876. It was the only institution for professional education in West Africa (enrolling 22 African males in 1922); and of the 548 students who had graduated from Fourah Bay College by the 1920s nearly half had taken university degrees. Normal production of the college was perhaps five or ten African males per year, many of whom left Sierra Leone for Ghana and Nigeria where they became key figures in the social and political life of these territories.[1]

The social significance of the foregoing educational development is seen in the emergence of a small educated, with an even smaller highly educated, sector within the African community. By the turn of the century, the educated group was already quite apparent, as Mary Kingsley noted in her *Travels in West Africa* (1897):

You will find, notably in Lagos, excellent pure-blooded negroes in European clothes, and with European culture. The best men among these are lawyers, doctors, and merchants. . . .

Though available data are few, some aspects of the evolution of this new social stratum in West Africa can be sketched. Not surprisingly, Sierra Leone witnessed the earliest and largest advances in this respect. As early as 1854, a Sierra Leonean, one William Rainy, was admitted to the English Bar, having earlier (1844–1847) been employed in the Sierra Leone Customs. The country's most prominent personality, Sir Samuel Lewis, entered the Bar in 1872, while some six Sierra Leoneans did so between 1878 and 1883, another in 1890, and more during the first two decades of the twentieth century.

[1] K. A. B. Jones-Quartey, "Sierra Leone's Role in the Development of Ghana—1820–1930", *Sierra Leone Studies*, June 1958.

Other well-educated Sierra Leoneans entered high posts in the civil service, with the number of senior service Africans reaching 20 by the 1920s. Still others filled leading positions in European mission undertakings, while larger numbers entered independent businesses or became very well-to-do merchants. Other occupations of educated Africans were as teachers (504), clerks in private concerns(700), and small shopkeepers (about 385).

A similar social stratum developed in Ghana from the late nineteenth century through the 1920s. By the mid-1920s, Ghana had, in professional occupations, nearly 60 lawyers, 14 doctors, 5 journalists and editors, 66 ministers of religion, and 458 teachers. As in Sierra Leone, educated Africans were employed in the colonial service, there being 311 general clerks in 1897 and a much larger number by the 1920s. On the lower level of the new social stratum, there were educated Africans in such trades or petty bourgeois endeavours as butchering (294), tailoring (1,204), printing (120), carpentry (2,159), and much larger numbers were traders (5,555). . . .

Politics of the Early African Middle Class

A fundamental condition of any concerted effort by the West African middle class (the African elite) to influence colonial government was the rise of a sense of corporate or class consciousness within it. The obvious question of the ability of members of the middle class to communicate with each other was of primary importance, inasmuch as such Africans came from a variety of tribal groups each having its own tongue. This problem was solved through the adoption of the English language. Communication among middle-class Africans, in the broader social sense, was also facilitated through their residence in the coastal towns and urban centres of West Africa, which emerged from European economic activity in the area. Compactness or propinquity always enables a particular group, when need and circumstance arise, to become conscious of its interests. This process was further facilitated by modern communication networks erected in urban centres by colonial governments. In 1898, for instance, Sierra Leone had 23 post offices, and by 1916 there were 45 post offices, telegraph, and telephone services in Freetown and Pendembu, 150 miles of roads, and 354 miles of railway. Ghana, in 1916, had 88 post offices, 55 telegraph offices, 4 telephone exchanges (Accra, Sekondi, Dodowa, and Tarkwa), with 182 telephones in use (66 for public and 116 for official use), over 400 miles of road, and 264 miles of railway.[1]

A more important contributor to the rise of class consciousness among the West African middle class was the development of newspapers. Newspapers in British West Africa go back some 150 years, the first one founded in Sierra Leone in 1801 and the first African-owned newspaper being established in 1855. By 1900, Sierra Leone's educated population had seen about 34 newspapers at one time or other, notable among which were *The Sierra Leone Gazette*, *The West African Herald* (1868–1872), *The West African Reporter* (1874–1884), *The Sierra Leone Weekly News* (1884–1951), *The Artisan* (1884–1888), and *The Sierra Leone Times* (1891–1912). Ghana's first newspaper was founded in 1822, and some 19 had emerged at one time or other by 1900, among which were the *Accra Herald* (1857–1859), *The West African Herald* (1859–1873), and *The Gold Goast Times* (1874). Nigeria lagged somewhat behind the former territories, though by 1900 seven newspapers had appeared, notable of which were *The Lagos Observer* (1882), *The Eagle and Lagos Critic* (1883), *The Mirror* (1887), *The Lagos Weekly Record* (1891), and *The Lagos Standard* (1895). The press during the late nineteenth century through the 1920s was not explicitly "nationalist" in its orientation or purpose. Its role was to discuss and criticize government policy and colonial developments generally, particularly in terms of their effect upon the African middle class. In this way, a significant contribution was performed in creating class consciousness among the middle class. As K. A. B. Jones-Quartey has noted, the press of this period "was published by the best educated and wealthiest—often the 'professional' classes, and read mostly by their own kind. In those conditions the public opinion which it created was compact, and effective. . . ."[2]

[1] Statistical data from *The Handbook of Sierra Leone*, 1925; *The Gold Coast Handbook*, 1928; G. W. Prathero, *Peace Handbook—British Possessions*, No. 2, 1922.

[2] K. A. B. Jones-Quartey, "The Institutions of Public Opinion in a Rapidly Changing Africa", Conference on Representative Government and National Progress, University of Ibadan, March 1959.

During the late nineteenth century and through the 1920s, the class consciousness apparent among middle-class Africans did not result in demands for control of state power. The demands that were put forth in the name of the middle class seldom extended beyond requesting more civil service posts for its professional members, obtaining direct and elective representation in the legislative and executive organs of colonial government, provision of better educational facilities, and policies favourable to African merchants. In nearly all cases, such demands were articulated through some sort of political grouping or organization among middle-class Africans. . . .

According to Maurice Dobb, self-uplift, however, has never been the sole mode of evolution and advancement for any bourgeoisie. And surely not the West African bourgeoisie. In the West African context of a colonial situation, the requisites of such evolution were dominated by the European bourgeoisie which formed a crucial part of the ruling group in the colonial system. Its reasons for entering the colonial situation were not to share its ingredients of power with an emerging African bourgeoisie—that is, to bring forth a competitor to its own supremacy. Admittedly, the colonial situation did impart aspects of these ingredients to some Africans, through the creation of a rudimentary capitalist sector in an otherwise primitive economic context and the spread of Western education. But all of this had its limitations; seldom actively carried beyond the point, as regards education, for example, of producing "a regulated supply of persons required in technical or professional posts in the public services".[1]

Such being the case, politics appeared as a logical and realistic means for further development of an African bourgeoisie. Political activity by the West African middle class first attempted to secure a representative foothold in the organs of colonial government, and through this to influence the government, to provide more and more of the conditions for its own development. As we have seen earlier, middle-class Africans in Sierra Leone secured political representation in the legislature in 1863, and in Ghana in 1888. By 1900, the middle class had

[1] Lord Hailey, *Native Administration and Political Development in British Tropical Africa—1940–41*, London, H. M. Government.

extended its political demands to include elected representation in legislative and executive organs of government. As an African friend of E. D. Morel, the British social reformer, put it in a letter to Morel: ". . . We should be allowed to elect non-official members of the Legislative Council, and two independent native members should be allowed to sit in the Executive Council [and] . . . we must have a voice in the expenditure of revenue."[1] The colonial situation moved slowly in respecting these and subsequent demands, but some were granted within limits. In 1893–1924, provisions were made in Sierra Leone for a Municipal Council of 15 seats, 12 of which were open, by direct elections, to Africans who could claim property ownership valued at £200 or more. Similarly, in Ghana the three major towns of Accra, Cape Coast, and Sekondi were granted, in 1894, Town Councils in which half of the seats were held by Africans who were elected by all rate-payers. By 1910, the electorate in these towns numbered 1,756, 1,600, and 811 respectively.

In the early 1920s, further demands were put forward by the West African middle class, mainly through a new political organization known as the National Congress of British West Africa. Much concern was now given to questions of senior service posts, professional occupations for Africans, and higher education facilities. In the course of a deputation to the Colonial Office in 1920–1921, Casely-Hayford informed a British audience that "Natives of West Africa, even those who had taken a high degree in European universities, are not allowed to occupy the better-paid posts in the Civil Service, and that West Africans, fully qualified to practise as doctors, are debarred from practising by reasons of their colour." On another occasion during the course of this deputation, T. Hutton-Mills called for "the establishment of a British West African University to give British Africans technical, industrial, and scientific training, and especially the training necessary for the holding of positions in the Civil Service." Political demands by middle-class Africans had also broadened during the 1920s, and the above-mentioned deputation of the National Congress of British West Africa requested that one-half of the

[1] E. D. Morel, "Administration of British West Africa", *West Africa*, 15 June 1900, p. 740.

members of the legislatures be elected African members, that the powers of municipal councils be expanded, and that an House of Assembly composed largely of Africans be instituted and granted "the power of imposing taxes and discussing freely and without reserve the items on the Annual Estimates of revenue and expenditure prepared by the Governor in the Executive Council and of approving them."[1]

Theoretically, the European ruling class in West Africa was powerful enough to ignore these demands altogether. Yet in practical terms such would not have been wise, in light of the role played by middle-class Africans in the functioning of the colonial system. Complete alienation of this class always involved possible non-cooperation on their part, which could impair colonial efficiency. Thus some of the demands put forward in the 1920s were acceded to, with newly structured legislatures being established in Nigeria, Sierra Leone, and Ghana in 1922, 1924, and 1925, respectively. Each territory was provided with increased African representation in Legislative Councils, including for the first time four elected members in Nigeria, three in Sierra Leone, and three in Ghana. The elected members represented the African middle class in the coastal towns, the total electorate numbering 4,000 in Nigeria, about 2,000 in Sierra Leone, and 7,063 in Ghana (1929).

Politics of a Developed Middle Class

The institution of elective franchise for middle-class African representation was bound to alter the form of middle-class politics in West Africa. Thus politics now involved not only power competition between the European ruling class and the African middle class, but competition within the African middle class itself. Especially was this true of Nigeria, where in 1923 and after, several "political parties" emerged among the middle class to contend the elections to the Legislative Council and to subsequent municipal council elections. Among these parties were the Peoples Union, the Union of Young Nigerians, the Nigerian National Democratic Party.[2] None of these so-

---

[1] From "Deputation to Colonial Office by National Congress of British West Africa 1920–21", *Journal of the African Society*, July 1920 and January 1921.

[2] Nnamdi Azikiwe, *Development of Political Parties in Nigeria*, 1957.

called "parties" developed modern party organization, nor did much to extend their influence beyond the confines of Lagos; but they did give some middle-class Africans experience at contesting modern elections, and continued advancing the claims of the middle class against colonial government.

Besides stimulating the rise of political competition within the middle class, the constitutional changes of the early 1920s also "nationalized" the middle-class politics of this period. That is to say, the political ambition and activity of the middle class were now directed exclusively—or nearly so—to the territorial entity in which it resided, as against the Pan-West-African politics of the National Congress of British West Africa. With this narrowing of the sphere of political activity of the different middle classes in West Africa, there was an increase in the opportunity of a particular middle class to influence its own territorial government. Especially was this the case in Nigeria and Ghana, where increased socio-economic changes during the 1930s through the postwar period provided the middle class with a territorial social basis from which the whole colonial system could be politically challenged.

A crucial element of the new social basis that emerged during the 1930s through the 1950s was the African wage-labouring class. By 1931 there were substantial increases in the wage-labouring population in Ghana, which then comprised some 14,107 labourers in mining industries, 4,309 in transport and motor industries, 5,128 domestics, 39,829 farm labourers, and thousands of semi-skilled or skilled labourers such as carpenters (5,216), mechanics (1,593), bricklayers and brickmakers (2,731), electricians (154), and telegraphists (55). At the close of the Second World War, Ghana's wage-labouring class had increased to 200,000 upwards, which included some 19,281 labourers in mining, 1,202 in timber, 9,768 in construction, and 11,453 in transport. Nigerian data for 1931 show 17,027 labourers in mining industries and 15,282 in transport and communication. During the next twenty years there was a fairly rapid growth in wage-labourers, the total figure being 300,000 upwards in 1954, which included 51,195 in transport, 51,552 in mining, 44,430 on cash-crop farms, 11,658 in timber, and 47,468 in construction.

The quantitative advance of the labouring class in West

CTCA

Africa brought with it the conditions for certain qualitative changes. Conditions of work were normally inferior to anything known in Western countries, and those of life compared, as Hodgkin has put it, quite "unfavourably with those described in Engels' *Conditions of the Working Class in England in 1844....*"[1] As might be expected, the step from here to organizing by labour for better conditions of existence was a short one. Though a few efforts at trade union organization occurred during the 1930s, it was not until the Second World War and after that trade union activity became widespread.[2] In 1941 Nigeria had 50 registered trade unions, 115 in 1950 and 135 in 1953 with a total membership of 153,000. Ghana also had 104 trade unions by 1954, with a membership of 46,309. Besides trade union organizations, other forms of voluntary associations emerged among urbanized African workers such as tribal unions, mutual benefit societies, welfare associations, youth clubs, and the like. Ghana, for instance, had in 1954 some 67 mutual benefit societies located in Accra with a total membership of 26,192. All of these associations endeavoured to provide "a measure of social security for persons living under urban conditions, where it is increasingly difficult for the traditional forms of security and mutual assistance to be adequate or applicable."[3]

Left to themselves, the foregoing developments among urban workers would hardly have constituted a situation capable of challenging the political positions of Europeans in West Africa. Such developments could be politically significant only to the extent that they provided new situations capable of manipulation by the sophisticated African middle class. The new generation of middle-class Africans which appeared in the 1930s recognized this situation, and endeavoured to create a new level of middle-class politics from it. One such endeavour was the founding of the Ghana Youth Conference in this period. Under the leadership of an able lawyer, J. B. Danquah, the Youth Conference expanded its influence beyond its middle-class base in the coastal towns. Within ten years the Youth

---

[1] Thomas Hodgkin, "Toward Self-Government in British West Africa" in Basil Davidson's *The New West Africa*, 1953.

[2] J. I. Roper, *Labour Problems in West Africa*, 1958.

[3] Ione Acquah, *Accra Survey*, London, 1958, pp. 87 ff.

Conference succeeded in affiliating some 18 voluntary associations with it, and attained a membership of 1,750. Whereas the earlier political groups concerned themselves with political representation for middle-class Africans, the Youth Conference extended its demands to include the whole Ghanaian "nation". It called for a "legislative Assembly for the *whole country*, with manhood suffrage or property qualification". A similar development in Nigeria was led by a lawyer, H. O. Davies, who founded the Nigerian Youth Movement in 1938. The Movement established some 20 branches in such centres as Ibadan, Ife, and Abeokuta, gained the support of a number of voluntary associations (e.g., the Producer's Union and the Motor Union, the latter having a membership of 2,000), and secured a total membership of 10,000 by 1940. Like the Youth Conference in Ghana, the Nigerian Youth Movement also proclaimed "complete independence" as its ultimate goal and conceived its role in "national" terms. Both of these so-called "youth organizations" were rather shortlived, due either to internal strife or opposition from colonial government.

With the end of the Second World War, the West African territories began to develop the kind of social basis that would permit attainment of the political activity striven for by the youth movements. As we have seen, the rise of a fairly substantial wage-labouring class was fundamental to the development of a new social basis for West African politics. By the 1950s this new social basis was more accessible to political organizations than at any other period, due to an expanding communication system. Taking the press as an example: Ghana's press increased from 8 newspapers in 1937 with a circulation around 17,000 to 23 newspapers in the 1950s with a circulation of 185,000 upwards; similarly, Nigeria's press expanded from 13 in 1926 to 35 newspapers in the 1950s with a circulation around 471,500. The use of wireless sets was another form of an expanding communication system. Ghana, for instance, imported 357 wireless sets in 1937 and 11,180 in 1955, while the number of relay service subscribers increased from 1,306 to 20,792.

At the same time that a new mass social basis was being effected, the middle class itself was becoming a more substantial and developed social group. Already in the late 1930s, Margery

Perham keenly observed a qualitative change in the living standards of middle-class Nigerians: "[Lagos] . . . is evidence of the prosperity of [middle-class] Africans . . . and of the drive towards European standards of life which impels them. . . . Houses, built by African contractors, are worth £400 on the average, though some run up to £1,000. They have fences, paths, and flower beds; their servants' quarters at the back; sometimes their tennis-courts. . . . There are lawyers . . . some of whom are rich enough to send their children to school and university in England and to visit them there."[1] By the time of the Second World War, commercial members of the middle class, especially traders, had increased their numbers to hundreds of thousands, with the average trader claiming new incomes of £650 while larger operators had new incomes of £2,000 upwards. Well-to-do cash-crop farmers had also registered substantial progress by the postwar period, with one wealthy Yoruba farmer being described by one observer as follows: ". . . [He] has an estate of approximately £50,000, he owns a shop, several lorries, two cars, many houses including the one in which he lives which has probably cost £3,000 to build."[2] On the professional and semi-professional level, lawyers in Nigeria increased from 15 in the early 1920s to 150 in the early 1950s and nearly 400 in 1959; doctors increased from 12 in the early 1920s to 160 in the 1950s and teachers and clerks increased from 21,000 to 70,000 in the same period.[3] This same period saw a number of Nigerians entering business and managerial fields, with some 11 African banks emerging in 1945–1952 having 45 banking offices in the country. One need hardly add that the general affluency of the postwar middle class was quite an advance of that observed by Perham in 1937.[4]

On first glance, one might expect that the foregoing advances in the position of middle-class West Africans would have satisfied their bourgeois aspirations. But such advances among

[1] Margery Perham, *Native Administration in Nigeria*, London, Oxford University Press, 1937.

[2] P. C. Lloyd, "Cocoa, Politics, and the Yoruba Middle Class", *West Africa*, 17 January 1953.

[3] James Coleman, *Nigeria: Background to Nationalism*, 1958.

[4] W. B. Birmingham and D. Tait, "Standards of Living; a Comment", *Universitas*, University College of Gold Coast, December 1954.

a developing bourgeois class have seldom, if ever, softened or weakened its urge and need for near total control of the political, and through this the social and economic, situation in which it finds itself. These advances did little more than whet its appetite, and more important still prepare it more adequately to launch its drive for total hegemony. Thus postwar West Africa saw a significant expansion in both the extent and influence of middle-class-led political organizations. In Nigeria, for instance, the National Council of Nigeria and the Cameroons (founded under the leadership of Dr Nnamdi Azikiwe in 1944, himself a banker and newspaper magnate) embraced over 100 voluntary associations within its organizational framework. Similarly, Kwame Nkrumah's Convention Peoples Party, founded in 1949, contained in its nationwide structure some 2,885 local branches (1,135 in the Colony, 1,043 in Ashanti, 204 in the Northern Territories, and 502 in Southern Togoland), which embraced a paid-up membership of 1,000,053. With the masses now constituting the organizational backbone of West African politics, there was little chance for this politics to neglect expressing the needs and interests of the masses. And having been born in an international context where modern nationalism frequently spoke, though did not necessarily accept, the language and principles of socialism, West African nationalist parties were likewise inclined. In the first programme declaration of the National Council of Nigeria and the Cameroons in 1945, its purposes included, *inter alia*, (1) provision for "economic security" which involved "the control by the local administration of the means of production and distribution of the mineral resources of the country [and] . . . legislation against trade monopolies so as to avoid the exploitation of the country and its people"; (2) provision for "social security" which meant the "abolition of all forms of discrimination and segregation based on race, colour, tribe or creeds . . . [and the establishment of] a national system of free and compulsory education for all children up to the age of sixteen"; and (3) the institution of "free medical and surgical treatment . . . by the central and local government. . . ." Similarly, the Constitution of the Convention Peoples Party in Ghana calls for "the Political, Social, and Economic emancipation of the people, more particularly of those who depend directly upon their own exertions by hand or by brain for the means of life." The fulfilment of these rather socialistically oriented declarations would certainly be a long-run affair; but their embodiment in the programmes of the postwar parties was important in winning mass support for their immediate goals.

Political independence was the primary goal of the postwar parties in West Africa, and by 1954–1955 much of this had been secured. At this time, Nigeria had 184 Africans in the central legislature, 10 in the executive council, as well as regional legislative and executive bodies including prime ministers. And Ghana, at this time, had 104 Africans in the central legislature, and an executive body of 8 Africans including an African prime minister. Not surprisingly, most of these new governmental posts were taken over by members of the African middle class. For instance, data presented by Professor Coleman on attributes of members in the Nigerian House of Representatives in 1957 show, for the Western Region representatives, that 20% were teachers, 23% professionals (viz., lawyers— 20%; doctors, pharmacists, journalists, and ministers of religion—together constituting 3%), 43% entrepreneurs, and 6% managers in European firms; and for Eastern Region representatives there were 28% teachers, 20% professionals (viz., lawyers—15%; doctors, pharmacists, journalists, and ministers of religion—together constituting 5%), 26% entrepreneurs, 3% managers in European firms, and 15% employees in local government. Similarly, data for members of the Ghana Legislative Assembly in 1954 show 31 teachers, 17 professionals, 22 entrepreneurs, 5 employees in commercial firms, 5 civil servants, 11 clerks, and 7 professional politicians, among others.

The new governmental positions secured by middle-class West Africans in the early 1950s were immediately employed to open the whole administrative system to Africans. Whereas Ghana had only 23 Africans in senior service posts in the mid-1920s, within a year after the first General Election in February 1951, the number increased to 530 African senior civil servants with a salary of £650 or over, and to 1,364 by 1956 as against 1,227 oversea officers. Similarly, there were 245 Africans in the Nigerian senior service in 1948, but a year after the enactment of the Macpherson Constitution of 1951 the number increased to 685 and 937 in 1957, as against nearly 3,000 oversea officers. In both cases, the placing of Africans in senior service posts is part of an unrelenting drive by the middle class to control the total state apparatus, and this drive is not likely to cease until this becomes a reality. As a recent report (1959) by the Federal Government of Nigeria has put it:

It is only when we begin to count the number of Nigerians in the superscale posts—the control room—of the civil service that we discover how slow has been the pace of *effective* Nigerianisation. At the moment virtually all the posts concerned with control and direction of the Administrative machine are in the hands of officers subject ultimately to the authority of the Secretary of State for the Colonies. . . . 58 Nigerians can and must be found and trained to take over the superscale posts in the Administrative Service.

It should also be noted that the new West African governments now in the hands of the middle class have sought the "Africanization" of the managerial staffs of European firms, and being keen to the meaning of the new political situation in West Africa, these firms have moved to adjust themselves accordingly. For instance, by the mid-1950s there were some 99 Nigerians holding managerial positions in the United Africa Company out of 365 such posts. And in British West Africa generally, whereas only 7% of the U.A.C.'s managerial posts were held by Africans in 1939, 22% were held by Africans in 1958—that is, 323 posts were held by Africans out of a total management strength of 1,483.[1]

What has become a rather total concentration upon state power as the main avenue for class and national development, is a phenomenon which fairly well distinguishes the contemporary middle class in West Africa from that of an earlier period—what we have characterized as "bourgeois, old style. . . ." Whereas the latter tended to view its own and its countries' future in terms of the adaptation of traditional bourgeois patterns of thrift, hardwork, and self-uplift, the contemporary middle class conceives its development in terms of its capacity to secure control of the state apparatus and to employ it for its own purposes. Part of this situation was

[1] Jocelyn G. Clark, "The Africanization of Private Enterprise", in *The Task of the Private Sector in the Actual Development of Africa*, Ghent, 1959.

recognized by the International Bank Mission to Nigeria, which noted that "the need for *self-help* is not understood by the African businessman who looks to the government . . . for financial assistance in the expansion of his business. . . ." On the other hand, West African governments have followed policies which assist this pattern, as in the case of the Nigerian government which recently earmarked some £300,000 for aiding the growth of African entrepreneurs. Similarly, the professional sector of the middle class need no longer depend upon the old bourgeois pattern of advancement, for West African governments have come actively to their assistance. In Nigeria, for instance, there were nearly 700 government scholarships for higher education in 1954, and the Western Region government plans to spend £800,000 for this purpose by 1960. Such developments do not necessarily mean that the old bourgeois pattern of evolution has been discarded altogether. They do mean, however, that, to an extent far beyond that in any other period in West Africa, access to state power has proved a major means of social and class mobility, and that the present-day middle class considers this perfectly normal. Actually, the social and economic position of the African middle class never really permitted the true operation of the old bourgeois pattern of development. As one observer has put it: "The emergent African state has been attracted to state enterprise . . . because of the absence of indigenous African private capital for productive investment, and because of the predominant position of metropolitan country 'expatriate' private capital."[1] Furthermore, the pscyhology and logic of West African nationalism, combined with the expensive social habits adopted and cherished by the emergent middle class, compelled it to seek a shorter route for its advancement. . . .

[1] Bernard Blankenheimer, "Economic Policy in Emergent Africa", *SAIS Review*, Winter 1959.

2. Changing patterns of leadership

P. GARIGUE *Africa* Vol. 24, No. 2, 1954 Oxford University Press for International African Institute; pages 222–30

(a) *Among the Yoruba*

Among the Yoruba the spread of British administration at first only directly affected those who, like the military chiefs, had an immediate interest in the continuation of the old way of life. Slowly, however, the first resentment of the chiefs gave place to a willing collaboration. By 1903 the relations of the Senior Chiefs with the Administration had become good enough for the latter to report that 'there is no reason to believe that there is a single disloyal chief'.[1] Not only was the position of the Senior Chiefs maintained, but it was sometimes reinforced. This was so, for instance, in the case of the *Alafin* of Oyo, of whom it has been said that the Administration 'has given him a security which has dislocated the checks and balances of the old consti-tion'.[2] It was longer, however, before the Junior Chiefs, nearly all of whom had lost some of their political importance, could accept the new system of centralization under the 'indirect rule' of the Administration. The rapid economic development of Yorubaland, and the passing away of the pre-colonial generation of Junior Chiefs, helped to minimize the friction, and by the 1920s the structure of authority built by the Admini-stration had become an accepted fact among the Yoruba.

A new stage was reached in the late 1920s with the formation, in practically every large Yoruba town, of associations led by European-educated Yoruba. Each town developed its own pattern with different attitudes to the Native Authority Council and to the administrator. Abeokuta, for instance, acquired the reputation of having more radical literate leaders than towns like Oyo or Ife, where being a progressive meant nothing more than wanting a voice in the framing of local policies. Administrators came to recognize that the demands made by the 'Progress Unions', as they were called, were often legitimate, and they frequently brought pressure to bear on the local councils to co-opt literate members as councillors. The

[1] *Lagos Annual Report*, 1903, p. 43.
[2] Perham, M., *Native Administration in Nigeria*, Oxford, 1937, p. 172.

chiefs themselves were pressed by the Administration to move with the times and in 1937 the most important Yoruba chiefs, who were traditionally supposed never to meet, were brought together to a conference which became a yearly event. Furthermore, the earlier cleavage between European-educated Yoruba and illiterate chiefs was gradually broken down, and an increasing number of new appointments as chiefs went to European-educated persons.

Just before the Second World War new associations were started in Lagos which aimed to link into national organizations the political groups which had been formed in the Yoruba towns. The most important of these was the Nigerian Youth Movement, which rapidly grew to a membership of nearly 10,000. This movement was characterized by the much more radical opinions held by its leaders compared to those of the 'Progress Unions', and by its strong anti-colonial attitude. Similar in their rapid expansion were the associations formed on a professional basis, such as the Nigerian Teachers Union, which was formed under Yoruba leadership. Dominating the political life of these new associations was the personality of Dr Azikiwe, and the ideas of the 'Zikist' movement, in a near messianic form, became the political creed of many young Yoruba.[1] Other Yoruba turned to socialism for a political theory to guide them in their actions. Among these, university students returned from Britain were the most prominent, and it was often they who supplied the leadership of these new movements.[2] It was during this period that trade-unions began to

[1] Dr Nnamdi Azikiwe, Ibo by birth (1904), student in Lagos and the U.S.A. until 1925; returned to Nigeria in 1937 and became a journalist, creating a chain of newspapers. Joined the Nigerian Youth Movement, but later resigned over policy, and became the leader of the National Congress of Nigeria and the Cameroons (NCNC), and the most important of the Ibo political leaders. A description of what is meant by 'Zikism' is given by Nwafor Orizu, in *Without Bitterness*, New York, 1944, pp. 287–344.

[2] Among these was H. O. Davies (born 1905), a student in Lagos and later in London; he was the manager of the C.M.S. bookshop in Lagos. He entered active politics at the foundation of the Nigerian Youth Movement, and was its secretary and its chairman. He returned to London to become a barrister in 1947. On his return he broke away from the Nigerian Youth Movement to create in 1950 the Nigerian People's Congress (on the lines of the British Labour Party). He was installed as chief in his home town in 1952.

develop in Nigeria. In 1945 there were already thirty-eight of them; by 1952 they had become fifty-six.[1]

The leadership of these new political groups was predominantly personal in character, the political life of the inner councils of the movement being dominated by a small group, or often by a single person, whose personality gave a sort of unity to the movement. It was partly in answer to this personal influence and partly in reaction from the dominant leadership of Azikiwe that a new type of political organization appeared among the Yoruba, the *Egbe Omo Oduduwa*. This organization was strictly political and had no connexion with the old Yoruba cult of Oduduwa. It provided, however, a common meeting-ground for the European-educated Yoruba and the chiefs, by placing foremost in its programme the demand for a return to the traditional Yoruba political institutions, 'freed' from any integration into the colonial administration. The organizing spirit behind this movement was a new type of political leader, the professional organizer, exemplified in Obafami Awolowo,[2] who was later to start the Action Group and become one of the foremost political leaders of the Yoruba. The difference between the *Egbe Omo Oduduwa* and the Action Group was that the former rested primarily on the tribal organization and depended on the support of the chiefs, while the Action Group relied directly on the political activities of its individual members and especially on its *cadre* of paid officials. This new type of organization was tested at the election

[1] The type of man who led these trade-unions can be illustrated from the life of H. P. Adebola (born 1916), a student of a Moslem school until he entered a Grammar School. He has been the secretary of the Railway Station Staff Union since 1945 and general secretary of the Nigerian Union of Railwaymen since 1946. He was elected to the Western House of Assembly on a NCNC party ticket.

[2] Awolowo (born 1909) came of a small farming family and went to school at the local mission at Ijebu-Ode until he was 11. He then began to earn his living and was successively a clerk, journalist, and trade-union secretary. He came to London in 1944 and took the degrees of B.Com. and LL.B., returning to Nigeria as a solicitor. He has been active in politics since the formation of the Nigerian Youth Movement and helped to create the *Egbe Omo Oduduwa* of which he was the secretary. He later became the leader of the Action Group. It was in answer to the leadership of the Yoruba Action Group that Azikiwe reorganized the NCNC with a *cadre* of full-time organizers.

of 1951, when the Action Group, as the political party of the Yoruba, supported by its connexion with the *Egbe Omo Oduduwa*, proved successful and gained an overwhelming majority of seats in the Western House of Assembly.

The arrangements for the election favoured political organizations based on tribal organization. The election procedure was complicated, and the elections were held at three levels— primary, secondary, and final. The primary elections were held within the wards of the towns or in the small villages. All the persons who had been elected at the primary level came together with the members of the local Native Authority (the chief and his council) and elected a number of persons for the secondary level. These persons in each Division then met in a final college to select two or more persons to represent the Division in the House of Assembly. It has been held that among the Yoruba the power of the chiefs in the primary elections was very strong. In some towns the ward chiefs held private meetings several days before the election and decided whom they wished to see elected. By the day of the election everything had been arranged and no meeting was necessary.[1] While, however, the success of the Action Group was due to the support it received from the traditional elements, as well as from those who had accepted new political ideas, the elected representatives all came from the occupational groups which were acquiring greater importance in the social life of Nigeria.

Professions of the elected members for the Egba, Egbado, Ijebu-Remo, Ijesha, Oyo, and Lagos Divisions, 1951

Trader-businessmen	12	Doctor	1
Teachers	7	Minister of religion	1
Lawyers	6	Trade-union secretary	1
Civil servant	1	Moslem society secretary	1

The pattern of political leadership among the Yoruba in 1950 was thus a balance between the traditional authority structure and the European-educated Yoruba organized into political movements. Most of the chiefs had joined hands with the leaders of these movements and some had become 'new'

[1] Lloyd, P. C., 'Some comments on the elections in Nigeria', *Journal of African Administration*, vol. iv, no. 3, 1952, pp. 82–92.

political leaders in their own right within these movements. This unification was made closer by transfers from the ranks of the successful 'new' political leaders into the 'traditional' authority structure; certain of the former, who would not otherwise have any claim to such appointments, are being given titles as chiefs. The successful merging of the chiefs and the elected political leaders can be clearly seen from the personal histories of the three leaders of the Action Group, who were, in 1950, sent to represent the Western Provinces in the Nigerian Council of Ministers.[1]

(b) *Among the Ashanti*

Until 1900 (the date of the last rebellion) Ashanti political leaders derived their importance from their position in the traditional authority structure, and it was the Kumasi chiefs who decided to rise against the British. But the political unity of the Ashanti as a single people had gone, and only a few of the *Omanhene* (chiefs of local 'states') joined the Kumasi chiefs in the rising. The rising itself was the last effort of the Kumasi chiefs and those among the Divisional chiefs who wanted a

[1] Sir Adosoji Aderemi (born 1889), *Oni* of Ife, was a student at the local Ife Mission and became a railway clerk. After saving some money he resigned and went into business on his own. Was very successful and rose to a position of influence before he became *Oni*. He was given a C.M.G. in 1943 and a knighthood in 1950. He became a leading member of the *Egbe Omo Oduduwa* at its formation, and later became an Action Group leader. He is a member of many Government committees and a director of the Cocoa Control Board.

Chief Bode Thomas, Minister of Transport (born 1918), son of a wealthy trader, was a student at the C.M.S. Grammar School, Lagos, and later became a railway clerk. He came to London to become a barrister in 1939. On his return to Lagos he established one of the foremost legal firms of Nigeria. He became a leader of the Nigerian Youth Movement and was at one time its Federal Treasurer. He also became a leader of the *Egbe Omo Oduduwa* on its formation, and was one of the founders of the Action Group. He was given the title of *Balogun* of Oyo, and is also a Chancellor of the African Churches Association.

Samuel Ladoke Akintola, Minister of Labour (born 1910), was a student at the Ogbomosho Mission school. He became a teacher and later took up journalism. After the Second World War he went to Oxford to qualify as a barrister, and set up in practice in Lagos in 1949. He then entered politics and became the chairman of the Lagos branch of the Nigerian Youth Movement, and later joined the Action Group.

return to the days of the slave-trade. The crushing of the revolt meant the end of the political supremacy of the Ashanti military leaders. After the rising one Senior Chief was hanged, sixteen others were deported, while thirty-one more were imprisoned for some years. The stools which had become vacant were filled by the British administration with persons who had supported it in the rising. Ten *Omanhene* were replaced, as well as six of the Senior Kumasi Chiefs, and a large number of Junior Chiefs.

The chiefs who had been appointed by the Administration were not to remain unchallenged by the commoners who, in many Divisions during 1905–6, refused to serve under them. In all cases of rebellion against the appointed chiefs the Administration supported the chiefs, and it is therefore not surprising that the Administration was able to report that the chiefs were showing themselves 'willing to co-operate',[1] while the commoners soon learned that their traditional right to destool a chief was no longer effective without the authorization of the Administration. Within a few years the wealthy cocoa-farmers were beginning to take a lead in political affairs, and it was between them and the Senior Chiefs that clashes were most often reported. The Administration's report for 1922 specifically mentions the growth of a new class of wealthy cocoa-farmers as one of the features of the political tension.

With the return of the *Asantehene* to Kumasi in 1925 and his enstoolment as Prempeh II, and the formation of the Ashanti Confederacy Council as a Native Authority in 1927, the traditional authority structure was partly restored. The administratively created Ashanti Confederacy and the position of the *Asantehene* in it did not, however, succeed in making the position of the Senior Chiefs more secure. The Confederacy Council did indeed deliberately change Native laws and customs so as to deal more severely with the leaders of movements to destool a chief, and it abolished the traditional *Nwankaa*, or association of commoners, which had an important constitutional role. But these measures were not effective. Between 1942 and 1946, for instance, among the twenty-one *Omanhene* members of the Confederacy Council, who were also Native Authorities in their own right, there were fourteen destoolments and two *Omanhene*

[1] *Ashanti Annual Report*, 1908, p. 7.

were replaced twice in that period.[1] With the increase in literacy a new development was taking place. In nearly every large town the European-educated formed themselves into associations under the name of 'Progress Unions'. The spread of literacy also meant that more chiefs had had a European education previous to their appointment. Of the twelve *Omanhene* appointed between 1942 and 1946, six were literate. This is an indication that the conflict between Senior Chiefs and Ashanti commoners was not always a conflict between educated and illiterate, but was concerned rather with the form of authority which should prevail. This conflict increased with the development of Gold Coast nationalism in the coastal towns, which slowly affected Ashanti. The cocoa 'hold-up' of the late twenties, for instance, was carried out by Ashanti who had come under the influence of political movements in the coastal towns. The *Omanhene*, as Native Authorities, were responsible for the maintenance of law and order, and had to punish those among their subjects who broke the law, which they frequently did during the period of the 'hold-up'. The more efficient the *Omanhene* was as an administrator of the Native Authority of which he was the head, the less of a political leader could he be to his people. Resentment against the *Omanhene* and the Native Authorities grew to include the person of the *Asantehene*, who until then had been regarded as the symbol of the Ashanti nation rather than as an active participant in the political situation.

From the thirties onwards Ashanti was to develop ever closer ties with the coastal towns of the Gold Coast. The end of the Second World War saw the appearance in Ashanti of political organizations which were no longer based on tribal affiliations, but on a common Gold Coast consciousness. There already existed, in the thirties, the Youth Movement founded by Dr J. B. Danquah, which held a number of meetings in Kumasi; but only a small number of the European-educated Ashanti had become members of it, or of the more widely known West African National Congress.

All these movements were characterized by a restricted appeal. It was only after the Second World War that new

[1] Busia, K. A., *The Position of the Chief in the Modern Political System of Ashanti*, London, 1951, pp. 215–16.

movements with a much wider appeal were created. The first
of this kind was the United Gold Coast Convention (UGCC)
founded in Accra in 1947. The leadership of that movement
included many of the leaders of earlier political movements,
and it appealed mainly to the European-educated. When,
however, Kwane Nkrumah, then a student in London, was
invited to become its paid secretary, he transformed the UGCC
and began a drive for mass membership. By 1949, however, a
split had developed among the leaders of the UGCC over the
methods and aims of Nkrumah, which finally led to a breach
and the formation of Nkrumah's party, the Convention
People's Party (CPP). Until then the leadership of the various
'new' political movements had always been in the hands of a
small number of lawyers and wealthy business men. In the
CPP the leadership came to include clerks, teachers, and small
farmers. Its rapid development in Ashanti can be traced to the
fact that, for the first time since the abolition of the *Nkwankwaa*,
the latent discontent present in Ashanti communities was given
an opportunity to express itself on a national level and through
leaders whose status was similar to that of the traditional
Nkwankwaahene, or head of the commoners. An examination of
what happened in Ashanti during the 1951 election shows this
very clearly. With the exception of Kumasi, where a single
secret ballot was held, the procedure in the other towns and in
rural areas was in two stages: primary and secondary. There
were 730 sub-districts in the primary election, each returning
one member for the twelve electoral colleges of the secondary
election. There was a 40·4 per cent. poll and 534 uncontested
elections at the primary stage. The high proportion of uncontested elections has been attributed to the fact that the person
elected to represent the sub-district had often been already
chosen by an unofficial ward or village meeting, without
recourse to the ballot box.[1] At these meetings the leading
persons were the Junior Chiefs or the wealthy villagers.

The different methods used by the various political groups
show more clearly than anything else the political differences
in their leadership. On the one side there were those groups,
like the UGCC and the Kosoko Society, which depended on
the support given to them by the Senior Chiefs. Although the

[1] Colonial Office, *Gold Coast 1951*, H.M.S.O., 1952, pp. 105–6.

Asantehene stated that he himself stood as an impartial onlooker, various members of the Confederacy Council took an active part in the elections. In Sunyani, for instance, the *Omanhene* himself stood for election, and was defeated by a commoner from his own town who was supported by the CPP. Other candidates supported by the Senior Chiefs included a university lecturer and a number of other professional men. On the CPP's side there was, first and foremost, the party organization which had been built up in nearly every village and town, and upon which all CPP candidates depended. While their opponents seldom left Kumasi, or the main roads to the large towns, and preferred to rely on the Senior Chiefs, an enormous amount of voluntary work was done by the CPP members who enthusiastically canvassed and encouraged the villagers to vote for their candidates. The CPP won nine of the twelve Ashanti constituencies, the other three going to independents. The occupational status of the elected CPP candidates included a letter-writer, a druggist, a journalist, a school-teacher, a produce-buyer, and, a sign of the strength of the party machinery, three full-time party organizers.[1] Only two of the returned CPP candidates had been university students, while most of their opponents had been university-educated. The most spectacular win for the CPP was in Kumasi itself, where its candidate, who was not even an Ashanti, won by 8,338 votes to 570.

Equally significant, as an indication of the trend in political leadership among the Ashanti, was the fact that the chiefs, who were allowed to return six persons to represent them in the Legislative Council, chose no less than three non-chiefs to do so. Underlying this transfer of political leadership was the recommendation made in 1951 by a Commission of Inquiry, that Local Government, which was what the Native Authorities were to become under the new centralized Gold Coast Goverment, should be clearly separated from the traditional authority

---

[1] A leading example of the new type of political leader in Ashanti is Edusei Krobo (born 1919). He was educated at a government school and became a journalist in 1931. When the CPP was formed he became full-time Ashanti Region propaganda secretary, and was chairman of the boycott committee in Ashanti in 1948. He became a member of the central commitee of the CPP, and was imprisoned for twelve months for 'positive action' in 1950. After his election he was appointed Government Chief Whip and Under-Secretary to the Minister of Justice.

DTCA

structure. This was intended to avoid 'involving the stools in the hurly-burly of local politics',[1] that is to say, recommending that the chiefs should cease to be active politicians.

(c) *In Dahomey*

After the conquest of the kingdom of Dahomey by the French in 1893, the deportation of the king, and the advance to the Niger, a decree made the whole of the conquered area a colony under the name of Dahomey. The new colony was far larger than the original kingdom, but nearly two-thirds of its population was made up of groups which had been within the kingdom of Dahomey. The whole colony was divided into *Cercles* under French administrators, and each of these *Cercles* was then divided into *Cantons* headed by loyal traditional chiefs or commoners appointed by the French administrator in charge of the *Cercle*. The authority structure which had been built by the Dahomean kings was thus broken, and the special position enjoyed by members of the royal lineage was ended. The town of Abomey, which had been the capital of the kingdom, lost its political importance, and the new economic and political changes transferred the centre of political activity to the coastal towns. In these towns the presence of a large number of Portuguese and Brazilian 'creoles' permitted the formation of a group of Europeanized Dahomeans, who in a few years completely accepted French assimilation. These 'creoles', who were later to be joined by the European-educated Dahomeans, the *akoues*, provided the traders, planters, middlemen, clerks, and so on, of the new colony. With the granting of French citizenship to those who had become assimilated, two distinct political groups were formed. The first was composed of those who identified themselves with France, and took out French nationality, and the second consisted of those Dahomeans whose social status derived from tradition. The first group was the more wealthy, and from 1893 to 1950 its members provided the 'new' political leadership in Dahomey.

The earliest political action which gained widespread support among the Dahomeans can be traced to a protest movement among the commercial groups in Whydah and

---

[1] *Report of the Select Committee of the Legislative Council appointed to make recommendations concerning Local Government in Ashanti*, Accra, 1951, p. 10.

Porto-Novo, against the land concessions given in 1900 to the railway company. During the visit of a French Deputy to Dahomey in 1902, a deputation met him carrying a petition which had been signed by 9,000 Dahomeans occupied in the palm-oil trade.[1] No similar collective movement took place in the coastal towns until 1925, when, as a protest against the laws differentiating between French citizens and French subjects, some of the latter showed their resentment by a series of disturbances, which were quickly stopped by the declaration of martial law.[2] After the First World War the towns of Whydah, Cotonou, and Porto-Novo, and later Agoue and Abomey, were given the status of mixed communes and were administered by a Municipal Council composed of persons appointed by the Governor and elected from a restricted electoral list. The elected members were practically always drawn from among the 'creole' population. 'Creoles' were also prominent in the foundation of the first newspapers, whose circulations were, however, very small.[3] This small group of journalists nevertheless figured prominently in the agitation for political changes in Dahomey, and the Administration regarded many of them with suspicion and barred a number from practising their profession.

During the Second World War Dahomey followed the fortunes of French West Africa, first under the Vichy Government and later under the Free French Forces. In the Vichy period the shortages due to the almost complete cessation of European imports led to a rise in the cost of living, while the presence of German and Italian Commissions created a feeling of frustration. After the coming of the Free French Forces in 1942 hopes

[1] Le Hérissé, R., *Voyage au Dahomey*, Paris, 1903, pp. 108–9.

[2] Buell, R. L., *The Native Problem in Africa*, 2 vols., New York, 1928, vol. ii, p. 16, and vol. i, p. 109.

[3] Among the best known of these journalists were the following two. J. M. Dorothe Lima (born 1885) was a student at the local Catholic mission in Porto-Novo, and became a clerk in the Administration in 1914. He became a French citizen in 1916, and served in France until 1918. On his return to Dahomey he bought a printing-shop and began newspaper publishing. Jose Firmito Santos was a student at the local Catholic Mission of Agoue. He entered the Administration as a clerk and later also became a Municipal Councillor. He was the principal accused in the case against the newspaper *La Voix du Dahomey*, which was charged with stirring up the people against the Administration and of stealing official documents.

of political changes began to develop and were stimulated by widespread publicity given to the Brazzaville Conference of 1944. This conference provoked widespread political discussion and created a demand among many Dahomeans for the recognition of their participation in the war. Immediately after 1945, when the French Union was created by decree, a number of 'electoral committees' were formed among the Dahomeans to support the candidature of individuals to represent Dahomey in the Constituent Assembly in Paris. A number of these electoral committees supported the candidature of a French missionary priest, Father Aupias, and of S. M. Apithy, a Dahomean who had lived for long in Paris. When Father Aupias died shortly after his election, Apithy became the most prominent political leader in post-war Dahomey.[1]

In Dahomey the immediate result of the French Union Decree, and the declaration that all inhabitants of the territory were French citizens, was the creation of a widespread electorate, which grew from 57,000 in 1946 to 352,000 in 1951; with the growth of this electorate various political organizations emerged to organize it. The first of these to develop from the electoral committees was the Union Progressive Dahoméenne (UPD), in which were to be found not only those who had acted as leaders for the small, politically active minority between the two World Wars, but also new leaders from other social groups which were increasing in political importance. Trade-unions, for instance, grew rapidly to number 34 in 1947, with a total membership of about 16,000. But the efforts of the leaders of the UPD to create a national party were unsuccessful, and it began to disintegrate along territorial lines. One of the reasons for this was the retention by the Administration of the old political

[1] Sourou-Migan Apithy, born 1913 in Porto-Novo, where he studied at the local mission school; later went to France where he obtained diplomas in political science and accountancy; joined the French Socialist Party 1945–7, and the Rassemblement Démocratique Africain (RDA) 1947–8, and the Parliamentary Group of the Oversea Independents in 1948. He was elected to the French National Assembly in 1946, after having been a member of the Interim Assembly in 1945, and was re-elected in 1951. He is president of the Dahomean Territorial Assembly. He founded the Dahomean Republican Party in 1951. He is also secretary of the French National Assembly, and a judge of the High Court of Justice, and the director of the newspaper *Ouest-Africain*.

differentiation between Dahomeans who were full French citizens and those who had retained their local status. The citizens of full metropolitan status quickly formed themselves into branches of French political parties, while those of local status seem to have been influenced less by an established political organization than by the personality of single individuals. Thus in 1946 the Dahomean Territorial Assembly consisted of thirty members, twelve of whom were elected by citizens of metropolitan status, and eighteen by those of local status. Of these thirty members, twenty-eight belonged to some sort of political organization at the moment of their election. There were only two independents. The 1951 Assembly, on the contrary, was composed of fifty members, of which eighteen were elected by citizens of metropolitan status, and thirty-two by those of local status. Of the fifty members, eleven were members of a political organization, while the rest were all independents at the moment of their election. The eleven who were members of a political organization had all been elected by citizens of metropolitan status, but the citizens of local status returned only independents. Since 1951 a number of independents have joined Apithy's Dahomean Republican Party.

The new balance of political interests in Dahomey has not affected the occupational and social status of the political leaders, as may be seen from the composition of the 1951 Assembly:

Occupational status of the members of the 1951
Dahomean Territorial Assembly

First college (18 seats)	Second college (32 seats)
3 civil servants	7 teachers
3 missionaries	6 traders/shopkeepers
3 doctors	5 clerks
2 clerks	3 doctors
1 teacher	3 civil servants
1 lawyer	2 hospital assistants
1 ex-colonial administrator	1 police officer
1 trader	1 Senior Peul Chief
1 railway station-master	1 chartered accountant
1 engineer	2 professions unknown
1 profession unknown	

This is shown equally clearly by the occupational status of the six most important Dahomean political leaders who have represented Dahomey in Paris since the 1951 election, and who comprise three teachers, one chartered accountant, one doctor, and one lawyer.

CONCLUSION

The foregoing account has shown that, during the period of colonial rule the Yoruba, Ashanti, and Dahomey peoples have experienced far-reaching changes in their economic, religious, social, and political life. The most notable of these changes have been the growth of a middle class and the rise of nationalism. The new political loyalties which were created, though by no means obliterating the lines of tribal cleavage, were able to produce a wider community of interest and action. Changes in political leadership can thus be directly related to changes in the location of political authority. Presented in its simplest form the first main change in political leadership can be seen in the transference of political authority from the pre-colonial tribal hierarchy to the authority structure created by the colonial Administration in which loyal chiefs were included in a subordinate position. On the whole the leadership of the colonial Administration was accepted and the transfer was thereby facilitated. As more and more of the people came under the influence of the social changes which allowed them to act independently of their lineage, village or territorial allegiance, the myths supporting the 'traditional' authority were shorn of their validity. But the rise of the new attitudes and beliefs also prevented the stabilization of the colonial authority structure. Western concepts of the legitimacy of political authority came to support the demands made by nationalists and others for a new political system.

3. The Ivory Coast

A. R. ZOLBERG *One-Party Government in the Ivory Coast* Princeton
University Press 1964; pages 322–7, 329–34, 335–7

The Ivory Coast exemplifies the growth of a regime in which a
single mass party is clearly dominant. As suggested in the introduction, this political form is a common one throughout the
modern world. Because it is not as well known as others that
cluster around the two polar types of liberal democracy and
totalitarianism, much exploration is necessary. Comparative
analysis, a prelude to greater understanding of single-party
systems, has begun only recently. The detailed study of
particular cases such as this one will make further work of this
type possible.

I have distinguished three major phases of development,
which correspond to successive stages of constitutional evolution
but which I have analysed in terms of the structure, the strategies, and the goals of the dominant political organization. In
spite of differences in timing, in style of rhetoric or action, and
in institutional arrangements, similar phases characterize the
political growth of many other former British and French
dependencies. The *Parti Démocratique de Côte d'Ivoire* began its
career as a protest movement within a framework that afforded
but limited opportunities for political participation by Africans
(1946–1951); it was transformed into a political party during
the period of terminal colonialism (1952–1958); and it became
synonymous with government when the Ivory Coast Republic
was founded (1959).

The movement began as an agglomerate of affiliated associations, a "congress", but was soon to become more formally
structured through the efforts of its leaders and with the help
of European sympathizers. Its objectives were both highly
specific, in that they constituted the sum of the particular
grievances of the various component groups, and highly general,
in that they had as their common denominator resentment
against alien rule. A desire for some form of autonomy, if not
outright independence, was shared by members of the élite and
communicated to their followers. Common discontent, together
with a reorientation of individuals away from traditional

authority, provided the cement for organizational solidarity. These processes were precipitated by one man who embodied the new aspirations, possessed the skills needed for leadership, and thus acted as the catalyst.

Like Nkrumah in Ghana, Houphouet-Boigny is a charismatic leader. Apter's analysis of the role of such leaders is applicable:

The efficiency of charisma lies in the fact that it satisfied the same functional requisites of leadership as did traditional leadership in the past. Nkrumah's charismatic authority has replaced the chief's traditional authority by meeting the same functional requirements, but by introducing new types of structures for their satisfaction.

The functional requirements involved are: serving as a source of norms, which become a standard for followers; serving as a symbol, which helps disparate groups in the territorial society acquire a sense of identity with one another; serving as a focus for political integration, by appearing as the central figure of authority within the new institutional framework; and finally, serving as a living symbol of the new territorial community, encouraging individuals to transcend traditional ethnic group affiliations. Although during this protest period the nationalist movement opposes the colonial government, the resulting conflict helps promote the goal of the colonial authorities: the institutionalization of a centralized secular political structure.

Incentives for leaders and followers during this period are not material. It is the era of the true believer; those who are frustrated and dissatisfied are willing to make sacrifices for a cause which has, at the time, little tangible prospect of success, because "things which are not are indeed mightier than things that are". It is a period of myth making, of selflessness, during which schoolteachers and junior civil servants, often recent graduates, are presented with an opportunity to become immortal historical actors. There is little need to compromise, little doubt, few pressures to dampen enthusiasm with political realism. Frustrations, grievances, malajustments stemming from the colonial situation, serve to reinforce the movement. Although one leader overshadows all others, he is not remote, for there has been little time to fully differentiate roles. Fraternal fervour prevails.

Since the colonial framework provides *some* opportunities for political participation by means of elections, nationalist strategy usually involves electoral pursuits. Hence, the movement exhibits from the very beginning some of the features of a vote-getting organization. Nevertheless, since suffrage is limited and elected representatives do not wield much authority, it can be argued that results are not a significant index of support and that elections are not the sole legitimate avenue to political power. The movement demonstrates its strength by engaging in agitational activities, probably easier to promote than any other form of political action. The upheaval that accompanies social change is thus useful to organizations based on protest and which have no responsibility for government.

After a relatively brief period of suppression, sufficient however to create an enduring mythology relating the struggle for national emancipation, the colonial government becomes more accommodating. The foremost nationalist leader is acknowledged to be an *interlocuteur valable*. Institutions are modified, either by means of a new constitution or less formally by a more liberal interpretation of existing rules, to broaden popular participation and to give modern élites a greater role in the structure of decision making. This is the period of dyarchy or terminal colonialism, during which nationalist movements become political parties. Although ultimate responsibility for government still belongs to colonial officials, who can be blamed for inadequacies of the system and for other ills that befall the country, the party can take credit for the greater emphasis on social welfare and economic development reflected in an expansion of government personnel and in the allocation of a larger share of the budget to tangible items such as new roads, educational and health facilities, or urban construction. Since its leaders participate in government, the party has some control over the allocation of offices, goods, and services. Its distributive capacity is vastly increased.

Earlier, support was often spontaneous. Now, the faithful have grown middle-aged physically and emotionally. They seek rewards more tangible than the knowledge that they are in the mainstream of history. The organization becomes more dependent upon material incentives, not only to satisfy its own members but also to secure the support of former enemies. Because the party's goals can be attained through institutionalized channels, regular demonstration of strength by means of electoral turnout takes priority over agitational tactics. The good party bureaucrat, who can be relied upon to bring out the vote, rather than the firebrand, who can arouse the market crowds, is needed and prized. Differentiations between leaders and followers become more pronounced as the former gain access to a new style of life that is associated with the high positions in the institutional structure they now occupy. The leaders not only derive status from these positions but also endow the institutions of which they are the pinnacle with renewed legitimacy in the eyes of their followers.

Although the party towers over other organizations and is politically secure, there is, during this period, increasing concern with the achievement of a political monopoly. This is justified on the ground that national unity is the primordial goal; since the nationalist movement represents all the people, national unity is defined as being synonymous with political unity. What is sought, the leaders maintain, is not a "unitary" party, but rather a "unified" party. The emphasis is not on exclusiveness but on inclusiveness: opponents are not to be eliminated; they are to be amalgamated. That this was accomplished earlier in the Ivory Coast than in other West African countries, or indeed that it was accomplished at all, remains a source of puzzlement. Disagreement among leaders over policies, together with the existence of consistent cleavages, would lead one to expect that several parties, rather than a single all-encompassing organization, would emerge and sustain themselves. Why did this not occur? No single factor can provide an adequate explanation. The first political body that moves into an organizational vacuum gains a considerable advantage over all competitors. Later, it is easier to hold this position than to conquer it.

The dominant organization also benefits from a bandwagon effect, observed not only in the Ivory Coast but in many other countries as well. During the period of terminal colonialism, opponents find that it is increasingly costly to pass up immediate opportunities in exchange for the uncertainty of future electoral success. More generally, the bandwagon effect can be ascribed to the widespread belief among members of the political élite that there is room for only one nationalist movement, that only one organization can speak validly for an entire country when dealing with alien rulers, that political competition jeopardizes national unity, and, as Ouezzin Coulibaly stated in 1956, that the primacy of a single political party is a prerequisite for the achievement of political maturity and territorial self-government. This belief becomes a social fact which in turn helps transform the belief into political reality. It is a case of self-fulfilling prophecy, an illustration of W. I. Thomas' basic theorem, "if men define situations as real, they are real in their consequences.". . .

During the period of terminal colonialism, the transfer of conciliar and democratic institutions inspired from the metropolitan model is completed. After independence, the framework of government is modified to suit local needs and to reflect more faithfully political realities. Provisions are made to insure the dominance of the executive over the legislature. Parliamentary bodies are reduced to the status of deliberative or consultative assemblies. Paradoxically, this step can be thought of as a return to an earlier state of affairs, following Napoleonic precepts such as the ones that guided colonial decision makers. Although universal suffrage is maintained, elections become plebiscitary in tone rather than competitive. Institutional devices may even be introduced to buttress the political monopoly of the government party. Even where the constitution proclaims separation of powers in keeping with liberal prescriptions, one-man rule becomes official. The man who led the movement for national emancipation now becomes the paramount executive, legislator, and judge. In case he is made vulnerable to criticism, as the result of his personal involvement in day-to-day government, his heroic stature is bolstered by mechanical devices of public glorification. Tradition is also invoked to reinforce the legitimacy of his role, either through the public bestowal of formal titles or by more subtle means.

In the course of meeting various contingencies, the rulers extend their control to new spheres. In some countries this is done in accordance with the directives of an ideological blueprint which prescribes total control as the essential strategy for rapid modernization. Although the Ivory Coast has explicitly rejected commitment to such an ideology, its leaders have in fact followed a similar path on an *ad hoc* basis. Their actions are visible in both the traditional and the modern sector. Because the survival of primordial ties is thought to be incompatible with modernity, the government seizes every available opportunity to accelerate the deterioration of the fabric of traditional society. Here, the strategy is a Fabian one; elsewhere, where statesmen have embraced a more militant style, a frontal assault may be preferred. Turning to the modern sector, the rulers view the growth of autonomous voluntary associations with much suspicion. They remember from their own beginnings that such groups can easily become politicized and that they can serve as stepping stones for political entrepreneurs. Two approaches are used simultaneously to meet this threat: on the one hand, secondary associations are transformed into ancillary organizations, subservient to the party; on the other hand, legal controls over associational life and over communications, inherited from the colonial regime, are revived or reinforced.

The lesser importance of parliamentary organs has already been noted. Although the national assembly remains the principal representative body, there is a growing dissatisfaction with the geographical basis of representation. Electoral districts tend to be identified as the home of particular ethnic groups. For this reason, as well as to facilitate control over recruitment of office-holders, the Ivory Coast began to enlarge constituencies until they disappeared altogether. An increasing number of representatives are designated as the spokesmen for occupational groups, "estates", or sectors of the population defined on some other non-geographical basis: they represent government employees, workers in the private sector, women, youth, small or large farmers, coffee or banana growers, foreigners. At the same time, after voluntary associations have been transformed into semi-official organs, they are granted a consultative role in policy making. These developments suggest a possible trend toward corporatism. This has not yet been formally institutionalized, except through the creation of advisory social and economic councils, perhaps because there is little familiarity with European models and because the corporate state has been associated in continental Europe with the right rather than with the left. Here is perhaps the nucleus of a trend more fully visible in the *P.R.I.* of Mexico.

Many of these changes have repercussions inside the party as well. Having merged with the government, the party becomes the coordinator of administration. It must disseminate information and directives from the centre to the local level as well as supervise their execution. Its major task is to engineer consent among the population: it must induce consumer demands that are compatible with the product government wants to sell. Since the party is an important component of the bureaucratic apparatus, it must perform its new functions efficiently. Competition within the organization, factionalism, and open debate, all of which had maintained an atmosphere of freedom and had contributed to inner cohesion by providing opportunities for the expression of conflict, must be eliminated because they are thought to endanger the effectiveness of government. There is much ado concerning the revival of party life and of internal democracy. In order to combat apathy, there is renewed emphasis on political pageantry as well. But the good party man, or in a mass-party state, the good citizen, is defined as one who follows directives without questioning the wisdom of his leaders.

The use of coercion to engender support and enforce adherence to the regime grows considerably. Techniques include warning and threats, backed by restriction upon freedom of movement, jailing, banishment, and exile. Although much publicity has been given to such events in African states, several things must be noted: first, that coercion is used *after* other tactics have failed; secondly, that these sanctions, however severe, are usually temporary; and thirdly, that coercion is not used methodically to induce a climate of terror. Relationships between rulers and dissenters retain the air of a family quarrel, followed by grand reconciliations when the crisis is over. This may be attributed in part to the intimate nature of politics in countries that have a small élite bound by a network of personal relationships. Almost anyone of sufficient consequence to be jailed is bound to be a member of at least the extended family of someone high in the ruling hierarchy. Furthermore, it is possible that prescriptions governing the use of coercion have been inspired from their experience under colonial rule. In almost every country of French- and English-speaking Africa, the colonial government eventually recognized that today's troublemakers benefited from popular support, that they had to be coopted in order to secure the consent of the governed, and that they might well become tomorrow's legitimate representatives of the people. The expression of grievances through agitation against the government and retaliatory sanctions may thus be viewed as complementary parts of an intricate process of institutionalized bargaining.

During the period of alien rule, the physical presence of European officials, traders, or colonists, as well as the colonial situation in general, contributes to the maintenance of internal cohesion by providing an external enemy against whom common energies can be directed. Although these objects are removed after independence, others are substituted. Particular choices reflect the more or less militant style of the regime. In some cases, the leadership will emphasize the threat of neo-colonialism, the desirability of liberating hitherto unfree African countries, and the need to create a powerful, unified pan-African whole, capable of intervening positively in world affairs. In other cases, among which the Ivory Coast may be included, the threats are identified somewhat differently. They have included other African countries suspected of having designs on Ivory Coast wealth; nations of the more militant type to which irridentist propensities can be attributed; and more recently, there have been occasional references to the dangers of Chinese communism. The choice of objects used to externalize inner tensions helps explain the different stand African countries with similar regimes have taken on international issues. Finally, it is not unusual to find that some group within the country inherits the unfortunate role of scapegoat. Immigrant African communities are particularly vulnerable in this respect.

Reliance on coercion to obtain support, the use of external threats to strengthen cohesion, the appearance of a scapegoat mechanism, must not be allowed to overshadow the fact that the priority assigned to these tactics remains lower than that which is attributed to others in the regime's panoply. Cooptation, distribution of tangible rewards, and persuasion remain significant. Similarly, the gap between constitutional theory and political practice, the growth of executive dominance and of personal rule, must not be allowed to hide the responsiveness of the regime, its concern with goals shared by most of the people, and the constant practice of formal and informal consultation. The rulers continue to benefit from a vast store of trust and consent. The most important source of support continues to stem from the ties thinner than air but stronger than steel that bind the people to the national hero. Although corrosion has attacked these bonds as the result of new political difficulties, they have not yet been destroyed. The people continue to believe in the benevolent intentions of their leader, in his wisdom in choosing policies, and in his power to overcome obstacles as long as he continues to fulfil the mission for which he assumed responsibility long ago: yesterday, to terminate alien rule; today and tomorrow, to secure rapid improvement of economic and social conditions at the least possible cost to his people. . . .

The Ivory Coast is not a political democracy in the sense usually attributed to this concept in the West. There is no institutionalized competition between two or more political parties to determine who will govern. Although in a one-party system it is possible for internal contests to serve as a substitute this does not occur in the P.D.C.I. Furthermore, civil liberties, which never flourished under French tutelage, have been severely curtailed by the new rulers. While in external appearance it is a government of laws rather than of men, these laws, including the constitution itself, have been tailored to suit a specific set of governors and can easily be altered at their discretion.

It is not difficult to argue, however, that the regime is more democratic than its traditional or colonial predecessors. The Ivory Coast and other new nations that are governed by a modern élite, ruling through a mass party which has a broad popular base, which is inclusive rather than exclusive, and which is genuinely representative of most strata in the population, have passed a point of no return on the road towards political modernization. Further development may be arrested; oligarchical tendencies may become more pronounced; controls may be greatly extended; but whatever else political change may bring, never again will rulers base their legitimacy solely on traditional claims, on the right of conquest, or on racial superiority. Today's rulers must proclaim their adherence to democratic values even when they depart from them. That they should do so must be seen less as a sign of hypocrisy than as the mark of a bad conscience. Ivory Coast leaders acknowledge the desirability of democracy but justify undemocratic practices on the basis of expediency. They view the regime they have helped to create as a tutelary democracy. As Shils has indicated, there is something instinctive about this:

Tutelary democracy is a variant of political democracy which recommends itself to the elites of the new states. It does so because it is more authoritative than political democracy, and also because the institutions of public opinion and the civil order do not seem qualified to carry the burden which political democracy would impose on them. It is not the object of a theory in the way in which political democracy and totalitarian oligarchy have become theories; it is the 'natural theory' of men brought up to believe in themselves as democrats, who have, for various reasons, considerable attachment to democratic institutions and who have, for good or poor reasons, little confidence in their people's present capacity to operate democratic institutions effectively amidst the tasks of the new states.

This type of regime is characterized by an adaptation of the institutions of political democracy in the direction of executive dominance. There tends to be a merger of party and government, with emphasis on discipline. Although freedom of expression, of assembly, and of association may be impaired, the rule of law must be maintained: "When it goes, then tutelary democracy turns more determinedly toward oligarchy." The regime must truly attempt to reinstate the institutions of political democracy whenever feasible. Furthermore, the incumbents must tolerate some criticism and accept at least in principle the idea of an opposition. The opposition, on its side, must overcome the twin dangers of self-destruction in the face of great odds and transformation into a subversive organization.

The distinction between a tutelary democracy and a modernizing oligarchy is a subtle one. Similar aspirations among the élite underlie both types. The oligarchy, whether it is manned by a military or a civilian élite, is characterized by the elimination of parliament or by a drastic reduction in its role. There is greater interference with the rule of law than in the tutelary democracy. Opposition is definitely not tolerated. It is important to note, however, that the term encompasses regimes that are representative, responsive, and concerned with eliciting consent among the governed. Tutelary democracies and modernizing oligarchies can be thought of as being part of a continuum, with the latter being more distant from the pole of political democracy than the former. If we use the actions of the Ivory Coast rulers rather than their stated intentions as classificatory criteria, then we must consider the country as a modernizing oligarchy. It is ruled by a set of benevolent managers. Like that of its colonial predecessor, its mood is one of paternalism. . . .

4. Ghana

DAVID KIMBLE *Political History of Ghana* Clarendon Press, Oxford 1963; pages 128–31, 135–41

Societies in Transition
Economic development was the main mediating force whereby the individualist, competitive, acquisitive attitudes and values of the West were introduced into African society. The impact was least, however, during the centuries of pre-colonial coastal trade, greatest during the comparatively short colonial era. The early European traders brought new means to wealth and power: their guns and gunpowder profoundly altered the balance of power among the coastal States with which they came in contact, and contributed significantly to the rise of the interior kingdoms, notably Akwamu and Ashanti.[1] But before

[1] This tendency is well illustrated in the new material brought to light by the research of I. G. Wilkes into the rise of the Akwamu Empire from 1650. He shows that the direction of expansion was dictated not only by political expediency, but also by the economic attraction of the coastal trade. At first the aim of the Akwamus was to obtain control of the Accra–interior trade routes as a source of revenue from tolls, with which to purchase guns and gunpowder; but economic ascendancy soon led to the conquest of Accra itself, 1677–81, and the emergence of Akwamu as a coastal power. (In 1963
ETCA

the nineteenth century, external trade brought little disturbance to the social order within these States, and scarcely affected the more loosely-knit societies of the hinterland.

The progressive assumption by the British of jurisdiction and political control brought about a gradual acceleration of the pace of social change. The isolated, autonomous States and tribal societies were brought into a new relationship with a central power, and hence with one another. The super-imposition of external authority seriously weakened the powers of the Chiefs, and the sanctions at their disposal. The prevention of inter-State warfare, for example, deprived them of their main means of gaining new prestige, territory, and wealth, and of providing an outlet for the aggressive impulses of their young men.[1] British interference with traditional judicial systems was initially prompted by humanitarian motives; but the prohibition of some common punishments—such as the chaining, mutilation, or enslavement of prisoners—deprived the Chiefs of their most important physical sanctions. Europeans also failed to understand the nature of many of the offences punishable by death. African customary law, like English law, aimed to protect society from unscrupulous individuals; but its definition of anti-social acts extended much farther, and there was little concern with protecting the rights of the individual during the processes of law.

Economic sanctions, especially the control of wealth by the traditional authorities, were also weakened by the creation of new openings for individual trade and enrichment. More important, perhaps, the religious authority of the Chief and his ability to invoke supernatural sanctions were undermined by the introduction of a new religion, Christianity; this offered not only the prestige of association with the ruling race, but also the utilitarian advantage of education, which in turn led to wider economic opportunities.

the Akwamus even captured Christiansborg Castle from the Danes, and appointed their own Governor for a year.) 'The Rise of the Akwamu Empire, 1650–1710', in *Transactions of the Historical Society of Ghana* (Achimota, 1957), vol. iii, pt. 2.

[1] Cf. W. Bosman, *A New and Accurate Description of the Coast of Guinea* (London, 1705), p. 70: 'The chief employments of the inhabitants are merchandise, agriculture, and war; to which last they are particularly addicted.'

British protection—and later, direct rule—meant far greater security for the individual. Within his society, he was no longer at the mercy of physical cruelty and exploitation, even when authorized by the Chief; outside, he was protected from molestation by hostile tribes or slave-raiders, and his territorial mobility was greatly increased. Some fugitives from traditional justice were thereby enabled to escape and claim refuge with the British; far more important, however, was the fact that many traders were enabled to extend the area of their operations, or to seek new markets farther afield. There was also much greater scope for anti-social individuals to evade traditional obligations within their own community.

The superimposition of external authority which brought these changes did not supplant the rule of the Chiefs, but it led to considerable tension between the Chiefs and the British Government on the one hand, and increasingly between the Chiefs and their subjects on the other. Similarly, the time-honoured relationships between groups and individuals were seriously affected by the economic and political changes of the nineteenth and twentieth centuries, even though these did not mean the complete destruction of the older social order. The expanding economy brought intercommunication and inter-dependence on an ever-widening scale. The kinship group or extended family began to lose its importance as an economic unit, and hence to some extent its social self-sufficiency; meanwhile, new associations began to emerge, based on common economic, cultural, or political interests, instead of kinship and age-structure.

A radical change of status for a substantial class of people was implied—though not at first strictly enforced—with the aboli-tion of domestic slavery in 1874. This, however, did not present a serious social problem since the ex-slaves were gradually absorbed into the emerging wage economy, and many found new patrons in Christian missionaries anxious to demonstrate the brotherhood of man. More significant was the fact that, as money incomes increased, wealth tended to accumu-late in the hands of the younger men, who were more adaptable and more susceptible to outside influences; the introduction of Western education threw emphasis even upon the children. In a society in which respect and high standing had been accorded to age—to such an extent as to make some communities almost a gerontocracy—this reversal of status brought about a widening dichotomy between the generations, which found strong political expression during the twentieth century.[1]

The significance of all these changes, as far as the individual was concerned, might be summed up as a movement towards achieved—as opposed to ascribed—status. It must be remembered, however, that the traditional system allowed certain scope for achievement, as already shown, and that the shift was gradual and partial, not sudden and total. Allied to this was the increasing emphasis upon the role of the individual, and the undermining of communal values and sanctions. Yet, though kinship ties might often be weakened, and new social groupings began to emerge, the tenacity of family and tribal loyalties often considerably modified the pace and direction of economic change; and they certainly had a strong influence upon the development of nationalism in the Gold Coast.

The Nineteenth-Century Conflict of Cultures

The establishment of permanent European administration on the coast brought a new, alien culture-group into close juxtaposition with African society. Even though British officials never became an integral part of the community, they introduced novel economic requirements, political prohibitions, judicial decisions, religious attitudes, and patterns of behaviour; and all these profoundly modified social norms and orientation in the coastal towns, their influence gradually penetrating to the interior.

During the nineteenth century there was some friction at nearly every point of culture-contact; it appeared that Africans had to reject the old entirely if they were to reap the benefits of the new, and since this was virtually impossible the attempt must often have set up severe psychological conflicts. British officials, however, were serenely confident of their civilizing

[1] Cf. G. Balandier's comment: 'The colonial situation involves not only . . . the appearance of new processes of social differentiation; it entails . . . a reorientation of the social structure. In overturning the traditional equilibriums, it lets come to the surface some of the very antagonisms repressed in order to maintain these equilibriums. This is particularly apparent in the relations between sexes and between generations.' 'Social Changes and Social Problems in Negro Africa', in *Africa in the Modern World*, p. 56.

mission, and increasingly attempted to exert their influence beyond the coastal forts. Certain customs, such as human sacrifice, slavery, and pawning, were obviously un-Christian; others, such as the cruel treatment of prisoners, or riotous celebrations that often ended in needless bloodshed, revolted the humanitarianism of Victorian administrators; while the scarcity or total absence of clothing offended their sense of propriety.[1]

There was a great deal of ignorance and misunderstanding about the significance of local beliefs and institutions. The Chief was treated primarily as a secular ruler, whose powers, suitably modified, could be incorporated within a new institutional framework, while fetish practices were expected to wither away, if not actually suppressed. Images of barbarism, bloodshed, and slavery tended to dominate European thinking about Gold Coast society,[2] and many honestly felt that the solution was to suppress all the savage and heathen customs. Then, surely, it would be only a matter of time and suitable Ordinances before superstitions were dispelled, and replaced by more enlightened modes of conduct.

It was perhaps the superficial manifestations of the Western way of life that were most readily taken over and consciously imitated during the process of acculturation. It was also these that attracted most controversy and were most earnestly rejected in later years, as cultural nationalism gathered force. Yet deeper and more subtle influences were at work, especially in the schools, the churches, and the market-place. No matter what clothes people wore, what language they spoke, what type of houses they lived in, an alien culture had come to stay in the Gold Coast, and could neither be wholly accepted nor wholly

[1] In 1872 some British merchants registered a complaint after seeing two young girls parading through Cape Coast, naked and decorated with beads, in celebration of puberty rites. There was considerable argument as to the degree of indecency involved. CO/96/94.

[2] Cf. Winwood Reade, *Savage Africa* (London, 1863), the narrative of a tour through West and Equatorial Africa, 'with notes on the habits of the gorilla; on the existence of unicorns and tailed men . . . on the origin, character and capabilities of the negro and on the future civilisation of Western Africa'. Although generally a fair-minded observer, Reade retained his belief that 'The typical negro is the true savage of Africa . . . unrestrained by moral laws' (pp. 554–5).

rejected. It was assimilated primarily by educated Africans, and their role in the changing social structure merits closer examination.

The New Élite

Changes in social structure, as opposed to patterns of behaviour, are less documented and more difficult to assess in detail. There is no doubt that economic development led to the enrichment of certain groups and individuals. At first it was the traditional authorities who benefited from the process of land alienation, and to some extent from the growth of cocoa farming. But they had no monopoly of economic opportunities; even in the nineteenth century there were some land speculators and a few professional men earning large incomes, which were later invested in cocoa farming or buying. Increasingly, the wealth from cocoa came into the hands of those whose status was simply that of 'youngmen' in the old society, but who now helped to focus discontent against both the Chiefs and the colonial authorities. It was the professional handful, in particular, who had sufficient wealth and leisure to devote to politics, and from whose ranks the early leadership of the national movement was drawn.

One of the most important means of expressing nationalist grievances was the expensive technique of sending deputations to London. The way in which these were financed is an interesting index of the change in their social and economic backing. In 1865 King Aggery of Cape Coast sent two educated commissioners to appear before the Select Committee; the money for this was borrowed in advance, and in default of payment the guarantors (including one of the commissioners) were imprisoned. Thirty years later, when the Asantehene sent an embassy of eight, consisting mainly of traditional office-bearers, in the vain hope of securing the independence of his kingdom, he levied a special tax throughout Ashanti, since the State coffers were then running low. In 1898, however, the three prosperous merchants sent by the A.R.P.S. to protest against the Lands Bill were probably able to pay their own expenses initially, until these were refunded by the grateful Chiefs. The success of this mission inspired the Chiefs to pay up handsomely in advance for a deputation to protest against the 1911

Forest Bill, and £3,000 was available for the merchant, doctor, and two lawyers who appeared before the West African Lands Committee. But in 1920, when the National Congress of British West Africa organized a deputation that forfeited the support of the Chiefs, they had to contribute largely towards their own expenses, and several of the members had their own commercial reasons for visiting London. The technique of organizing mass support and securing a multitude of small subscriptions had not yet been studied.

By the 1920s there was a small but growing group of African business men and traders, who might be regarded as constituting the nucleus of a middle class. But it is risky to apply the analysis appropriate to Western society in the different social situation of the Gold Coast. Complicating factors arise not only from the persistence of traditional patterns and values, but also from the explosive force of Western education. Some writers assume that the end-product of education was the creation of a new class in West Africa. J. S. Coleman, for example, emphasizes the isolation of educated Nigerians, due to their 'Conversion to Christianity, knowledge of and preference for English, imitation of European behaviour, and postschool employment in an urban milieu'; it is doubtful, however, whether these common factors are sufficient to justify his grouping them together as a single class, especially since he makes no reference to their economic interests.

Various attempts have been made to define an African middle class. Some would place it between 'the wealthy aristocracy and the impoverished masses of the old economy', but this hardly seems relevant to the Gold Coast. One writer distinguishes a middle class somewhere in between the lower class of peasants and wage-earning labourers, and the European 'upper class' of officials and entrepreneurs; but it seems unsatisfactory to lump together in theory all Africans engaged, at whatever level, in commerce, teaching, and the civil service, as well as members of the professions. T. L. Hodgkin, however, is careful not to include the infinitesimally small group of lawyers, doctors, property owners, and senior civil servants, and defines the middle class as consisting of relatively small-scale entrepreneurs, traders, and the less exalted ranks of the educated salariat. His analysis of their ambiguous status, patterns of consumption, and political and social attitudes, is useful and suggestive.[1]

But it seems clear that the concept of class structure is not particularly helpful in analysing the shifting patterns of African society.[2] Even today, when the process of social differentiation has been carried to considerable lengths, the network of kinship ties, involving obligations towards members of the extended family at all social levels, prevents the formation of rigid class barriers. Gold Coast society in the nineteenth century saw the emergence of a significant educated group, dependent on non-traditional sources of income, who set patterns of social behaviour in the towns, and from time to time exerted a strong political influence upon rural Chiefs. But they do not easily fall within any rigorous definition of a social class. This is true whether one chooses an economic interpretation—such as Max Weber's, in terms of common interest in the possession of goods, opportunities for income, and market situation[3]—or whether, with J. Schumpeter, one defines a class by the purely social criterion that intermarriage prevails among its members.[4]

One is left sharing G. Balandier's doubts whether the new social strata which transform the traditional African status system can be regarded as classes, in the sense in which modern industrial societies understand them. His study of modern Brazzaville has shown the emergence of some aspects of a

[1] T. L. Hodgkin, 'The African Middle Class', in *Corona* (London, 1956), pp. 86–7.

[2] Even a Soviet scholar has recently admitted that it is not always possible to determine the nature of the class structure emerging from what he calls the 'primaeval community system'. I. I. Potekhin, 'The Origin and Development of National Capital on the Gold Coast'; Lecture, University College of Ghana, Dec. 1957.

[3] Weber offers some applicable generalizations concerning the transition from status to class: 'When the bases of the acquisition and the distribution of goods are relatively stable, stratification by status is favoured. Every technological and economic transformation threatens stratification by status and pushes the class situation into the foreground.' He suggests that ' "Property" and "lack of property" are . . . the basic categories of all class situations'; but West Africa has not yet fully reached this stage. From *Max Weber: Essays in Sociology*, edited and translated by H. H. Gerth and C. W. Mills (New York, 1946), pp. 180–95.

[4] *Imperialism and Social Classes* (Oxford, 1951), pp. 137–47.

middle-class spirit among what he calls the 'educated progressives'.[1] But he concludes that in general 'the maintenance (even at a low level) of the familial economies and the persistence of certain traditional relations between individuals of unequal economic status', as well as the shallowness of modern economic distinctions, and the tendency to unite in opposition to foreign rule, counteract 'the formation of those radically incompatible groups which are the social classes'.[2]

The concept of *élites* appears far more relevant to the analysis of changing social structure in West Africa. Here, the definition of S. F. Nadel seems most useful: 'a stratum of the population which, for whatever reason, can claim a position of superiority and hence a corresponding measure of influence over the fate of the community'. He emphasizes that an *élite* must have some degree of corporateness and exclusiveness, forming a more or less self-conscious unit within the society.[3] This enables us to classify the Western-educated group as an *élite* in Gold Coast society, without any assumption as to identity of economic interests or of marriageable status. Still more illuminating is Nadel's discussion of the *élite* as a standard-setting group; the recognition of their superiority tends to be attached not merely to their special advantages, such as the wealth of the rich or the learning of the educated, but is extended to cover their general interests, manners—and, one might add, styles of dress—so that their status is enhanced by being in some respects imitable. Furthermore, the extent of their social influence may depend upon the close personal relations between the members of the *élite* and the rest of the community, and on their readiness or wish to communicate their values to other people. The stronger

---

[1] *Sociologie des brazzavilles noires* (Paris, 1955), ch. iv, 'Les problèmes de l'organisation sociale et de la vie politique'.

[2] 'Social Changes and Social Problems in Negro Africa', in *Africa in the Modern World*, pp. 61–3.

[3] Cf. K. Mannheim's analysis of the function of *élites* in creating and assimilating culture. He points out that if the necessary 'minimum of exclusiveness is lost, then the deliberate formation of taste, of a guiding principle of style, becomes impossible'. At the same time, the *élites* should be 'reasonably accessible' and recruited from society in certain definite ways— in the Gold Coast, largely by education—if their culture is not to lose life and vigour through social in-breeding. *Man and Society* (London, 1940 edn.), pp. 86–8.

such links, the greater the power of the *élite* to facilitate or hinder developments and to make new ideas acceptable to the new group at large.[1]

Here we have the key to the tremendous social and political influence of the Gold Coast educated *élite*. They normally remained bound by family obligations (especially where the extended family had raised the funds for educating one or two chosen members) and by personal allegiance to their Chiefs; even if they had moved away from their traditional communities, their enhanced status gave them a strong potential influence there. During the latter half of the nineteenth century many Chiefs anxiously sought the guidance of educated advisers to help them in their new relations with one another, and with an alien central Government beyond the confines of their own States. European administrators, seeing only the gulf that divided the educated few from the illiterate many, failed to realize the close personal and social ties that were able to bridge it. Consequently they refused to acknowledge the claim of the *élite* to speak on behalf of the masses, or to make constructive use of them in a mediating role.

The situation was, however, complicated by the existence of more than one *élite*, with potential and actual rivalries between them. K. A. Busia suggests that there are three main classes of *élite* in the Gold Coast: 'the traditional "royal" families, the European or alien rulers, and the educated Africans'.[2] It is possible to trace the social origins of nationalism to the fundamental conflict between the European *élite* and the educated African *élite*. As Balandier points out, 'The colonizing power has created a situation involving profound social changes, but the control which it exercises imposes an upper limit to these processes'.[3] As soon as Gold Coast Africans became sufficiently educated to hold European-type posts and to demand European status, they found increasing discrimination; and the resulting social frustration and resentment was channelled into a demand

[1] S. F. Nadel, 'The Concept of Social Élites', in *International Social Science Bulletin* (Paris, 1956), vol. viii, no. 3.

[2] Busia, 'The Present Situation and Aspirations of Élites in the Gold Coast', in *International Social Science Bulletin*, vol. viii, no. 3.

[3] Balandier, 'Social Changes and Social Problems in Negro Africa', in *Africa in the Modern World*, p. 63.

for political power, partly as a means of controlling the sources of status and influence.

During the twentieth century, however, a more significant conflict among Africans began to emerge, between the educated and the traditional *élites*. 'The Chiefs,' as Busia puts it, 'secure as a standard-setting group in the traditional culture, wish also to exercise some degree of effective political authority, since this has been an aspect of their traditional role.' He is writing of the period immediately preceding Independence, but his analysis is equally applicable to the attitudes of the paramount Chiefs—the 'Natural Rulers', as they somewhat nostalgically preferred to call themselves—during the 1920s. They were then asserting a claim to participation in the central Government, against opposition from the educated *élite*, who considered that their training for the problems of the modern world gave them a prescriptive right to leadership on the national scale. This conflict was to remain unresolved for many years, with the scales becoming increasingly weighted against the Chiefs.

The changing social situation between 1850 and 1928 may be summed up in terms of the principles governing the selection of *élites*. Mannheim suggests that, historically, these have always been selected on the basis of blood, property, and achievement.[1] In the Gold Coast the traditional *élite* was based on blood or lineage. Western education then introduced the principle of achievement, and economic development attached a growing importance to wealth. But a barrier was imposed by the growing racial exclusiveness of the European *élite*—especially in the higher ranks of the civil service—and here the potential conflict provided strong motivation for nationalist agitation. The aspirations of the new *élite* towards political leadership were at first expressed in alliance with traditional rulers; but during the twentieth century they began to challenge the Chiefs directly, with a new claim to leadership on a national scale.

This *élite*[2] covered a wide range of educational attainments, income levels, and occupational interests, from the junior

[1] *Man and Society*, p. 89.
[2] One might perhaps attempt to distinguish a semi-educated 'mid-*élite*' between the higher educated *élite* on the one hand, and the illiterate 'mass' on the other hand. Cf. H. D. Lasswell and A. Kaplan, *Power and Society* (London, 1952), pp. 201–3.

clerk employed at an annual salary of £36 to the self-employed professional or business man earning over £1,000 a year. The growing emphasis upon individual wealth and achievement gave some additional status to those at the top; but it would be rash to classify African society in terms of income received, since this often bore little relation to disposable income, which depended also on the financial help available from, or expected by, other relatives. The individual accumulation of capital, which had been virtually unknown under the traditional system, became possible to some extent, at first in trade; but towards the end of the nineteenth century the increase in the scale of expatriate enterprise eclipsed the efforts of the small African trader. Later, however, private practice in the professions (such as the law and medicine) enabled the fortunate few to invest their surplus income in house renting, cocoa farming, or cocoa buying. By the 1920s it was noticeably the wealthier professional minority who took the lead in the National Congress movement.

The growth in numbers of the educated *élite*, taken as a whole, built up increasing political power behind nationalist demands. There was indeed a hierarchy of status within the *élite*; but this depended more on educational attainment than on income level as such; and the remarkable vertical mobility of individuals should prevent the assumption that there was any rigid stratification even among the educated. Participation in 'modernist-orientated'—i.e. in the Gold Coast context, nationalist—politics was effectively limited to those with some command of English. They alone were able to look beyond the tribe or State, to negotiate with the British governing *élite*, to use new concepts not readily assimilated into the vernacular, and to read the nationalist press. But an examination of the correspondence columns of these newspapers shows that an interest in politics and national affairs was not confined to the most highly educated; the illiterate majority, in so far as they became aware of any specific political grievance, increasingly gave what support they could.

It would be an over-simplification to regard the towns as the province of the new educated *élite*, and the rural areas of the traditional *élite*. In both there was conflict between the old and the new social order. Cocoa farming, in particular, brought modern social and economic change into the villages; and the position of the Chiefs in the towns raised some interesting problems of their relationship to the new political leaders. The cross-ties of kinship prevented any serious urban-rural dichotomy. Nevertheless, it was in the towns that the forces of social change were most uncomfortably at work.

5. Progress towards independence in Nigeria: a review

Nigeria Oxford University Press for Royal Institute of International Affairs 1960; pages 42–53

The pace of constitutional development after 1945 progressively quickened and in little over a decade Nigeria moved forward from a colonial dependent status to self-government and independence. The first steps in this great surge forward came before the end of the war in proposals for constitutional change outlined by the then Governor of Nigeria, Sir Arthur Richards (later Lord Milverton), in a White Paper published in March 1945. During the war the spirit of nationalism had grown in Nigeria, as in other parts of Africa and Asia, and it was realized that with the advent of peace fundamental changes in the form of government would be necessary. From these proposals emerged in 1946 a new Constitution which Sir Arthur Richards hoped would help to 'promote the unity of Nigeria; to provide adequately within that unity for the diverse elements which make up the country; and to secure greater participation by Africans in the discussion of their own affairs'.[1] It provided for Houses of Assembly in the Northern, Eastern, and Western Provinces (and in the North a House of Chiefs also) and the setting up at the centre of a new Legislative Council which for the first time was to have an unofficial African majority. The

[1] Cmd. 6599.

members of the Houses of Assembly were chosen by native authorities from among the members of their councils, together with a number of officials and members appointed to represent special interests, but here also there were African majorities. However, the Assemblies had no legislative powers but acted in an advisory capacity only, and so were criticized by the more radical political elements. Nevertheless, they afforded an opportunity to learn and practise parliamentary procedure being particularly valuable in the North, which hitherto had not even been represented on the Legislative Council. The Governor was President of the new Council, which was made up of 16 other official members and 28 unofficial, of whom 4 were elected and 24 were nominated by the four Assemblies. Thus a link was established between them and the Central Government at Lagos. The Governor's Executive Council was not changed when the new Constitution was introduced but in 1949 four African members were appointed to it, making a total of five, since one of the official members, the Director of Medical Services, was an African. The Governor still retained the right to make into law measures which were refused by the Legislative Council though he never in fact exercised this right.

It was intended originally that the Richards Constitution should operate without revision for six years, but although it marked considerable political progress and worked well within its limited scope it did not satisfy the ever-increasing political consciousness in the country. It was opposed strongly, for example, by the NCNC who alleged that it had been introduced without consulting representative Nigerian opinion. In 1947 Dr Azikiwe visited the United Kingdom—where he led a delegation to see the Colonial Secretary, Mr Creech Jones—and the United States to demand more rapid moves towards self-government. In response to criticism the new Governor, Sir John Macpherson, proposed to the Legislative Council in 1948 that the situation should be reconsidered. To ascertain the form of constitution that Nigerians themselves wanted he initiated consultations at various levels throughout the country, culminating in a general conference held at Ibadan in January 1950 at which all but three members were Africans. At this conference an attempt was made to reconcile marked differences in opinion which were becoming apparent between the three groups of provinces, the main issue being between the North's insistence that in any central legislature that might be established its representation should be equal to that of the East and West together on the basis of its having more than twice their combined population. With two other unresolved issues, the representation of Lagos and the proposal that the central legislature should be empowered to refer back legislation to the regional Assemblies, this demand was referred to a committee of the Legislative Council for consideration. In July 1950 the Colonial Secretary, Mr James Griffiths, gave his approval in principle to the constitutional proposals and in September the committee announced that it had reached agreement on all points including the proposal for a single central legislative chamber in which the North would hold half the seats.

The Macpherson Constitution

The new Constitution was promulgated by an Order in Council in June 1951 and came into operation in January 1952. Its life was short but it represented the beginning of semi-responsible government and was thus an important landmark in Nigeria's constitutional development. While giving a considerable amount of regional autonomy, it was specifically designed to preserve the unity of the country. A House of Representatives was set up at the centre with 68 members from the North, 34 each from the East and the West (chosen by and from the respective regional Assemblies), 6 ex-officio members, and 6 nominated to represent special interests. A Council of Ministers replaced the Executive Council, composed of 6 officials and 12 Africans (4 from each region) drawn from the House of Representatives.

Executive Councils were set up in the East, West, and North, including some officials but with an African majority in each case. In the East one minister was appointed from the Southern Cameroons. The regional Assemblies were enlarged and given legislative and financial powers over a specified but considerable range of subjects. In the West a House of Chiefs was established.

The governor retained his reserve powers, but in the general

working of the Constitution power rested with the central
House of Representatives which could reject legislation passed
by the Assemblies. Success in working therefore depended on
the ability of the regional representatives in the Council of
Ministers to resolve their differences and so preserve the unity
of the country. This task was not made easier by the insistence
of the North that all executive decisions should be taken by the
full Council and not by ministers independently. It was soon
evident that wide differences between the Regions—mostly
between the North on the one hand and the East and West on
the other—could not be satisfactorily resolved and that further
regionalization of the Government would have to come.

The 1951 Elections and the Political Parties

The elections following the introduction of the Macpherson
Constitution—the first nation-wide elections in the country's
history—lasted several months and were not completed until
January 1952. They were indirect through electoral Colleges
except in the case of Lagos, and the system varied in the
different regions.

The elections were fought more on a party basis than had
been expected, reflecting the rapid development of political
parties since the Ibadan conference two years earlier. In the
East the NCNC, which had campaigned for a strong unitary
state, gained its expected majority while in the West Chief
Obafemi Awolowo's Action Group party, formed almost
simultaneously with the elections, gained a working majority,
which was soon increased by the accession of many independent
members. The Action Group grew out of the Egbe Omo
Oduduwa, a cultural organization of the Yoruba people of
which Chief Awololo was Secretary, and was strengthened
politically by the support of anti-Ibo nationalists in the South
who had been former members of the Nigerian Youth Movement. Like the NCNC, the Action Group stood for the rapid
attainment of self-government, and Chief Awololo subsequently
contested the leadership of the independence movement with
Dr Azikiwe. In marked contrast to the NCNC, the Action
Group supported the principle of strong regional government
at the expense of the Central Government. In the less politically
organized North the election was not fought along political

lines and political parties were not established firmly there until afterwards. The Northern People's Congress (NPC), which emerged as the dominant party, found its origin in a loosely-organized Hausa cultural organization with an anti-Southern bias. From its inception the party had at least the overt support of the Fulani emirs and ruling families, who supplied most of its candidates. The NPC was led by Alhaji Ahmadu Bello, the Chief Scribe of Sokoto Native Authority, who is a descendant of Usuman dan Fodio and is usually referred to by his traditional title, the Sardauna of Sokoto.

The selection of members for the House of Representatives by the regional Assemblies produced some unexpected results. Although his main support came from the Ibo people of the Eastern Region, Dr Azikiwe chose to stand for one of the Lagos seats and was returned to the Western House of Assembly. Under the constitutional arrangements, of the five (all NCNC) members who had been elected to represent Lagos, two had to be selected to go to the House of Representatives. The selection, however, was to be made by the Western House of Assembly, in which the Action Group was paramount. In the outcome two of the NCNC members were persuaded to accept selection and so assisted in the exclusion of their leader from the House of Representatives.

Events Leading to the Breakdown of the 1951 Constitution

The first Parliament of Nigeria met in January 1952. The Action Group and NPC, both of which stood for strong regional government and distrusted the more politically adept NCNC, formed an uneasy alliance, and for a year Nigerian politicians made considerable efforts to work the Constitution, subordinating party differences in an effort to prevent a political impasse. But by 1953 the strain had become too great and two events eventually combined to bring about the breakdown of the Constitution.

The exclusion of Dr Azikiwe from the House of Representatives tended to weaken the support his party gave to the new Constitution. The Eastern Regional ministers and the Eastern representatives on the Council of Ministers had been nominated after consultation with Dr Azikiwe as leader of the NCNC and they set about operating the Constitution, but not many months

FTCA

elapsed before an NCNC party convention declared it to be unworkable and ordered its ministers to resign. Most of them refused to do so, and instead formed a new party, the National Independence Party (NIP), in February 1953 led by Professor Eyo Ita, the senior minister in the East. NIP then attempted to carry on as a minority Government in the East and a constitutional deadlock resulted. Under the terms of the Constitution, a fresh regional Assembly could not be elected without a corresponding dissolution of the House of Representatives. Special provision was therefore necessary before the Eastern House was finally dissolved and elections held which swept Dr Azikiwe (now resigned from the Western House) to power in the East and to his seat in the House of Representatives.

While the Eastern Region crisis was still unresolved, an Action Group member in the House of Representatives put forward a motion demanding the acceptance of the principle of 'self-government by 1956'. No other issue could have been better calculated to arouse the North's intense fears of southern domination. The influx of Southerners, particularly Ibos, into the Northern Region to take clerical and administrative posts, which through the lack of trained personnel the Northerners themselves could not fill, had increased the fear that self-government would lead to domination by the more politically advanced East and West. Though committed to the principle of self-government, the NPC therefore refused to commit itself to a date by which this should be achieved. As was revealed afterwards, the motion was first discussed by the Council of Ministers where it was agreed on a majority vote that ministers should not take part or vote in the debate. The Action Group ministers, who had dissented, subsequently resigned. The NPC then tabled in the House a motion substituting 'as soon as practicable' for '1956'. In the debate that followed the former Action Group ministers protested at the ruling of the Council of Ministers and attacked the Governor. When, after a series of bitter exchanges, a Northern member moved the adjournment, the Action Group and the NCNC members walked out. Although the NPC's superior voting power had secured the rejection of the Action Group motion, its members deeply resented the attack made on the North by the Action Group and NCNC members during the debate and incidents outside the House afterwards, and their threat of secession might well have been carried out had not the Region been dependent on the South for its access to the sea. The depth of feeling was further displayed two months later when, during a visit by Action Group delegates, lawless elements in Kano caused serious rioting in which forty people were killed.

The political impasse in Lagos was due primarily to the regional basis of the parties which meant that no one party could command a clear majority in the House of Representatives and ministers tended to regard themselves as regional delegates with little feeling of collective responsibility. Apart from the self-government issue, it was evident that there were fundamental differences of opinion in the country as to the form which the Constitution should take, and on 21 May 1953 the Colonial Secretary (Mr Oliver Lyttelton, later Lord Chandos) announced in the House of Commons that it would 'have to be withdrawn to provide for greater regional autonomy and the removal of powers of intervention by the Centre in matters which can, without detriment to other Regions, be placed entirely within regional competence'.

The 1953 London Conference

It was with some difficulty that the Colonial Secretary succeeded in persuading the representatives of the leading Nigerian political parties to come to London to attend a constitutional Conference. Its meetings reflected the strong regional antipathies. During them, two delegations, those of the National Independence Party and the Action Group, withdrew from the Conference, the latter when its demand for the reinstatement of the four ministers who had resigned over the self-government issue was not immediately conceded. When this matter was satisfactorily resolved, however, the Action Group returned to the Conference and, with the exception of certain points, agreed the final report.

The degree of agreement reached was far greater than had been anticipated and was made possible by the NCNC's somewhat reluctant concession to the demand for greater regional autonomy. With this point accepted it was easier to find a solution to the problem of self-government. Each Region in fact secured most of its demands. The East and West gained a big reduction in Colonial Office control and a large measure of self-government at the regional level with a promise that this would become complete in 1956. The North retained its existing status and, by the establishment of a regional civil service, was safeguarded to some extent against the possibility of Southern domination. All these achievements were at the expense of the centre, whose powers were now further reduced. But one major difficulty remained unresolved.

The Lagos Question

In the absence of agreement among the delegates themselves, the London Conference asked the Colonial Secretary to arbitrate on the problems of Lagos. The Action Group was bitterly opposed to separating Lagos, a traditionally Yoruba city, from the West and sought a solution whereby the municipal area could be kept within the region and special protection accorded to Federal interests there. This solution was not acceptable to the representatives of the North, for most of the Northern trade passed through the ports of Lagos and Apapa and their suspicions of the Action Group's intentions remained unabated. The possibility of a new Federal capital was ruled out on the grounds of expense and the difficulty of finding a site acceptable to all parties. It was probably the wider concept of Lagos serving Nigeria as a whole which finally made the United Kingdom Government decide that Lagos should remain the Federal capital and that the municipal area should become Federal territory directly under the Federal Government.

Despite threats of Western secession, the issue was not raised when the constitutional Conference resumed its meetings in Lagos in January 1954 to clear outstanding matters. In response to a request from the Southern Cameroons it was then agreed that this part of the Trusteeship Territory should be separated from the Eastern Region and given quasi-regional status with its own House of Assembly. The Northern Cameroons continued to be administered as part of the Northern Region. In addition it was decided to regionalize the Marketing Boards and the proposals of Sir Louis Chick for the allocation of revenue on the principle of derivation—a basis which the Eastern Region as the poorest region had consistently opposed—was agreed subject to minor adjustments.

The basis of Nigerian federation was thus established. Each region gained its own Governor, Premier, independent civil service and judiciary, whilst in the East and West British officials, with the exception of the Governor, were no longer included in the Executive Council. The Governor of Nigeria was raised to the status of Governor-General and continued to preside over the Council of Ministers. The Central Government was weakened by the transfer of residual and other powers to the Regions, but its position was enhanced by the introduction of direct elections to the House of Representatives instead of its members being chosen by the regional Houses of Assembly as formerly. Within this broad federal structure Nigeria continued to evolve towards her goal of complete self-government.

The Federal Elections, 1954

Before the new Constitution had been finally agreed, the NCNC had been returned to power in the Eastern Region, winning 72 out of the 97 seats in the House of Assembly and Dr Azikiwe (who had resigned his Lagos seat to stand for the Eastern House) had become Premier of the Region. His come-back was made more complete by his party's unexpected gains in the Federal elections held at the end of 1954.

When the Macpherson Constitution was drawn up it was assumed that the leading party in each Region would secure a majority of Federal seats in that region. Events proved otherwise and in 1954 one party (the NCNC) secured a majority in both the Southern regions. In the North where, because of the continuing system of indirect election, the results took longer to come in, the NPC secured its expected majority, although losing some seats to the Northern Elements Progressive Union (NEPU, which was allied to the NCNC) and the separatist United Middle Belt Congress (UMBC).

The NCNC victory marked the full return of Dr Azikiwe after his tactical error in 1951, but it could not be said that as a result of this election political parties in Nigeria acquired a national rather than a tribal basis. In the West the Action Group's relative unpopularity was probably due to the increased taxation levied to pay for an ambitious programme of social improvement and this, together with the NCNC's play upon tribal divisions in the non-Yoruba areas of the West, combined to give to the latter its unexpected victory in the region.

Significantly, none of the three main party leaders—Dr Azikiwe, Chief Awolowo, or the Sardauna of Sokoto—chose to resign his seat in the regional House of Assembly in order to contest the elections to the Federal House, but the senior NPC minister at Lagos, Alhaji Abubakar Tafawa Balewa, Vice-President of the NPC, did so among others and thus became, in August 1957, the first Prime Minister of the Federation of Nigeria.

Federal and Regional Government, 1955–7

As a result of the Federal elections the NCNC found itself with a majority of Federal ministers (six, three representing each of the Southern regions) and, as the North continued to return half the members of the House, a minority of Federal seats. This unexpected development led to many forebodings that the Action Group would not submit to being excluded altogether from the Council of Ministers and that the Northern People's Congress would refuse to work in coalition with the NCNC. In fact neither of these things happened. The Action Group agreed to accept an opposition role and sustained it with intelligence and vigour, while the NCNC and NPC formed a coalition Government which outwardly at least had the appearance of working satisfactorily.

There followed a period which, apart from a serious disagreement between the regional Governor and the Premier of the Eastern Region, was marked by peaceful political and material progress. It was a period also when much necessary administrative reorganization resulting from the establishment of the Federation was carried out. In each of the Regions, though particularly in the more prosperous North and West, great strides were made in putting into effect educational, social, and development programmes. . . .

The 1957 Independence Resolution

The unanimous decision of the House of Representatives to instruct the Federal delegates to the May Constitutional Conference to demand independence for Nigeria in 1959 is the most important event in Nigeria's history since 1900 and, for Africa, scarcely less important than Ghana's independence to which the decision was mainly due.[1]

[1] *West Africa*, 6 April 1957.

This commentary on the House of Representatives debate of 26 March 1957 fully reflects the tremendous achievement underlying it. Only three years earlier a similar motion introduced in the same place had brought the breakdown of the Constitution and threatened the permanent separation of North and South. A greater degree of unity had been achieved in the country than had ever before seemed possible. Whilst this change could be partly explained by the influence and example of Ghana's newly-won independence, its origin lay in the fact that the past three years of political bargaining and negotiation had brought home the realities of the situation to all sides. The North had found in the safeguards provided by the Federal Constitution much of the security it had previously sought. Nigeria thus embarked on its long-promised and long-planned constitutional Conference with a greater degree of unanimity than had characterized such conferences in the past.

The 1957 Constitutional Conference
The Conference, which was held in London, raised few new issues but brought about two changes of great significance. Although the NCNC had declared itself to be more concerned with the attainment of Federal than Regional self-government, the party nevertheless decided to follow the West's example and take up the promise of self-government made in 1953. For matters within their competence under the Constitution, both territories became independent and no longer subject to the Governor's power of veto; the Governor-General was however empowered to issue such directions to a Region as he considered necessary to ensure that the executive authority of the Region was not exercised in such a way as to 'impede or prejudice the performance by the Federal Government of any of its functions or to endanger the continuance of federal government in Nigeria'.[1]
It was agreed that the three remaining *ex-officio* members,

[1] The Federal Government has exclusive power to legislate on more than 40 subjects the most important of which are External Affairs, Citizenship, Defence, External Trade, Currency, Mining, Police (other than local government police), Communications, &c. A list of some 30 subjects is within the competence of both Federal and Regional Governments, Federal law prevailing in the case of conflict. This list includes public order, higher education, electricity, water, &c. The Regions alone make laws on all subjects not included on the two lists.

the Chief Secretary, Financial Secretary, and Attorney-General, should surrender their seats in the Council of Ministers and House of Representatives and that an all-African Cabinet under a Federal Prime Minister should be established. (It was later announced that Alhaji Abubakar Tafawa Balewa, the leader of the NPC in the Federal House and formerly Minister of Transport, had accepted the invitation of the Governor-General, Sir James Robertson, to be first Federal Prime Minister, and that the new 'national' cabinet would include two Action Group members.)

On the question of independence for the Federation of Nigeria, the Conference came to no definite conclusion. The report issued at the end of the meetings[1] showed that because a great number of problems remained to be solved, the delegates had recognized that self-government could not be granted in 1959. Mr Lennox-Boyd agreed however that the British Government would do its best to implement a request for self-government in 1960 but could not commit itself without knowing how the changes decided by the Conference would work out.

The Conference showed that the most important new issue to arise since 1954 was the demand for safeguards for minorities and the splitting up of existing Regions and it was agreed that this question, together with boundary matters in general, should be submitted to a Commission of Inquiry. On another contentious question, that of the regionalization of the Nigeria Police, a compromise was reached and it was agreed that efforts should be made to strengthen the Nigeria Police stationed in the Regions, so that they could, if it was so decided, become the nucleus of Regional forces at a later date. It was specifically stated however that no region should legislate to establish its own force unless the Colonial Secretary, after consultation with all the Nigerian Governments, decided that Regions should set up their own forces. The Conference also agreed that there should be a nominated Federal Senate, that the status of the Southern Cameroons should be raised to that of a full, though not yet self-governing, region, that direct elections based upon adult male suffrage should be adopted henceforth for Federal elections in the Northern Region (universal adult suffrage already applied elsewhere), and that

[1] Cmnd. 207, p. 8.

the Colonial Secretary should appoint a Fiscal Commission to review the revenue allocation system.

The Minorities Commission

A Commission under the Chairmanship of Sir Henry Willink, Master of Magdalene College, Cambridge, was subsequently appointed by the Colonial Secretary and studied the problem of the 'fears of minorities and the means of allaying them', collecting evidence in Nigeria during the latter part of 1957 and during the early part of 1958. Its report[1] was published in August 1958. It recommended that no new states should be created and that human rights in general and the rights of minorities within the present Regions in particular should be safeguarded in the Constitution. 'Minority Areas' should be established in the Western Region (the Edo Area) and the Eastern Region (the Calabar Area) with Councils to foster inter-well-being, cultural advancement, and economic and social development, and to bring to the notice of the Regional Government any discrimination shown against them. A 'Special Area' should be established in the Niger Delta and a survey made of its special problems with a view to drawing up a plan for its development. On the question of the boundary between the Northern and Western Regions, and the demand that the Yorubas of Ilorin and Kabba Provinces should be reunited with their kinsmen in the Western Region, the Commission advised against a change except as a result of a plebiscite with at least 60 per cent. of the votes in favour of transfer. The question of whether or not to hold a plebiscite was left to the constitutional Conference. The view that there should be only one Nigeria Police Force to serve both Federal and Regional purposes was supported.

The 1958 Constitutional Conference

A Conference was held in London in September 1958 to review progress and to consider the reports of the commissions appointed by the 1957 Conference. The representatives of the Northern Region, who had previously stated that they did not propose to ask for Regional self-government before 1959, now requested that the Region should become self-governing on 15 March

[1] Cmnd. 505.

1959. This was approved. On the question of the grant of independence to the Federation as a whole, the Secretary of State announced that Her Majesty's Government would agree to a resolution seeking the grant of independence if passed by a newly-elected Federal Parliament in Lagos early in 1960. In this event, legislation would be introduced in the United Kingdom Parliament to enable Nigeria to become fully independent on 1 October 1960.

After considering the report of the Minorities Commission, the Conference agreed that provision should be made in the new Constitution for safeguarding human rights; that there should continue to be one police force, to be administered by a joint body; and that no new regions or states should be established, and no plebiscite held on the future of Ilorin and Kabba before independence. The report of the Fiscal Commission,[1] varying the arrangements approved by the 1953 Conference, was adopted. Among minor changes it was agreed to establish a House of Chiefs in the Eastern Region and to increase the membership of those in the North and West.

The Federal Elections, 1959

The period after the 1958 constitutional Conference was dominated by preparations for independence and the Federal elections which were held on 12 December 1959. The Northern Region became self-governing on 15 March and the celebrations, held later after the Muslim festival of Ramadan, were attended by the Duke and Duchess of Gloucester.

The approach of independence lent an added significance to the Federal elections, which were conducted simultaneously all over the country by the direct method and with secret ballot. Interest was increased by the decision of Dr Azikiwe and Chief Awolowo to resign their regional premierships in order to seek election to the House of Representatives, and the election campaign was fought by all parties with unprecedented vigour and resources. The Action Group used a helicopter to carry its leaders around the country on campaign tours.

Polling was conducted peacefully everywhere and results confirmed the existing tripartite political division of the country. No one party gained an overall majority of the 312 seats in the

[1] Cmd. 9026.

House; but each gained a majority of the seats in its home region. The NPC gained 142 of the 174 Northern seats, losing the others to the Action Group and the Northern Elements Progressive Union, the Northern ally of the NCNC. In the South the NCNC and Action Group each gained seats in the minority areas of its opponent's region, the NCNC also capturing some seats in the Yoruba areas. The detailed results were:

Party	North	East	West	Lagos	Total
NPC	142	—	—	—	142
NCNC/NEPU	8 (NEPU)	58	21	2	89
Action Gp.	24	14	34	1	73
Independents	—	—	8	—	8
	174	72	63	3	312

Alhaji Abubakar Tafawa Balewa (whose knighthood was announced in the New Year's Honours) was reappointed Prime Minister on 15 December and subsequently formed a Government consisting of 10 members of the NPC, 7 members of the NCNC, and 2 independent members of the Senate, which held its first meeting in January 1960. Dr Azikiwe, the NCNC leader, chose to remain outside the Government and was appointed President of the Senate. Chief Awolowo, whose party had previously unsuccessfully made overtures to each of the others with a view to a coalition, became Leader of the Opposition.

The appointment of Alhaji Sir Abubakar Tafawa Balewa made it virtually certain that he would lead the country to independence on 1 October 1960. This is a fitting climax to the career of the most experienced of the Nigerian ministers. He was born in Bauchi in 1912, the son of a district head, and takes his name from Tafawa Balewa, a small town on the banks of the river Gongola where he spent his childhood. Unlike most Northern leaders, Sir Abubakar is not a Fulani, but belongs to the Jere tribe of Bauchi Province. He was educated at Bauchi Provincial School and Katsina College, which most of the present Northern leaders also attended. He was subsequently employed by Bauchi Native Authority as a teacher and, while headmaster of Bauchi Middle School in 1945, spent a year in London gaining his Teachers' Professional Certificate.

Soon after his return to Nigeria he was appointed a member of the House of Assembly and, in turn, of the Legislative Council at Lagos, under the provisions of the Richards Constitution. At Lagos he made a reputation for being a rather chauvinistic Northerner. A quotation from a speech he made in the Legislative Council in 1948 throws an interesting light on the part played by the British Government in fostering Nigerian unity:

Since 1914 the British Government has been trying to make Nigeria into one country, but the Nigerian people themselves are historically different in their backgrounds, in their religious beliefs and customs and do not show themselves any sign of willingness to unite. Nigerian unity is only a British intention for the country.[1]

It is fair to add that Sir Abubakar has since become the foremost exponent of the ideal of Nigerian unity. He was one of the founders of the Northern People's Congress, in the form in which it existed before it was declared a political party to fight the 1951 elections, and is now the Deputy Leader of the party. After the 1951 elections Sir Abubakar was appointed Central Minister of Works in January 1952 and thus began what has proved to be an uninterrupted ministerial career. He transferred to the Ministry of Transport in 1954 and became Prime Minister for the first time in August 1957.

Lacking the conventional aristocratic background of most Northern leaders, and not being leader of his party, Sir Abubakar is sometimes unfairly underrated. His extreme dislike of personal publicity, contrasting with other Nigerian leaders, has not helped to correct this wrong impression. A strict Muslim, he belongs to a conservative and moderate school of politics not often favoured by West African political leaders, but his reputation for integrity and judgement, his industry behind the scenes, and the personal ascendancy which he enjoys over the House of Representatives have lifted him above the level of an ordinary party leader, and have given him a reputation in the country of a non-party character which may be his greatest asset.

Sir Abubakar greeted Mr Harold Macmillan, the British Prime Minister, when the latter arrived in Nigeria during his tour of Africa in January 1960, and in the House of Representatives, in Mr Macmillan's presence, he moved the resolution

[1] Nigeria, Legislative Council Debates, 4 March 1948.

requesting the grant of self-government for Nigeria on 1 October 1960 and admission to the Commonwealth. The resolution was carried unanimously.

6. Élites in French-speaking West Africa

IMMANUEL WALLERSTEIN *Journal of Modern African Studies* Vol. 3, No. 1, 1965 Cambridge University Press; pages 1–33

The Colonial Situation and Social Stratification

When French administration was established in West Africa, largely at the turn of the century (with the principal exception of parts of Senegal, which have been French-administered for some 300 years), the existing social structures ranged widely from some quite simple, egalitarian groups to some very highly stratified and centralised political systems, often conquest states where the distinction between 'noble' and 'commoner' was clearly recognised and had consequences in the style of life and the possibilities of a career.

The French created new territorial units within which social action would henceforth take place, as well as a federal administrative entity, *Afrique occidentale française* (AOF).[1] This meant the establishment of a modern educational system, relatively more extensive in Senegal because of its long history of colonisation and in Dahomey and Togo because of the freer play allowed to missionary activity. It meant the establishment in West Africa of productive enterprises linked to the world market: cash crops, such as coffee and cocoa in the Ivory Coast and Togo, bananas in Guinea, peanuts in Senegal and Soudan, cotton in Upper Volta, palm oil in Dahomey; extractive industries, particularly iron and diamonds in Guinea; a few light processing industries, such as flour mills in Senegal; and

[1] A.O.F. was composed throughout most of its history of eight territorial units: Dahomey, (French) Guinea, the Ivory Coast, Mauritania, Niger, Senegal, (French) Soudan—now Mali—and Upper Volta. Upper Volta was dismembered from 1932 to 1947. (French) Togo became a mandated, later trust, territory after World War I, and did not, because of its legal status, become part of A.O.F. It is, however, included in 'French-speaking West Africa', which in the colonial era was termed A.O.F.-Togo.

the extension of commercial activity, at first in Senegal, but later embracing the Ivory Coast and to a lesser extent Guinea.

The territorial structures with their administrative centres, the schools, and the new economic activities combined to produce a migratory movement to the towns and the emergence of non-traditional élites centred in or geared towards the urban areas. The unwillingness of the new educated groups to render as much deference to the traditional chiefs as had been customary, plus the rather peremptory overlordship the French were wont to exercise in some rural areas, led to a sharp curtailment of the role of traditional rulers and to their ability to enforce traditional norms.

Even in French colonies, where traditional systems found little solace in the colonial ideology of '*la mission civilisatrice*', it would be a mistake to assume that traditional groups declined to an insignificant role. Often, traditional structures seemed to survive best in cash-crop areas, where those with high status in the traditional system could use this advantage to acquire modern economic power which could sustain their traditional prestige.

Still, many of the new educated town-dwellers came from groups that were underprivileged in the traditional systems. In any case, there seems to be little question that their new roles called for different kinds of values, and there seems equally to be little question that the changeover in value-systems has been imperfect and not smooth. This strain seems to have been even greater among those converted to Christianity.

If, however, the urbanised, educated, sometimes Christianised élites had, and have, some difficulties in finding a consistent set of values, they have had less difficulty in locating advantageous social roles which fit their training. Indeed, it may be argued that although these values were at first imperfectly internalised, individuals in these new positions discovered the usefulness of modern values as a defence against untoward demands of their kin-groups. And thus, by practising these values, they increasingly internalised them.

It was primarily these individuals who up to World War II made up the administrative cadres in the public and private sector of the economies (the latter including principally the European export-import houses, the few industrial and mining enterprises, and the missions). In addition they served as teachers, religious personnel, health personnel (up to the role of *médecin africain*), and a few as skilled workers. There were no professional men, except in Senegal, where a thin crust of lawyers existed. There were some traditional traders, such as the Dioula, who extended and consolidated their position and their relative wealth, but they operated within the framework of a commercial economy dominated by European export-import firms and, to a lesser extent, by Syrian-Lebanese traders. Finally, there grew up in the rural areas, as we have mentioned, a rural planter class.

This new occupational structure was more interrelated than it might have seemed, for many successful cash-crop farmers became traders, and the sons of traders as well as of planters went to school. The great medium of advancement was the educational system and the great goal of advancement was administrative work. The coherence of this system was rein-forced by the fact that the structure of education was centralised. The apex in A.O.F. was the secondary school at Dakar known as the *Ecole William-Ponty*.

Thus came into existence a small modern élite, who had great prestige and were distinct from the traditional élites, although in many cases they came from families with high traditional prestige. Membership was obtained through educa-tion. In this sense, it was a relatively open élite, in that access to education was available to lower-caste persons in the tradi-tional systems, albeit not in absolute proportion to their numbers. Education was translated into occupations, particu-larly administrative positions, which in turn were the most stable and one of the most lucrative sources of income. A social class, an administrative bourgeoisie, was coming into being. What this élite could not gain access to was political power or indeed even political office, except to a very limited degree, mainly in the four *communes* of Senegal.

There was little upward mobility to be achieved by starting as an unskilled labourer in the towns. Most unskilled workers were migratory and returned to their villages after a period of years. While this spread urban values to the countryside, it was not a channel for advancement, except in the indirect sense that returned migrants were often anxious to place their children in educational institutions and so pressed the administration and missions to expand their facilities.

As with most middle classes in an economy whose expansion was limited, in many ways they felt threatened more by the pressure of other, 'lower' elements seeking to gain admission to their midst than by the lack of expanding opportunity in the system. The classic mechanism of defence is to turn a social class into a status-group, to tend towards closure of entry, to the transmission of social position through the family. This process was furthest advanced by World War II in Senegal; then Dahomey; then Togo, the Ivory Coast and Guinea. The other territories scarcely had an administrative bourgeoisie in the first place.

The signs that this new élite was seeking to consolidate itself into a status-group were clear. There was the emergence of exclusive African clubs, established to be sure as counterparts to European clubs, but operating to exclude those urban Africans who did not share the style of life of the new élite. There was the disdain for manual labour widely observed as a value of this group, one which served to reinforce their separate status. There was the fact that an administrative position or employment as a free professional was much preferred to commercial activity. Sons of successful merchants became senior civil servants. Mercier notes of Senegal, for example:

High prestige, more or less definitely acknowledged by the whole population, crystallizes around professions; functions or situations which are considered to be 'intellectual'—implying in fact a minimum of western-type learning. Prestige on economic grounds seems definitely on the decline.

How successful this group was in transforming itself into a status-group is hard to assess. One would want to have some knowledge of rates of intermarriage in the group. One would want to know more of the social recruitment of students. One has the impression from the literature that endogamy within the new class was favoured, if far from a rigid rule, and that the children of the educated formed the larger part of those who went to school in, let us say, the period 1930–45. To this degree, then, the administrative élite tended towards being a status-group in the same sense as the traditional élites. The key difference was that the former laid claim to prestige and position in the urban, territorial social structure rather than the rural, traditional one.

When in the aftermath of the war the French decided to make some political concessions, a critical social issue was posed. As positions of political power became available, it would be possible for the administrative élite to complete the process of becoming a status-group, provided they could gain control of the political machinery and enact various kinds of legal protection for themselves.

Post-war Nationalism and its Ideology

World War II brought about an expansion of the numbers of skilled workers and junior administrative personnel. They sought to maintain the middle class as a fairly open group, which would include them. When the French allowed some partial devolution of political power, they combined with those traders and planters who were also not admitted to the limited circle of the 'old' urban élite. It was in this new alliance that the mass nationalist movements found their impetus—in particular, the interterritorial *Rassemblement démocratique africain* (R.D.A.), but also the *Bloc démocratique sénégalais* (B.D.S.), and the *Comité de l'unité togolaise* (C.U.T.). These parties found themselves opposed by a combination of the French administration, the 'old' urban élite, and the traditional chiefs, all of whom were threatened by the nationalists.

Because the 'old' urban élite and the traditional chiefs were by and large rather weak, and the French were ultimately constrained by a changing world context, the nationalists attained their goals with relative ease in the period 1945–60. They did so by emphasising certain central political values which had widespread popular appeal: the importance of full political control of one's destiny and the moral right to organise to attain this end; the value of modern education for all; the possibility of radically improving economic standards of living; the validity of cultural self-assertion. It is as an expression of these values that the history of nationalism in French West Africa from 1945 to 1960 must be appreciated.

As a consequence of the decisions taken at the Brazzaville conference of 1944, the French African territories were called upon to send elected representatives to the First and Second

National Constituent Assemblies chosen in 1945 and 1946, as well as to participate in municipal elections. Several political facts must be noted about these elections. The number of representatives to be chosen was very small, in terms of both the over-all membership of the Assembly in Paris and the propor-tion of population they represented. Nevertheless, these were, in most territories, the first such elections, and thus were in-vested with great political significance by the participants. Secondly, because these elections were often the first, there were no political party structures in existence. The notable exception was Senegal, where a section of the S.F.I.O. (French Socialist Party) had been created during the Popular Front period before the war. Since no parties existed in most areas, *ad hoc* groups called *blocs* came into existence, which had no solid base.

The third political fact to underline is that the suffrage was very limited. The only persons who could vote, besides Africans who were French citizens,[1] were in effect members of the élite. This, however, included the traditional élites, the 'old' urban élite, the merchants, and the school teachers and others of the 'new' modern élite. In addition, white Frenchmen resident in these areas could vote—sometimes in the same electoral college, sometimes in a separate one[2]—and because of the restricted franchise they contributed a not negligible propor-tion of the electorate. In other cases, the *blocs* broke down into

---

[1] Until 1946 Africans were legally divided into 'subjects' and 'citizens'. Citizens were a minute percentage of the population, who were admitted to this status of equality with Frenchmen on the basis of passing certain tests. In addition, persons born in the so-called 'four *communes*' of Senegal—Dakar, Gorée, St. Louis, and Rufisque—were all citizens. The *Loi Lamine Guèye*, passed in 1946, made all subjects citizens without requiring them to re-nounce their right to have personal affairs regulated by customary law, which had formerly been a prerequisite to citizenship. See Doudou Thiam, *La Portée de la citoyenneté dans les territoires d'outre-mer* (Paris, 1953).

[2] In those instances where there were two colleges, which was never the case in Senegal or Togo, the distinction was based on 'personal status', that is, adherence to French civil law or to customary law. This was the old citizen-subject distinction. Consequently, the few Africans who had been citizens voted in the 'first college'. However, under the pressure of the new political atmosphere, even a few of these renounced this status to be grouped in the 'second college'. On the complications of the double-college system and where and how it applied, see L. G. Cowan, *Local Government in West Africa* (New York, 1958), pp. 101–7.

several factions, each representing one of the élites. A prime example was the 1945 election in the Ivory Coast of the second-college deputy to the First National Constituent Assembly. There were three candidates: Kouamé Binzème, lawyer, representative of the 'party of intellectuals' and coming from the most 'advanced' ethnic group, the Agni; Félix Houphouet-Boigny, *médecin africain*, president of the *Syndicat agricole africain*, representative of the 'new' modern élite and sub-chief of the large Baoulé tribe, traditional rivals of the Agni; and the Baloum Naba, an important traditional chief of the large, hierarchical, less 'advanced' Mossi, a man who could not speak French. Houphouet won by a narrow margin on the second round.

The 'new' modern élites saw clearly that elections in such circumstances would continue to be hazardous unless they could create a political organisation that could mobilise votes and win a broader-based electorate. Thus the period 1945–51 was one in which these men sought to create mass political parties. The key events in this process were the creation of the interterritorial R.D.A. in Bamako in 1946, and the breakaway of the B.D.S. from the S.F.I.O. in Senegal in 1948. In addition, a number of the same individuals participated in organising trade unions, principally in the form of branches of the French *Confédération général du travail* (C.G.T.), the trade union movement linked to the French Communist Party. In France, the university students, who did not exist before the war, except for a few Senegalese, organised the *Etudiants du R.D.A.*

These organisations were regarded by the French administration in most areas as threats to the stability of the colonial régime, and pressure-groups for reform whose programmes had dangerous revolutionary implications. Since the traditional rulers and the 'old' urban élite took the same view, the latter, encouraged by the authorities, established various ethnic-regional parties (in some cases calling them branches of the S.F.I.O.). These came to be known as *les partis administratifs*. The mass parties countered by trying to include various ethnic organisations within their own structures.[1]

---

[1] The ideological and organisational difficulties this entailed I have discussed in my 'Class, Tribe, and Party in West African Politics', in *Transactions of the Fifth World Congress of Sociology* (Brussels, 1964), III, pp. 203–16.

In addition to encouraging the *administratif* parties, the French administration actively harassed the mass parties by attacking the largest and most vulnerable sector of the 'new' modern élite, the civil servants and school teachers, who were militant party advocates. By means of transfers, denying them promotion, and actual dismissals, the French sought to break the allegiance of party and trade union leaders to the mass parties. Partly as a cause, partly as a consequence, of this repression, the largest group of mass parties, the R.D.A., became affiliated (*apparenté*) on the French parliamentary level to the French Communist Party.[1] The repression increased in crescendo up to 1951, and its success could be measured by the relative failure of the mass parties in the elections of 1951, a failure that was in part the consequence of falsification of returns, in part of intimidation.

The mass parties resisted *relatively* best in Senegal, Togo, Dahomey, and the Ivory Coast. In the first three, non-affiliation to the Communists was a factor of strength. In all four, however, what was perhaps more important was the relatively larger percentage in the party cadres of those who were *not* civil servants or school teachers and could therefore resist French *economic* pressure better. Most notable was this among the cocoa and coffee planters in the Ivory Coast, the territory where repression was in fact heaviest.

In 1950–1, the French administration under the leadership of the then Minister of Overseas Territories, François Mitterand, decided to shift its tactics, from systematic opposition to the 'new' modern élite, the emergent, enlarged bourgeois class, to co-operation with it. The policy was marked by new

[1] Two other French parties played a role in this period. The S.F.I.O. lent the cover of its name to largely ethnic-traditional parties in Guinea, the Soudan, and the Ivory Coast as well as to the party of the 'old' urban élite in Senegal. The socialist trade union structure, the C.G.T.–F.O., consisted largely of white members plus very senior African civil servants. The M.R.P. played a far more complex role. It lent support in some areas to parties of the 'new' modern élite, as in Senegal and in the eastern part of Upper Volta, and in other areas to *administratif* parties. The Catholic trade union, C.F.T.C., organised sections in Africa; though it numbered only a small percentage of the total trade union membership (the majority adhering to the C.G.T.), it recruited Africans, rather than whites like the C.G.T.–F.O., and in some cases the least-skilled workers (the opposite of the C.G.T.–F.O. deflection from the C.G.T. norm).

administrative appointments (most notably, as Governor-General of A.O.F., Bernard Cornut-Gentille) and by decisions to refrain from tampering with elections, to terminate support for *administratif* parties, and to end repressive measures against mass-party cadres. The counterpart to this was the decision of the R.D.A. (and the C.G.T. of A.O.F.) to break its links with the French (and world) Communist movements,[1] and to lay ideological stress on the creation of a 'Franco-African community'. This bargain was progressively put into practice between 1951–8, and may be said to have been sealed by the three elections of 1955 and 1956 and the passage that same year of the *loi-cadres*, which permitted the establishment of semi-autonomous governments in A.O.F.[2]

In the elections—for mayors in the large cities in 1955, for members of the French National Assembly in January 1956, and for members of the Territorial Assemblies in May 1956—the mass parties won successively more striking victories. The January elections brought the *Front républican* Government to power in France, and this Government, in conjunction with the African deputies, enacted the *loi-cadre*.

The establishment, in July 1957 under the *loi-cadre*, of

[1] The break with the Communists represented however more than a mere expedient. It resulted as well from an ideological commitment to nationalism and cultural self-assertion. In 1956 Aimé Césaire expressed this quite succinctly in a pamphlet that was itself extremely influential among French-speaking West African élites.

> In the case of Stalin and his sectarians, it is not perhaps a question of paternalism. But it is surely something so close as to be easily mistaken for it. Let us invent the word: it is 'fraternalism'. For it is precisely a question of a brother, of a big brother who, imbued with his superiority and sure of his experience, takes you by the hand (with a hand, alas! that is sometimes rough) to lead you on the road where he knows will be found Reason and Progress.
>
> Now that is exactly what we do not want. What we no longer want.
>
> *Lettre à Maurice Thorez* (Paris, 1956), p. 11.

[2] The time-schedule for Togo was slightly different because of its status as a trust territory. It was granted a semi-autonomous government in 1955 but the mass party was not allowed to take power until 1958. The reason for the greater reluctance of the French Government to come to terms with the Togo nationalist movement, the C.U.T., was because of the explicit commitment of the latter to the goal of independence. This commitment derived in turn from the normative reinforcement provided by the special legal status under the U.N. Charter.

territorial governments in which the mass parties predominated marked the crucial victory of those elements of the emergent middle classes which we have called here the 'new' modern élite. It gave them the essential legal and political tools with which to consolidate their power against traditional élites, the 'old' urban élite, and the colonial administration.

They used their control of the government first of all to expand educational facilities considerably at all levels, thus ensuring wider access to middle-class positions and also creating the base for expanded economic activity.[1] They exercised their control of the administration to force traditional rulers to 'renounce politics'—which meant, in effect, pledging loyalty to the mass party, and also to 'democratise' the chieftaincy, which meant increasing the role of rural 'non-traditional' or 'modern' elements in the choice of local authorities. They began to place nationalists in the higher civil service and keep an eye on the technicians, both the new ones recently returned from the university in France, and the older ones, some of whom were suspect because of 'collaborationist' biographies; they created party structures, composed of men who were less educated than the technicians but more committed to the new governmental structures, to keep watch over the administrators.

They used their governmental positions to consolidate the party structures, forcing smaller parties to merge or inducing the leaders of these parties to desert them. They could do this all the more easily since the most lucrative and prestige-laden occupations had now shifted from the administration to politics (and even the administrative jobs were, for the time being at least, filled more according to political than to educational criteria). Access to wealth, power, and prestige came increasingly through the party, the single party in power. Thus arose, alongside the old administrative and commercial bourgeoisies (the former much expanded), what might be termed a proper

---

[1] To be sure, this only continued an expansion in facilities which had been going on since World War II, under the pressure of the insistent demands of these mass nationalist movements as well as of the expansion of the economy. Unfortunately most of the statistics available take us only to this point in time, thus making it difficult to see whether the expansion since 1957 is significantly different from that of 1945–57.

political bourgeoisie, men who literally could not afford to lose political power.

Finally, they sought to consolidate their power by rapid economic expansion, thus securing for themselves as a class larger incomes, which they could use to invest, to create a more expensive style of life, and to retain mass support through some mass distribution of benefits. The latter feature was perhaps less emphasised than the former, an imbalance not without its difficulties, and sometimes compensated for by a radical terminology. Economic expansion was most likely through increased foreign investment, especially in infrastructure. France seemed (and seems) the most likely source of such capital. It was precisely at this time, however, that Raymond Cartier wrote his famous articles in *Paris-Match* in which he asserted that, political independence being inevitable for French Africa, France should cut down on its costly contributions to African territorial budgets.

The spectre of *cartiérisme* evoked two contrary reactions within the mass parties. One position, championed by Houphouet, was to cajole and blackmail France into heavy investment by the sacrifice of Africa's international political rights, and by permitting large-scale participation by French capital in the profitable sectors of the African economy. It entailed also retaining large numbers of French civil servants and technicians in the private sector, both as employment outlets for these men and as surety for the French Government. The advantage of this position was that it ensured a continuing outflow of capital and maintained a general level of relative prosperity. On the other hand, it was disadvantageous to at least some of the very commercial and administrative bourgeois elements upon whose support the government rested.

The alternative reaction to *cartiérisme* was to strengthen the political bargaining position of the African states vis-à-vis France and the world, so that they could in the long run 'force' capital investment at rates and terms that were not dependent on the 'charity' of France. This position came to be championed by Sékou Touré. Its advantage was that ideologically it was more consonant with the ideals that had dominated A.O.F. nationalism up to 1956 and were standard throughout Africa. One could talk of independence rather than of a 'Franco-African community'. It thereby won the allegiance of the party cadres. It further lessened dependence on a single power, France, by reaching out to the U.S.S.R. and the U.S.A. ('neutralism'). The disadvantage of this position was that France could retaliate economically more swiftly than the African states might be able to balance the economic loss with the gains resulting from their new political leverage.

This argument first came to the surface in the Third Inter-territorial Congress of the R.D.A. in Bamako, in September 1957, where it took the form of a debate over the importance of 'democratising the federal structure' of A.O.F. The supporters of Sékou Touré, who were in the majority, argued for a federal state in A.O.F., which presumably would have increased political leverage against France. Houphouet argued against federation, presumably because, being rightly associated by the French with the drive towards independence, it would frighten off French capital from A.O.F. as a whole and, of course, from the Ivory Coast in particular. Houphouet, knowing that time was on his side because of the latent 'local' nationalism of the new political bourgeoisies of the several territories, won the debate by adjourning it.

The point of view expressed at this meeting by Sékou Touré was also reflected in the organisational developments among trade unions, youth groups, and student associations, where defenders of this opinion sought to create positions of strength to counterbalance the party 'in-groups', who were seen as increasingly 'conservative' because of self-interest.

The break of the trade unions led by Sékou Touré with the world Communist movement came later than that of the R.D.A. as a party. R.D.A. had disaffiliated (*désapparenté*) from the French Communist Party in 1950. It was at the meeting of the Co-ordinating Committee of the R.D.A. in Conakry in 1955 that Touré read a report advocating the disaffiliation of the trade unions from the C.G.T. At first, Touré could only carry about half the unions with him, the others arguing that this was a betrayal both of the nationalist and the international proletarian struggles. Touré and his supporters argued that the logic of their mutual position—the primacy of political considerations over economic—applied here as it did in the argument with Houphouet, and that the organisational conclusion must be an autonomous, united trade union federation, free from European political links and dedicated to the attainment of independence. This end was achieved by the creation in January 1957 of the *Union générale des travailleurs d'Afrique noire* (U.G.T.A.N.), which included the large majority of the trade unions and refused to be affiliated to any of the international confederations.

If historically in French West Africa the trade unions had been run by men active in the nationalist movements, the majority of the youth organisations had been captured by elements neutral—sometimes hostile—towards the mass movements, and in particular to the R.D.A. This was partly because so many of the youth movements were church-related and hence were never affiliated to Communist groups. Nationalist elements however obtained control in Senegal in 1952, and in co-operation with other groups established an interterritorial structure in 1955, which was rebaptised in October 1957 the *Conseil de la jeunesse d'Afrique* (C.J.A.), and by then included all the major youth organisations of A.O.F., united in territorial co-ordinating councils, which largely refused international affiliations.[1] Thus, while U.G.T.A.N. involved the majority of trade unions moving from Communist international affiliations to none, the C.J.A. involved moving from non-Communist international affiliations to none.

Among African students in France, the picture was somewhat different again. Here the disaffiliation of the R.D.A. from the Communist movements was simply not accepted. It meant instead the death of *Etudiants du R.D.A.*, and the growing importance in the 1950s of the *Fédération des étudiants d'Afrique noire en France* (F.E.A.N.F.), which moved from a position of non-affiliation to membership of the International Union of

---

[1] The word 'largely' reflects the compromise formula adopted in 1957. In each of the eight territories of A.O.F. the member of the C.J.A. was the single territorial co-ordinating council (except in Mauritania, where, because of the paucity of groups, the member was a single youth group). The compromise was that the C.J.A. would remain unaffiliated but that its affiliates would have the option of direct international affiliation. Two of them, Dahomey and the Ivory Coast Youth Councils, remained affiliated to the World Assembly of Youth. In addition, some small groups, affiliated to the territorial youth councils, remained affiliated to the World Federation of Democratic Youth.

Students. Nevertheless, it was direct membership, not mediated by any French organisation, and it was membership as a 'united' group, and thus was at least partially consonant with the growing theme of 'unity and autonomy' in A.O.F. The common intellectual ground of U.G.T.A.N., C.J.A., and F.E.A.N.F. was shown by their declaration in December 1957 of joint efforts in favour of 'national independence', whereas the R.D.A. at its September 1957 meeting had restrained itself to demanding 'the right to independence'.

The momentum towards unity led to pressures for a united political movement, whereby the majority R.D.A. would join together with the other mass parties (most notably that of Senegal). Negotiations were conducted in early 1958; but they failed, and most of the parties outside the R.D.A. (both mass and smaller parties) joined together in the *Parti du regroupement africain* (P.R.A.), which, at its inaugural congress in Cotono, in July 1958, was swept into outbidding the R.D.A. ideologically and adopting a position in favour of 'national independence'.

It was in this atmosphere, in the summer of 1958, that General de Gaulle prepared his referendum, which was aimed primarily at resolving certain problems in France itself and in Algeria. Black Africa was only relevant in so far as de Gaulle was anxious not to have any difficulties there which might interfere with the overwhelming support that he desired for the new constitution. He therefore offered full internal autonomy, the 'right to independence', and immediate independence 'outside the Community' for any state that voted 'no' in the referendum.

As is well known, only Guinea under the leadership of Sékou Touré voted 'no' and became independent. The economic retaliation of France was swift, urged on by Houphouet, who insisted that his prophecy of catastrophe be fulfilled. In the course of 1958–60, therefore, enormous strains emerged between Guinea and the other states of A.O.F. The interterritorial structures of U.G.T.A.N. and C.J.A., both of which had recommended a 'no' vote on the referendum and were thus identified with the Guinea position, were destroyed by the governments in power, who were unwilling to allow non-'loyal' structures to exist within their body politic. F.E.A.N.F.

felt these pressures less, as indeed it had even before the referendum, because of its remoteness and because in a certain sense the mass movements never took the students seriously.

The consequences of the independence of Guinea, however, partially fulfilled the prophecy of Touré in that Guinea's independence forced the other states in A.O.F. to follow its political example, and France in 1960 to cede gracefully, first to the Federation of Mali, then to the four states of the *Conseil de l'entente*, then to Mauritania (thus to all of A.O.F.), what it had granted to Guinea only on pain of the implementation of *cartiérisme*.[1]

Thus 1958 to 1960 was a period of the further consolidation of state and party structures, the deepening of the hold of the 'new' modern élite on their countries, the further elimination or absorption of the traditional and 'old' urban élites, and finally the achievement of full political sovereignty.

Independence and Social Stratification

The various states of French-speaking West Africa, as they became independent in 1960 (Guinea in 1958), had comparatively little sense of territorial nationalism. This was particularly true because, at least until 1945, the major mass party, the R.D.A., was oriented to what has been called an *aofien* nationalism.[2] Even French West Africa was a creation only of this century; but the crisis in the R.D.A. from 1957 to 1960 and the break-up of the Federation of Mali in August 1960 led to much uncertainty about national identity. If one adds to this the fact that in some of the states the leaders were not willing to use blatantly national symbols or talk of independence until virtually the very moment of it, we can well understand why these states were weak in the loyalty they could command. In this sense, Guinea had the good fortune to be rejected by France for her first two years of independence;

[1] How Guinea's independence operated to achieve the end of independence for the other states in West Africa is analysed in my 'How Seven States were Born in French West Africa', in *Africa Report* (Washington), VI, 3, March 1961.

[2] An adjective formed from the initials A.O.F., which stand for French West Africa.

her beleaguered status helps to explain the relative solidity of popular support for the Guinean nation. At the other extreme, Mauritania obtained her independence essentially because her neighbours did, and because the French feared that a delay would only have pushed the more nationalist elements into an actively pro-Moroccan position.

The problem of the people's weak loyalty to the state, one common to newly independent nations, was then especially acute in French-speaking West Africa. Furthermore, all the nine countries were made up of several major ethnic groups, and it is fairly easy to identify a number of 'backward' regions (Casamance in Senegal; the north in Dahomey, Togo, and the Ivory Coast; the Forest in Guinea, etc.). These regions are distinctive culturally, and 'backward' often in both the traditional and the modern arenas. To be 'backward' in the traditional arena means to come from a group culturally despised by the majority of the others. To be 'backward' in the modern arena is to have fewer educated cadres, less involvement of the region in the money economy, a lower standard of living. There are also often major rivalries between 'advanced' ethnic groups (Fon and Goun in Dahomey, Agni and Baoulé in the Ivory Coast, Djerma and Haoussa in Niger, Malinké and Peul in Guinea, and so on). It is important to observe not only that these various ethnic regions have traditional élites of varying strengths but that each ethnic group has its representatives among the modern élite, especially of that segment we have called the 'new' modern élite. Various ethnic groups did see 'their' modern élite as indeed their 'representatives' not only within the state but within the party structures.

In addition to the weakness of loyalty to the state, and the social and economic differences between existing ethnic-cultural regions, the third fundamental political reality after independence was the relative lack of trained political and administrative personnel, especially since the nationalist movement had been pledged both to expand and Africanise the personnel.

The patterns of economic transformation begun in the colonial era continued after independence. In the agricultural sector, this meant the continued expansion of cash crops, selling at an artificially high level because of the arrangements of the franc zone. The world market for these products, however, has tended to fluctuate. Nevertheless, the national economies have remained dependent upon them, and cash-crop farming has still attracted many of the traditional cultivators because of its continuing, if uncertain, lucrative nature. Many of the major cash-crop enterprises required seasonal migrant labour (Mossi in the southern Ivory Coast, *navétanes* in Senegal) as well as various forms of share-cropping. Over the past 30 years, various 'stranger' groups have gained *de facto* control over land in many areas. The *de facto* transfer of land rights opened up the possibility of much judicial litigation over what is now valuable land. So did the inherent strains between matrilineal systems of inheritance and cash-cropping, which has created new *de facto* lines of transfer of property. This increasing legal fluidity (if not alienability) of land tenure has meant that the control of the political structure can have a great impact on the ability of families to control, expand, and transmit wealth. It has made 'stranger' groups fight for political power, a situation which has been particularly complicated when 'ethnic strangers' are also 'territorial strangers', since the latter can be attacked as being outside the new national entity.

The desire for economic development has led to demands for the reduction of costs in the commercial sector. A moral repugnancy for the 'middleman' has been part of the underlying ethos of African nationalism. The elimination of the small trader can be effected either by increasing the role of presumably more efficient large traders (such as European export-import houses), or by interposing various state organisms for trading (such as O.C.A. in Senegal, Somiex in Mali, the Comptoirs in Guinea), which presumably would take lower profit margins or apply their profits to national investment. In either case this puts a squeeze on traditional trading groups, such as the Dioula, who find ill-rewarded the support that they gave to early nationalist movements on the assumption that the nationalist protest against exploitation would be directed primarily against European capitalists.

As to the industrial and mining sector, the major problem is that it scarcely exists, and that even if the capital is obtained through forced savings or outside investment, the technicians to operate the enterprises are scarce and can most readily be supplied by outside capitalist firms. An indigenous industrial bourgeoisie does not exist, and can only come into existence with either considerable state aid or the partnership of private outsiders or both.

Faced with these political and economic factors at the moment of independence, the various French-speaking West African states have reacted with a basically similar three-fold programme. They have sought to ensure the creation of a strong, centralised state machinery. Lacking a really extensive bureaucracy, they have invested much energy in a single party which can utilise less technically trained personnel and integrate the country by using appeals to solidarity rather than the ties of rational interdependence. They have specifically urged the need to use all the skilled workers available as an argument against 'wasting' effort on opposition political parties. They have similarly argued for the subordination of auxiliary organisations (trade unions, youth, women, ex-servicemen) to the party. There is no exception to this pattern in French-speaking West Africa. The drive towards centralisation means that politics becomes primary not only in an ideological sense but also in the sense of being the primary vehicle of personal well-being and mobility for the élite. Such good positions as there are, such perquisities of life as are available, are obtained primarily by political activity.

The second basic reaction to the political and economic problems of the independent states is to seek to expand their educational system. This is done because the school system is a rapid mechanism for the creation of national loyalty. Its expansion is a way of rectifying the regional imbalances. It is a means of increasing the size and the number of economic institutions. The state pays for the largest proportion of university education. In 1961, 69 per cent of the university students from French-speaking Black Africa in Paris held government scholarships (and 58 per cent in the provincial universities).

The third basic reaction has been for the state to play a major role in economic development, but thus far largely to limit its role to one of support and encouragement of outside economic assistance. The attempt of the state to move directly into the organisation of co-operatives and to participate in and partially control the distribution sector has been largely restricted to Guinea, Mali, and Senegal. In the relatively free economies, those members of the élite who have large incomes from their political roles have found the most fruitful area of investment in collaboration with French capital. (This does not seem to hold true in Guinea and Mali.) This situation has created certain vested interests in maintaining the present economic structure among some sectors of the governmental élite.

The relatively common problems and common reactions of the independent governments of French-speaking West Africa have produced some relatively common dilemmas. The limited differentiation of the economy, and the correlative lack of skilled human resources to run both the administration and the modern economic institutions, is reflected in and contributes to a low over-all standard of living. However, the widespread acceptance of the objective of development means that some way of overcoming this self-contained cycle is sought; and the most likely instrument seems to be the creation of a strong, centralised state machinery to make the most efficient use of limited human and material resources and thus enable the most rapid progress towards development. In what may superficially seem a paradox, the overwhelming concern with the state of the economy has led to an ideology which proclaims the primacy of politics.

The concept of the primacy of politics produces the first major dilemma: whether one seeks to secure its maximum central control by a tight or an accommodating one-party structure. The way in which this dilemma is built up is easy to perceive. The primacy of politics means that the ladder of career advancement for the élite is concentrated in directly political positions. Political posts become a primary source of income, both licit and illicit, and the possibilities of successful private enterprise are heavily conditioned by political influence. This means then that students are attracted to political careers, whether in state or party, and in general many students tend to see educational training as a step to higher-level, non-technical posts. These posts are doubly attractive; as posts of national service they are worthy of high social approval, and they are also highly rewarded in a material sense. The material rewards do not contradict the sense of virtue in national service. Rather they are legitimate recompense for the high career risk of political activities. Such a tendency is further reinforced by the general sense that after independence technicians can be imported from abroad but not men to fill posts of high political responsibility—ministers, legislators, ambassadors.

This overloading of career possibilities in politics means that there is particular personal profit in political separatism for members of the élites from 'neglected' regions, since they can advance even further and faster in the politics of their own areas, which have fewer indigenous cadres. Furthermore, they receive support for such projects from 'their' populace because of the unevenness of development (which is blamed upon the central government) and because the populace fears, often quite rightly, that the methods of development of the central régime will lead to an even greater disparity of living standards and economic opportunities within the country.

If the government in such a situation opts for maintaining a tight party structure (which has been the original tendency of Guinea and Mali) it will presumably have the advantage of a more efficient use of resources, as well as more effective political control of outside influences and hence a better position in international economic bargaining. Furthermore, the egalitarian values presumably tend towards a more open class structure, with greater efficiency in the recruitment of personnel. The disadvantage is that it may be too difficult, given the small size of cadres, to administer effectively either the political (state or party) or the economic machinery. In this case, behind the façade of a one-party régime grows up a *de facto* acceptance of decentralised political power, thus in effect buying off 'local' élites both politically and financially. If, for immediate political reasons, it is thought wise to remove the local leader from actual contact with his people, the reward is often in the form of an ambassadorial post or, less desired because less rewarding, a post in an international institution. This is probably happening, to a greater or lesser extent, throughout French-speaking West Africa, including Guinea and Mali. It is the prevention of tribalism by a partial surrender, a most acceptable solution to 'local' élites. For as Mercier remarks:

Tribalist movements or 'tribal nationalisms' often express less a rejection of the political framework constituted by the territory, which tends in most cases to be accepted as 'given', than a search for an equilibrium within the system which is in process of being accepted by everyone. It is a refusal of *de facto* ethnic domination or monopoly, a claim for the equality of all, whatever their origin. Generally, the language alone is conservative, the perspectives are modernist.

The perspectives may not be modernist, however, if this 'localism' results in the reinforcement of various traditional structures. Or they may be modernist in the limited sense of providing an acceptable niche for traditional status-groups in the new national bourgeoisie. To sum up, then, the first dilemma is to what degree the state's accommodation of 'local' élites—in order to prevent separatist movements, maintain unity, and allow time for economic development—may, in fact, undermine the process of economic development by weakening the urban nationalist élites vis-à-vis both the traditional élites and the outside world.

This dilemma, if politically the most noticeable problem, is logically a sub-category of a larger dilemma involved in economic development. This is the problem of distributing the proceeds of increased production between rewards for those whose efforts brought it about, directly or indirectly, and investment in productive equipment. The state makes these decisions, even in self-styled 'free economies' like the Ivory Coast, because of its central economic role as mediator between outside capital and local enterprise. Indeed, a pattern of limited, non-direct intervention may for the present be largely forced on all these states, even those committed to a direct state role like Guinea. The collapse of the Guinean *Comptoirs* was caused by the lack of a bureaucracy large enough to administer it efficiently, and able to keep down favouritism and corruption to a reasonable level.

Still, if economic development is to progress at all, some decisions about forced savings must be made. To maximise the freedom of the central élite in this matter, it is essential to keep pressure groups under control. Thus, any claims from the trade unions, who largely represent the lower administrative bourgeoisie, for increased rewards have been quickly put down throughout French-speaking West Africa (viz. the suppression of civil service strikes in Senegal and Ivory Coast in 1959, and of the teachers' strike in Guinea in 1962). This freedom once maximised, the central political élite must make some decision, however, on the allocation of rewards; and it is understandable that, sitting at the point through which the money is funnelled, they tend to remove a relatively large proportion for themselves. This is all the more inevitable in that the central politicians use as their standard of comparison an international social world dominated by westerners of high incomes.

The problem is not that the economic rewards for the politico-economic élite are too expensive for the *economy* to bear. On the contrary, the history of economic development throughout the world has indicated that such large rewards are normal and perhaps even inevitable. It is rather that they are perhaps too large for the *polity* to bear, particularly in this modern era of rapid communication and a widespread, diffuse belief in equality. That is to say, if the way is wide open for a small group rapidly to acquire enormous wealth by virtue of positions which others think they have acquired 'accidentally' and not because of virtue or achievement, then others become disorientated in their values and resentful of privilege.[1]

How large are the rewards of the politico-economic élite is only one part of the question. Another is how their share compares to the rewards given to technicians. The financial demands of the latter are kept well in line because of the strict control over trade union activity. The technicians however may be satisfied with relatively smaller financial rewards than the politicians, provided they can obtain other, less tangible, satisfactions, for example in high professional performance— which may also be essential for economic development. Such satisfactions may, however, be denied by political interference, of two main kinds. One is the natural political pressure for log-rolling and nepotism, exacerbated by the concessions to 'local' élites spoken of above. The second is due to suspicion of the political motives of the technicians (expressed as a fear of 'radicalism' in Senegal and the Ivory Coast, and a fear of 'the complex of the colonised' in Guinea and Mali). Since, as we have argued, control of the political machinery is fundamental for the acquisition of money, prestige, and power, it is natural for politicians to fear the ambitions of some of the

[1] This is the spectre which Durkheim evoked, of limitless possibilities creating a loss of sense of proportion and *anomie*.

élite who may be willing and anxious and are certainly able to switch from their technical roles to directly political ones.

The value placed on economic development has thus reinforced the belief in the primacy of politics already developed in the anti-colonial revolution. This same value has led to an overwhelming approval for expanded education, both for itself and because it will contribute to increased development. But the expansion of educational facilities has probably created the greatest dilemma of all. As Di Tella argues, in an analysis of the impact of education on political attitudes in a developing economy at an early stage:

Education grows more rapidly than the economy. The higher aspirations produced by education remain for that reason frustrated, since occupational positions adequate for the products of the expanded educational system are not to be found, especially for secondary school leavers . . .

It would seem that in underdeveloped countries this difference between occupational aspirations and realities tends to produce racial attitudes, or more generally attitudes in favour of development . . . In consequence, we would hold that during the first stage of economic development the sources of social tension would not only be due to the rapidity of change from the rural to the urban sector, but in part traceable to the very occupational structure (rural and urban) which is generated by the first phases of development.[1]

Di Tella further argues that the social perception by educated persons of what constitutes appropriate middle-class employment is largely limited to urban positions, thus concentrating them in the towns, with the obvious political consequences.

This overproduction of the educational system operates both for primary school-leavers and university graduates in French-speaking West Africa. At the level of primary and intermediate schools (up to and including the *brevet*), it is probably true of all the countries, but is more serious in the relatively more developed coastal states (Senegal, Guinea, Ivory Coast, Togo, and Dahomey). The so-called 'problem of unemployed school-leavers' is not only an explosive one but will predictably become more and more severe until the economy makes a

---

[1] Di Tella gives statistical verification of his hypotheses with Chilean data. It is my presumption that a replication of his tests with data from French-speaking West Africa would give similar results.

major jump to provide sufficient salaried 'middle-class' positions. This may well be at least 20 years in the future. The alternative is to slow down the expansion of education, a course which is to some extent being quietly undertaken in parts of French-speaking West Africa. This risks unrest among those persons who, having entered the edges of the money economy themselves, are anxious to enable their children really to profit by it via the route of education.

If this latter course is not pursued, however, the governments will find those who are educated at the primary level turning against each other in competition for the limited jobs available. This has already occurred in two forms. One was the anti-stranger riots in the Ivory Coast in 1959, where unemployed school-leavers indigenous to the region secured the expulsion of Dahomeans and Togolese, who had held a large proportion of the better 'middle positions' in the Ivory Coast economy and administration. Less spectacular but equally effective anti-stranger campaigns have been seen in Niger and Senegal, and probably elsewhere. Strangers, being vulnerable in the atmosphere of the new nationalisms, are an easy target. Once they leave, however, the problem is not necessarily solved. The next stage is internal 'ethnic' competition (status-group politics), where those who are nearer to the control of force are likely to win. The army coup in Togo in 1963 is the prototype of the latter situation. Returned ex-servicemen, almost all from the 'backward' Cabré people, could not find employment, and prevailed upon their fellow Cabré still in the *gendarmerie* to undertake a coup aimed at giving them positions. Ultimately, the money allocated by the new Togo Government for the employment of these Cabré must be taken from some other sector of the economy, presumably peopled by non-Cabré.

If the problem of disparity between the numbers of primary school graduates and the jobs available seems almost unavoidable at this time in French-speaking West Africa, it does not seem that a similar problem exists at the secondary school level. It is surprising therefore that it seems to reappear for university graduates, given their relative paucity and the need of the economies for high-level trained men and women. Here, however, another factor intervenes. The commitment of a number of states to achieving economic development by close involvement with France has brought with it the corollary of *political* commitment by the leadership of these countries to the employment of French expatriates, even when indigenous university graduates are available. Furthermore, the French Government pays the salaries of its civil servants who are seconded to work with African governments, thus providing an important subsidy to African budgets that would be lost by Africanisation.

The slogan '*pas d'africanisation au rabais*' (no cut-rate Africanisation) has meant in effect the non-employment, at the level of their expectations, of many 'intellectuals'. This is particularly true of Senegal and the Ivory Coast, and was probably an important factor in the 1963 plots in these two countries. The problem is less in Guinea and Mali, committed as they are in theory to rapid Africanisation. While none of these governments has been willing to employ all the 'intellectuals' available, they have been following a procedure of 'divide and conquer' by buying off some of the most politically skilful of the student leaders with appropriate posts. The impact of this policy is in part measured by the bitterness of African students in France against the student leaders of a few years earlier who have 'renounced' their ideological opposition to the régimes in power.

If we now review the pattern of political tensions resulting from continuous economic development, we see three main stages in summary. Before World War II, there was a small emergent urban élite—we have called it the 'old' urban élite—which found itself vying with the traditional élites for the small crumbs of power and prestige available in the colonial system. This was particularly the case in the coastal states, since an urban élite scarcely existed in the interior states.

The expansion of the urban money economy during World War II produced a 'new' urban élite, a sort of 'lower' middle class. At first, the 'old' urban élite tried to hold this group back, partly by joining forces with their old rivals, the traditional élite. They formed the *administratif* parties, most of which were ethnic, as against the *mass* parties, which were dominated by the 'new' urban élite. The latter won power and with it their main objectives: internally, their full admission to élite status, and externally, their control of the legal institutions by obtaining independence. In doing this, they more or less obliterated the distinction between the 'old' and the 'new' urban élite, by absorbing the former with them into a single enlarged 'upper middle class'. This occurred largely during the period 1956–60.

Independence brought further expansion of the economies and of the educational systems. The problem now is that still more persons are knocking at the door for admission to 'middle-class' status and perquisites. But until the economy can absorb all of them roughly at the level of their expectations, there will be permanent tension. The 'outs' will be the weaker groups: élites coming from 'minority' or backward groups, 'stranger' farmers in cash-crop areas, traditional merchants squeezed out in the process of economic nationalisation, skilled workers and lower administrative staff as opposed to higher cadres in the towns. It will be these groups who will get the smaller portion of the economic pie, and among whose children the larger number of unemployed school-leavers will be found. If these groups are able to coalesce, and particularly if leadership can be provided by intellectuals who are unemployed (especially where the lack of employment is due to the presence of non-indigenous personnel), then a radicalised but pro-development ideology should have much appeal and much effect. We must now turn to the ideological biographies of African intellectuals in French-speaking West Africa to see what clothing such a pro-development ideology is likely to wear.

The Ideological Expression of Structural Strains

Political terms use themselves up quickly and their sense varies according to the time and place. The same word has not, today, the same meaning on the Left among African and metropolitan students who meet in our faculties. The African, for example, associates nationalism, Marxism, and Christianity, while the European in general considers these terms antithetical.[1]

The ideology of the nationalists of French West Africa in the period immediately following World War II was largely expressed in Marxist terminology. This is easy to understand. The climate of France was still imbued with the alliances and the values of the Resistance and, among the three major

---

[1] H. Brunschwig, 'Colonisation-décolonisation: essai sur le vocabulaire usuel de la politique colonial', in *Cahiers d'études africaines* (Paris), 1, 1960, p. 44.

parties that made up the coalition government, the French Communist Party (P.C.F.) showed the most sympathy for and gave the most practical aid to the movements of what we have called the 'new' urban élites. This found expression in the parliamentary *apparentement* of the R.D.A. to the P.C.F., and in the fact that African trade unionists affiliated to the C.G.T., besides the many individual African students who joined the P.C.F. African nationalism was a movement of protest against the powers-that-be in France; so was French Communism. The alliance seemed natural.

There was in France at this time only one other organised current of intellectual thought which was at the same time a protest movement within France and sympathetic to African aspirations. This was based on the 'personalist' ideas of Emmanuel Mounier, whose socialist ideology, though it rejected individualism and egoism, sought none the less the personal development of spiritual values within the framework of the collective society. This found expression in the work of the *Service social des étudiants d'outre-mer* in Paris, and in some, but not all, of the activities of the M.R.P., especially in its encouragement of some nationalist groups in Senegal and Upper Volta. It also found an echo in the activities of the C.F.T.C. in Africa.

The initial French support for African nationalists from both Marxists and Catholics in time came to be seen as limited by French national perspectives. Elements of paternalism suffused the atmosphere. French Marxists and Catholics were very ready to point at each other's motes in this regard, and the Africans came increasingly to resent their attitudes.

The classic statement of this discomfiture is the famous open letter written in 1956 by Aimé Césaire (a Martiniquais, but influential in French African intellectual circles) to Maurice Thorez, explaining his resignation from the P.C.F. in the following terms:

I think I have said enough to make it understood that it is neither Marxism nor Communism that I renounce, but it is the use that certain people have made of Marxism and Communism of which I disapprove. What I want is Marxism and Communism to be placed in the service of the black peoples and not the black peoples in the service of Marxism and Communism.

The reproach of a representative of the *Union des étudiants catholiques africains* speaking to French Catholic students reflects a similar attitude to Catholic doctrine:

We say that in Africa 'the explanation of revealed Truth must appeal to artistic, cultural and philosophical categories' which are authentically African. Whence the imperative necessity of rethinking the quality of institutions, traditions and cultural resources which express the catholicity of the Church . . . so that the peoples of Africa may, like everyone else, realise their own genius.
It is the best way of translating into reality this primary truth that Christianity is not tied to any civilisation, nor any culture.

Although the break with French Marxists was more 'opportune' and more bitter than the break with French Catholics, ideologically the process was the same. It was an assertion of a relative independence from French ideology, even the ideology of Frenchmen sympathetic to African aspirations, as a way of moving towards organisational autonomy and national independence. Intellectually, this was expressed in the doctrines of *négritude* and an eclectic version of socialism sometimes qualified by the adjective, African. The various versions of the new ideology shared one basic assumption, well expressed by Cheikh Hamidou Kane of Senegal:

The consciousness [*prise de conscience*] of its situation by the Third-World begins by charges [*une mise en accusation*] against the west, which is charged with the initial responsibility of having invented the world, and the later responsibility of having done poorly with it.

From this point of view, the Soviet Union was regarded as part of Europe, Marxism being but one strand of European thought; and it was against this common European tradition that Africa would assert its special qualities, not only those inherited from its own culture but those derived from the particular African cultural environment.

Négritude as a theme found organisational expression in the journal *Présence africaine*, and the two *Congrès des écrivains et des artistes noirs* convened under its aegis in 1956 and 1959. The organisational flourishing of *négritude* coincided with the efforts to create the autonomous political organisations, trade unions, and youth movements mentioned above. During the period (1956–60) of the *loi-cadre* and autonomous states within the

Community, various versions of *négritude* and African socialism suffused the ideology of all the nationalist movements in French-speaking West Africa; by contrast, during 1945–50 these movements had been intellectually dominated by Marxism and, to a much lesser extent, by personalist doctrines. This reaction of cultural nationalism—called by one French observer 'sour nostalgia'—was regarded by Africans as a way of restoring the equity of cultural exchange between Africa and Europe in the spirit of the traditional gift-exchange, wherein African spiritual values would be traded against western technology.[1]

Independence brought with it additional ideological emphases. We have already discussed the problem of creating a centralised state to resist the centrifugal forces that appear with the end of direct colonial rule. This led to the idea of the single-party state, elaborated between 1958 and 1960 in Guinea by Sékou Touré, but taken over, implicitly and quite often explicitly, by all the states of French-speaking West Africa. The three key elements of the theory may be said to be: the primacy of the party (over the administration, and over interest groups); the structure of the party as a mass party; the absence of an internal class struggle. While the first element is derived from Leninist theory, the two others are conscious rejections of Leninist theory and are recorded by African leaders as original ideas. In these matters Sékou Touré has served as the ideologist for the other states, even if they do not openly acknowledge it.

The only partial exception is Senegal, where the two leading

---

[1] Kane proposed: 'That for contemporary international relations we revive in a form adapted to modern realities the theory and practice of exchange which was in honour among the primitive tribes of North America or New Caledonia or elsewhere.

'Let us remember the analyses [Marcel] Mauss has made of them. The gift is not exclusively the movement, between two owners, of a material good with a market value. On the contrary, its market value is only the support, the vehicle, of a social message infinitely more important. The gift is a payment in full, bearing the maximum social utility. As, furthermore, each gift calls for a counter-gift, the latter also a vector of meaning, there is established a double current of both material and spiritual exchange, a true bond of solidarity.

'Comme si nous nous étions donnés rendez-vouz', in *Esprit* (Paris), October 1961, p. 387. *Esprit* is the journal founded by Mounier.

figures, Léopold Senghor and Mamadou Dia, have been
influenced by two leading products of French left-wing
Catholicism, Father Teilhard de Chardin and François
Perroux respectively. The difference with Sékou Touré has
been in fact rather slight. Both Senghor and Dia on one hand
and Touré on the other have criticised Marxist analysis as
irrelevant to the actual social situation of contemporary Africa.
Senghor has added his own emphasis on western materialism's
offence against African spiritual values:

What is most disturbing is that the predictions of Marx have not
been fulfilled, a fact by which ought to be judged the worth of his
theory—and of his *praxis*. The proletarian revolution was not made
in western Europe, but in eastern Europe, and as a result of a military defeat. The state has not *withered away*, neither in the west nor in
the east. It is the state, turned capitalist in both places, which
makes the revolutions: in eastern Europe by radical means, in
western Europe by reformist means. In the two areas, *white-collar
workers increase while proletarians diminish* in numbers. In the west,
technicians replace, little by little, private capitalists, while in
the east they are becoming technocrats. In sum, the two areas,
North America and the U.S.S.R., are coming to resemble each
other in their concern for technique and for comfort at a time
when, paradoxically, religious faith is reviving; when certain 'more
or less moral categories'—justice, humanity, liberty, equality,
fraternity—are being reinforced, categories which, according to
Marx, 'stand for absolutely nothing'.

Although there has been basic ideological agreement, among
the nationalist leaders in power, on the structure and role of
the state and of the party within the state, there has been open
division on the theory of economic development, which has
developed into a debate about pan-Africanism. This split can
be traced to the 1957 Congress of the R.D.A. in Bamako,
already mentioned, which considered the means by which
Africa could achieve a radical reallocation of the world's
income in its favour. Initially, the problem was phrased in
purely political terms: from 1956 to 1958 with reference to 'the
democratisation of the federal executive of A.O.F.'; from 1958
to 1960 with reference successively to the vote on the referendum, the creation of the Federation of Mali, and the path to
'international sovereignty'.

The string of independences in the summer of 1960 closed this version of the argument at the very moment that the Congo crisis brought into existence another political formulation of it—the division of Africa into the Casablanca and the Brazzaville powers. The Brazzaville powers stood for close and almost exclusive political and economic alignment with France, and associate membership in the E.E.C. Guinea and Mali stood for a more militant neutralism which would obtain economic aid from diverse sources while politically committed primarily to the African continent.

The argument of the Brazzaville powers, often called 'moderate', was that economic development requires considerable capital aid from the developed world, which must therefore not be frightened off, especially its two most wealthy sectors, the U.S.A. and the E.E.C. The greatest danger was *cartiérisme*, the economic neo-isolationism of the developed world, particularly Europe. A secondary danger was the substitution of American for European economic domination, which many considered even less advantageous to Africans; they therefore advocated membership in the E.E.C., the development of co-operatives at home, favourable conditions for foreign investment, and occasional gestures towards the Soviet Union (largely as blackmail).

The Casablanca group in effect scorned this approach as a trap, saying this is precisely what the sophisticated sectors of the developed world want. They argued that such aid would appease immediate needs but would not change the fundamental economic relationship with the developed world. They advocated belt-tightening, getting tough with Europe and America, and a policy aimed both at widening world channels of trade and at developing a common market in Africa.

Behind the analysis of this latter group lie two major hypotheses familiar in western European intellectual history. One is the Marxian hypothesis of the trend towards the polarisation of classes and 'immiserisation'. The other is the Sorelian hypothesis of the myth of the general strike as the method of revolutionary action. In both these hypotheses, there are two classes, the developed or 'bourgeois' nations, and the underdeveloped or 'proletarian' nations, whose lot is immiserisation. The way out is the myth of the general strike, which in this context means that if economic links, both trade and aid, were cut between the developed and under-developed world, the former rather than the latter would suffer most over any extended period.

In effect, both the Brazzaville and the Casablanca groups saw themselves as in a struggle with the developed world, in which their opponents are western Europe, the U.S.A., and the Soviet Union. They benefit by the divisions between these countries. What they fear most in this regard is an *entente* among the developed world. Thus for opposite reasons both Guinea and the Ivory Coast, for example, were pleased by the exclusion of Britain from the Common Market. The split between China and Russia aids their position, while the split between China and India harms it; nevertheless, for numerous diplomatic reasons, the various states do not feel free to express openly such attitudes.

The difficulties with the more militant position of the Casablanca powers lay in the objective world situation. The ability of African states to carry off such a posture depended on their unity and the capacity of the Soviet Union to supply alternative aid. But the experience of Guinea from 1958 to 1962 demonstrated that the U.S.S.R. was not in a position to furnish sufficient economic assistance to counterbalance western economic retaliation. This, combined with the lack of unity, made such a militant position even harder to sustain and pushed Guinea and Mali closer to the other states of French-speaking West Africa in terms of reliance on European economic aid. In return, the Brazzaville states have moved closer to the position of Guinea and Mali on the creation of African unity as a bargaining weapon with Europe.

This partial ideological synthesis has been under systematic intellectual attack from only one source, the university students, primarily those who have studied in France. University students have been the radical leaven in French-speaking West Africa continuously since 1945, despite being largely located in France. Paris was in many ways the centre of intellectual discourse, especially since African politicians were elected as representatives to French parliamentary bodies, with a freedom of action often greater in Paris than in their home territories because of repression. The students have pursued three themes since 1945:

independence, pan-Africanism, and internationalism. They were the first to talk persistently and systematically of independence, whether they were Marxists or Catholics or neither. Indeed, in 1952 Maghemout Diop wrote an article whose title expressed the student point of view, one considered quite *avant-garde* at the time: 'The only way out: total independence; the sole path: a wide movement of anti-imperialist union'. The theme of independence was picked up from the students by the youth and trade unionists and finally acceded to by the leadership of the mass nationalist movements.

Concerning the second theme, pan-Africanism, the argument was that 'in unity there is strength'. This was reflected in the perennial insistence of the students' organisation, F.E.A.N.F., that it can be recognised as the exclusive representative of African students, in preference to separate territorial students' associations. The basic approval was echoed even by coherent Marxists like Maghemout Diop, despite their concern with possible racist implications:

But the day is not far off when the truth will burst out and when every Negro, whoever he may be, will be proud to be a Negro. In preparation for that day, and for the pan-Negrism which will be its inevitable consequence, it would be prudent to consider organising it now, channelling it so that it does not turn into racism.[1]

The pan-Africanism of the students must however be distinguished from *négritude*, which was always received more sceptically, because of its anti-rationalist (and hence anti-universalist) overtones. Typical of this scepticism were the remarks of Albert Franklin:[2]

The theory of *négritude* [remains] ideologically a mystification, and practically a dangerous diversion. For the consequence (and perhaps the intended objective) is to separate Negro Africans from the united

[1] Cf. the similar point of view of a student leader, who is a Catholic: 'We do not want to be made into a mosaic of tiny dependent states, as in Central America. . . . Our goal must be to assure our own solidarity.' A. Tevoedjre, *L'Afrique révoltée* (Paris, 1958), p. 133. Tevoedjre later became secretary-general of the U.A.M., but was discharged after a short period of service.

[2] Franklin later returned home to become secretary-general of the Ministry of Foreign Affairs in the Government of Togo during the presidency of Sylvanus Olympio.

front of the oppressed against the oppressors. The practical argument which Sartre gives [in *Black Orpheus*] is that, whatever his situation, the white proletarian would be worse off without colonisation. Let us admit that at first sight this argument seems to have merit. But before accepting it let us reflect a little . . .
In any case colonisation has not saved the Euro-American proletarian. Only the fall of the bourgeoisie will save him. It seems that, whatever be the evolution of the colonies after independence, the European (or American) proletarian will have, over all, nothing to lose and everything to gain. Indeed we might say that if his revolution is delayed, one explanation is the existence of colonies . . . Let us even say that, on the absurd hypothesis that white proletarian and bourgeois would join forces against us, the most elementary tactical sense would tell us not to reinforce this coalition.

The criticism of *négritude* is in fact in the name of the third theme of the students: internationalism. This was reflected organisationally by the links established by F.E.A.N.F. with students' groups from North Africa, Madagascar, the Antilles and other areas, to form an anti-colonialist student front in Paris. It was also to be found in their insistence on affiliating with the Communist-dominated International Union of Students at a time when the youth movement and the trade unionists were insisting on international disaffiliation as an expression of neutralism and autonomy.[1]

By 1960, their position on independence had been accepted by the leaders at home, and their position on Pan-Africanism at least by the leaders of Guinea and Mali. In the heyday of new independence, internationalism was at best a muted theme. This did not prevent them from feeling still in the *avant-garde* of ideas; but there was a tone of discouragement, even with Guinea and Mali, especially as they noticed their own former leaders becoming integrated into the new independent governments. This attitude was reflected in the acute strain between the *Association des étudiants guinéens en France* and the party in Guinea after independence, not to speak of the difficulties of students from states such as the Ivory Coast or Upper Volta.

In the light of all this, and of the fact that the students

[1] The students' organisations had been, however, independent of French associations from their inception, unlike the youth and trade unions. Hence they did not feel the same need to disaffiliate from *international* organisations in order to emphasise their autonomy vis-à-vis *French* organisations.

continue to play an intellectual, *avant-garde* role, while still subject largely to contemporary French influences, what can one project about the values that élites will hold in the coming years in French-speaking West Africa? We can do this best by summarising the sources of strain in the social structures and indicating which current ideologies might serve the purposes of some social group.

We suggested that the middle-class groups in power in the various states are in a precarious position. Their political and economic systems are fragile, and they have promised more than they can probably deliver in the coming 10 years. The positions of real power, prestige, and wealth are few, and there are more individuals who can lay a legitimate claim to such positions than there is room for. That is to say, the belief in an open stratification system, one in which men may attain the status for which they have the ability, creates the maximum discontent in economies that are insufficiently expanding.[1] Accidents of ethnic group, of age, or of family often determine the difference between high and medium status. And the determinants are indeed seen as accidental.

In such a situation, the 'ins' will normally try to create or recreate status-groups which will legitimate their privilege. The 'outs', who are many and initially unrelated, will counter by urging radical egalitarian ideologies which will prevent the consolidation of 'accidental' advantage. By arguing that there are no accidents, that social conditions are determined (and hence scientifically determinable), they can thereby justify revolutionary action. For if, by the egalitarian values of the 'African revolution' (values to which the 'ins' are presumably publicly committed), the fate of the 'outs' is 'undeserved', and if there is no such thing as luck, then it is the system which is responsible and which must be changed. Or, to put it in the probable language of the 'outs', the revolution must be 'fulfilled'.

There are two likely ideological themes for the 'outs' to develop. One might be termed 'neo-traditionalism', a romanticising of ethnic and/or African characteristics. The idea of *négritude* could be developed and distorted in this direction.

[1] This is the now familiar problem of 'relative deprivation' in an anomic society.

It is easy to see how this could be combined with various kinds of appeals to violence and a deep antagonism to the developed world. Such doctrines could have an appeal to élites from 'minority' ethnic groups, to traditional merchants who are unable to compete in the ever more modern economy, to partially educated town dwellers who have 'failed' in the modern occupational system. One might point out diverse manifestations as precursors of such a movement: the *Ligue des originaires de la Côte d'Ivoire* who organised the riots against the Dahomeans in 1959, of the *Bloc des masses sénégalaises*, a political party of intellectuals like Cheikh Anta Diop, the historian of *négritude*, plus some traditional religious groups; even the group of Cabré army sergeants who arranged the *coup d'état* in Togo in 1963 might qualify.[1]

A second possible ideological theme is in a sense the direct opposite. It is the theme of the ultra-modernists, the proponents of the internal class struggle. This can be found in classical Leninist form in the *Parti africain de l'indépendance* or in the variety of Abdoulaye Ly and the P.R.A.-Senegal. It can be found more recently in the last book of Frantz Fanon, which has been so widely read in Africa. Fanon shares with Ly a belief in the revolutionary role of the peasantry and adds to it a strong emphasis on the necessity of violence. These doctrines may appeal more to those 'out' groups who see their future tied to further and more rapid modernisation: 'stranger' farmers in cash-crop areas, skilled workers and administrative personnel whose path is being blocked for reasons not related to their skills, and especially unemployed intellectuals.

These two groups of 'outs' share certain ideological presumptions. They are both fundamentally antagonistic to the status quo and hence to those at present in power. They are both opposed to continuing western influence, albeit for opposite reasons: the neo-traditionalists because of their cultural rejection of the west, the ultra-modernists because of their total espousal of western values. They are both willing to entertain seriously the prospect of violence. They both proclaim doctrines of ideas and of action and therefore have a continuing appeal

[1] Indeed it is probably because he saw the Togo sergeants as such a menace that President Sékou Touré of Guinea reacted so strongly to the assassination of Olympio.

to students, especially when their future careers are so uncertain. They are both Pan-Africanist, though here it must be noted that the neo-traditionalists would tend to mean only Black Africa whereas the ultra-modernists would usually include North Africa as well. Indeed, some of the latter would think in terms of the 'Third World'. The coming together of these two groups of 'outs' seems typically indicated in the Ivory Coast plot of 1963, in which the modernist intellectuals of the J.R.D.A.C.I. (the youth section of the governing party) were implicated along with those who had been responsible for the anti-Dahomean riots of 1959.

The two 'out' groups seek power in part through the organisation of dissident groups, but in part also by taking over the structure of the party and its auxiliaries. National youth movements, trade unions, and women's associations are natural places for ultra-modernists. Local party structures are natural places for neo-traditionalists. The national leaders, using the state machinery and the national party structures, are in a sense constantly struggling on both fronts, and have thus far managed to remain in power in all the states of French-speaking West Africa, except possibly Togo. They can only remain so, however, if they simultaneously reinvigorate their party structure and develop sufficiently rapidly, thus preventing the clear coalescence of a politically conscious opposition. This will be difficult, particularly if the death of de Gaulle were to mark a resurgence of *cartiérisme* in France.

The alternative would be a steady weakening of the centre, which would have one of two likely consequences. One would be the triumph of the neo-traditionalists, followed by further economic stagnation and the eventual ousting of the relatively modernist elements in the present régimes. (Some argue that this was the meaning of the Ivory Coast and Senegal crises of late 1962.) In this case, the modernist opposition might be in for a long winter and would be forced into revolutionary agitation. The other result might be a split in the present régimes, leading to the entry of some ultra-modernist elements into government. (Some argue that this was the meaning of the Dahomey revolution of late 1963.) The verbiage in which this élite would clothe its pro-development ideology would depend very much on the reaction of the outside world towards their

ITCA

assumption of power. Their early rise to power, however, would probably mean a minimum of actual revolutionary turmoil. If this occurred, the new régime would immediately find itself in the same dilemmas as the old, and again would have to produce rapid development or face in their turn the opposition of ever 'newer' élites.

II. FORCE AND INDEPENDENCE IN NORTH AFRICA

7. Emergence of a political party in Morocco

DOUGLAS E. ASHFORD *Political Change in Morocco* Princeton University Press 1961; pages 34–9

Emergence of a Political Party

From the small group of students at Rabat, led by Ahmen Balafrej, and the group at Qarawiyn University, led by Allal Al-Fassi, emerged the first political party of the French zone. Formed during the final steps of the pacification, its struggle in 1937 to become a rudimentary, poorly organized party was stifled with the approach of World War II. During this entire period the group of young nationalists never operated with complete freedom or with any legal protection. Although they were permitted for short intervals of a month or two to operate quite openly, most work was done clandestinely in anticipation of the next wave of suppression. Only in the brief period from December 1936 to March 1937 did they enjoy a measure of legality, when General Noguès granted a general amnesty and many new papers were started. This amnesty was partly due to the establishment of the Popular Front government in France in June 1936. Its desire to solidify the loyalty of the Moroccans was reinforced by the initiation of the revolution under Franco in Spain the next month. Before this time the nationalists had had the blessing of some Socialists. They had subsidized and written in the early French review of the nationalists, *Al-Maghreb*, in 1932 and 1933. For nearly all the first half of the period from 1926 to 1939 French Morocco was still in a state of open warfare and complete military occupation except for the secure areas along the coast. Under these conditions it is not surprising that little was done.

In April 1927 the Fès group, called the Students Union, and the Rabat group, called the Supporters of Truth, began collaborating and clandestinely took oaths in a new organization, the Moroccan League. The next month, after having been denounced by the head of the Kettani brotherhood, the first nationalist, Mohammed Ghazi, was arrested. Mohammed Ghazi had started the first free school of the nationalists in Fès in 1926. This school was an institution that was to take on its full political implications only after World War II. After these early meetings the young nationalists again returned to their studies, mostly at Qarawiyn or in Paris. Until the Berber *dahir* the most important goal of the group left in Morocco was their opposition to the increasing activity of the brotherhoods. Al-Fassi became famous for his lectures on this subject at Qarawiyn University. Indeed, the first primitive organization of the nationalists in Morocco consisted of groups of Islamic scholars and students who exchanged information throughout the regions of the country where orthodox Islam was strongest and who convened in the privileged sanctuary provided by the mosques.[1]

In view of the small percentage of the Moroccans who belonged to brotherhoods, this original goal of the nationalists was actually more an intellectual protest than a theme that could be developed into an imperative for political action. As has been noted, this need was admirably filled by the Berber *dahir* of May 1930. It brought the cause of the nationalists to the attention of the Socialists in France, who from this time on sympathized with the young nationalists. Shortly after the issue of the *dahir*, Chekib Arslan made his visit to Tetouan and made contact with the nationalists of the French zone.[2] Arslan made the *dahir* a central theme of his Pan-Arabism, and his protégé, Mohammed Hassan Ouazzani, started a French-language newspaper, *L'Action du Peuple*, in Fès, in 1933. While some nationalists with more French background, like Mohammed Lyazidi and Omar Abdeljalil, wrote for its columns, the nationalist *ulema* of Qarawiyn in the same city contributed nothing

[1] Rezette, pp. 7–11 gives some examples of the better-known meetings in mosques. These meetings were, of course, important throughout the period before the war and, in addition, in the absence of permission for the nationalists to meet publicly, were used to reach the public and to overcome the obstacle of illiteracy to political agitation.

[2] Rezette, pp. 68–71. Though not directly pertinent to this inquiry, it is indicative of the plight of the young nationalists between the appeal of France and the Arab world that Chekib Arslan declined an invitation to a Socialist-sponsored rally on behalf of the Moroccans in 1933.

and little appeared pertaining to their Islamic-inspired pro-tests.[1] Through Arslan's efforts the campaign reached all parts of the Arab world, and committees to defend Islam in Morocco were started in Egypt, India, and Indonesia. The young nationalists were convinced that the *dahir* was the initiation of a programme to divide Morocco into smaller colonies and to begin the proselytism of the Berbers by Christian missionaries.

In 1929 the Moroccan League had formed a loosely bound Committee of National Action, which included members from both the old Spanish and French zones. The committee took on new significance after the enactment of the 1930 *dahir* and was broken into separate parts for the north and south to facilitate its activities in the French Protectorate. Allal Al-Fassi continued his lectures at Qarawiyn and late in 1933 made visits to Tetouan, Madrid, and Paris. On his return in May 1934 he was received by the King—the first contact between the nationalists and Mohammed V. Shortly afterwards the nationalist newspapers, now four in number and coming from Tetouan and Paris as well as Fès, were banned. Allal Al-Fassi and his colleagues were forbidden to continue their public lectures.

During this same early period the organization of students and youth began. When Balafrej returned to Paris after the first meeting of 1926, he helped start the Association of North African Muslim Students. Congresses were held in Tunis in 1931 and in Algiers in 1932. The 1933 Congress, scheduled for Rabat, was forbidden there and was held in Paris. At the same time graduates of the Muslim colleges of Fès, Rabat, Marrakech, and Casablanca began to form alumni associations, though their initial reluctance to engage in direct political agitation drew the criticism of the *L'Action du Peuple*. An unsuccessful attempt was made by the alumni associations, in November 1933, to condemn the banning of the meeting of the Association of North African Muslim Students. Another source of potentially more aggressive support for the nationalists, the Movement of Moroccan Scouts, also started in 1933. Though under French auspices, its Moroccan directors were known for

---

[1] "*Ulema*" is the plural form of the word "*alim*", or "religious scholar in Islam". For a more detailed view on this early publication, see Rezette, p. 76.

their nationalist leanings, and by the end of World War II the scouts had become an important nationalist adjunct. Efforts of the nationalist press to establish as a national holiday November 18, the day on which Mohammed Ben Youssef became King, also succeeded from the fall of 1933.

Up to 1933 the French authorities had not forcefully inter-vened in nationalist activities, which were still largely confined to small groups in Rabat, its neighbouring city of Salé, and Fès. Allal Al-Fassi and his colleagues had been removed from their positions as *ulema* at Qarawiyn and a few of their students had been briefly detained by the police. Early in 1934 the King made a visit to Fès, where the spectacular ovation he received produced serious concern among the French authorities. They cancelled his trip to the mosque on the Friday of that week and abruptly hustled Mohammed V back to Rabat. The riots resulting from the arbitrarily foreshortened visit alerted the nationalists to the problem they would have in pursuing their activity among a population whose enthusiasm was so easily turned into violence. This incident was violently attacked by the nationalist press, which was forbidden soon afterward in Morocco. The nationalist leaders appear then to have entered a period of reflection and consultation, from which emerged the Plan of Reforms of 1934, described in the following paragraph. It must be remembered that at this time they possessed almost no organization outside of the small groups in the major cities, loosely held together in the Com-mittee of Action. From this incident of the riots following the King's forced return to Rabat came the more conciliatory opinion embodied in the Plan of Reforms and also the decline in the importance of Arslan and Mohammed Hassan Ouazzani, the most outspoken critics of France.

After the Fès riots a small committee of ten persons had been formed in Fès to work on a new plan of action.[1] Six were clearly of predominantly Arabic background and of the four who had some French background only Mohammed Hassan Ouazzani represented what might be termed an extreme modernist

---

[1] Julien, p. 151, lists them as Omar Abdeljalil, Abdelaziz Ben Driss, Ahmed Cherkaoui, Mohammed Diouri, Allal Al-Fassi, Mohammed Ghazi, Boucker Kadiri, Mohammed Lyazidi, Mohammed Mekki Naciri, and Mohammed Hassan Ouazzani.

viewpoint. In December 1934 the Plan of Reforms, which this committee had prepared, was presented to the King, Premier Laval, and the Resident General. The document justified Julien's evaluation that "[the] programme constitutes a catalogue of claims more than an elaborated plan of reforms". The first part of the Plan reiterated the original conditions under which the Protectorate had been established and outlined how this agreement had been violated. This was followed by five sections on proposed changes in the realm of political and administrative procedures, judicial and penal institutions, general social and health measures, economic and financial practices, and, last, special needs, including the abolition of the Berber *dahir* and the use of Arabic as the official language. The goal of independence was not discussed, nor was any suggestion made that the Moroccans be given a voice in foreign affairs or national defence. The section on economic reforms was probably the most naïve, starting off with the unexplained injunction to "raise the standard of living of Moroccans by the creation of work and the development of economic activity". The section on justice was outlined the most systematically and completely, which was to be expected since many members of the committee had a thorough knowledge of Islamic law and Moroccan history. The political and administrative section was a mixture of sound suggestions and obviously ambitious schemes, particularly in the area of representative institutions, as the authors of the document learned after three years of independence. The Plan of Reforms is valuable for this study not so much for what it specifically contained, as for its tacit testimony as to how little the nationalists changed their thinking over the next twenty years regarding the actual problems of running a nation.

To expect the young nationalists to be familiar with the intricacies of government while at the same time carrying on their campaign for independence would be unreasonable, but it is important in understanding events after independence. Their organized membership was restricted to Rabat, Casablanca, Fès, Salé, and Kenitra (Port Lyautey).[1] A few members

[1] Most of the organizational information in this paragraph is from Rezette, p. 255 and pp. 263–7. The cited figures were taken from "an official document", according to Rezette. Since he is known to have received

were just beginning nationalist activity in Safi, Meknes, and Marrakech. Finances were provided largely by contributions of a few wealthy members. Very little attention had been given to developing a disciplined following even in the cities, though it was possible to create a potentially violent demonstration. The nationalists' strength for the entire area of Morocco was reliably estimated to include 12 leaders, 150 militants, and from 200 to 300 sympathizers.[1]

The Plan of Reforms marked the entry of the nationalists into official politics. Though it is probably an exaggeration to say that the Plan "had far-reaching repercussions in French and Moroccan circles", it alerted the French to the growing threat to their control and showed the nationalists how difficult it would be to negotiate for reforms. The Plan was rejected in its entirety and the nationalists again were dispersed, many of them going to Paris to try to bring their case to the attention of officials there. Their efforts were renewed with vigour late in 1935, when the French residents demanded representative institutions. This was regarded by the nationalists as the first step in the incorporation of Morocco in the French Empire and also, of course, as the denial of equal privileges to Moroccans in their own affairs. Allal Al-Fassi and his colleagues met with the Resident General to discuss the matter on the eve of the formation of the Popular Front. This was the first meeting of the nationalists with a Resident General and soon broke down into a round of mutual incriminations, but the establishment of the Blum government postponed the controversial issue. The same Resident General also forbade the convening of the annual congress of the Association of North African Muslim Students in Morocco in the fall of 1936. By this time the nationalists had established their first local sections, four being formed in Casablanca, five at Fès, and one each at Kenitra, Rabat, and Salé. . . .

some assistance from French authorities in Rabat and Paris in writing his book, these figures are probably the work of the French administration. Even if minimized considerably, they indicate how small a group were active participants at this time.

[1] The two leaders in addition to the ten authors of the Plan of Reforms were probably Ahmed Balafrej and Mohammed Zeghari.

8. The politics of boundaries in North and West Africa

I. WILLIAM ZARTMAN *Journal of Modern African Studies* Vol. 3, No. 2, 1965 Cambridge University Press; pages 155–72

Problems created by boundaries are among the more frequent causes of war, and North and West Africa has some of the strangest boundary problems in the world. Unlike many of the world's borders, the boundaries here are not the walls and moats of history, natural defence lines whose traces mark the military conflicts and diplomatic compromises of the nation's past. The only exceptions are one-sided and even ironic: the treaty of Lalla Maghnia of 18 March 1845 defined 100 miles of the Algero-Moroccan border after the Moroccan defeat by France at Isly, and the line dividing Algeria from Mali and Niger was the result of an agreement in 1905 separating French military explorers in North Africa from rival French military explorers in West Africa. There is therefore none of the legitimacy of national history associated with the boundary lines. This has its advantages and disadvantages: the might of conquest and the right of diplomacy have not sanctified the borders, but the Schleswigs and the Alsace-Lorraines are not present either.

All boundaries in North and West Africa were colonial creations. Some were drawn as a result of the Berlin Conference of 1884–5, which stated that European states could claim the West African territories they effectively occupied; expansion started from coastal enclaves and riverine holdings, and the lines where Britain, France, Spain, and Portugal met were often drawn with no precise knowledge of the terrain and traditional nations (i.e. tribes) involved. Most of the boundaries were merely administrative divisions within French North Africa or French West Africa (A.O.F.), but were drawn with no greater awareness of human or physical geography. Thus, half the boundaries are geometrical, mainly straight lines. Such borders obviously correspond to no natural—human or physical—features.

Over a quarter of the boundaries, however, are physical. For the most part these follow small river-beds, although two major rivers—the Senegal between Senegal and Mauritania, and the Niger between Niger and Dahomey—are also used. Gambia combines the two criteria by being bounded by lines and arcs drawn on either side of the Gambia river. As a result, except in the case of the Senegal,[1] large parts of the most important river basins are found within a single state, a situation which favours development of this natural resource and reduces the need for co-operation among littoral states. Crest-line and water-shed boundaries are rare (less than 400 kilometres or two per cent) for there are few mountains and the colonial accident placed those that exist inside one country or another. In North Africa, the Atlas Mountains run perpendicular to the boundary lines. There are small stretches of watershed boundaries between Algeria and Mali (Ilforas), Guinea and Ivory Coast (Mimba), and Sierra Leone and Guinea (Loma), and along eastern Nigeria.

Boundaries and Human Geography

The most serious problem—and most frequent reproach—concerning the unnaturalness of North and West African boundaries relates to human geography. This complicated question requires much clarification. Although these African boundaries do not coincide with mountains—which elsewhere help to create conditions for a stable border by providing less populous frontier areas as well as natural defence lines—they do cross deserts, which have many of the same characteristics. All boundaries between the Atlas Mountains on the north and the Senegal and Niger rivers and the sixteenth parallel on the south run through regions averaging less than one person per square mile. Moreover, all boundaries that cross the poor middle belt of West Africa (running roughly parallel to the coast from the Futa Jallon to the Jos Plateau) traverse regions with an average of less than 25 persons per square mile. The only borders that

[1] Besides the Senegal, the only river planned for joint exploitation is the Mono, between Togo and Dahomey, under an agreement signed in March 1964. The Niamey Convention, negotiated in October 1963 between the riverine states of the Niger to replace the Berlin Agreement of 1885 and the Statute of St-Germain-en-Laye of 1919, has led to little co-operation as yet, and has nothing to do with boundaries.

cross regions of over 100 persons per square mile are those along a 100-mile-deep coastal strip (the Mauritanian, Spanish Saharan, and Ghana-Ivory Coast borders excluded), and those of northern Ghana and Nigeria. From the point of view of population density, therefore, there are encouraging factors of stability. Unfortunately, these statistical considerations, like considerations of physical geography, must bow to other, more important human factors if the permanence of a frontier is to be ascertained.

Boundaries separate nations. Their stability depends above all on the satisfaction or dissastisfaction with which a citizen accepts the order that he must turn his back on a particular neighbour, or the satisfaction or dissatisfaction with which a national leader accepts the fact that in certain areas people are turning their backs on him and his leadership. Nation-building is a back-turning process, as the government (and party) seeks to establish and inculcate coincidence between the nation and the territorial country. All boundaries are artificial in the sense that it is not natural to draw lines separating neighbours from contact with each other. Countries learn to live with boundaries as nations and states develop, a learning process imposed by the exigencies of government and of conducting international relations between territorial states. Nation-building is part of Africa's learning process. Boundaries are involved in many ways in this process, the first being the relation between the modern and the traditional nations.

The much-repeated charge of artificially directed against African boundaries refers specifically to their disregard of tribal geography. In these terms, there is nothing but truth in the charge; only in a few spots do North and West African boundaries coincide with tribal boundaries. More important, is such coincidence possible? It is desirable? Is it relevant? Few are the spots in the area where tribes themselves observe fine territorial distinctions; they intermingle, intermarry, and migrate. Even the great empires of the Sudan and the Maghreb were not territorial states. In modern times, the tribe may have a sense of community and a seat of authority, but it does not have fixed territorial limits. It is a human, not a geographical, unit. Thus, any line that cuts between some tribes will cut through others, and it would be difficult to find any boundary in either North or West Africa that would coincide with tribal geography. Whether such a boundary would be desirable or not is a less clearly answerable question. Some African leaders build their new nations by cementing old nations together;

Land boundaries in North and West Africa

State	Total	Geometric	River	Water-shed	Road	Scale of Maps Used[1]
	Km.	Km.	Km.	Km.	Km.	
Tunisia	1,402	362	53			2,000,000; 1,000,000
claims	1,514	462	53			
Algeria	5,970	4,000	800	75	142	2,000,000; 200,000
Morocco	1,938	1,020	762			2,000,000; 1,000,000
claims[2]	1,890	1,340	390			
Spanish Sahara	1,992	1,942				2,000,000
Mauritania	4,760	3,800	930		10	2,000,000; 500,000
Senegal[3]	1,700	192	1,046			2,000,000; 500,000
Gambia	750	750				1,000,000
Portuguese Guinea	715	206	80			500,000
Mali	7,030	3,713	1,600	75	10	2,000,000; 500,000
Guinea	2,923	153	1,132	138		2,000,000; 250,000
Sierra Leone	895	105	395	130		1,000,000; 250,000
Liberia	1,310	30	872			800,000; 250,000
Ivory Coast	2,930	125	1,750	8		800,000; 500,000
Ghana	1,994	428	963		9	500,000
Upper Volta	3,105	1,028	1,390			2,000,000; 250,000
Togo	1,507	438	536		9	2,000,000; 500,000
Dahomey	1,792	286	686			2,000,000; 1,000,000
Nigeria	3,732	60	320	140	210	2,000,000; 1,000,000
Niger	4,253	2,717	622			2,000,000; 1,000,000
Totals[4]	28,579	13,364	7,344	353	370	

[1] Distances have been measured by means of an instrument designed to follow irregular lines; the scale of the largest and smallest maps used for this purpose is given. Measurements will err by under-estimation; breakdowns for geometric, river, and other components are minimum figures.

[2] Boundary estimated along a straight line that follows the escarpment south of the Dra, leaving the *conaens* in Morocco and Tindouf in Algeria. No line has been suggested for putting Tindouf in Morocco.

[3] Senegal figures exclude Gambian boundary.

[4] Totals do not add up because shared boundaries are not counted twice.

tribal unity would fit this policy. Others seek to ignore or destroy the tribes (a remarkably difficult process); an intra-tribal boundary may coincide with, even if not facilitate, this policy. States in the latter category would presumably not find it desirable (assuming rationality) to rectify their border to coincide with inter-tribal lines, but states in the former category might seek to consolidate their tribal overhang or embark on conquest in the name of a former tribal empire. Morocco and Ghana have done this, although without much rationality, since they are among the latter category of states.

The basic question concerns the relevance of tribal geography to modern states. In the mid-twentieth century, the African tribe is no longer an organisational unit, comparable to the government or the party, any more than it was a territorial unit. The tribe is still the predominant national group in much of North and West Africa—the primary unit of allegiance and identification throughout the area between the Gulf of Guinea and the Atlas Mountains—until replaced by the modern nation state; but it has had little importance as a unit of political action. Border conflicts involving the Requeibat and their neighbours of Morocco, Algeria, and Mauritania (1958–60), the Tuareg of Mali, Niger, and Algeria (1963–4), the Manjaks of Senegal and Portuguese Guinea (1961, 1963), the Ntribus and Ewes of Togo and Ghana, the Assini of Ivory Coast and Ghana (1960), and the Fulani and Bariba of Niger and Dahomey (1963–4) are relatively rare exceptions when it is realised that the frontier of Ghana alone cuts through 17 major tribes. Even more important is the fact that the Tuaregs' was the only tribal action carried out autonomously, without outside instigation and assistance from a party or government.[1] Had it remained a political as well as a social group, as it had been in the past, the tribe would have posed such a threat to the modern government that it would have been necessary to

---

[1] Mali, however, claimed that the Tuareg were incited by French mercenaries; *Le Monde* (Paris), 15 September 1964; *L'Essor* (Bamako), 11 May and 28 September 1964. There has been no serious study on the tribal factor in North or West African politics, a challenging if difficult subject. Tribal data are provided in James S. Coleman and Carl G. Rosberg (eds.), *Political Parties and National Integration in Tropical Africa* (Berkeley, 1964), although conclusions remain to be drawn and verified.

destroy it outright or adopt it as the basis of government. But government and party have replaced the tribe's political functions, and state services and the nation slowly replace many of its social functions, leaving the traditional nation with little relevance as a basis for boundary determination.

True as this may be for the socio-political aspects of the North and West African tribe, it may be objected that it is less so for tribal socio-economic life, which is still vigorous. In fact in many of the above-mentioned tribes—Reqeibat, Tuareg, Assinis, Fulanis-Barabas, Ntribus—political unrest broke out only when triggered by economic troubles. Trade, migration, and marriage all are part of contemporary tribal life, even when the tribe is split by borders. Given the permeability of many African boundaries and the laxity of border control between most states, this condition usually poses few problems. However, when an attempt is made to close the border—as between Ghana and Togo, Ghana and Upper Volta, Senegal and Mali, Dahomey and Niger, and Algerian borders with Mauritania, Morocco, and Tunisia—a hardship is imposed on traditional ways of life. But the fact is that the whole process of modernisation imposes hardships on traditionalism, of which the clash between nation-building and tribal life is only one example. Nationalism means closer ties within and looser ties without; it means the construction of a coincident nation-state-government ensemble and the centralisation of allegiance towards the new entity, just as it means the redirection of economic and social patterns within the new unit. There is no reason why the construction of the new nation should make way before the criteria of traditionalism in boundary-making any more than in any other sector, although of course there is no reason not to expect tribal-based problems along the borders from time to time.

In sum, tribal criteria for borders in North and West Africa are neither possible, nor wholly desirable, nor relevant. For, in fact, it is not the boundary but the nation that is artificial. The coincidence of popular, territorial, and organisational units has not yet been achieved; boundary lines are still imprecise in human and political terms. As the nation consolidates, borders for the first time find their *raison d'être*. In the process, tribes slowly lose the importance they now have, although both new irredentist claims and minor rectifications may be expected to arise.

There is one tribal characteristic that does bear on North and West African boundaries. Throughout this area, the pre-colonial boundary concept was one of frontier marches, not of border lines. The classical West African empires were composed of one or more centres of power, with control and allegiance conceived in terms of people rather than land, concentrated about the centres and diminishing with distance. The Fula empire was where the Fulas lived and maintained control, and they could move long distances and keep the empire intact, as long as they preserved a cohesive society and independent political control. In a nomadic society such as that from which the Muslim legal ideas of North Africa sprung, it was the people—the *umma* or community of believers—that determined the geographic scope of the state, not the territorial limit of the state or its effective control that determined the allegiance of the people. Morocco was traditionally divided into *bled al-makhzen* (government region) and *bled as-siba* (dissident region), both of which considered themselves part of the Sherifian Empire and owed religious allegiance to the sultan as *imam* (religious leader); but only the former owed political allegiance to the sultanate. In the Maghreb, the Sudan, and along the Guinea coast, the nation determined the state and was an ethnic unit. Today, the state and its boundaries are the framework for nation-building, and the state is a territorial unit. At the present time, however, the state is a state of becoming, not a state of being. As a result, although boundary lines are drawn on a map and customs posts are (sometimes) located along them,[1] effective government control has not yet become coterminous with the limits of the state. Boundaries still tend to be frontier marches.

This situation goes far to explain the infrequency of border wars and border claims. It also reinforces the suggestion that such disputes may become more frequent in the future, as the frontier zones shrink to lines and authority meets authority. At the present time, nearly every African state has a buffer zone between itself and its next-door neighbour, a semi

---

[1] In Mali, for example, in May 1963, this traveller passed customs in Bamako, both coming from the Ivory Coast and going to Senegal. Usually in West Africa, customs posts are located in major towns near the border, leaving a 'no-customs-land' frontier zone around each country.

no-man's-land of incomplete government control and much human intercourse across the formal boundary. The general nature of West African geography reinforces this concept, for the area is made up of vast zones across which no natural boundary is visible. It is hard to draw a meaningful line through the Sahara, although the desert itself forms a huge natural boundary-in-depth. The forest zone of West Africa performed the same function during the time of the classical empires, as did the poor middle belt between the Sudan and the forest. Thus the inter-tribal frontier march, the natural zone, and the buffer area are three distinct concepts that reinforce each other.

Other than unification, few alternatives to the present North and West African boundaries have ever been proposed. The greatest deterrent to territorial revisionism has been the fear of 'opening Pandora's box'. If any boundary is seriously questioned, why not all boundaries in Africa? And then what is natural? One alternative is to redraw borders according to physical features; but the absence of sharp geographic divisions in the area is as troublesome to territorial revisionists as it was to the colonial boundary makers. The one case of a long geographic border—the Senegal river—has cut up a natural demographic and agricultural region, and made river basin development dependent on international co-operation. In an age of boats and bridges it is no more logical to set a boundary in a river than it is to set it on a road or railroad, which serve the same purpose.[1] Another alternative is to reconstitute states in natural geographic regions. Treatises on artificiality have also shown how North and West African borders cut across the area's latitudinal vegetation belts, but wisely no one has taken up the implied suggestion that the states be rearranged to fit these zones. The colonial practice of setting up territories stretching from harbour to hinterland—Senegal, Guinea, Ivory Coast, Ghana, Togo, Dahomey, Nigeria, and the Maghreb—gives the advantage of diversity, whereas more homogeneous states—Liberia, Sierra Leone, Mali, Niger—have more limited development possibilities. (If the Congo had been confined to a geographically homogeneous region, it would never have

[1] About 400 kms. or more of western African boundaries are defined by roads and tracks.

had an outlet to the sea.) Two other alternatives are left. Regional unity pools the resources of several states and increases the possibilities of development. Tribally-based irredentism, reviving memories of historic empires, poses problems of international conflict.

Unresolved Problems

On the basis of this general appreciation of the North and West African boundary situation, it is possible to examine specific border disputes and rectifications. Problems of delimitation, demarcation, administration, and territorial claims are all involved; but this study seeks to focus on the foreign relations rather than the technicalities of boundary-making.

The case of the southern Moroccan boundary is certainly the most complex. It includes two problems, inextricably related: the actual border problem with Algeria between Teniet as-Sassi and the western Tarfaya boundary (9° 40 W), and the broader problem of Morocco irredenta. The narrow boundary problem results from a Franco-Moroccan judgment over a century ago that no border was necessary because 'a country which is found without water is uninhabitable and a delimitation thereof would be superfluous', and from a Moroccan decision after 1956 to await the independence of Algeria before finally drawing a border which, in this century, has appeared clearly necessary. Between 1956 and 1960, a bilateral commission accepted in principle by both Morocco and France met rarely and never agreed on a settlement of the southern border. In May 1958, an incident involving Moroccan and French troops in the contested territory resulted in an agreement to constitute a no-man's-land in the Algero-Moroccan *confins* (frontier region).

Morocco's hope that an independent Algerian Government would prove more understanding than the French appears to have had no concrete basis beyond a too literal interpretation of mutual professions of North African brotherhood, until 1960, 1961, and 1962, when Premier Ferhat Abbas and then his successor, Benyussef ben Khedda, gave assurances that the problem would be negotiated after independence. Similar assurances were refused by Ahmed ben Bella, however, during his visit to Morocco in 1962, and when independence came and

KTCA

Moroccan troops moved in to occupy the *confins*, they found Algerian troops there first. The new situation was worse than the old, since Algeria refused to discuss the border and both sides began occupying the no man's land, with not even a presumed border running through it. When Moroccan and Algerian troops met over contested positions during 1963, a number of incidents arose which finally blew up into the Algero-Moroccan border war in October.

In addition to the previous Franco-Moroccan agreement not to draw a border and the Moroccan decision to await Algerian independence before solving the problem, a third element hindered a boundary solution: Morocco irredenta. The Moroccan thesis was that the nineteenth-century Sherifian empire was dismembered by colonial conquest since the early 1900s, the French annexing parts to Algeria and French West Africa and occupying the core as a protectorate, and the Spanish acting similarly. Underneath this foreign rule, say the Moroccans, the people continued to consider themselves subjects of the Sultan and members of the Muslim community (*umma*) which he headed. In 1956 the core area, made up of the French and Spanish protectorates and Tangier, was restored to complete sovereignty, and two years later the southern Spanish protectorate (Tarfaya) rejoined the kingdom. However, this left unredeemed parts of the country and nation still under colonial (Spanish), 'neo-colonial' (Mauritanian), or simply neighbouring (Algerian) rule. The attempt to secure the return of these lands is really a nutshell case of western African relations, for it involved the use of warfare, subversion, breaking off relations, propaganda, alliances, and mediation, as well as continuing diplomacy, and it concerned basic elements of security, ideology, identity, sentiment, and national interest.

Sentimental attachment to irredentism was the major theme in Morocco's African relations between February 1958, when the cause was formally espoused by Mohammed V, and May 1963, when Hassan II refused to sit next to Ould Daddah at the African summit at Addis Ababa; since then, the problem has primarily affected relations with Algeria, although as late as October 1964 Hassan was absent from the Maghreb reconciliation meeting at Tunis in order to avoid the Mauritanian President. The guerrilla phase of the policy lasted from

November 1957, when irregular forces from the Saharan army of liberation took over most of the Spanish enclave of Sidi Ifni, to mid-1962, when the last raids of the National Council of Mauritanian Liberation took place against Mauritania from Malian territory; in between, in February 1960, a joint Franco-Spanish 'Operation Swab' cleared Spanish Sahara and Mauritania of bands of roving guerrillas, and two years later about 6,000 members of the Saharan army of liberation were brought under minimal control on the Moroccan side by being integrated into the Moroccan army. However, as late as mid-1963, after the return from Morocco of the leading Mauritanian defectors, Mauritania displayed evidence that they were merely acting as a local fifth column in collaboration with subversive agents sent in from Morocco.

The propaganda and diplomacy phase of the policy began unofficially soon after Moroccan independence; it was first reflected in official Moroccan diplomacy with protests beginning in August 1956 over French exploitation of the Sahara, and continued through the various steps by which Mauritania acceded to full sovereignty. The diplomatic offensive, however, was ineffective and even counter-productive. It resulted in diplomatic ruptures with Tunisia, Senegal, and Algeria; provoked a Moroccan boycott of meetings of the United Nations Economic Commission for Africa, the African National Radio and Television Union, the Inter-African and Malagasy Organisation (Monrovia group), and the Organisation for African Unity, and of Maghreb co-operation generally; and ended in Morocco's isolation after the collapse of the Casablanca group. Repeated mediation efforts by Senegal and Tunisia stumbled over Mauritania's precondition of recognition by Morocco although a limited element of conciliation has been present in Moroccan policy since 1961; O.A.U. mediation—largely by Mali and Ethiopia—in the subsequent border dispute between Morocco and Algeria achieved a cessation of hostilities but no political solution of the boundary problem.

Indeed, the only positive contribution of Morocco's irredentism to the African diplomatic scene was its role in the formation of the Casablanca group, its importance in holding together the Brazzaville group, and its place among the local issues that kept the two groups apart while the pressure for a single African unity organisation could mature. Certainly none of these effects was a part of Morocco's intended goals. The case of Moroccan irredentism is an example among many others of the primacy of national independence as a goal (perceived and defined by the national policy-makers) over other, conflicting values of unity and development.

The case of the Togo-Ghana border involves an entire state rather than a boundary. Ghana came into being in 1957 with a border that followed tribal lines for 170 of its 498 miles. The unification of British Togoland with the Gold Coast through the May 1956 plebiscite placed the Kusasi, Mamprusi, Dagomba, Busanga, and Mchumburu tribesmen totally within Ghana. But it left nearly 100,000 Ewes (along with lesser tribal groups of Bmobas, Konkombas, Ntribus, and others) split between the two states. No border problem better illustrates the fact that a line which unites some tribes in Africa will divide others.

Elections of April 1958 in the French trusteeship territory of Togo brought to power a government headed by the Ewe leader, Sylvanus Olympio, whose policy had until 1952 paralleled that of Ewe unificationists under British rule but had thereafter changed to champion independent unity of the two Togos. Although Ghana supported Olympio's régime as one working towards independence from colonial rule, the permeable nature of the border and the uncertain allegiance of the Ewes posed problems to the Ghanaian policy of national integration. Late in 1958, a number of Ghanaian Ewes (including two members of parliament) were imprisoned in Ghana, and others who had moved freely across the border were threatened with arrest for showing Togolese sympathies. A year later, as Togo moved towards independence, Nkrumah predicted that it would become the seventh region of Ghana, and relations again turned for the worse.

In the spring of 1960, the Ghanaian army held its annual exercises 10 miles from the border. Hearing rumours of a Ghanaian attack on Togo, Olympio merely questioned Ghana's ability to execute militarily and defend diplomatically such an action; after rumours of a Togolese plot to unite the Ewes by force (despite the fact that there was no Togolese army), Ghana made more arrests, and on 10 March 1960

addressed a note to France alleging that the Togolese constitution (in fact, still unwritten) contained irredentist clauses. In
July, three months after Togolese independence, however,
Nkrumah was in Lomé on a state visit, discussing plans for a
return of economic co-operation between the two countries. By
September, relations had swung to bitter again; Ghana closed
its eastern border, charging Olympio with failing to produce the
promised plans for co-operation. Togolese elections in April
1961 were the next occasion for bad blood, as opposition groups
(mainly Juvento) alleged repression by Togo and fled to
Ghana. Togo in September unanimously adopted a national
assembly resolution favouring reunification of the two Togos,
and in early December announced the discovery of a plot
supported by Ghana against Olympio. When the attempts were
made on Nkrumah's life in 1961 and 1962, he accused Togo of
harbouring the assassins.

The situation turned predictably for the better when
Olympio was assassinated in January 1963 and Antoine
Meatchi, a Togolese refugee in Ghana, became the vice-
president of the new régime. The Ghana newspapers
proclaimed, 'Ghana and Togo are one', and after several
weeks' hesitation Ghana opened its border again. But, as might
also have been expected, when the new Togolese Government
did not move towards Ghana but continued to act as an independent régime aware of the delicacy of its position, relations
returned to mere politeness, lightened only by the passing of
the personality clash between Nkrumah and Olympio. The Ewe
border problem, which was left far behind in the exchange of
plots and charges since 1958, remains unsolved, except to the
extent that awareness of Ghanaian and Togolese nationality
may very slowly begin to spread along the border regions. Instead,
the situation has served both sides in their efforts to consolidate
their régimes and divert dissatisfaction to external problems.

The dispute between the Ivory Coast and Ghana over the
'Sanwi state' is a tribal matter, exacerbated by uneven modernisation and Ghanaian interference. The south-eastern corner
of Ivory Coast was 'outside the mainstream of African organizational life' since the early beginnings of Houphouet's nationalist
movement; in the elections of 1957, 1959, and 1960, it either
supported opposition candidates or had a high rate of

abstention. Economically, too, it was alien; although the region was a rich coffee and cocoa area, the farmers were immigrants from elsewhere in the country or were tribesmen the Assinis had long considered vassals. In early 1959, the Fraternal Society of the Sanwi sent a delegation to General de Gaulle asking for autonomy under a treaty signed in 1834, and when no results were forthcoming, in early May they set up the Sanwi independence movement under Chief Amon Ndouffou III. Some leaders fled to neighbouring independent Ghana, where they received arms and aid in subversion. Others were arrested and tried in Abidjan in early 1960, were imprisoned for violating the external security of the state, but were released a few months later.

The coming of independence to the Ivory Coast and the consolidation of the régime reduced the importance of the Sanwi movement. Dissidents petitioned Houphouet-Boigny and were granted a reprieve in December 1961; they returned under a general amnesty in April. Nevertheless a number of leaders remained in contact with the African Affairs Bureau in Accra, and a small Ivory Coast colony continued to camp on the eastern side of the border among their fellow-tribesmen in Ghana. In September 1962, those who remained in Ghana joined a Freedom Fighters Front, and in June reissued their 'constitution' and programme. Their representatives turned up in Morocco and Algeria early the next year, but received little support there for their movement.[1] Ghana openly claimed the area in the name of tribal unity in 1960, the 40,000 Sanwis being related to Nkrumah's native Nzima tribe, but Accra has denied both aid and claims since then.

The southern Algero-Tunisian border was left undelimited at the time of Tunisian independence, with treaties of 1910 and 1955–6 giving grounds for questioning the usual map version. A mixed inspection commission sought to trace the frontier in April 1957; after an initial rebuff, Tunisia succeeded in

[1] The Ivory Coast sent a parliamentary delegation to Algiers to warn them, 'hands off'. For the Sanwi programme, see *Mouvement de Libération du Sanwi: status et programme* (10 May 1958, Kringobo, Ivory Coast, reissued 5 June 1962, Winneba, Ghana). On 17 September 1962, however, the Ghanaian Ambassador to Abidjan denied the existence of a Sanwi movement in Ghana!

gaining recognition of its ownership over Fort Saint only by linking the matter with current negotiations with France. In a subsequent note to Paris, Tunisia reserved its rights over the uninhabited desert south of the line between Fort Saint (marker 220) and Bir Romane. In one of his weekly radio talks in 1959, Bourguiba specifically raised the question of the Tunisian Sahara, suggesting either a 'natural prolongation' of Tunisian territory south from Bir Romane to about 30° N (the parallel near marker 233, south of Ghadames), 'just as parts of Libya, Algeria, Morocco or Senegal [sic] will be their prolongation', or a common agreement that beyond a certain limit 'the door opens on an area undivided and shared by all, where communications, water points, pasturage, and underground wealth are at the disposal of all.'

This view was subsequently reiterated in negotiations with France and then in a Tuniso-Malian communiqué of June 1961, when the Franco-Algerian negotiations at Evian turned on the Saharan question; Keita and Bourguiba wished to emphasise the non-French nature of the Sahara, but the declaration also stated Tunisia's claim to part of the desert. Morocco and Tunisia repeated these views in a second pair of statements later in the same month. The resultant ill-feelings between the Provisional Algerian Government and Tunis over the subject were temporarily smoothed over as Tunisian policy took a militant turn during the Bizerta crisis of July, and a detachment of volunteers was sent to marker 233 to indicate Tunisia's determination. The volunteers were annihilated, de Gaulle recognised Algeria's territorial integrity, and the matter was dropped on the Tunisian side. Broad negotiations between Tunisia and independent Algeria finally ended in a number of agreements in September and November 1963, the November accord providing for the joint use of Saharan oil and gas, but leaving details undecided and the border unsettled.

Bourguiba's entire policy appears to have been directed towards affirming Tunisia's right to share raw materials from the 'North African desert', rather than towards acquiring the uninhabited 15,000-square-mile triangle of the Great Eastern Erg between Bir Romane and Ghadames. Out of this problem has come Bourguiba's 'theory of *dépassement*', according to which border problems can be left behind as solutions are found on a higher level of co-operation. A rich oil strike in mid-1964 at al-Borma, right on the contested border, showed, however, the necessity for a specific border settlement; in line with Bourguiba's theories, it is conceived in the novel form of joint sovereignty over the contested oil area, to be ratified during the proposed visit of Bourguiba to ben Bella in early 1965.

Another unresolved boundary problem concerns the insignificant island of Lete in the Niger river between Dahomey and Niger. In this case the boundary was merely a symptom of deeper troubles between the two states. In late October 1963, the *Parti dahoméen de l'unité* Government of Hubert Maga was overthrown by a military coup under Colonel Christophe Soglo, who installed a provisional unity Government including Maga, Soro Migan Apithy, and Justin Adhomadegbe, the leaders of the country's three regional factions. However, in early December, Maga and some of his supporters from northern Dahomey were arrested on charges of plotting to restore the former régime; some citizens of Niger were killed or arrested in the process, and Niger was accused of supporting the plot of its former R.D.A. ally. Later in the month, Niger announced that it would expel all Dahomeyans (variously estimated at 15,000 to 50,000) living on the northern side of the Niger river, probably to disturb the new Dahomeyan Government, already laden with social problems and internal demands, and thus reduce the pressure on Niger of a revolutionary example next door. Dahomey closed the border, and Niger announced the dissolution of the two states' joint commercial organisation. Both sides mobilised, Niger charging that Dahomey was preparing to seize the five-mile-long island of Lete in the Niger river.[1] Gabon, Togo, Nigeria, and Liberia offered good offices, and Soglo appealed to the U.N. and the O.A.U. A special meeting of the *Union africaine et malgache*

[1] It is alleged that French control over Niger ammunition stocks was the element that prevented the outbreak of hostilities. There seems to be no detailed documentation on the Lete problem. Reportedly, Maga's supporters among the Baribas wanted to be part of Niger in order to avoid domination by the south Dahomey Fons; Virginia Thompson, 'Dahomey', in Gwendolen Carter (ed.), *Five African States* (Ithaca, 1963), p. 248. Troubles in 1963 apparently began in Niamey on 20 November with riots between Dahomeyans and Nigerois set off by a Dahomeyan who killed his Nigeroise wife and himself.

(U.A.M.) to handle the problem in mid-January was post-poned after the two parties had already met on the border on their own initiative. During the same month, elections were held under the new Dahomeyan constitution, and Soglo's régime gave way to a new civilian Government under Apithy and Ahomadegbe, combining their forces in a new, single Dahomeyan Democratic Party (P.D.D.).

With the passing of the provisional Government, the crisis temporarily subsided. At the March conference of the U.A.M. at Dakar, the two Presidents, Diori and Apithy, signed a reconciliation agreement. A meeting of the two parties at Dosso in early June restored commercial co-operation and scheduled new negotiations in Cotonou to solve the expatriate and border problems. However, the Cotonou meeting at the end of the month brought no decision on either partition or ownership of the island of Lete. The matter was of reduced importance as long as the general climate of relations between the two countries was improved; but when the internal stability of both régimes weakened in late 1964, the problem was revived in the bitter terms of the previous year.

There have also been a number of smaller claims and conflicts that have neither turned into major disputes nor been solved. One series concerns the borders of Upper Volta, which have never been demarcated. A Ghanaian claim on Voltaic territory along the north-eastern corner of Ghana kept President Yameogo away from the second O.A.U. summit at Cairo in July 1964, although the matter was smoothed over in the pre-summit foreign ministers' meeting. Problems of demarcation along the north-eastern border of Upper Volta were discussed with Niger the previous month; along the northern Upper Volta border, Mali occupied a large, marshy strip in 1963, despite vigorous Voltaic protests. In late 1960, after Dahomeyan and Nigerian independence, the Nigerian Action Group published a series of articles suggesting the incorporation of Dahomey as the fourth region of Nigeria; there was some favourable echo from the Dahomeyan Yorubas, who had not benefited as much as they had expected from Dahomeyan independence, but the claims were implicitly disavowed by the Nigerian Premier, Abubakar Tafawa Balewa, and the matter blew over.[1]

[1] Demarcation was undertaken between 1960 and 1962, for the first time.

Similarly, there have been fears in Niamey that Algeria may claim the Tuareg region of northern Niger or, alternatively, that Bakary Djibo's Sawaba movement may encourage Tuareg pretensions at self-determination. The problem is less one of Algerian irredentism or Tuareg separatism than one of combined traditional dissidence by the Tuareg and subversion by the Sawaba.[1] These and new problems of the same type can be expected to reappear from time to time as the new nations try to fit comfortably into their territorial frame. Usually, they involve technical problems of demarcation, aggravated by political differences between régimes.

Solved Problems

Other conflicts have already been settled, often with a show of maturity. The Mali-Mauritanian frontier underwent the first rectification ever to be made between two independent African states. The problem arose from the mixture of nomadic and semi-nomadic populations along the desert and savannah border region. An attempt to stabilise administration was made in July 1944, when the Hodh district was transferred from Soudan to Mauritania, but demarcation of the border was unclear. Administrative means of dealing with the nomads were worked out in meetings between the two territories between 1958 and early 1960, but attempts by a commission of experts to settle the border itself at the same time ran into continual deadlock, each side buttressing its position with sound legal, geographic, and sociological evidence. In the autumn of 1960, a number of tribal incidents along the disputed frontier embittered Mali—already sensitive over the break-up of its federation with Senegal—and led to two years of bad blood between the two neighbours, marked by raids by pro-Moroccan bands on Mauritania from Malian territory.

A realisation of the fruitlessness of the quarrel, particularly on the Malian side, led to attempts at *rapprochement* in late 1962. In November and again in January 1963, interior ministers and then a mixed commission met to re-examine the border,

---

[1] Fears of Algerian claims have appeared on occasion in *Le Monde*, but further evidence from this area of rare news is slim. Suggestions that Niger might claim parts of Algeria, on the other hand, were denied by President Hamani Diori, in a Niamey broadcast, 2 August 1962.

but they ended on the same positions of intransigence. More than any territory or population, the issue at stake was prestige. Mali, having lost the Hodh, did not want to give up any more land, and Mauritania, feeling its territory 'incomplete' in abridged form, rebuffed Malian demands. The negotiators did manage to arrange a meeting between Keita and Ould Daddah, and in mid-February 1963 the two heads of state met at Kayes to begin negotiations all over again. After two days of deadlock, the expectation of an agreement—the contrary of pressure on the lesser officials, who were expected to uphold a point of view—pushed the Presidents into a settlement. Mali gained a rectified straight-line frontier across the Saharan region, while Mauritania won recognition of a southerly line in the savannah region near Kayes. In the absence of natural social or geographical lines, the determination of the border was political.

Two other frontier problems were solved easily and peaceably. Liberia, which had defended its independence against its colonial neighbours during the past century only at the price of hunks and slivers of territory, made a serious diplomatic attempt to regain a portion in negotiations with France during the first months of 1958. The territory in question was the Mount Nimba region of Guinea and the land between the Cavally and the Cess rivers in Ivory Coast. At the time of independence, it was suggested in the French press that Liberia would take advantage of the isolation of its neighbour to press its claims. Instead Tubman used the occasion of Touré's visit in mid-November 1958 to renounce all claims to the Guinean region. Since then there have been negotiations on Guinean use of the new Liberian ore railroad from Buchanan to the mountains to carry iron ore, resulting in an agreement signed in January 1962.

Liberia's border with the Ivory Coast was stabilised with equal ease. During a state visit by Houphouet-Boigny to Tubman in mid-November 1961, the two Presidents agreed to accept the present borders, thus ending Liberia's claim to land west of the upper Cavally river, and recognised the river boundary lines on the right (west) bank, thus perpetuating the classic error of a Liberian diplomat who unwittingly had given up control over the entire river. But the boundary rivers were opened for use by citizens of both states, thus removing an old obstacle to traffic from Liberian rubber plantations. Similarly, a protocol between Niger and Upper Volta, signed in June 1964, settled border problems between the two allies; delimitation, population movement, administrative and security coordination, and provision for a census to facilitate tax collection were the points involved in the agreement.

9. French Algeria: reality to myth

DAVID PICKLES *Algeria and France* Methuen and Praeger 1963; pages 26–32, 106–8, 109–13, 119

From French Liberation to the Algerian Statute

Important steps to improve the status of the Moslem population had been taken, however, even before the war was over. While still in Algiers, the Committee of National Liberation had extended to certain Moslems the right to become citizens without relinquishing their personal status, and the Constitution of the Fourth Republic abolished entirely the distinction between French "subjects" and French "citizens". All overseas territories of the French Republic were henceforth guaranteed the rights and liberties of French citizens. Of the thirty deputies and fourteen senators representing Algeria in the Parliament of the Fourth Republic, half were elected by the Moslem electoral college. The distinction between Frenchmen subject to the French civil code and those subject to Koranic law still remained, however, roughly coinciding with the distinction between Europeans and Moslems. The fifteen deputies elected by the first college represented a population of about a million, while the fifteen elected by the second college represented 8–9 million Moslems. But the "native code" had already been suppressed in 1944, and equality before the law now existed.

By this time, however, there were Algerian nationalist movements in existence which were no longer prepared for mere progress towards first-class French citizenship within the Republic, and two important warning signs of changing Moslem ideas were ignored. The first was the revolt at Sétif in May,

1945, on the occasion of the victory celebrations. The second was the total rejection of the programme put forward by the moderate nationalist leader, M. Ferhat Abbas, at the time of the drawing up of the new French Constitution. At no time during the parliamentary debates on the Constitution did any section of French opinion contemplate for a moment any break with the assimilationist tradition. Instead of trying to come to terms with moderate nationalism, French governments relied on the suppression of the more extremist expressions of nationalism, together with the traditional manipulation of elections, to weaken the parliamentary expression of opinions unpleasing to the administration.

Even so, if these activities had been accompanied by a sincere attempt to recognize more fully what it became fashionable to call "the Algerian personality", it might still not have been too late to retain the assimilative framework, at least for some time. Of course, integration on a basis of complete social and political equality had always been out of the question within any forseeable future. Political equality would have meant 100 Moslem deputies in the French National Assembly instead of 15, and social equality would rapidly have bankrupted the state and led to an even more spectacular increase in the Moslem birthrate, which was already becoming a serious problem. From less than 2·5 million in the middle of the nineteenth century, the Moslem population had risen to more than 6 million by the outbreak of the 1939 war, and it had passed 7·5 million by 1948. Population was, indeed, perpetually outrunning subsistance, in spite of the economic progress that had been made. There were, however, certain reforms to which the Moslem population attached considerable importance and which the French government undertook but failed to carry out. This failure was the second nail in the coffin of French Algeria (the first having been the failure in 1936 to provide for easier access of the Moslem élite to citizenship).

The Sétif revolt was transformed by French repression into a rehearsal for 1954. Previous revolts had been sporadic expressions of discontent with French rule. This was a nationalist revolt and, as they were to do in December, 1960, in Algiers, the Moslems came out with green and white nationalist flags and with banners inscribed: "Vive l'Algérie indépendante". But it was a small demonstration, savagely repressed by the police and followed by even more savage reprisals by the Moslems, including atrocities, which led in turn to systematic and widespread punitive measures, including the bombing and burning of Algerian villages. Reliable figures of casualties were never published, but they certainly ran into thousands. M. Ferhat Abbas (whose home town was Sétif, but who had not been involved in the demonstration) was arrested, and his movement, the Amis du Manifeste, dissolved. Some of those arrested were later to be among the rebels of 1954. The scale of the revolt alarmed the colons, and the result was a step backward by the French government at the precise moment when it was essential to take steps forward. In 1947, the Algerian Statute was voted. It made some concessions to Moslem demands, but colon opposition meant that they were never applied. From 1947 to 1948, Algiers gave orders to Paris.

The Algerian Statute was an affirmation of Algérie française. Its first articles proclaimed that Algeria was "a group of départements, enjoying corporate personality, financial autonomy, and a special organization. . . . All inhabitants of French nationality in the départements of Algeria enjoy, without distinction of origin, race, language, or religion, the rights attached to French citizenship, and are subject to the same obligations." Executive power belonged to a Governor-General, appointed by and responsible to the French government, and assisted by a government council. Legislative power belonged to the French Parliament in matters concerned with the Constitution and the civil and penal codes, and, in matters concerning Algeria, to a new body, the Algerian Assembly, in conjunction with the Governor-General. This, in practice, meant that the approval of the Governor-General was necessary for the Assembly's decisions to be effective. The Algerian Assembly consisted of 120 members, of whom half were elected by the predominantly European college and half by the Moslem college. But one-fourth of its members, or the Finance Commission, or the Governor-General could at any time request that a vote should be taken by a two-thirds instead of a simple majority. This device ensured that the presence of a certain number of Moslems in the first, or European, college could not enable a Moslem majority to outvote the Europeans.[1]

The Statute satisfied neither colons nor Moslems in Algeria, and neither Right nor Left in France. For the Right and the colons, it went too far, for the Moslems not far enough. The latter resented the provisions for the equal representation of something less than a million Europeans and 8–9 million Moslems,[2] just as they did the built-in European majority. Of the thirty Algerian deputies only four (all elected by the first college) voted for the Statute, for by then a growing number of them were thinking in terms of independence. But it did provide for increasing Moslem participation in administration and also made two important concessions to Moslems, namely, the separation of the Moslem religion from the state, and the use of the Arabic language in schools. It also accorded Moslem women the vote.

All three provisions remained, however, a dead letter, as did the provisions for transforming *communes mixtes* into fully elective municipal councils, and for gradually including the Saharan *territoires du sud* in the départements and increasing the number of départements so as to remedy Algeria's serious under-administration. It was not until the rebellion had been in existence for over a year that M. Mollet's government made a belated effort to carry out the administrative reforms, and it was by then probably too late politically, even without the difficulties caused by the war itself. By then, the Algerian Assembly had ceased to function, partly as a result of FLN intimidation of its Moslem members. It had never had any real authority, for elections had been manipulated so as to provide a majority of Moslem members favourable to the administration.

The terms of the Statute, the attitude of the colons to it, and the debates in the National Assembly preceding the vote showed how far apart French opinion and that of the Algerian

---

[1] Electors of the first college included 464,000 citizens subject to the French civil code and 58,000 Moslems; electors of the second college included 1,400,000 Moslems subject to Koranic law. The Statute somewhat restricted the possibilities for Moslem to pass from the second to the first college in the future. Universal suffrage with a common roll did not exist in Algeria until 1958.

[2] The population figures over-emphasize Moslem under-representation because of the high Moslem birth rate. Almost half the population is under twenty-one.

nationalists had grown. While more moderate nationalist opinion, led by Dr Bendjelloul and M. Ferhat Abbas, would have been content at this stage with "autonomy", or self-government for Algeria within the framework of the French Union, this was still something that French opinion was no more ready to accept than were the colons. Much of the debate was taken up with a long and technical argument put forward by a European Algerian, Professor Viard, claiming that the Algerian départements were juridically French in the same sense as metropolitan départements such as Corsica, which, though separated from the mainland by sea, is classed as a "metropolitan" and not as an "overseas" département. Colon opinion was thus illogically seeking to maintain, at one and the same time, the Frenchness of Algeria and distinctions between European and Moslem Frenchmen which would perpetuate the domination of the European minority.[1]

From Unfulfilled Promises to Rebellion

The immediate reaction of Moslem opinion was the return of large numbers of M. Messali Hadj's extreme nationalist MTLD in the municipal elections held some weeks after the voting of the Statute. There was also an increase in the revolutionary propaganda of the movement. This led to a move by the administration to redress the situation by systematic falsification of electoral returns, both in 1948 and in 1951.[2]

---

[1] It was also illogical to maintain, on the one hand, that Algeria was a French "province", as integrationists like M. Soustelle liked to put it, and yet in the Assembly of the Union, to provide for separate representation for metropolitan France (considered as a single unit), the Algerian départements, the Saharan regions, and the overseas départements.

[2] According to M. Julien, the prefects had estimated that, if nationalist propaganda were allowed to be carried on unchecked, the MTLD would obtain 90 per cent of the Moslem votes at the elections for the Algerian Assembly in 1948, some of them owing to the intimidation practised by the movement. The problem facing the administration was, therefore, not whether to allow honest elections or to "manipulate" them. The choice was, as Pierre Frederix put it, "between elections cooked by the Messalist leaders, and by the Governor-General". (*Le Monde*, April 3, 1952.) The administration naturally chose the second alternative in 1948, and again in 1951 at the first partial renewal of the Algerian Assembly. There were a number of protests by Socialists and the MRP, and the Governor-General of Algeria, a Socialist, M. Marcel-Edmond Naegelen, felt obliged to resign.

Neither in the pseudo-parliamentary Algerian Assembly nor in the French Parliament was Moslem opinion validly represented. It is ironic to reflect that, after the outbreak of the rebellion, one of the most persistent French objections to negotiations with the FLN leaders was that they were not "valid spokesmen" (*des interlocuteurs valables*) for Algeria. And that was true enough, at least during the first years of the rebellion. But the absence of valid Algerian spokesmen was something for which France bore a large share of the blame.[1] The result was, on the Moslem side, further disillusionment and loss of confidence in French promises and intentions. The creation of a façade of relative harmony between the two communities made it easier for the colons to oppose the application of either political or economic measures designed to improve Moslem status. The pre-occupation of French governments during these years with struggles at home against inflation and against the anti-parliamentary extremes of Communism and Gaullism, and with the struggle abroad against independence in Indochina, made it only too easy for them to take the line of least resistance in Algeria and to allow the colons effectively to sabotage the provisions of the Statute and impose their policies in Paris. And so a vicious circle was constituted, to be broken only by the rebellion in 1954.

The years between saw a great deal of quarrelling between as well as within the different Moslem movements on both tactical and personal grounds, together with some disputes between Arabs and Berbers. One of the reasons why Algeria lacked valid spokesmen, at a time when the Tunisian Neo-Destour and the Moroccan Istiqlal were both establishing themselves as indisputably valid spokesmen for the nationalist aspirations of their respective countries, was the inability of Algerian political movements ever to establish any degree of unity except for very brief periods of time. An attempt to achieve unity was made in 1944, shortly after the publication

[1] The unrepresentativeness of the Algerian Assembly was such as to worry a number of progressive Frenchmen, particularly M. Jacques Chevallier, Deputy for Algiers and later Mayor. He pointed out that the danger of neglecting a dynamic and moderate Algerian élite would be to encourage extremist opinion and so lead to a conflict between colonialists and separatists. This prophecy turned out to be accurate. For examples of the falsification of election results, see Julien, op. cit., pp. 326 ff.

LTCA

of the Manifesto. In 1946, there was further effort at union between moderate and federalist Algerian representatives in the Assembly, and again in 1951, between the UDMA, the MTLD, the Ulemas, and the Algerian Communist Party. All these attempts failed.

The persistent quarrels between the older, established leaders ended by driving nationalists of the younger generation into support for direct, underground resistance, as a reaction against what seemed increasingly to them to be purely verbal revolutionary fervour or affirmations of personal ambition on the part of some older leaders, in particular, M. Messali Hadj. The so-called "special organization", formed in 1947 after the vote of the Algerian Statute, and which developed into the revolutionary movement eventually responsible for launching the rebellion, consisted very largely of younger men. It emphasized from the start the principle of collective, as opposed to personal leadership, a principle that was to become that of the rebel FLN movement. . . .

The cease-fire agreement was signed on March 18 and became effective the following day. Along with it, there were also published agreements on future Franco-Algerian cooperation, after the referendum on self-determination. These constituted a series of ingenious and face-saving compromises on issues on which the two sides had hitherto found compromise impossible. The first was the French objection to concluding any agreement other than a cease-fire with what was, juridically speaking, a rebel organization without governmental status. This difficulty was dealt with in two ways. First, French *de jure* sovereignty was to be retained throughout the transitional period and exercised through a High Commissioner, while the Algerian provisional executive, responsible *de facto* for much of the administration, was to consist of both Moslems and Europeans and to include Moslem representatives who were not members of the FLN. This met the French requirement that "all tendencies" should have a say in Algerian affairs. After the cease-fire, the twelve members of the provisional executive were nominated by the French government. The President was a Moslem, the Vice-President and two other members European. It included five members of the FLN (other than the President) and three "neutral" Moslems. Its functions were twofold. They were, first, to administer the country, through the regular administrative machinery, except for those matters still reserved to the French, represented by a High Commissioner. These were foreign affairs, defence, security, justice, currency, economic relations, education, telecommunications, ports, and airfields. The second function of the provisional executive was the preparation of the referendum.

The second compromise was the acceptance by both sides of a series of "declarations of principles", dealing with future economic and financial cooperation, military matters, cooperation in the economic development of the Sahara, and so on— six of them in all (together with an annex on Mers-el-Kebir), filling twenty-eight columns of the *Journal Officiel*. They constituted an ingenious solution of the problem of devising an agreement which would be binding on a future Algerian state, although none could come into existence until after a cease-fire had been concluded and referendum and elections had taken place. The "declarations" were preceded by a "general declaration", announcing the joint decision of the French government and the FLN to conclude a cease-fire and provide for the government of Algeria during the subsequent interim period. The conditions of future cooperation between France and Algeria were determined on the assumption that the referendum would result in a vote of independence in cooperation with France. The vote in the referendum would be, at the same time, on self-determination and the ratification of these declarations. The declarations would then be binding on the future Algerian state, and any disagreements would be submitted to the International Court of Justice.

No provisions were made to meet the situation that would arise if the majority of the Algerian electors were to refuse to accept this package deal.[1] It was by now taken for granted by opinion in France that the overwhelming majority of the electors would vote in favour of the agreements. And the FLN now felt sure enough of its dominating hold over the country not to fear an electoral consultation, even though it was to be

[1] It was generally suggested that in this highly unlikely eventuality, a second referendum would have to be held to enable Algerians to choose between the remaining options originally envisaged, namely, integration and secession.

held before the FLN leaders had taken over control of the Algerian governmental machine. In fact, of course, the members of the provisional executive, though not officially nominated by the FLN, were obviously acceptable to the GPRA and were working in harmony with, if not on instructions from, the FLN. The maintenance of French sovereignty during the interim period was a convenient fiction, which enabled a tactful and progressive High Commissioner, in cooperation with a Westernized and liberal Moslem President of the provisional executive, who was also a member of the FLN, to deal with the delicate and dangerous situation that existed during the three months between the cease-fire agreements and the referendum. . . .

The important thing about these Evian agreements was that, on paper at least, they did, as both sides in fact claimed, safeguard the points that each had regarded as essential. On the French side, the Europeans were assured of keeping their French nationality. True, they could not have double nationality in the sense in which they had wanted it. They were free at any time, unless they specifically renounced French citizenship, to return to France with the status of French citizens. But at the end of three years, if they remained in Algeria, they were to be obliged to choose between Algerian citizenship and the status of a French minority, enjoying certain guaranteed rights—linguistic, cultural, and religious—but no longer that of Algerian citizenship. Those who chose Algerian citizenship, however, were guaranteed, along with the above minority rights, that of adequate minority representation, a certain number of seats being reserved in both central and local Algerian assemblies for representatives of the European population, in proportion to their numbers in the area.

The second important safeguard, from the French point of view, was the maintenance of France's existing economic rights in the Sahara. French mineral rights were to be unaffected, and Franco-Algerian cooperation in the exploitation of Saharan resources was to be provided for by the setting up of joint technical bodies. In the granting of future mining rights, France was to be given preference.

The guarantee of French military and strategic rights was the most surprising in view of what was known of FLN attitudes.

France was to have the right to maintain permanent communications with the trans-Saharan states, to continue her atomic tests in the Sahara for five years, and to keep her airfields there for the same length of time. She was to retain occupation of the naval base at Mers-el-Kebir, at least for fifteen years, and after that by agreement. French forces were to be allowed to set up the necessary military establishments around the base. Withdrawal of French forces from Algeria was to begin immediately after the referendum on self-determination, and their numbers were to be reduced to 80,000 at the end of a year. Withdrawal was to be completed by the end of three years, by which time the European population was to opt definitely for Algerian or foreign status.

The solution of the thorny problem of responsibility for maintaining order was no less ingenious than the solution of juridical problems. The transition to independence was bound to be difficult in a country just emerging from a long war, and where the party that was expected to form the government was still a banned underground movement. All along, the FLN had refused to consider the possibility of supervision of the referendum by the French Army, and this attitude was comprehensible enough. The trouble was to find an alternative. The OAS threat at least helped the two sides to reach a compromise on this point, and one that the French hoped would reassure the European population and help to save the face of the French Army, while at the same time satisfying the need of the FLN leaders to appear henceforth in the eyes of their own people as being in charge in Algeria.

In principle, the maintenance of order remained the responsibility of the Algerian provisional executive, which was to have a security force made up of Moslem auxiliaries of the gendarmerie, local Moslem auxiliary police, and Moslem recruits. No member of the ALN was to be included, for France was still *de jure* sovereign until the constitution of a regular Algerian government. In Algiers and Oran, however, French Army units were to be responsible for keeping order, since only they could deal with the OAS. To employ a Moslem local force would, indeed, have achieved immediately one of the OAS objectives, which was to provoke Moslems into taking reprisals and so prevent the application of a cease-fire. The

French government faced a twofold dilemma. On the one hand, the French were determined, as they had been all along, to prevent out-and-out civil war at almost any cost, and so tried to keep action against the OAS as far as possible within the limits of police action, using riot squads and gendarmerie instead of the army wherever they could. They thus laid themselves open to FLN charges of half-heartedness in repressing the OAS. On the other hand, when the army was brought in, the French were bound to rely on Moslem auxiliaries, and thus further inflamed European opinion.

One problem, at least, settled itself, though at the cost of increasing temporarily the difficulties of the French Army. It may be wondered why the French Army, with several hundreds of thousands of men in Algeria, would need to employ Moslem auxiliaries. Army organization was under great strain at this time, for, since the agreement ruled out the use of ALN units, the Moslem local force had necessarily to be recruited from Moslem units either in the French Army or in the police or gendarmerie. This disorganized French units considerably, since the local force was to number some 60,000 members. In addition, Moslems were by this time deserting from the French Army in such large numbers that the President of the provisional executive even contemplated intervening at one point to request them to stay where they were. The constitution of the local force, together with the desertions, helped to minimize one danger which it had been feared might be serious when the war ended, namely, that of FLN reprisals against Moslems who had fought or cooperated with the French against the nationalists. Reliance on them now to defend their compatriots against the OAS helped them to "whitewash" themselves, so to speak, before the ALN fighters over the border came back, and before those inside the country had regained their freedom of movement.[1] But the deserters, many of whom wanted to be "last-minute resisters", also created a new problem because, in their anxiety

[1] The agreements provided for ALN units to be "frozen" in certain regions until after the referendum, in order to minimize the risk of clashes with French forces or of savage reprisals against the OAS or other Europeans, which might provoke the French Army to retaliate. In practice, however, the conditions were evaded in many regions.

to provide evidence of their *bona fides*, they were liable to be overzealous and take independent action against the OAS, thus increasing the danger of a breakdown of the Evian agreements and of consequent anarchy.

The Evian agreements gave France, at least on paper, guarantees that she had fought to obtain in previous negotiations. General de Gaulle, in his broadcast to the nation on the cease-fire agreements, emphasized the good sense that they represented, the real safeguards of France's national interests that they provided, and the possibilities that they could open up for the rebuilding of Franco-Algerian fraternity, even after seven and a half years of war. On the Algerian side, M. Ben Khedda also expressed his satisfaction at what he described as "a great victory of the Algerian people". He emphasized mainly the FLN's attainment of its political objectives: the recognition by France of Algerian sovereignty over the traditional territory of the Sahara, and the avoidance of partition; the recognition of full independence, including Algerian responsibility for her own defence and diplomacy and her right to control both her internal and external affairs; and finally, the recognition of the provisional Algerian government as the authentic and exclusive spokesman of the Algerian people.

This last achievement was, as has already been said, a *de facto*, not a *de jure*, recognition, but this was a distinction not apparent to the mass of the Moslem population and, in any case, not to be permanent. For one of the first acts of the provisional executive was to fix the date of the referendum, not, as had been originally envisaged by General de Gaulle, within one to four years of a *de facto* cease-fire, but within three to six months, a period already agreed to in principle in the general declaration.

M. Ben Khedda's announcement made no mention of the economic price that the French government was to pay for the achievement of France's essential objectives. Yet without the provisions for economic and technical aid contained in the agreements, the political advantages won by the Algerians would obviously be a hollow, and brief, victory. France was contracting to provide, for at least three years, and with the possibility of renewal, both technical and financial aid on a scale at least equal to that of the economic and social programme then being carried out under the Constantine plan. Algerian exports were to be admitted to France either duty-free or on a preferential basis—a promise that seems likely to create some difficulties for France in the European Economic Community. Algerian workers were to be free to remain in France and to enjoy all the rights of French nationals, except, of course, political rights. France was also undertaking to enable Algeria to buy back property held by French nationals, to guarantee to all Algerians the payment of disability or retirement pensions to which they were entitled at the time of the referendum on self-determination (whether payable by French or Algerian organizations), and to be responsible for paying pensions to Moslem ex-servicemen. French schools were to continue, and France was to supply Algeria with civil servants and technicians and to agree to receive Algerian students in France. . . .

Nevertheless, in spite of all the uncertainties that surrounded the future both of Algeria and of Franco-Algerian relations, for the overwhelming majority of the French people the Evian agreements did at least three things that made the acceptance of them worth while. The first was to provide a device by which the French Army and, it was hoped, the European Algerians, along with other right-wing elements, could be brought to swallow the unpalatable facts of Algerian independence with the minimum loss of face possible under the circumstances.

The second was to free France from her Algerian incubus. For over seven years, hundreds of thousands of young Frenchmen had had to spend up to twenty-seven months of their lives in military service in Algeria. For years, in NATO, United Nations committees, and the UN General Assembly, French government delegations had been defending increasingly unconvincing Algerian policies. French politics had been dominated by the Algerian problem, and political parties had been divided by it. Algeria had now gained her independence, and France had regained her freedom.

The third achievement was that, with Algerian independence, France had completed, or virtually completed, her decolonization. The long series of hopeless and demoralizing colonial and quasi-colonial wars was ended. On July 14, 1962, for the first time since 1946, France's national day was celebrated by a nation at peace.

10. Libya 1911–51

NEVILLE BARBOUR *A Survey of North Africa* Oxford University Press for Royal Institute of International Affairs 1959; pages 351–7

From the Italian Occupation (1911) till Independence (1951)

On 3 October 1911 the Italians launched an attack on Tripoli; and subsequently landed troops at Derna, Homs, Misurata, and Tobruk. They employed large forces, both naval and military, and met with little opposition, since their invasion was well-timed. Though they had little difficulty in establishing bridgeheads, their progress inland was slow. They had only advanced a dozen miles from their base when the Sultan, alarmed by the threat of war in the Balkans, began to negotiate for peace. In October 1912 he signed the Treaty of Ouchy (or Lausanne) by which he gave up his rights in Libya; he did not, however, recognize Italian sovereignty but by a curious diplomatic device granted the Libyans 'full autonomy'. For their part the Italians had already proclaimed in 1911 their sovereignty as conquerors of the country. By the spring of 1914 they had completed their military occupation, although the Sanusi almost immediately began to attack their outposts in the Fezzan. The outbreak of the First World War weakened Italy's position; and when she joined the Allies she automatically came into direct conflict with Turkey at a time when she could ill spare troops for Africa. The Sanusi, supplied with Turkish and German arms and ammunition, attacked the British in Egypt, while the Tripolitanians turned upon their Italian masters. By 1917 the Italians held only the towns of Homs, Tripoli, Zuara, and the Cyrenaican ports, and were on the verge of losing their new possession altogether.

At the end of the war the Tripolitanian leaders, advised by Abdurrahman Azzam, later first Secretary-General of the Arab League, felt strong enough to proclaim a republic. To counter this the Italians offered to set up locally elected Parliaments in Tripolitania and Cyrenaica, under Italian Governors. For two years the Italian Government negotiated with the Libyans, who continued to press for self-government, finally offering the Amirate of united Libya to Sayyid Idris el Senussi (the present

King). The Sayyid's followers had always been the backbone of opposition to Italian rule, and he alone could unite the country. In July 1921 the Italian Government took a decisive step by appointing the dynamic Giuseppe Volpi (later Count Volpi of Misurata) to be Governor of Tripolitania. He proceeded to subdue the Tripolitanians by force of arms, without reference to the liberal and hesitant ministers in Rome. The advent of Fascism a year later strengthened his hand. By vigorous and ruthless action he and his military commander—Graziani—reconquered northern Tripolitania by the end of 1923. Fighting continued intermittently for the next six years, by which time even the Fezzan had been reoccupied. Graziani then passed on to Cyrenaica and reduced it to exhausted quiescence, which he called 'Pax Romana', by the end of 1932. His success was achieved by herding the civilian population into concentration camps and so depriving the Sanusi fighters of supplies and auxiliaries. The subsequent loss of life among human beings and livestock was very heavy. By the time that the 'pacification' was completed, the numbers of the population had been very greatly reduced. The inhumanity of these methods caused a bitterness which outlived the Italian régime.

As soon as the Italian occupation was secure, the Italian Government turned its thoughts to colonization. Count Volpi proposed to grant large concessions of land to wealthy Italians who could develop the resources of the country. Mussolini, however, favoured the establishment of large numbers of peasant proprietors, thinking more of rural overpopulation in Italy than of the economic aspect of the schemes. Libya was to become the 'fourth shore of our sea'. But there were innumerable difficulties and by 1933 it had become clear that if the Government wanted to people North Africa with metropolitan peasants within a reasonable time it would have to do so out of state funds. Accordingly the many small-scale schemes for assisting colonists were finally abandoned, and plans for mass emigration of peasant families were adopted. In 1938 20,000 persons in family groups from the most densely populated rural areas in Italy left Genoa in a blaze of publicity. In 1939 10,000 others left more quietly from Venice. They were settled on the Jefara plain of Tripoli and the Green Hills of Cyrenaica, in small, neat houses, in which everything down to a box of matches was provided before their arrival. The fields were already sown, and the animals in the stalls. The plan provided for hire-purchase of the farm by the peasant tenant who could become his own master after twenty years. The outbreak of the Second World War prevented a third mass migration, and made it impossible to judge the success of the earlier ventures.

When Italy declared war in June 1940, there were large military forces in Libya under the command of Marshal Graziani. With great circumspection they moved to attack the British in Egypt, only to be promptly driven back by General Wavell who captured Benghazi in February 1941 and cut off the retreating mass of the army on the coast road south of the city. Thereafter the war ebbed and flowed over Cyrenaica until, in the autumn of 1942, the British Eighth Army swept the Axis forces out of Libya for ever. On 23 January 1943 the British forces captured Tripoli city and passed rapidly on to link up with the Anglo-American forces in Tunisia. From the beginning of the war Sayyid Idris el Senussi had supported the Allied cause and on his initiative a Libyan Arab Force had been raised in Egypt and trained to fight beside their British allies.

During the several British occupations of Cyrenaica, and the final advance into Tripolitania, British Military Administrations were established. These derived their powers from the Commander-in-Chief of the Middle East Land Forces. Their position, like that of all military administrations, was both curious and difficult. Under the Hague Convention of 1906 they were bound to enforce the laws and methods of administration of the enemy. But in the case of Libya these were entirely Fascist in origin, and were repudiated by the Italian Government set up under Marshal Badoglio in 1944. The Hague Rules had therefore to be liberally interpreted and, even so, it was impossible to remove all traces of twenty years of Fascism. The problem was further complicated by the fact that the future of the former Italian colonies was so obscure that the military administrations appeared likely to continue for several years, and, in fact, lasted longer than such administrations generally do.

In September 1945 the Foreign Ministers of the United States of America, France, Russia, and Great Britain first met to discuss the future of the Italian colonies, upon which they held most divergent views. The Americans wished to place all the territories under United Nations trusteeship (the Byrnes plan). France favoured the return of her colonies to Italy under trusteeship. Russia unexpectedly demanded the trusteeship of Tripolitania for herself; and Great Britain, upholding Mr Eden's pledge of 1942 that the Sanusi of Cyrenaica should never again come under Italian rule, was opposed to the return of the colonies to Italy. No conclusion was reached, and the matter was left for discussion before the meeting of the Peace Conference in Paris in May 1946. In April 1946 Mr Bevin, the British Foreign Secretary, announced that Great Britain was in favour of 'the unity and independence of Libya'. He was, however, unable to obtain any support for this policy from the other Foreign Ministers, and by June declared himself to be leaning towards the French view which had remained unchanged. This announcement produced such violent reactions in Tripolitania that the British and Americans were deeply impressed. The latter suggested that the future of the colonies should not be decided until one year after the ratification of the peace treaties, and that meanwhile a Four-Power Commission should investigate the wishes of the inhabitants and report to the Foreign Ministers. This was adopted.

Since Italy, Russia, and France did not ratify the treaties until September 1947, the temporary military administrations automatically continued until the autumn of 1948. The Four-Power Commission visited the three territories in turn during the spring of 1948 and submitted a report to the Foreign Ministers that summer, which was unanimous only in considering that the Libyans were not yet fitted for independence. In September the Foreign Ministers handed separate and quite different reports to their respective Governments. A decision was therefore not reached and the matter was automatically referred to the Assembly of the United Nations.

The question was first discussed by the Political Committee, at Flushing Meadows in April 1949, where it was suggested that Great Britain should have the trusteeship of Cyrenaica and France of the Fezzan. The future of Tripolitania remained obscure. The French alone proposed to hand it back to the Italians as trustees. The Russians, who had declared themselves in 1948 in favour of the return to Italy of all her colonies, reverted to the Byrnes plan for United Nations trusteeship. After much discussion, during which Count Sforza made an impassioned plea for the return of Tripolitania to Italy, it became clear that the chances of agreement were scanty, since the Latin American bloc opposed all plans ousting Italy entirely from Libya, and the Arab states boycotted all proposals by which she returned. In a desperate effort to end the controversy Mr Bevin secured the agreement of Count Sforza to a compromise. Tripolitania was to attain independence in ten years, remaining under the existing British rule for three, and reverting to Italian rule for the remaining seven years. In a dramatic midnight session of the General Assembly, the vital Tripolitanian clause failed by one vote to gain the necessary two-thirds majority; this brought down with it the whole compromise plan. Its rejection caused universal rejoicing in the Arab world, and particularly in Tripolitania, where its adoption had produced consternation, demonstrations, and threats of violent opposition.

Six months later, the Political Committee at last settled the fate of the Italian colonies. In the interval, all the powers concerned had abandoned their claims to trusteeship and adopted various methods of establishing an independent and united Libya. The Russians proposed immediate independence, the Italians after six months, the Americans and the British after a period of several years. Finally the Political Committee agreed that independence should become effective 'as soon as possible and in any case not later than 1 January 1952'. Cyrenaica, Tripolitania, and the Fezzan were granted full freedom to determine the form of their union. A United Nations Commissioner was appointed to assist them in framing a constitution. To advise him, an international Council was set up on which Great Britain, France, Italy, the United States, Egypt, and Pakistan were represented.

The Commissioner, Dr Adrian Pelt of Holland, arrived in Tripoli in January 1950. Three months later the Council of Libya met for the first time and appointed a committee of twenty-one—seven from each territory—to make plans for the convening of a National Assembly to draw up the constitution. This body, which was finally composed of sixty members, on the basis of equal representation for the three territories, managed to complete its work by the end of 1951, and the independence of the United Kingdom of Libya was proclaimed in December by its first hereditary ruler, Sayyid Mohammed Idris el Senussi.

The Independent Government

The first act of the new state was to hold elections for Parliament. They were not conducted on party lines, except in Tripolitania, where a National Congress Party in opposition to the Sanusi had been organized by Beshir el Saadawi, a returned exile who had held the post of adviser to the King in Saudi Arabia. His party was defeated; riots ensued, in which 17 people were killed and 200 injured; the party was dissolved and Beshir deported. The second general election, held in January 1956, was not contested on party lines but on the grounds of personality and family influence.

Even without organized parliamentary opposition, the task of the King and his ministers was not easy. The three provinces had little in common, and the King's special connexion with Cyrenaica did not help to bind them more closely together. There was a complete absence of educated Libyans to carry on the work of government. Technical assistance could only be expected from the west, but Libya as an Islamic state naturally wished for the closest association with other independent Arab states. The King was the most substantial link between the three provinces, but he was far from young and the succession was in doubt, since he had no son to succeed him. A boy, born in February 1953, lived only for a few hours, and the King's second marriage in June 1955 produced no male heir. The King's brother, Mohammed el Rida, who was heir presumptive, died in 1954, to be succeeded by his second son el Hassan Rida, the present heir presumptive.

During these years of uncertainty the royal family was a centre of intrigue. Much of it was directed against Ibrahim Shelhi, Controller of the Royal Household, a loyal and able counsellor of many years service. In October 1954 he was assassinated by a young nephew of Queen Fatima. As a result, almost the whole royal family were divested of their titles and privileges, and banished to the Tripolitanian desert oasis of Jadu. Busairi Shelhi, the son of the murdered man, took his father's place, and enjoys much of the same influence and authority.

Two further problems spring from the federal and democratic organization of the state. The King has preferred to reside in Cyrenaica, particularly since an attempt was made on his life during a visit to Tripoli. In theory the Government should alternate between Tripoli and Benghazi, but practical convenience and the expense of moving have caused it to remain principally in Tripoli, thus causing dissatisfaction in Cyrenaica. There has been constant competition between the provinces for money, and between the King and Parliament for authority. Of the second, it is said that insistence on legislation by royal decree has caused the resignation of three Prime Ministers, Mahmud el Muntasser in 1954, Mohammed Sakesli a few weeks later, and Mustapha ben Halim in 1957. The present (December 1957) Prime Minister, Abdul Majid Koobar, has been President of the Chamber of Deputies, with two short intervals as a Minister, since the proclamation of independence. It is, however, easy to make too much of differences between the Throne and Parliament. A measure of direct action by the sovereign may well be essential while the legislature is still immature. The position of King Idris I is extremely difficult. He is driving three unwilling horses in harness, hampered by the activities of some of his family, and harassed by thoughts of the uncertain future. In these circumstances, the faltering or still more the disappearance of the coachman or the bolting of a horse could easily result in the overturning of the coach. . . .

11. Beginning of Tunisian nationalism

L. HAHN *North Africa: Nationalism to Nationhood* Public Affairs Press 1960; pages 10–17

Tunisian nationalism was born approximately twenty years after the signing of the Treaty of La Marsa—after a generation of Tunisians had grown up under the *présence française*. From the very beginning, it demonstrated that characteristic typical of virtually every twentieth century nationalist movement, particularly in French-colonized areas: the fact that the colonizing country, by trying to graft its own culture onto the colonized, was digging its own grave.

For the people who organized "Young Tunisians" in 1907, led by Ali Bach-Hamba and Bechir Sfar, were for the most part young men who had just returned from studying in Paris. The French, by opening their schools to young North Africans, and teaching them the philosophies of Voltaire and Rousseau, were hoping eventually to make Frenchmen—or at least pro-Frenchmen—out of them. Since the young students were delighted and overwhelmed, on the whole, by what they found on the continent, this policy might well have worked out had the French remembered to treat the young Moslems as equals. Instead, however, the Tunisian students often found themselves discriminated against in France, and, worse yet, in their own country once they returned. The net result was a bitter disillusionment, and a bewilderment at "Why don't the French practice the equality that they have taught us?"

They therefore founded a movement which aimed at giving the Tunisians equal opportunities and equal treatment in the economic and special spheres, if not yet in the political. To these ends they began the publication of newspapers and pamphlets which would acquaint people with the various goals for which they were striving. Self-improvement groups, such as an agricultural school for the teaching of more modern farming methods, which would better enable the Tunisian *fellahin* to compete with the *colons*, were also organized.

In the matter of religion, they felt that the Tunisians need not be ashamed of their Moslem heritage—to the contrary, they should be proud of its past achievements. But religion should be modernized—a concept which they borrowed from the programme of the Young Turks, and from the teachings of Jamal' addine al-Afghani and Cheikh Mohammed Abdou, leading figures in the Moslem Renaissance.

It must be borne in mind, however, that although all the Young Tunisians were able to agree on a vague platform declaring the rights of peoples to express themselves and the needs for modernization and reform, not all the members were, as yet, "nationalists" in our sense of the term. For the concept of the "nation"—a geographical entity wherein live people of many religions who share certain customs and interests in common, and where national law is separated from religious law—was something totally new to the world of Islam. Here all laws, whether dealing specifically with religion, with the individual or with government, were based on the Koran. There was, in other words, no separation of "church" and "state", and the criterion for judging what sort of laws an individual must follow depended on whether or not he was a Moslem, not on what particular area he inhabited. The traditional emphasis was thus always on "what should we Moslems do?" not on "what should we who happen to inhabit Tunisia (or Egypt or Mesopotamia or India) do?"

Thus the earliest movement in the Islamic world which aimed at combatting colonialism, formed towards the end of the nineteenth century, was pan-Islamism. This held that all Moslems in the world should unite behind the man who was then the spiritual head of most of Islam, the Sultan of Turkey, and jointly combat imperialism. When unity of all Moslems appeared to be a practical impossibility, it was replaced in the minds of many by what seemed to be a more feasible scheme: pan-Arabism, or the concept that all Arabs, sharing a more or less common racial and cultural as well as religious heritage, should fight for freedom from colonialism, with the eventual goal of uniting into one Arab state. These ideas, held by many Arab leaders at the turn of the nineteenth century, were publicized widely in North Africa by Chekib Arslan, a learned man of Syrian origin who operated from various points of exile, usually Geneva. His ideas influenced many of the Young Tunisians in the wing led by Sfar and Cheikh Abdelaziz Taalbi (of whom more will be said later), making them think in terms of eventually obtaining independence for Tunisia— but only as a first step towards the formation of the greater Arab state. Eventually, of course, these ideas as to the future of a free Tunisia would conflict with the plans of others, who wanted to be just plain Tunisians. But for the time being, this was all academic—the problem was to get some immediate changes in the protectorate system, and begin preparing people for life in the twentieth century.

Ironically, the Young Tunisians' first clash with the French authorities occurred not over a question of these reforms, but over a traditional religious issue. In 1911, when the French

Mtca

attempted to register a highly venerated cemetery at Dzellaz under European laws, they gathered with other Tunisians to stage mass protests. The result was an open skirmish with French troops—the first since 1881—and the proclamation by protectorate authorities of a state of siege which was to last for ten years. When another protest demonstration occurred the following year, the French retaliated by exiling many of the nationalist leaders, and forcing the movement to go underground until the end of World War I.

The French were not the only group with whom the Young Tunisians came into conflict. As in all countries where European civilization was rather suddenly thrust into a decaying society, whose rulers were primarily interested in preserving their traditional privileges, groups with vested interests tended to fear young native reformers who might upset the whole system more than the foreign conquerors. For the latter were usually more than content to leave alone the decadent institutions, which kept the masses in a state of apathy, and which thus made the country far easier to rule. In Tunisia, the "Old Turbans", a conservative and intensely religious group interested in maintaining traditional Moslem institutions and the privileged religious fraternities, found little reason to object to the French, who, except for the brief incident in 1911, left religious institutions intact. But they did object to the modernist tendencies of Young Tunisians, whom they fought ever since their founding, and whom they were happy to see driven into the pale of disrepute.

The latter grew steadily even after their declared illegality. In the first place, their ranks were constantly swelled with the batches of newly French-trained youths who returned eager to put their skills into operation, only to find that there was no place for them within the protectorate system. But in addition the self-determination ideal so clearly expressed by President Wilson in his fourteen points fired the imagination of people who had never really thought of "nationalism" before, or, if they did, never thought of it in terms of a natural right. Finally, a French blunder in 1919 was to cause even the once-antagonistic (or at least apathetic) Old Turbans to co-operate with the Young Tunisians.

This event was the attempt by the French to open up sizeable sections of the *habous* (lands controlled by religious groups) for settlement by *colons*. This of course brought home to the Old Turbans the fact that colonialism might indeed be a bad thing, and that France might not really be the true defender and respecter of Moslem institutions they had supposed. They thus decided to overlook their past differences with the Young Tunisians and present a common front in protest. At the same time, still enveloped in the wave of idealism so difficult for later generations to comprehend, both groups sent delegations to President Wilson at Versailles, hoping the great emancipator would do something for them. As was true with most other "oppressed peoples"—he could not. But the Tunisians then decided to do something for themselves. The following year both groups joined forces and formed what was the country's first real political party, the *Destour* (constitution).

The founder and leader of the party was the reformer Cheikh Taalbi, author of the pamphlet *La Tunisie Martyre*, which encouraged the nationalists to continue their efforts despite the first (of what was to be many) rebuffs in Paris. The Tunisian people, said Taalbi, were at least entitled to have certain fundamental rights guaranteed by a constitution. For this there had been a precedent in the short-lived constitution granted by the Bey in 1857 after a revolt. This document was revolutionary by Moslem standards, since it guaranteed the equality before the law of all people, regardless of race or religion. It was partly to revoke memories of this that the name Destour was chosen for his party. But the name also signified that Taalbi wanted France to grant "the emancipation of the Tunisian people from the bonds of slavery", and give them certain rights within the protectorate system, by granting a constitution. This, he felt, should provide for a government responsible to a popularly elected assembly composed of French and Tunisian representatives elected by universal suffrage, in a system based on the separation of powers (a concept recently learned in France). Also demanded was the opening of official posts to Tunisians, with pay equal to that of French civil servants in the same posts, freedom of press and assembly, and other related rights learned from the West.

Although this westernized programme attracted a great

deal of attention, it was a matter of religious nature which was to do the most to interest Tunisians in nationalism. The Destour Party, although fairly well organized on a hierarchical basis, suffered from lack of well-laid, co-ordinated planning. These were the causes of its eventual eclipse. It was, however, able to clarify the issues between France and Tunisia so that future nationalist leaders, trained in its ranks, could know how to operate more effectively. To be specific: it was able to make the people very conscious of being Tunisians—the thing that France was trying so hard to avoid.

France, ever anxious to make Frenchmen out of the Tunisians, passed a law in 1923 offering French citizenship to educated or "qualified" Tunisians. This offer of a presumably better nationality would in itself have doubtless aroused antagonism, even among those who were until then more or less apathetic to the Destour and its programme. But the French offer had a more direct and offensive implication: accepting another nationality would have meant committing heresy to many Tunisian Moslems. For it would have meant accepting the jurisdiction of French law and French courts instead of the Islamic courts and law, since under Islam church and state law are inseparable. Thus the 1923 decree aroused the biggest protest to date, with religious leaders joining nationalist leaders in opposing naturalization. Although Taalbi and other leaders were forced to leave the country, and the Destour was forced underground until 1930, strikes and demonstrations continued. Their climax was reached in the tremendous outbreaks of violence which occurred in 1933 when the French attempted to bury a naturalized Tunisian in a Moslem cemetery in Monastir and the Tunisians protested on the grounds that she was a renegade and a traitor.

These demonstrations were important in that they marked a setback for the French, who finally yielded to public demands by burying the *naturalizes* in a special cemetery. But they were also important for another reason: they brought into the limelight a young man who was destined to become Tunisia's nationalist Number I, and eventually the elder statesman of North Africa: Habib Bourguiba.

To assume that Bourguiba is the entire story of modern Tunisian nationalism would be as naïve as to assume that

George Washington was solely responsible for American independence. There were a score of others, now heading departments in Tunisia's government or directing its embassies abroad, in some cases dead as martyrs, who were responsible for important decisions and for tactical victories. There were countless others whose names will never appear in any Tunisian history book—petty businessmen in the *souk*, workers, teachers —without whose grass-roots co-operation Tunisian nationalism could never have become a force to be reckoned with. But the fact that Bourguiba was able to capture the imagination of these diversified elements, to sell them on a moderate, unglamorous course of action, to weld them into a faithful and disciplined striking force, and to become while alive a hero whom school-boys emulate, testifies to a political acumen rare in any part of the world.

Bourguiba is the big exception to the rule that Tunisians generally dislike politics—he thrives on it. A superb orator who can speak with equal facility to a party caucus, a Berber peasant woman or the cream of French diplomats, a born leader who uses to the best advantage his flashing blue eyes and his training in dramatics (the theatre has always been one of his major hobbies), he plays the role of *chef* to the hilt, and could be content with nothing else. But the role is a real one, as real as the philosophy of "Bourguibism", which he created. For Bourguiba is above all a realist with special *mélange* of vision, *weltanschaung*, patience and just plain know-how.

Born in the small town of Monastir on August 3, 1903, Bourguiba was the youngest of eight children (his oldest brother Mohammed was 22 at the time). At five he was sent to live with two brothers in Tunis, where he began the studies at Sadiki College which he was forced to interrupt in 1919. In that year he developed a serious case of bronchial pneumonia, and went for a long rest cure at La Kef, where Mohammed was in charge of a hospital.

The following two-year intermezzo at La Kef was in the narrow sense a setback, but it also turned out to be the turning point in Bourguiba's life. For along with his medicine, he absorbed the strongly individualistic philsophy of Mohammed, a free thinker with no respect for the traditions he himself decided were contrary to human dignity. Young and impressionable, Bourguiba then became obsessed with the idea (so omnipresent in his recent speeches to western leaders) that something should be done to give all people a sense of dignity, and like so many schoolboys at that time, he interested himself in the cause of nationalism. When he returned to his studies in Tunis in 1922 at the Lycée Carnot, he investigated the activities of the Destour, joined in several demonstrations, and decided to study law in Paris, as was the pattern among most young intellectuals.

Student life in Paris—the wines, the women without veils, the lack of traditional family obligations which ensnared a young Tunisian at home, no matter how he might oppose such things intellectually—were France at its best. It is sometimes hard for a western observer to understand how a North African can devote his life to fighting the French, and yet be attached to their language and culture, as are virtually all. The Tunisian might try to explain it by saying "The French in France are different from the French in Tunisia", or, in more intellectual terms, "The French language can express *nuances*, particularly philosophical concepts, which Arabic can not", or "We wanted to know modern concepts and western ways and those of France were the only ones available to us". Perhaps. But in most cases, the attachment can be explained mainly by the fact that France provided the young Tunisians with an intellectual and moral freedom, opened to them new vistas which they could never have dreamed of in Tunisia, and provided them with some of the happiest years of their lives. France helped make them the westernized "sensible" people they are today; to reject French influence would be to repudiate themselves.

Bourguiba, probably more than any other North African, symbolizes the emotional attachment to France which his famous political formula "I do not hate France—only colonialism" only begins to describe. In Paris he learned to speak French better than many Frenchmen, and better than his native Arabic—to the point, in fact, where he finds it a bit difficult to understand how any foreigner can consider himself educated unless he can speak French fluently. He also acquired a French wife, Mathilde Lorraine ("love is love," he explains it, "and besides, she was ashamed of being French"). Finally, he developed that feeling which, admittedly or not, has coloured his every action *vis-à-vis* the French: a desire to be respected by them and to be accepted as an equal.

Returning to Tunis in August of 1927 with Mathilde, four-month old Habib Jr. and degrees in law and political science, he opened what promised to be a successful law practice, and more or less as a matter of course, officially joined the Destour. Soon, the latter—or rather, what he felt should be the latter—was sequestering all his energies.

For a time, Bourguiba fully co-operated with the "old crocodiles" of the Destour, then directed by Salah Ferhat and Ahmed as Aafi. He soon rose to become a member of its executive committee, and of the editorial staff of its newspaper *La Voix du Tunisien*. But he was young, nervous and impatient, and soon concluded that this party, with its endless impertinent discussions and its platonic protestations of anti-colonialism, was dying, both from lack of contact with the people and from lack of courage.

"If we are supposed to be working for our country," he observed, "we should obviously work with our countrymen." There were others within the party who shared these sentiments. There was, for example, the physician Mohammed Materi, a man five years Bourguiba's senior who had long been a faithful Destour member, but who finally concluded he was accomplishing nothing within its stilted atmosphere. There was his brother Mohammed, who had aroused his interest originally, and Tahar Sfar. There was a man five years Bourguiba's junior, a small, intense, ambitious young man named Salah ben Youssef. There was also a precocious youth who joined the party in 1930 at the age of sixteen, and from the start insisted that nationalism was a question not of congresses and coffee klatches, but of organization, sincere devotion and action—Bahi Ladgham.

Bourguiba and his friends tried to push a programme of mass organization and frequent, open congresses, but to no avail. In 1932, in protest, they started their own newspaper, *L'Action Tunisienne*, which sought: (1) to seek, "with prudence and sincerity", a remedy for the serious economic, moral and political crisis which gripped Tunisia; (2) to defend "free from all spirit of caste or of demagogic sterility" the interests of all Tunisians "without distinction as to religion"; (3) to accomplish all the aims of the Destour, "educator and organizer of the masses", and to even go beyond this in the attempt to further Tunisian interests; and (4) to serve as an intermediator between French opinion and Tunisian opinion in advocating, as much as possible, "the idea of justice and of understanding, without useless haranguing, but without any degrading of our national identity". The group did succeed in publicizing many administrative abuses by the French in their attempts to increase their hold on Tunisia. For example, they took the part of one M. Mohammed Chenik, who was trying to organize a credit organization for Tunisians, even though he was known to be a French "collaborator". They did a great deal in arranging the demonstrations in "the affair of the cemeteries". But they could do little in the way of building an effective nationalism so long as they were fettered by the conservative—to the point of cowardice —directors of the Destour. And the more they protested, the more the chasm opened by their launching of *L'Action* widened.

The cord was finally clipped at the memorable party congress held in Ksar Hillal in March, 1934, where the old guard, through some political pyrotechnics, attempted to muzzle permanently the new. The move, however, backfired. The result was that the Bourguiba group gained control over most of the membership, and organized themselves as a new party, the Neo-Destour, with Materi as President and Bourguiba as Secretary General. The old Destour was started on the road to near oblivion.

From then on Tunisian nationalism was virtually synonymous with Neo-Destour, which was in turn almost synonymous with Bourguiba—or at least his ideas. And a new term— "Bourguibism"—was to enter political vocabularies.

III. REVOLUTIONS IN EGYPT

12. Populist control in Egypt

M. BERGER *The Arab World Today* Weidenfeld & Nicolson and Doubleday 1962; pages 422–3

...The Egypt of King Farouk and the Egypt of Colonel Nasser are in a sense opposite models of the political evolution of countries that seek to change from a traditional agricultural to a modern industrial society. Though Farouk's regime was not liberal, it allowed a certain amount of freedom and political dissent. Partly, this was the result of a balance of forces among the palace, the British, and the various Egyptian groups who opposed both; the hesitation or fear of each one to assume all power enabled the others to survive and express themselves. But it stemmed also from the nature of the monarchy as a pre-populist regime. Such a regime and social system does not rest on public opinion. It retains considerable latitude by ignoring the masses, by not drawing them into political life, by leaving them undisturbed in their private misery and political apathy. It can therefore allow greater freedom at the top to the articulate groups—the press, political parties, professionals, students. By leaving the masses dormant, it affords a modicum of freedom for the elites.

Nasser's populist Egypt is something else. Having destroyed the organizations (especially the political parties and the economic bases of the groups that supported them) which enjoyed that modicum of freedom under its predecessor, the populist regime cannot allow these esrtwhile elites or their remnants the same degree of freedom in politics. Instead, it seeks mass support by drawing new classes into the political process. These are the peasants and urban workers, who are wooed to give the strength of numbers to the regime's support in the army and the upper levels of the civilian bureaucracy. The political process no longer embraces competing parties and relatively free parliaments but means (1) the single mass organization to arouse and channel political consciousness, (2) the professional associations, peasant co-operatives, trade unions, and religious groups harnessed to the regime's goals, and (3) plebiscites, and parliaments without parties.

Because the populist regime depends on the systematic cultivation of formerly isolated and ignored groups, it must rely on exhortation and propaganda to a greater extent than does the pre-populist regime. That is to say, it communicates with the masses more directly and more often, creates opinions in them, arouses their passions, stimulates their desires and tries to make them work harder for the elite's goal of modernization. In such a society, where mass opinion is stirred, the expression of any opinion becomes all the more significant because it is no longer confined to the homogenous and articulate thin layer at the top. The populist regime suppresses freedom at the top because freedom may now penetrate the lower levels and have serious consequences. And precisely because opinion and communication may now move the masses being brought into the political spectrum, the populist regime seeks to control expression everywhere. . . .

13. Coup and consolidation

K. WHEELOCK *Nasser's New Egypt* Stevens and Praeger 1960; pages 11–25

. . . It was surprising how ill-prepared the Free Officers were for success. After finding that their swift military action was welcomed by much of the country, they hastily improvised an *ad hoc* plan of action. Upon deciding in favour of Ali Maher as the Prime Minister, they had to ask a local journalist to guide Anwar Sadat to the home of the new head of government. With Maher sworn in, the next problem was how to deal with the King. According to some sources, the Free Officers, until July 24, were willing to retain the monarch; initial statements by Naguib and Sadat seemed to support this impression. But even after Farouk accepted the military group's original list of demands, there was strong sentiment in favour of deposing the monarch. On the night of July 25, two groups, one under Naguib and Sadat in Alexandria, the other under Nasser in

Cairo, decided the King's fate. Although there was strong feeling that he should be placed on trial for his many crimes against the state, Nasser's moderate view prevailed. The following day, while British troops in Suez made no move to save the King, he abdicated in favour of his six-month-old son. At six in the evening, Farouk left Egypt.

Rout of the "Old Order"

The day after Farouk's departure, General Naguib, publicly recognized as leader of the Free Officers, declared: "Our military movement has nothing to do with politics." Refusing to make a statement on foreign affairs, he asserted that the military accepted responsibility for an investigation of the Palestinian arms scandal and for the defence of Gaza against possible Israeli attack. These objectives were added to a previous Free Officer commitment to a campaign against graft and nepotism. The absence of more detailed plans was understandable, for the Free Officers never had expected to govern. As Colonel Gamal Abdul Nasser has somewhat naïvely written: the army's role was that of a "commando vanguard"; he and his associates sincerely felt that "good politicians" would run the country once the army had eliminated the "bad elements". Later, a member of the Free Officers' executive council, Khaled Mohieddine, commented frankly: "We didn't discuss what we would do after the Revolution." It was on an *ad hoc* basis that the military had to cope with the problems of governing.

The first week's achievements were impressive. Some of the King's closest advisers were arrested, and a number of political prisoners were released; investigations were reopened in the Palestinian arms case and in the murder of Hassan el Banna, founder of the Moslem Brethren. The inefficient practice of moving the government to the sea resort of Alexandria during the summer months was ended, and all officials were ordered to return immediately to Cairo. The titles of "pasha" and "bey", claimed to be representative of Egypt's past social inequality, were abolished. A purge against Farouk's supporters was initiated by the army, and a Regency Council, including Colonel Rashad Mohanna, was established to substitute for the absent infant, King Fuad II. An anti-corruption law was enacted, and political parties were ordered to purge themselves.

By the end of the week, however, many of the Free Officers openly had become disillusioned. Some of them had thought at first that the new regime could function with the old politicians. Nasser and Major Khaled Mohieddine even favoured the immediate recall of the suspended Parliament. But it soon became evident that the powerful Wafdist Party's as well as the dangerous Moslem Brethren's alliances with the Ali Maher government were only tactical and temporary ones. Upon Mustapha Nahas' hasty return from France, the leader of the Wafdist Party publicly supported the proposed Regency Council on the condition that the Wafd-dominated Parliament be recalled to ratify it. Invoking Naguib's pledge to "uphold the Constitution", Nahas further suggested that nationwide elections be held. Observers agreed that they would result in an overwhelming Wafdist victory.

The Moslem Brethren, pleased that one of their followers, Rashad Mohanna, held such an important position, felt that they could also depend upon support from former sympathizers such as Nasser, Anwar Sadat, Hussein Shafei, and Kamel el din Hussein. Although the Brethren, on two occasions before the overthrow of Farouk, had refused actively to support the Free Officers, the Supreme Guide, Hassan el Hodeiby, informed Nasser in late July that any law which was to be promulgated had first to be approved by the Moslem Brethren. Moreover, on August 3, the Brethren issued a "White Paper" which stated that "the Koran is our only Constitution", thus pressing their concept of a theocracy. The Free Officers, in rejecting a coalition with the Brethren, realized that the army was now opposed by the two most powerful political forces in the country.

What started as a simple *coup d'état* soon became a struggle for political survival. The Free Officers, in an effort to consolidate their power, substantially raised military salaries and added Lt. Colonel Zacharia Mohieddine, Lt. Colonel Hussein Shafei, Lt. Colonel Abdel Moneim Amin, Lt. Colonel Yussef Saddik Mansour, and, according to many reports, Major General Mohammed Naguib to their executive council. While a political parties reorganization law was being implemented, Naguib and his colleagues believed that the country could be governed by the non-party civilian government of Ali Maher. But they were soon disillusioned even on this score. Ali Maher was a conservative politician of the old regime. Although he was willing to accept the premiership after the coup, he displayed strong reluctance to implement the sweeping reforms urged by the military. When an agrarian reform bill was first discussed, the Premier was loath to impose such severe financial penalties upon members of his own social class. Moreover, in opposition to Naguib's expressed wishes, he authorized additional indirect regressive taxes on such commodities as tobacco.

By August 8, the die had been cast. Naguib publicly set the campaign in motion with the warning that it might become necessary to proclaim a dictatorship unless Egypt's political parties thoroughly "cleansed" themselves. Referring to the Wafd, he declared: "Most of the evil element extending to the very top still remains untouched. What I think of the Wafd clean-up goes for all the other parties, too." Two days later, Naguib continued his attack in a leading Cairo newspaper, *Al Misri*: "We have advised. Now we warn. Next we shall act. We have had enough of corruption. Political parties must get rid of bad elements. The next step should be to bring these bad elements to book and let justice take its course. . . . Our parties are founded on personalities, not on principles." The Free Officers, however, were labouring under a self-imposed handicap: they had committed themselves to peaceful means. And the opposition to the army, taking heart from the absence of forceful measures, became increasingly virulent.

The first serious challenge to the new regime came from the Delta. On August 12, riots broke out in the mill town of Kafr el Dawar. An organized band of workers, shouting "Long live the army's Revolution, the people's Revolution!", seized the factory installations, setting fire to several buildings and damaging equipment. When the police force could not cope with the rioters, army troops had to be called from Alexandria to subdue the workers in a pitched battle; nine were reported dead and twenty-two wounded. The Free Officers, panicked by this show of violence, took forceful action. Naguib, until then represented as a mild and moderate leader, declared bluntly: "All sections of the population. and particularly labour, should notice that any disorder or infringement of public security will be considered as an act of treason against the country, the penalty for which is well known to all." A special military court, headed by Abdel Moneim Amin of the Free Officers executive council, was created to try the arrested textile workers.

Government officials to this day have failed to give a consistent account of the riots. The controlled local press strongly suggested that the same "secret hands" which had organized the January burning of Cairo were behind the Kafr el Dawar rising. General Naguib stated flatly that it was a "Communist-inspired" strike, and Major Ahmed Abdullah Toiema, the military coordinator of labour affairs since 1952, declared in 1958 that the responsible individuals were Communists. On the other hand, leading figures in Egypt's labour movement claim that no definite proof of Communist involvement has yet been established. It is generally accepted, however, that Communist influence in labour unions at the time was strongest in the textile industry. At any rate, the public prosecutor obtained the first death sentence within five days of the strike and, during the following week, another worker was given the death penalty, while a score of others received prison terms. The two condemned to death were offered clemency if they turned state's evidence; but when they refused to name the instigators of the disturbance, the Free Officers upheld the original sentences and the two were hanged early in September.

On the Monday following the strike, the Ministry of Interior announced the formation of a "State Security Department" to fight against Communism and Zionism, and before the Kafr el Dawar trials ended, the Ministry announced the break-up of a major Communist cell and the arrest of twenty-four persons charged with belonging to the outlawed Communist movement. This vigorous campaign against the Left alienated a leading Communist faction which previously had supported the Free Officers. The MDLN (Democratic Movement for National Liberation), which claimed Colonel Yussef Saddik Mansour and Khaled Mohieddine among its members, soon became openly antagonistic; it denounced the "military dictatorship which, after sparing Farouk, the feudal lords, traitors, and embezzlers, spilled only the workers' blood".

In an impromptu address, Naguib told a group of soldiers that the army would "crush" anyone caught spreading the false idea that the army was tainted with Communism. Then, in an apparent reference to right-wing politicians, he continued: "'Elements belonging to the corrupt era are still at large and they are actively working to frustrate our movement. But we will crush them. We will shoot them, if necessary." This blunt warning followed his announcement that parliamentary elections, originally scheduled for October, would be held in February, 1953. It was felt that, before the elections, the army, after implementing a retroactive illegal profits act and after initiating a general purge, would approve only substantially reconstituted parties. The Free Officers believed, also, that the agrarian reform law, once enacted, would destroy the dominant influence of large landowners in Egyptian politics. As was to be expected, most political parties reacted sluggishly to official orders for a purge, awaiting the outcome of the expected show-down between the Wafd and the regime.

Naguib and other Free Officers met with various leaders of the Wafd in an effort to reach a compromise. But, in a speech at Alexandria on August 23, Mustapha Nahas claimed that violence had been done to the Constitution and demanded a return to parliamentary rule. The army, fearing that wealthy landowners and others affected by recent reform measures might rally in support of the Wafd, moved tanks to strategic positions throughout Cairo, only to withdraw them the following day. Then, on September 5, the Wafd defiantly announced that the decisions of purge committees should be regarded as accusations, subject to approval in duly constituted courts of law.

Ali Maher's position, during these turbulent days, was fast becoming untenable. The Free Officers group, impatient for reform, accused Maher of deliberately delaying the land reform bill and other measures. Early on September 7, 1952, simultaneous with the arrest of forty-three politicians of the old regime, General Naguib, prodded by the more impatient members of the Free Officers' junta, established himself as Prime Minister of a new civilian Cabinet.

Yet, the struggle was far from over. The Egyptian masses, although disgruntled at the failures of the "old order", still were not captivated by the minor reforms initiated by the new regime for the benefit of the poorer classes. So the Free Officers, realizing their lack of firm popular support, sought an alliance with the Moslem Brethren against the Wafd. Supreme Guide Hodeiby was approached with an offer of two ministries in return for Brethren support. But Hodeiby's candidates, Munir Dallah and Hassan Ashmawi, were unacceptable to the Free Officers. When the new Cabinet accepted a more moderate Brethren member, Sheikh Ahmed Hassan Baquory, he was immediately expelled by the Brotherhood. A coalition with Hodeiby consequently being out of the question, the Free Officers nevertheless decided to challenge the Wafd. Thus Suliman Hafez, a bitter foe of the Wafd, was appointed Deputy Premier and Minister of the Interior.

The mass arrest of old-regime politicians did not appear to be directed solely against the Wafd. Rather, the coming struggle was foreshadowed by the new Cabinet's first meeting. After a session of nine and one-half hours, Minister Fathy Radwan announced, on September 9, that the Agrarian Reform Law had been enacted and a law for the compulsory reorganization of political parties had been approved. The Agrarian Reform Law was, of course, more than a purely political move. Nevertheless, it was clear to many observers that the legislation, aimed at breaking up the feudal hierarchy of the countryside, was designed—at least in the short run—to cripple Wafdist power in the villages. Nor was there any mistaking the fact that the party reorganization act was directed against Mustapha Nahas' leadership, for the Free Officers had made it amply clear that a Nahas-dominated Wafd would be unacceptable.

The septuagenarian Nahas struggled against the October 8 deadline set by the government for "political reorganization". Meanwhile, a Wafdist faction friendly to the military regime urged the dismissal of Nahas and his replacement by a former senator from Tanta, Salem Fahmi Gomaa. While the Wafd was thus split internally, other parties hastened to reorganize in compliance with the law. Four cabinet ministers founded a new party, and the Moslem Brethren, after fighting bitterly over the decision of whether to register as a religious society or political party, finally enrolled as a political organization.

But the Wafd had not yet come to heel. Indeed, as the other parties complied meekly with the government's ultimatum, the Wafd was becoming the rallying ground for civilian opponents of the Free Officers. Wafd leaders realized that their backs were against the wall—that the party, having already been humiliated several times since the July coup, could not retreat further without forfeiting its political future. Nahas, therefore, launched a counter-offensive with the declaration that "No power, Allah and the Egyptian people excepted, can oust me." He followed this up, on September 27, with an attack against Deputy Premier Hafez, when he referred to "those who exploit political events to feather their own nest". The government, realizing that a compromise was impossible, decided to act. After placing the military under a "state of alert", Naguib and his fellow officers left on a tour of the Delta, traditionally the Wafdist stronghold. His trip turned into a triumphal procession. As one veteran newsman commented: "The Wafd is dead."

Ultimately, the Wafd elected Nahas as Honorary President. Deputy Premier Hafez, however, refused to recognize this reorganization. A Wafdist attempt to challenge this ruling through the courts was countered by a Cabinet decree which conferred supreme powers, not subject to judicial review, upon General Naguib for six months, retroactive to July 23, 1952.

This decree was not the only indication of the government's drift toward complete military dictatorship. New round-ups of civilian politicians were conducted, and, on September 25, the Cabinet retired 450 army officers of all ranks. Five days later, staff officers were assigned to many of the more important government departments. It came, therefore, as no surprise when Naguib declared in early October: "We have already declared that our principal aim is to establish a 'true democratic government' in Egypt. *If political parties will become perfectly reorganized by that date* [February, 1953], elections will take place at the fixed time, and without undue delay." (Italics added.) Obviously, the military junta, becoming accustomed to governing, was reluctant to surrender its newly acquired powers to civilian politicians.

With the Wafd subdued, the government turned to the Moslem Brethren, still a major threat because of their widespread religious appeal and its many active supporters even within the army and the police. Two days after pardoning Brethren members imprisoned for political crimes, the government dropped a leading Brethren sympathizer, the popular

NTCA

Colonel Rashad Mohanna, from his position on the Regency Council, charging that Mohanna had opposed the agrarian reform programme, had sought to gain undue personal influence, and had refused "to conform with the principles of the military movement". A local newspaper charged that he tried to proclaim himself as Caliph of Islam, and a government source revealed that Mohanna had summoned the Prime Minister to inform him that he did not wish to remain a mere figurehead. It is entirely possible that Colonel Mohanna did seek greater personal recognition, for the Regency Council possessed no real power. More significantly, however, Mohanna had attracted attention by his criticism of the existing "godless" government, and it is likely that he was chastised primarily for his close working relationship with Hassan el Hodeiby. Upon his removal he was placed under house arrest; the Regency Council was thus reduced to a single man, the affable Prince Mohamed Abdul Moneim.

The Military Takes Over

With some of the more formidable organized opposition thus eliminated, the regime felt ready to lay the groundwork for a new political structure. Ali Maher, still on friendly terms with General Naguib, publicly announced, on November 15, what many believed to be the political beliefs of the Free Officers' junta. He declared that

the Constitution must be modern. The present Constitution does not meet the needs of a free and developed democracy because it was based on nineteenth-century principles of democracy. Parliament must actually represent all sections of the nation, political and economic, workers and technicians. It must be a living mirror of the nation. The major outlines for this project must be submitted to a Constituent Assembly or to a National Congress, so that the people may make its choice.

While the press carried reports of army efforts to form an "organization of liberation youth" (thought by some to be a new political party), continued publicity was given to the need for a "truly sound Constitution".

Ahmed Abdul Fath, the Wafdist editor of *Al Misri*, was not alone when he declared that "the people are looking forward to the day when they will be able to enjoy the freedom of speech and the freedom of assembly, as well as all other basic rights". But by the time Naguib announced, on December 10, that the Constitution had been abrogated and authority had passed to a "transitional government", a majority of the population was conditioned to accept this *fait accompli*.

Through December and much of January, the drive against existing political parties continued. A government decree, retroactive to 1939, barred all persons convicted of corruption or abuse of power from political activity and public office. Still another court, consisting primarily of army officers, was established to try cases of corruption, and a number of former ministers, including Wafdist Fuad Serag el Din, were indicted. Then, shortly after a fifty-man constitutional committee was set up under Ali Maher's direction, twenty-five officers, the most prominent being Colonel Mohanna, were arrested on charges of conspiring to overthrow the government; Colonel Nasser, then acting Army Chief of Staff, also announced that fifteen civilians had been taken into custody and that the arrest of every known Communist was planned. These arrests preceded Naguib's announcement that there would be a "transitional period" of three years before constitutional government would be resumed. Moreover, the Cabinet decreed a ban on all political parties and authorized the seizure of party funds. And so, on the six-month commemoration of the coup, with the announcement of the formation of a "Liberation Front" to replace the dissolved political parties, military dictatorship was a fact. The authority of government was transferred to a newly created Revolutionary Command Council (RCC), composed entirely of Free Officers' executive council members.

Thus, a small band of officers, who had initiated a modest *coup d'état* with no professed desire to govern, had become, within the brief period of six months, rulers of their country. A historian, looking back upon this turbulent period, will find cause to indict Nasser and his group: their systematic elimination of political opposition and their abandonment of principles which they had held aloft in the battle against the "old order". But in fairness to these young insurgents, one cannot escape the conclusion that their hand, at least in part, was forced by circumstances. Dedicated nationalists, and imbued with a devotion and honesty rare in Egyptian public life, they entered the political arena with the naïve preconception that a simple change at the top could halt the deterioration of Egypt's national life. This attitude was natural in men whose military careers had kept them relatively removed from the miasma of Egyptian politics. Once they came face to face with the corruption and irresponsibility of the "old order", the conclusion became inevitable: the implementation of reforms could not be entrusted to the old politicians with their vested interests and their cynical disdain for the public good. A new system had to be wrought.

The efforts at reform were praiseworthy. Inheriting a nation close to bankruptcy, the new Cabinet bravely introduced an austerity budget which was not expected to gain favour with many civil servants and local businessmen. Furthermore, the reduction of rents and food prices, the introduction of minimum agricultural wages, the establishment of "anti-corruption courts", the enactment of a land reform programme, the drafting of new labour laws, the introduction of more progressive taxes, and a host of other measures all reflected the spirit of the military group.

By January, 1953, what had begun as a coup turned into a revolution. No longer was the old political system to be tolerated; no longer would the traditional social and economic structure remain intact. The Revolutionary Command Council, rapidly consolidating its power, pressed the Revolution which had begun to take form during the preceding months. Perhaps some of the Free Officers still remembered the aims which had been expressed in their pamphlet of March, 1952, entitled *Down With Martial Law*:

1. The abolition of martial law.
2. The lifting of censorship.
3. The shattering of the political police.
4. The release of political detainees.
5. Amnesty for political prisoners.
6. The abrogation of all previous reactionary laws.
7. The restoration of the Constitution.

But what had become of these lofty goals? Martial law, in January, 1953, was still in force. The press already had threatened to strike over local censorship. Sections of the old political police had been disbanded—only to be replaced by army personnel. Many political victims of the old regime had been released from prison—only to be replaced by new detainees, arrested in January "for the security of the State". The Constitution had been abrogated. Political freedom was sacrificed as the RCC undertook the reconstruction of Egypt.

The first phase of the Revolution had been easy, perhaps deceptively so. The Free Officers, by virtue of their physical control of the government, were able to split, isolate, and contain their immediate opposition. Their success, however, was due largely to the apathy and submissiveness of the Egyptian people. Egyptians traditionally have been accustomed to domination. But there is also a deep-rooted passive resistance among Egyptians against any authority beyond that of the family or the local village. This refusal to cooperate with the central government had plagued Cairene rulers for many centuries. Destroying the "old order" by degrading leading political figures, by confiscating party funds, and by redistributing existing wealth was one thing; creating a viable alternative system was quite another. The RCC was determined to initiate a political revolution which, by necessity, also entailed an economic and social transformation of the first magnitude.

The new "Liberation Rally", headed by Colonel Nasser, was expected to provide the new regime with popular support. Nasser, by recruiting Abdel Latif Boghdadi as Comptroller-General, Major Ahmed Tahawy as Deputy Secretary-General, and Major Ahmed Abdullah Toiema as Deputy Secretary-General in charge of Labour Affairs, and by appointing other officers like Major Wahid Ramadan and Captain Adel Tahir to manage the Rally's youth activities and its para-military formations, sought to create a Falange-type organization whose loyalty to the government would be unquestioned. As Colonel Nasser expressed it:

Liberation Rally is not a political party and was never intended to be. The creation was prompted by the desire to establish a body that would organize the people's forces and overhaul the social set-up. The Liberation Rally is the school where the people will be taught how to elect their representatives properly.

It was apparent that the Liberation Rally would wean few members from the old political organizations. Since the Rally was determined to create a new political base, it decided to cast its appeals to labour and the youth. Ever since the Kafr el Dawar incident, the military had consciously wooed the working classes. Although legislation was passed which for all practical purposes outlawed strikes, efforts were made to expand trade unionism, and a new conciliation and arbitration law was enacted. Certain key union leaders were allegedly placed on the government payroll. The other target group, the youth, was more difficult to control, for the universities traditionally had been arenas for paid political agents; moreover, the Moslem Brethren had unusually strong support among Cairo's students. Brethren members had explicit orders to infiltrate the Rally and, as Major Toiema later observed, it was the Brethren members who were most anxious to receive para-military training.

The government had become an unwieldy mechanism for policy implementation. Final authority rested in the RCC, which scheduled weekly joint sessions with the civilian Cabinet headed by General Naguib. The RCC, however, exercised little executive control since, except for Naguib, none of its members occupied official administrative posts. Moreover, RCC decisions were determined by majority vote, each officer, including Naguib, casting but a single ballot. Understandably, some of the members deemed this system burdensome; and Naguib himself felt bridled by the equal votes of his young, often unknown, colleagues. It is surprising, indeed, that decisive action resulted from such an awkward arrangement; and as operational decisions became more pressing, the group appointed a vice-chairman, Colonel Nasser.

The political climate during the spring of 1953 was calm. Colonel Mohanna and a number of other officers, arrested on the eve of the start of the "transitional period", were tried before a Revolutionary Tribunal headed by Nasser and including eight other RCC members. After a trial in which the defendants were not permitted counsel, all the accused were found guilty, with some sentenced to life imprisonment. Later, still another committee was established, this time composed of Minister Fathy Radwan and RCC representative Sadat, charged with screening defendants for yet another "treachery court"; public accusations were directed against Mustapha Nahas' wife and against Fuad Serag el Din of the Wafd, who already had been arrested on three previous occasions. In June the Palestinian "arms scandal case" came to a surprising end. Since Naguib and his associates long had claimed that defective arms were mainly responsible for the army's poor performance in Palestine, it was generally expected that scapegoats would be produced from ex-King Farouk's entourage. Instead, eleven of the thirteen defendants, including Prince Abbas Halim, second cousin to Farouk, were acquitted; the other two were let off with fines.

Beginning in early 1953, the rumour was current in Cairo that the RCC, with Ali Maher's hearty approval, had decided to proclaim Egypt a republic, and that Nasser, now recognized by many as the *primum mobile* of the Free Officers, would supplant Naguib as premier. The General was scheduled for elevation to a new position of president. Indeed, this had been the plan, but Naguib strongly protested the proposed change. Naguib's objection confronted the other RCC members with a difficult decision. While the younger officers had remained in the background, Naguib had become the popular figure of the Free Officers movement. His humble manner, the cheap cigarette tobacco in his musty pipe, his simple honesty—these had become the symbol of the Revolution, and he its only personality. The Free Officers, having created the image of Naguib the leader, found it impolitic to deny his wishes.

On June 18, 1953, the Republic was proclaimed, with Mohammed Naguib as its first President. Since Naguib also retained the Premiership, Nasser was sworn in as Deputy Premier and Minister of the Interior; Wing Commander Abdel Latif Boghdadi became Minister of War and Marine; Major Abdel Hakim Amer, close friend of Nasser and once director of Naguib's office, was promoted to Major General for his new job as military Commander-in-Chief; and Major Salah Salem assumed office as Minister of National Guidance and Minister of State for Sudanese Affairs. These changes were significant, for they drastically reduced what civilian participation there had been in the government. Nearly all of the key posts were now held by officers. The only critical ministry not headed or staffed by officers was that of Finance, for the Free Officers still felt incapable of coping with the intricacies of economics. . . .

14. The Egyptian revolution

GAMEL ABDUL NASSER *Egypt's Revolution, the philosophy of the Revolution* Government Printing Offices, Cairo 1958; pages 26–30

. . . Was it incumbent upon us—the Army—to undertake what we carried out on July 23rd?

The answer to this question was definitely in the affirmative. It was inevitable. There was no escaping it.

Indeed, I can now say that we are going through two revolutions, not one.

Every people on earth go through two revolutions—a political revolution that helps them recover their right to self-government from the hands of a despot who had imposed himself upon them, or free themselves from the domination of alien armed forces which had installed themselves in the land against their will; and a social revolution—a class conflict that ultimately ends in the realisation of social justices for all the inhabitants of the country.

People who preceded us on the path of human progress have all passed through those two revolutions, but not simultaneously. In certain cases, centuries have separated the one from the other. In our case, we are passing through the gruelling ordeal of experiencing the two revolutions together.

This gruelling ordeal, this acid test, lies in the fact that each of these two revolutions has peculiar circumstances which are strangely conflicting and highly contradictory.

Unity, solidarity and co-operation of all elements of the nation, and self-denial and self-sacrifice on the part of the individual to ensure the safety, prosperity and integrity of the Mother-country are the fundamental factors for the success of a Political Revolution.

The disintegration of values, disruption of principles, dissension and discord among both classes and individuals, and the domination of corruption, suspicion, perversion of egoism form the foundation of a social upheaval.

And between these two millstones we find ourselves today destined to go through two revolutions—one calling for unity, solidarity, self-sacrifice and devotion to sacred duty, while the other imposes upon us, against our will, disunity, dissension and nothing else but envy, hatred, vindictiveness and egoism.

Between these two millstones, to cite a case in point, the 1919 Revolution failed to reach the results it ought to have realised. Hardly had the ranks designed to meet oppression been formed before they dispersed to fall out and engage in nothing else but strife, fighting among themselves, classes and individuals.

Ignominious failure was the result—the oppressors tightened the screw, whether through the Occupation Forces or through their tools and instruments who were then led by Sultan Fuad and later by Farouk, his son. All that the people reaped was distrust, doubt, dissension, hatred, rancour and strife among themselves, both classes and individuals.

Thus faded the hope that was expected to be realised by the 1919 Revolution.

I said the hope faded. I did not say the hope disappeared, because the natural forces of resistance driven by the People's great hopes were still active and getting ready for yet another trial.

Such was the situation that prevailed after 1919—a situation which made it imperative for the Army to be the only force capable of any action.

In fact, the situation demanded a force concentrated within a framework that separates its members to a certain extent from the continual conflict between individuals and classes, a force drawn from the very heart of the people whose members can trust one another and have full confidence in themselves, a force so equipped as to be capable of a swift and decisive action, and these conditions only prevailed in the Army.

Thus it was not the Army, as I said before, that determined the role it was to play in the course of events. The reverse was nearer to the truth. It was the events and their development that determined the Army's part in the supreme struggle for the liberation of the Homeland.

I realised from the outset that our success depended on our

complete understanding of the nature of the circumstances in which we live in the present phase of our country's history. We could not with a mere stroke of the pen change these circumstances. We could not put back or forward the hands of the clock, and be masters of time. We also could not act the part of a traffic officer on the road of History, holding up the passage of one revolution to allow another revolution to pass through, and thus avert a collision. All that we could do was to act as best we could to escape being crushed between two millstones.

There was no alternative to carrying out the two revolutions together.

In fact, the day we proceeded on the road to the political revolution and dethroned Farouk, we took a similar step on the road to the social revolution and limited the ownership of land.

I still believe that the July 23 Revolution should continue to retain the initiative and its ability of rapid movement so that it would be able to accomplish the miracle of carrying out the two revolutions simultaneously, no matter how contradictory our action may seem at times.

Once a friend of mine remarked: "How is it that you ask for unity to face the British, yet allow the Graft Courts to continue functioning at the same time?"

I listened to him with the thought of our great millstones crisis predominant in my mind.

One revolution demanding that we should stand united and forget the past.

And another revolution demanding that we should restore the lost dignity of moral values, and not to forget the past.

Yet I did not tell that friend that our only way to safety was to retain, as I said before, the initiative and our ability of rapid movement, together with the ability of simultaneously following two roads.

This was not my will, nor was it the will of those who took part in the July 23 Revolution. It was the will of Fate, the will of our people's history and the stage through which they are passing today.

IV. MODERN ETHIOPIA

15. The Italian dispute

ARNOLD TOYNBEE *R.I.I.A. Survey of International Affairs 1935*
Oxford University Press for Royal Institute of International
Affairs 1936; pages 8–16

(a) Introductory Note

... The narrative can be divided into several distinct chapters:
the five years of relative quiescence which came to an end when
the Walwal incident occurred on the 5th December, 1934; the
history of the Walwal incident itself and the long ensuing
controversy which ended in a settlement that was as fruitless
as it was unexpected; the history of the military operations
which were precipitated by the Italian army's invasion of
Abyssinia on the 3rd October, 1935, without declaration of
war; and the history of the action taken by the Council and
Assembly of the League of Nations and by the states members
acting both jointly and severally in fulfilment of their obligations under the Covenant. As the Italo-Abyssinian conflict thus
becomes the focus of the international relations of the greater
part of the World, the bulk of the events to be recorded swells
to such dimensions as to leave no space in this volume for
recapitulating the historical antecedents of the crisis on a corresponding scale; and the reader must therefore be referred to the
retrospect—inadequate though this is—that has been given in
previous volumes. On the other hand, the events that are the
subject of this volume can hardly be made comprehensible
without a preliminary survey of the motives and the attitudes
of the *dramatis personae*—a cast which came to embrace a
majority of the principal Governments, nations, churches and
races of the World.

By the January of 1936 ... the war in East Africa had already
become a burning question everywhere. It was being discussed
by illiterate Negro villagers on the Gold Coast as eagerly as it
was being debated in the press and in the parliaments and on
the wireless of the great cities of the White Man's World. It had
already produced inter-racial disturbances, west of the Atlantic,
in the West Indian Island of St. Vincent and in Harlem, the

Negro quarter of New York. It had brought about the fall of a British Secretary of State for Foreign Affairs, and had had much to do with the subsequent fall of a French Prime Minister. It had made what might prove to be a permanent impress on the foreign policy of the United States, as well as on that of the United Kingdom and France. And it had precipitated a stubborn contest of wills over the question of whether the legally declared aggressor was to be further restrained from his transgression against the Covenant by the imposition of an 'oil sanction'—a now universally current term of public controversy which would have been quite unintelligible to all but a handful of experts even as lately as a few months back.

The situation thus created was shot through with paradoxes. The country which was now the hub of the wheel of world affairs was one of the most backward—and hitherto the most obscure—of the existing sixty or seventy fully self-governing states among which the living generation of Mankind was partitioned at this moment. The Amharic-speaking masters of this Empire of Ethiopia were being vilified by their Italian assailants, in one and the same breath, as Negroes and as the alien oppressors of Negro victims; and both these at first sight contradictory grounds of vituperation had a certain plausibility, since the Amharas were a people of Semitic speech and of Arabian origin who in the course of some two thousand years had imposed themselves as conquerors upon an African Hamite and Negro population and in the process had acquired a potent and perhaps predominant strain of native African blood. At the same time these unwarrantably race-proud Amharas, who believed that their earliest dynasty was descended from Solomon, and who styled their reigning emperor 'the Lion of the Tribe of Judah', were being hailed as champions of the Black Race by the Negroes of the Old World and the New beyond the Ethiopian frontiers; while simultaneously the international crime which was being committed against Abyssinia by one of the White nations of Western Christendom whose leader was posing as the liberator of the Negus's oppressed Negro subjects, was being taken by other White Men—and this not only in Europe, but also in Russia and in North America and in the Antipodes—as a test case of the ability of a Westernized (and to that extent a White

Man's) World to substitute the rule of law and justice for the inherited social and moral chaos of its international relations.

In attempting to comprehend this agitated and complicated scene we shall perhaps do well to take a bird's-eye view of the motives and attitudes of the principal actors before we immerse ourselves in the turbid stream of events; and, in making this preliminary survey, we will follow the natural course of beginning with the two protagonists.

(b) The Abyssinian Standpoint

The dominant feeling in the hearts of the Abyssinians, as they awaited and eventually met the Italian assault in the year 1935, is expressed in two sentences which the Emperor Haile Selassie had addressed nine years back, when he was serving as Regent of the Empire, to the Governments of Abyssinia's fellow states members of the League of Nations.

Throughout their history [the people of Abyssinia] have seldom met with foreigners who did not desire to possess themselves of Abyssinian territory and to destroy their independence. With God's help, and thanks to the courage of our soldiers, we have always, come what might, stood proud and free upon our native mountains.[1]

Both the indictment and the claim that are made in this passage are justified by the facts of the history of Abyssinia, which in this aspect displays a close resemblance to the history of Japan.[2] The successive Muslim and Frankish attacks upon Abyssinian independence had been repelled as valiantly and as victoriously as the successive Mongol and Frankish attacks upon Japanese independence;[3] and the living memory of these past achievements had inspired the Amharas, like the Japanese, with a national pride and self-confidence which caused both peoples to reject resentfully the role of 'natives' for which their European and American visitors would have liked to cast them.

[1] Circular note of the 19th June, 1926, addressed by Ras Tafari Makonnen (as he then was) to the states members of the League. The passage has been quoted already in the Survey for 1929, p. 209.

[2] The parallel has been drawn in the Survey for 1929, p. 210.

[3] The first Frankish threat to Abyssinian and to Japanese independence came from the same quarter at the same date. In the latter part of the sixteenth and the early part of the seventeenth century of the Christian Era, both Abyssinia and Japan nearly fell under the dominion of the Portuguese.

In the year 1935 the social order in the Empire of Ethiopia was still feudal, and the proneness of a feudal society to sedition and civil war was a factor of which the Italians were not slow to take advantage. Moreover, Abyssinia was grievously handi-capped by a division against herself of which the Emperor Haile Selassie was perhaps more acutely conscious than were his Italian adversaries. This was not the division between Christians and Muslims or between Amharas and non-Amharas or between overlord and vassals, but the division between a progressive minority, with the Emperor at its head, and a reactionary majority which included most of the Rases.[1]

This slowness of the majority of the Abyssinians to realize, and conform to, the necessities of the times gives the measure of their backwardness in culture by comparison with their Japanese contemporaries. In Japan the lesson taught by Commodore Perry's forcible entry into Yedo Bay in 1853 and by the bombardment of the Shimonoseki forts by an inter-national squadron in 1863 was learnt so promptly and so thoroughly that all but a fraction of the feudal nobility and their retainers had voluntarily renounced their ancient privileges as early as 1868 in order to clear the ground for a reconstruction of Japanese society on a basis on which Japan would be competent to hold her own in an irretrievably Westernized World. In that very year 1868 the Abyssinians had been given just such a lesson in the shape of Lord Napier's victorious march to Magdala and unscathed return to the coast; and this lesson had been driven home, between 1882 and 1896, by the first Italian attempt to conquer the country. Yet, sixty-seven years after Napier's ominous passage, an enlightened Emperor, supported by a tiny band of Western-educated young men, was still struggling to impress the necessity for a radical reform of Abyssinian life upon a feudal nobility which was still apparently blind to the urgency of the Emperor's programme. The Amharas' pride in their glorious military history ought to have been tempered by the recollection that on two occasions already—in the sixteenth century and in the nineteenth—their forefathers' valour had not availed to save them from all but succumbing to enemies armed with new-

[1] i.e. feudal lords: literally 'heads'.

fangled products of the Frankish genius for lethal blacksmith's work. In the sixteenth century Abyssinia had been overrun by a handful of 'Osmanli matchlockmen and in the nineteenth century by a handful of Italian riflemen; and on each occasion the Lion of the Tribe of Judah had only been saved because, in the nick of time, a supply of the new weapons had been thrust into his hand by a friend in need—a Portuguese friend in the one case and a French friend in the other. This history of unearned good fortune could not be expected to continue to repeat itself—especially after the 7th January, 1935, when, for European reasons, Abyssinia's French patron had gone over to the Italian side. Ultimately the Abyssinians could only save themselves by Westernizing themselves sufficiently to hold their own in warfare against a Western Power without Western aid; and this would mean Westernizing themselves through and through. The deadly weakness of Abyssinia in her fearful ordeal of A.D. 1935–6 was the failure of the majority of her people to realise this home truth sixty years before. They had allowed two precious generations to pass without waking from their sluggish self-complacency; and in June, 1936—when, after a seven months' war, the Amharas lay prostrate under the nozzle of the Italian invader's gas-sprayer—it seemed possible that the wages of this mortal sin of omission might prove to be nothing less than the capital punishment of losing, not only their dominion over the more backward African peoples around them, but also their own two-thousand-years-old existence as an independent national community.

(c) The Italian Standpoint

It was a combination of a number of different considerations—material and psychological, economic and political—that moved Signor Mussolini to impose on Italy the heavy immediate sacrifices, and the still more formidable risks, that his East African adventure entailed. The most potent of these considerations had nothing to do with Abyssinia or with Italo-Abyssinian relations, but were concerned either with Italy herself or with Italy's relations to the rest of the World.

Italy's economic grievance was closely akin to the economic grievance of Japan, which had been one of the causes of the Japanese militarists' outbreak in the autumn of 1931. Like

Japan, Italy was a country with a dense and rapidly increasing population and with an unusually poor natural endowment of material resources. Only 41·4 per cent. of the total land-surface of Italy was cultivable—even when the cultivated area had been extended to the verge of diminishing returns in the Fascist 'Battle of the Grain'—and a strictly circumscribed agriculture could not be supplemented out of home resources by an extensive manufacturing industry because the subsoil was notably deficient in those minerals, particularly coal and iron ore, which were the indispensable basis of industrial production according to the modern Western technique. During the past half-century, the pressure of Italian population upon Italian means of subsistence had been accentuated by a diminution of the death-rate (through an improvement in public health and also—in the teeth of adverse circumstances—in the standard of living) which outstripped the contemporaneous fall in the birth-rate;[1] and during the post-war years the congestion had been seriously increased owing to the arbitrary restriction of immigration from Europe into the overseas countries of European origin—first and foremost, the United States.[2] The last blow had been the progressive exclusion of Italian exports from the world market under the influence of the wave of economic nationalism that swept over all countries—including the British mother-country of Free Trade—after the onset of the World Economic Crisis since the autumn of 1929. It is true that this economic nationalism was both the faith and the practice of Italy herself, and that Signor Mussolini had retorted to foreign restrictions upon Italian immigration by discouraging Italian emigration, on the ground that Italy's human crop, which was her most precious product, ought not to be exported in order to enrich soils under foreign flags. Yet, since Man—or at any rate *Homo Politicus*—is not a rational animal, the Italian resentment at the economic difficulties that were being placed in Italy's path by the policy of other countries was not diminished by the fact that Italy was all the time doing her

---

[1] The birth-rate had fallen from an average of 36·8 per 1,000 in the years 1872–5 to 23·7 in 1933. There had, however, been a corresponding fall in the death-rate from 30·5 to 13·7 per 1,000.

[2] For the effect of the United States Immigration Restriction Acts of 1921 and 1924 upon Italian life, see the *Survey for 1924*, Part I B, section (ii).

worst to place the same difficulties in the path of her neighbours as far as this lay in her power.

By the beginning of the year 1935 Italy's financial and economic position was undoubtedly serious—partly by reason of Italy's own inherent material weakness; partly by reason of the World Economic Crisis which was afflicting her in common with other countries; and partly in consequence of the measures with which the Fascist régime was attempting to combat both the temporary and the permanent economic evil. The public works of which these measures largely consisted might perhaps have been beneficial in themselves if their value could have been calculated apart from the strain that they imposed upon the general economic stamina of the country; but, on a comprehensively framed account of profit and loss, they were showing themselves to be not worth their price—and this the more so inasmuch as the scale on which these works were being executed was not determined purely by economic calculations, but was largely governed by motives of political prestige, and even personal megalomania, which tended towards a quite uneconomic grandiosity.[1] Yet, in spite of all this—and in spite of the toll that had been taken from Italian prosperity by Italy's belligerency in the General War of 1914–18—the standard of living of the agricultural and industrial working-class in Italy was distinctly higher in 1935, on the eve of the Italo-Abyssinian War, than it had been in 1870, on the morrow of the completion of the political unification of the peninsula. If they had been content to measure their material prosperity in terms of their own Italian past, the Italians of this generation of 1935 would have had no great cause to complain of the material progress that the Italian people had made over a span of sixty-five years. The actual measure, however, by which the

[1] A monument of this spirit which thrust itself upon the attention of foreign visitors to Italy was the colossal railway station at Milan which was opened in July 1931 to replace an unassuming but serviceable predecessor. A visitor who was familiar with the United States could hardly fail to receive the impression that in this colossal structure Signor Mussolini was deliberately setting himself to outdo the architects of the Grand Central Station, New York. The same megalomania had shown itself in 1927 in the stabilization of the lira at an excessive value which was manifestly chosen, not on an expert estimate of the lira's natural level, but in order to put the previously stabilized French franc out of countenance.

Italians reckoned at this date was the contemporary prosperity of their non-Italian neighbours of their own status, and here they were setting themselves the highest possible standard; for, in virtue of her political unification, Italy had come to rank as a Great Power. The material resources—in cultivable land and minerals, in raw materials and markets—of the greatest of the Great Powers of the day, the British Empire, the French Republic, the Soviet Union, the United States, thus gave the measure of the material endowment which Fascist Italy demanded for herself as her right.

In stating their demands in these terms, the Italians were pressing beyond the limits of the field of absolute material needs into the vast, and perhaps boundless, domain of relative requirements which might still be material in form (in the shape of territory or of raw materials) but were psychological in essence inasmuch as the craving that chiefly prompted them was a thirst for status and not a hunger for bread.[1] For example, in Article

[1] The writer of this *Survey* does not, of course, mean to imply that the material deficiences under which Italy was labouring were not in fact severe or not severely felt. The depth and the consistency of the Italian feeling on this matter are attested by Signor Tittoni's speech of the 10th November, 1920, at the Eighth Plenary Meeting of the First Assembly of the League of Nations. Fifteen years in advance, Italy's economic case in 1935 had been put by Signor Mussolini's predecessor perhaps as forcibly, and certainly as convincingly, as it could have been put by Signor Mussolini himself. The following extracts may encourage the reader to turn to the original:

'Henceforth, it must be frankly admitted that the existence of nations depends on the solution of the economic question. If the war [of 1914–18] has fulfilled the expectations of those who desired the triumph of liberty and justice in the sphere of politics, it has completely failed to satisfy the expectations of those who desired justice and equality in the sphere of economics. We are bound to admit, as a matter of fact, that the relations existing between states have become more difficult and more acrimonious than was the case before the war. Protectionist barriers have been erected everywhere; export duties and differential duties have been established. I appeal to the states which have had recourse to this system. I say to them that if, up to the present, there has been no actual quarrel between the different states, that is only because there have been no reprisals. If the victims of this system should seek to defend themselves, and resort to the same methods, they would let loose on the World an economic war: and, if that should happen, how could you hope to preserve peace?

'I desire to draw the attention of the Assembly to the gravity of this question, for these are undeniably very weighty and very serious matters,

13 of the quadripartite London Treaty of the 26th April, 1915, in virtue of which Italy had intervened in the General War of 1914–18, the Italian Government had stipulated for some 'equitable' compensation in the event of France and Great Britain increasing their colonial territories in Africa at the expense of Germany,[1] and though 'equitable' was not synonymous with 'equal' (as British and French statesmen were quick to point out), the word did carry the implication that Italy, as a member of the privileged order of Great Powers, had a right to that ownership of colonies which was one of the hallmarks of her older and more fortunate peers.

involving interests of the highest importance, which cannot be settled perfunctorily, and with regard to which I have no easy solution to offer.

'To those privileged states which enjoy a monopoly with regard to raw materials, and to those whose wealth has permitted them to acquire a monopoly of these materials outside their boundaries, I say: Do not wait to be appealed to by the poorer states which are at the mercy of your economic policy, but come forward spontaneously and declare to this Assembly that you renounce all selfish aims, and before the bar of the League of Nations declare yourselves ready to support the cause of international solidarity.'

It is significant that this appeal of Signor Tittoni's was evoked by a foregoing speech from the representative of Canada, in which Mr Rowell had contended that the economic functions of the League were of secondary importance, and that, in general, economic matters were domestic questions. 'I think it is unfortunate', Mr Rowell had observed in this context, 'to throw out to this Assembly and to the public any proposal to the effect that the Covenant of the League covers the question of raw materials.'

[1] See the *Survey for 1920–23*, pp. 360–1, and the *Survey for 1924*, pp. 463–70. The text of Article 13 of the Treaty of the 26th April, 1915, ran as follows:

'Dans le cas où la France et la Grande-Bretagne augmenteraient leurs domaines coloniaux d'Afrique aux dépens de l'Allemagne, ces deux Puissances reconnaissent en principe que l'Italie pourrait réclamer quelques compensations équitables, notamment dans le règlement en sa faveur des questions concernant les frontières des colonies italiennes de l'Érythrée, de la Somalie et de la Lybie et des colonies voisines de la France et de la Grande-Bretagne.'

The Foreign Office in Whitehall appears to have taken the view that the meaning of the word 'équitables' in this article was defined—and limited— by the concluding phrases beginning with the word 'notamment'. On this interpretation, Italy's claim under the article amounted to no more than a right to demand a rectification, in her favour, of the frontiers of her African possessions where these marched with those of Great Britain and France; and she was not entitled to demand compensations proportionate in extent to the British and French acquisitions at Germany's expense.

The feeling that Italy had received unduly short measure in the distribution of colonial assets, owing to the unfortunate accident of the lateness of her entry into the goodly company of imperialists, was a powerful political driving force in Italian souls; and this grievance over a question of status—or pique of *amour propre*—was not only distinct from, but was also not necessarily related with, any absolute material Italian need of colonies as outlets for population or as sources of supply for raw materials or as markets for exports. In the colonial field Italy had been ambitious to emulate the past achievements of England and France, ever since the completion of the political unification of Italy herself in 1870. And Signor Mussolini was undoubtedly expressing sentiments that a majority of the Italian people heard with approval from the lips of a national leader when he declared to a sympathetically Fascist-minded French journalist in the summer of 1935:

I think for Italy as the Great Englishmen who have made the British Empire have thought for England, as the great French colonisers have thought for France.[1]

Evidently it did not occur to Signor Mussolini that, in his own day, this kind of thinking might have become an anachronism, and that on this account his own, and his Italy's, misfortune of having been born too late might in fact be irreparable. . . .

16. The intractable frontier

J. DRYSDALE *The Somali Dispute* Pall Mall and Praeger 1964; pages 88–92, 95–9

For the first half of Somalia's ten-year period of trusteeship under Italian administration, the United Nations urged at each session that the Ethiopian and Italian governments should speedily resolve their dispute over Somalia's frontier with Ethiopia. This frontier, it will be recalled, was traced on

[1] Interview given by Signor Mussolini to Monsieur de Kerillis of the *Echo de Paris*, quoted in *The Times*, 1st August, 1935.

two maps in 1897 by Major Nerazzini and King Menelik. Neither map could subsequently be found and no living person can testify to the exact nature of the agreement. Today, the border is still undefined, still disputed, and this sector of the frontier between the Somali Republic and Ethiopia, though provisionally drawn, has no legal basis.

The background to this dispute is that in 1908 a convention was drawn up between Italy and Ethiopia "for the settlement of the Frontier between the Italian Possessions of Somalia and the Provinces of the Ethiopian Empire". The first three articles of the convention describe the border from Dolo to the Shibeli river (Map 2) as a line drawn between various Somali clans, some of whom are dependent on Ethiopia and others are dependent on Italy. Article 4 states that from the Shibeli river "the frontier proceeds in a north-easterly direction, following the line accepted by the Italian government in 1897, all the territory belonging to the tribes towards the coast shall remain dependent on Italy; all the territory of the Ogaden, and all that of the tribes towards the Ogaden, shall remain dependent on Abyssinia." The two governments undertook, in Article 5, to delimit the border on the ground. We have seen what took place thereafter.

When Somalia became a Trust Territory in 1950, the Trusteeship Agreement stipulated that the boundary in question "shall be those fixed by international agreements and, in so far as they are not already delimited, shall be delimited in accordance with a procedure approved by the General Assembly".

In order to resolve any differences arising in the course of such negotiations, the respective parties were urged to agree, at the request of either party, "to a procedure of mediation by a U.N. mediator to be appointed by the Secretary-General and, further, in the event of the inability of the parties to accept the recommendations of the mediator, to a procedure of arbitration".

A limit of ten years had been imposed for the duration of the trusteeship, and a speedy settlement of this dispute was clearly in everyone's interests. It was not, however, until 1955 that a real start to negotiations between Italy and Ethiopia began, but the impetus soon flagged when the Ethiopian government declined to permit Somalis to join the Italian delegation as experts. A Somali spokesman told the United Nations Fourth Committee in November 1955 that "agreements made between alien powers without the consent . . . of the inhabitants are unacceptable to us". Ethiopia subsequently agreed to the inclusion of Somali experts but objected to the possibility of mediation.

As A. A. Castagno has observed, "the arbitral technique is favoured by Ethiopia because it contends that the dispute is restricted to different interpretations of the 1908 Convention". The Somalis wanted the more flexible technique of mediation. A further problem was posed, in the words of an Ethiopian review, "by the revival of an old Italian claim, that has been advanced, in exactly the same words, by the government of Fascist Italy in its dispute with Ethiopia at the League of Nations in regard to this territory. This sought to establish that the boundary should be determined primarily in accordance with the principles of *de facto* occupation prior to the year 1935 . . . and only secondarily on the basis of the Convention of 1908". But this stand, according to another official Ethiopian narrative, was "completely abandoned in the course of the discussions and Italy further recognised the obvious truth that agreements concluded by Italy with a third state (U.K) were without legal validity as regards Ethiopia".

Again, according to an official Ethiopian account, both parties agreed to adopt the principles that the 1908 Convention should be the "sole criterion" for the delimitation of the boundary; that no third party agreements should apply; that the interpretation of the words of the convention should first be agreed upon before delimitation on the ground; that this interpretation should be reached through a juridical process; that no compromise was possible on juridical principles; that the interpretation should relate to the situation prevailing in 1908 and to the intentions of the negotiators of the convention; and finally that their respective juridical positions were capable of dealing with the problem.

To avoid lengthy negotiations, the Ethiopian government proposed a compromise. She would accept the existing provisional boundary and thereby renounce "more than 47,000 square kilometres of territory to which she was entitled on the

basis of the Convention of 1908". The Italian delegation rejected this on legal grounds and because it "did not meet the needs
of the local population".

Both parties then offered their respective views on the crucial
phrase in the 1908 Convention: *starting from the Webi-Shebeli
the frontier proceeds to the north-east, following the line accepted in 1897
by the Italian Government.* The Italians considered that the line
followed the coast at a distance of 180 miles to meet the
Protectorate border at the 47° meridian. Their evidence was
drawn from four main sources: the report referring to the 180-
mile limit which Major Nerazzini made to his government on
his return to Italy after concluding the 1897 agreement with
Menelik; the news-agency report on August 9, 1897, also
referring to a delimitation of 180 miles from the coast; a
telegram from the Italian government to Menelik accepting the
line agreed upon by Nerazzini; and an Ethiopian memorandum
submitted to the League of Nations in 1934 which referred to a
line of delimitation "which runs at a distance of 180 miles
parallel to the coast of the Indian Ocean".

For their part, the Ethiopian government contended that
the line in question was far nearer to the sea. Supporting
evidence consisted of nine maps published mainly in Italy
between 1912–35, all of which showed the frontier to be east
of the 47° meridian. Ethiopia also attached much importance
to a statement by the Italian Foreign Minister on June 16,
1908, in which he said that sovereignty over the "territory
bounded by the Lugh and Bardera lines" remained with
Ethiopia, but during the 1908 negotiations an area of about
50,000 sq. km. was purchased from the Emperor for three
million lire, pushing the border northwards to Dolo. Thus it was
before 1908 that the southern part of the frontier, at any rate,
had characteristics in common with Ethiopia's present interpretation of the boundary. Evidence from other sources
included a British map, and others reproduced in Italian
publications, particularly in Caroselli's *Ferro e Fuoco in Somalia*
which, unlike the other maps, deliberately set out to interpret
the Nerazzini line. This work carried authority because of a
preface by General de Bono, formerly an Italian Minister for
the Colonies.

As Y. Jame observes, of all the maps only one was prepared

originally for the purpose of identifying the elusive boundary: that of Caroselli, which supported the 180-mile theory but favoured the tri-junction point on the Protectorate boundary at 48° and not at 47°. The value to the Ethiopian delegation of the other maps was not that they purported to trace the line of the 1897 frontier, but that all boundaries shown met at the 48° tri-junction point on the former British Somaliland border.

The Ethiopian delegates also argued that the Amharic version of Article 1 of the 1908 Convention reads that the frontier "starts from Dolo . . . proceeds eastwards by the sources of the Baideba . . .", and that Baideba is the same as Iscia Baidoa. The Italians claimed that Maidaba and not Baideba was meant and that the southern sector of the present provisional line is substantially in accord with this view.

In December 1957 both parties reported to the General Assembly that direct negotiations had failed and the Italian delegation proposed that the two parties should proceed to mediation. Ethiopia favoured immediate arbitration and the Assembly approved this course on the grounds that "a final settlement can be achieved more expeditiously by a procedure of arbitration". The arbitral tribunal, by a resolution the previous year, was to consist of three jurists, one to be appointed by Ethiopia, one by Italy and the third by agreement between the jurists so appointed. Failing agreement, the third jurist was to be appointed by the King of Norway. The tribunal would delimit the frontier in accordance with terms of reference to be decided upon by the two governments, with the assistance, if necessary, of an 'independent person' mutually acceptable to both parties.

In August 1958 the tribunal was formed with Dr Bolla, former President of the Swiss Federal Court; Professor Radojkovic, Dean of the Faculty of Law and Professor of International Law at Belgrade University. Professor Castren, Professor of International Law at Helsinki University, was nominated as the third jurist by the two arbitrators. Ethiopia and Italy, meanwhile, attempted to reach agreement on the terms of reference for the tribunal. They were unable to agree on an 'independent person' to assist them with the framing of the terms of reference, but nevertheless they were still able to exchange draft *compromis*.

The focal point of the dispute over the terms of reference was Italy's departure from the previously agreed basis for negotiation. According to the Ethiopian government, the Italian delegation did not consider that the basis arrived at during the early stages in negotiation was necessarily relevant to arbitration and that there could be other applicable agreements concerning this territory. Italy wished the tribunal "to give its decision on the basis of all the international conventions relating thereto and of the interests and well-being of the populations, in harmony with the principles of the United Nations".

Ethiopia objected to these proposals. She maintained, as she had done during the earlier negotiations, that the arbitration tribunal should confine itself strictly to an interpretation of the 1908 Convention only and that "no other issues or questions for decision . . . may be proposed . . .". Evidence of facts which existed on or before May 16, 1908, could be brought before the tribunal, but facts subsequent to this date were only relevant if they assisted in clarifying facts which existed before that date. Political factors occurring after 1908 and all questions relating to the well-being of the inhabitants concerned were excluded from the purview of the tribunal. Neither third parties nor representatives of other governments or organisations could appear before the tribunal. A number of escape clauses were also included. For example, differences which may have arisen out of an interpretation of the terms of reference were to be settled by the parties to the dispute, and not by the tribunal, likewise any differences arising out of an interpretation of the tribunal's award. Moreover, this award would only be binding after the frontier had been delimited by both parties and duly ratified in the appropriate legislatures. This last provision was presumably inserted to ensure that the future Somali government was also bound by the arbitration award.

The Ethiopian government also objected to Italy's inclusion in her draft *compromis* of "international conventions", other than the 1908 Convention, and of matters relating to "the interests and well-being of the populations, in harmony with the principles of the United Nations". They protested that the agreements referred to in the Italian draft *compromis* "were the imperialist third party agreements, carving that territory into spheres of influence . . .". As for taking into account the interests and well-being of the people, the Ethiopian government made the rejoinder that "Italy apparently persisted in looking upon African territories as subject to a rule of colonial law which can be modified to fit political *desiderata*". Ethiopia also resented the inclusion of non-legal concepts, such as those of the "interests (undefined of course) and welfare (undefined of course) of the populations, in harmony with the principles of the United Nations"; and added that "it is apparent that the principles of the Charter have no conceivable application to the precise problems of delimitation which alone are involved . . .". She maintained that Italy's attitude was designed only to delay a solution to the problem.

As the two parties failed to agree on an "independent person" to assist with the resolution of the terms of reference for the arbitration commission, the King of Norway, in accordance with a resolution of the General Assembly, appointed Mr Trygve Lie, the former United Nations Secretary-General, to undertake this task in August 1959, ten months before Somalia's independence.

In their submissions to Mr Trygve Lie, the Ethiopian government held to their former draft *compromis*, but the Italian delegation submitted a new draft "based on the general principles and model rules on arbitration adopted by the General Assembly at the thirteenth session". The Italians insisted that the tribunal should not only examine relevant international instruments but should rule as to the admissibility of evidence and as to the probatory value of same. Moreover, legal effect should be given to the arbitration award, as soon as it was announced, and should be binding on both parties without reservation. Ethiopia rejected the Italian draft *compromis* for three reasons: it ignored the agreement reached by both parties during preliminary negotiations; it required the tribunal to consider international agreements concluded with third parties; it would empower the tribunal to consider the well-being of the inhabitants as if there had never been a frontier agreement and "as if the tribunal was a legislator".

Mr Trygve Lie's proposals threaded their way through both points of view. Ethiopia offered twenty-one amendments to these proposals, of which Italy accepted six (three with reservations), but rejected the remainder. Italy offered ten amendments to the draft but there is no record of Ethiopia's comment on these amendments. At that point the arbitration came to an end; and at the fourteenth session of the United Nations General Assembly, the last session before Somalia's independence on July 1, 1960, no resolution was passed as the Fourth Committee was unable to make a recommendation. Thus Somalia moved into independence with five hundred miles of frontier undelimited and hotly disputed.

Without entering into the relative merits of the positions taken up by the Ethiopian and Italian delegations during these years of abortive negotiations, some aspects of this dispute are relevant to Ethiopia and to the Somali Republic on whom this legacy had fallen since her accession to independence in 1960. The first question to be answered is whether both countries wish to settle this dispute, and, if so, in what manner?

The Somali Republic claims that all Somalis living on her frontiers are entitled to the right of self-determination; that she would accept the results of a plebiscite, provided it was conducted impartially, and that inter-state boundaries should be delimited accordingly. In other words, the Somali Republic does not wish to conduct negotiations on the basis of ancient treaties or conventions made between colonial powers and Ethiopia. This includes that part of the Republic's border with Ethiopia which was negotiated in 1897 between Rodd and Menelik. This Treaty was not recognised by the Somaliland government when they attained independence on June 26, 1960, in spite of the grazing agreement which forms an integral part of this treaty.

Leaving aside, for a moment, Ethiopia's attitude to the frontier question with the former Trust Territory of Somalia, it will be recalled that the Anglo-Ethiopian agreement of 1954 was abrogated on Somaliland's independence. This reaffirmed the grazing rights of clans from the former Somaliland Protectorate in the Haud and Reserved Area. The grazing rights were entrenched, however, in the 1897 Treaty; but on June 5, 1960, three weeks before Somaliland's independence, it was reported from Addis Ababa that the Ethiopian government had announced that, as from June 26th, it would regard the provisions of the 1954 agreement relating to the grazing rights as automatically invalid. As D. J. Latham Brown points out, however, this announcement in no way calls into question the frontier demarcation of 1897.

There is [he concludes] an implicit distinction in its terms between the frontier provisions and those relating to the grazing rights. Hence it would seem that, in the opinion of the Ethiopian Government, the 1897 frontier delimitation is capable of surviving a succession of states in Somaliland, whereas the grazing rights are not, at least without a fresh agreement between the successor state and Ethiopia.

Ethiopia did, however, modify this attitude in a speech by the Emperor, reported to have been made two days before Somaliland's independence, in which he intimated that, so long as the Somali Republic was willing to accept the 1897 frontier, Ethiopia would continue to allow Somali clans to cross the border and make use of the grazing lands in Ethiopian territory. This uneasy arrangement remains to this day as a permanent source of anxiety to the nomads concerned, who are frequently in armed conflict with Ethiopian authority, and as an acute irritation in relations between the Republic and Ethiopia, to say nothing of the problems of maladministration and injustice which these absurd conditions create. Threats of closing the border are still made by the Ethiopian government, which regards the granting of these facilities as a favour to the Somali Republic. The Ethiopians complain that the Republic sends armed men across the frontier under the guise of nomads. But, as Latham-Brown observes, "if the Ethiopian Government expects to retain the fruits of what some observer might describe as an 'unconscionable bargain' made in 1897, they must be prepared to continue to pay for those fruits".

To return now to the Republic's undefined western border. Ethiopia regards the issue as a simple matter of delimiting the boundary in accordance with her 1908 Treaty with Italy. We have already seen that Ethiopia, in her negotiations with Italy, followed an exclusively juridical approach which discounted the interests and well-being of the inhabitants. There would be some sympathy for this view if the inhabitants concerned were a settled people without common ties across the border, but it scarcely seems an appropriate attitude to adopt in the circumstances of nomadic people. Since neither party appears to have broached the subject yet, it can only be assumed that, for their part, the Ethiopian government, in their official account of *Ethio-Somalia Relations,* are sincere when they state that in regard to "the demarcation of the frontier between the two countries, the Ethiopian Government are ever ready and willing, as in the past, to consider just and honourable proposals for mutual agreement by the two governments concerned". Yet, when such protestations of good will are seen against the background of Ethiopia's uncompromising stand with Italy over the interpretation of the 1908 agreement, which declined to take into account the well-being of the people concerned, it is not perhaps surprising that the Somali government have failed to respond. Moreover, Ethiopia's concern to exclude "imperialist third-party agreements" is absurd and only weakens her case with the Somali Republic. As Castagno observes, "Somalis protest that if this is a valid point, then there is no reason why they should be bound by any agreements at all, since none of them was drafted with Somali consultations." At present the issue lies between the Somali view that a plebiscite should be held, on the basis of self-determination, and the Ethiopian view that the boundary should be delimited according to the 1908 Convention with Italy. If a third factor, oil, should enter into the dispute, the *status quo* is unlikely to be preserved.

But before we leave the Somali Republic's northern frontiers and turn towards Kenya, we should look briefly at another baffling problem: the future of French Somaliland, France's last African possession. Some Frenchmen believe that the economic incentives for a continuing French presence in the territory are so great that a concerted demand for independence among its divided inhabitants is unlikely in the foreseeable future. Whilst it is true that the thirty thousand or so who live in the flourishing little port of Jibuti owe their salary scales (twice those of neighbouring territories) and a high percentage of employment to French capital, management and foresight— the Somali and Danakil inhabitants of this territory are not political freaks, although their political and economic interests often conflict.

Ethiopia is still dependent on her railway link with Jibuti as an outlet for foreign trade, in spite of her newly acquired, and developed, Eritrean ports of Massawa and Assab. She has special facilities in the port of Jibuti and is a major partner in the ownership of the Franco-Ethiopian railway, which, according to reports, is to be extended to the Sidamo Province to the south of Addis Ababa. Clearly, the future status of this little French Protectorate will be influenced largely by the attitude of Ethiopia, for she could exert formidable economic pressure on Somali and Danakil politicians by threatening to switch her trade to Assab.

Yet the Somali Republic is still the focus of much nationalistic feeling, and if the unlikely choice had to be made, without prejudicing economic links with Addis Ababa, it is probable that majority opinion would favour some form of political association with the Somali Republic rather than with Ethiopia. But the more likely course of events is neutrality and independence with close links with France. It is doubtful, though, how long this vulnerable and divisive little country, half-Danaki and half-Somali, could maintain its independent status with acquisitive and rival nations at its gates.

17. The Ethiopian no-party state

ROBERT L. HESS and GERHARD LOEWENBERG *American Political Science Review* Vol. LVIII, No. 4; pages 947–50

The emergence of political parties performing important functions in the political system has characterized the recent history of much of the African continent. The new party systems have taken various forms, including single parties with a narrow ruling elite, as in Liberia, or with mass support, as in Guinea; two-party systems where one mass party is dominant, as is the case in Kenya; and multi-party systems, as in Nigeria and Somalia. In two states, Libya and Sudan, once-flourishing political parties have been banned. Only in Ethiopia (Eritrea excluded) have there never been political parties. The Empire of the Conquering Lion of Judah can well be termed a no-party state. In Ethiopia today no organization exists that would or could describe itself as a political party.

Writing in 1951, Professor Duverger concluded that "a regime without parties is of necessity a conservative regime". That only a handful of partyless political systems remain today is the consequence, apparently, of the rapid pace of political modernization in the past decade. In the "non-Western" world, wherever new states have been created out of former colonial territories, the movement driving for independence has itself provided the nucleus for at least one political party and, sometimes, for more in response to the first. These parties have performed a variety of functions associated with both political and economic modernization: they have provided a communications network transcending parochial boundaries, have helped to organize and express the new interests, have recruited and established the new political elite, and have contributed to the legitimation of the new authorities.

Political parties developed in association with economic and political modernization, not just in Asia and Africa, where parties were formed for the purpose of creating independent states, but also in Latin America, where parties grew in an independent situation. The correlation between political party development and economic modernization is not therefore limited to newly independent Africa. However, the evidence does not point to a general inter-dependence between the two processes. In the earlier "Western" experience, in which there was a relatively slow transition to modern forms, there are notable examples of economic development without political parties. The political systems of the remaining no-party states, especially those showing signs of undergoing economic development, should therefore be viewed with special care by those interested in the relationship between economic and political change. The example of Ethiopia is particularly relevant because it is the case of a state facing the challenges of economic modernization within the framework of a traditional political system.

The absence of political parties from the Ethiopian scene can be explained by the role of the Emperor and the lack of those historical factors that elsewhere stimulated the development of African political parties. Most African political parties arose as the result of the colonial situation; in Ethiopia the "colonial" period lasted only for the brief five years of the Italian military occupation. Elsewhere, economic development in the colonial period provided one of the bases for the educational development of the personnel which later participated in political organizations; in Ethiopia the noticeable lack of economic development until recently may very well have retarded such political development. For reasons of economic underdevelopment, the rise of an African middle class through detribalization is less evident in Ethiopia than elsewhere. Political parties in other countries were aided by the development of a modern communications network by the colonial power; Ethiopia until recently had one of the poorest such systems on the continent, and strict supervision by the Government ensured that it was not used for political purposes. Elsewhere the decline of chiefly power was the result of European intervention, and a new elite, itself the creation of the Europeans, was able to take advantage of the disruption of traditional society to develop as a potential political force; in Ethiopia, however, the destruction of chiefly power came about as the result of the Emperor's consolidation of his own power and his appropriation of the authority of other traditional elements.[1] No potentially independent elite was directly involved in the process, although the Emperor did and does provide for the Western education of a growing number of closely controlled bureaucrats recruited from the traditional aristocracy and from an aristocracy of talented young men from humble origins or from ethnic minorities like the Galla. Finally, in the isolated and conservative Ethiopian social context, remarkably little attention has been paid to Western organizational forms, like the mass party and modern bureaucracy, and, until very recently, to Western ideas like nationalism or democracy, while in other countries these forms and ideas have had a noticeable influence.

The impetus to modernization in Ethiopia has come not from a new elite and its political parties but from the Emperor himself as a result of his contact with Western states over the past forty years and, more recently, from his association with

[1] A distinction should be made between the power of chiefs over clans, tribes, and larger ethnic groups and that of the village head, who has often been erroneously called chief in the literature of African exploration.

the new states of Africa. The emphasis in Ethiopia has therefore been on economic and administrative, but not on political modernization. Through skilful diplomacy Haile Selassie was able, first to preserve Ethiopia's independence except during the short period of Italian domination, and, second, to develop for Ethiopia an important role among the new African states. But these expanded relations with the world outside Ethiopia have brought his country into contact with Western technology, especially in the form of modern weapons, with Western entrepreneurs and technicians—most recently under the auspices of United States economic and military aid programmes—and with Western political ideas and institutions, notably nationalism, law, and bureaucracy. Successes derived from his new international position have strengthened his domestic position, which was strong in any case because of his effective use of traditional myths of the Emperor's legitimacy. Because neither Africanization nor national independence was an issue, he faced no challenge from domestic political movements analogous to those of colonial Africa. His powerful situation permitted him to control the strongest traditional centres of authority, notably the church, the army, and the nobility, by making personal appointments within these institutional groups.

The effective transfer of authority to the Emperor was limited, however, to the regional and national level. It did not extend to the villages, where traditional authority patterns remain intact. It created no new elite structures. It left largely unchanged the linguistic, ethnic, and religious divisions of the nation. The Ethiopian economy remains the least developed in Africa. The five per cent literacy rate is the lowest of any African state, and per capita income is also extremely low. Ninety per cent of the population is still in the subsistence agricultural sector of the economy. The money economy is dependent on monoculture, since coffee accounts for 45 per cent of the total value of exports. The economic development of the nation, which the Emperor seeks to promote through a series of five-year plans, is therefore taking off from a very low base and within a remarkably traditional political and social system. Whatever economic development there is may be attributed to the Emperor's initiative. But in Ethiopia there is a lack of the

PTCA

fervour, excitement, and enthusiasm for economic development
that can be found wherever political parties in Africa have
striven to mobilize the population for economic change.
Although there is a sentimental attachment to the Emperor
in almost all ethnic sections of the country, it is doubtful whether
the central authorities can succeed in winning the support of the
rural population, which is still under the influence of traditional
landlords and village heads. This raises the question of how the
masses can be mobilized for economic change without political
parties. More generally, how can the political functions
nowadays performed by the parties in the process of economic
change be performed by other structures, and with what
consequences?

The absence of political parties and the existence of a traditional pattern of government have not precluded at least some
political change. A new constitution was promulgated by the
Emperor in 1955. While it largely confirmed the concentration
of powers in his hands, it did provide for an elected Chamber
of Deputies in a bicameral Parliament which also included a
Senate whose 101 members are all appointed by the Emperor.

The unusual phenomenon of contested elections in a state
without political parties occurred in Ethiopia in 1957 and again
in 1961. The country was divided into 100 electoral districts of
approximately 200,000 inhabitants on the average. Each
constituency elected two deputies. Those towns with 30,000
or more inhabitants (that is, Addis Ababa and four other
municipalities) were given one representative plus an additional
deputy for each 50,000 inhabitants above the base figure, some
measure of urban over-representation. Under the old constitution there had been only 72 deputies, none of whom had been
popularly elected.

According to the Central Board of Registration and Election,
a government agency, 491 candidates qualified to stand for the
210 seats. Candidacy required wealth of 1000 Ethiopian dollars
and property ownership of twice this amount, total holdings in
U.S. terms of $1200. In a nation then having a per capita in-
come of US $56, the Chamber of Deputies was bound to consist
overwhelmingly of members of the traditional nobility. There is
evidence that many of the candidates were self-nominated
notables who commanded local respect. Others may very well

have been sponsored by the Government. Despite the absence of political parties many individual candidates vigorously campaigned in competition with each other on the basis of their personal records and their positions in local society.

Of the 6,000,000 potential voters who had the necessary property qualifications in the nation of 19,000,000, slightly more than 3,000,000 registered, and apparently 80 per cent of registered voters cast their ballots in 1957. A process of selection in which over three million voters chose 210 deputies from over twice that number of candidates took place again in 1961 and will probably recur in 1965. But the sole function of this elected Parliament has been that of legitimating the Emperor's acts.

A new elite group has not been recruited by elections. Rather it has developed among those members of traditionally privileged classes and among a new aristocracy of talent appointed by the Emperor which is participating in new or reorganized institutions created in the process of economic and administrative modernization. The establishment of the Haile Selassie I University in Addis Ababa, the legalization of the trade unions in 1962, the creation of a special palace military guard, the expansion of the bureaucracy and the judiciary, the training of army and air force officers, have all contributed to the growth, at least in the capital, of a new corps of leaders.

There has been much speculation about the aspirations of the youthful civil servants, bureaucrats, and university students who comprise a small but growing intelligentsia. In informal discussions they exhibit a general distaste for the *status quo* and often sharply criticize the distribution of political power. For them too much of Ethiopia is too far from modernization. Whether or not their impatience is a function of their age or an indication of real disaffection, they are not ardent nationalists or revolutionaries. Moreover, for westernized youths few opportunities exist other than those in government service. For them talk has been an adequate substitute for action, and the intelligentsia are noteworthy for their political ineffectiveness. Significantly, they played no major part in the 1960 coup, and it remains to be seen how they would behave during the uncertainty of a future crisis.

During the Emperor's absence from the country in 1960, an apparently haphazard collection of members drawn from these new elites engaged in an unsuccessful coup. It gave evidence of little planning and organization, the result, basic- ally, of the failure of communication among its participants. But it also demonstrated the existence of demands for political change and briefly challenged the myths of the Emperor's legitimacy. Significantly, during the days of the rebellion the formation of political parties was promised by its leaders, some of whom had studied in the United States. Since 1960, the process of modernization has apparently again been under the Emperor's control, and, in view of the severe penalties against free political expression, there has been no evidence of any moves to form new political organizations.

The educated elite is still very narrowly recruited. The use, primarily, of ascriptive criteria of selection preserves existing class lines and assures, if not complete loyalty to the Emperor, at least loyalty to the existing class structure. The absence of political organization has meant the lack of a ready-made communications network among the members of this elite, thus reducing its ability to take concerted political or economic action. The interests favouring change are therefore highly fragmented. If the Emperor's authority is in this way protected, it also leaves the vast majority of the population unaffected by economic change. Untouched by new political organizations, politically informed only by the government's communications monopoly and by the traditional local aristocracy, it is beyond the reach of political appeals from the new elites. But it remains also beyond the reach of economic and social changes. It is still illiterate, engaged in subsistence agriculture, governed by traditional village authorities, divided ethnically and religiously. The question of how it can be mobilized for economic purposes without being politically organized is still unanswered.

Another unanswered question concerns the chances of survival of the traditional political system when the Emperor's powers pass to a successor. Although the position of the present Emperor appears strong, it depends in part on his special international reputation, in part on the personal loyalty of his appointees, and in part on his highly personal use of legitimacy myths. Can these sources of power be transferred to a successor except through a new political organization?

Where African political parties have arisen in opposition to colonial regimes, they have developed as institutions parallel to the colonial administration, with judicial, administrative, police, education, and social welfare functions. They have provided a new set of values and given expression to new interests, in opposition to those of both the colonial regime and the traditional African milieu. They have been powerful agents for political agitation, education, and communications. In the process they have from time to time produced their cult of martyrs, their charismatic leaders, but above all they have created a new political elite. They have given Africans a new sense of solidarity, and have resolutely sought the modernization of African economies. They have given legitimacy to new political systems. In Ethiopia, however, all of these functions have been monopolized by the Emperor and an elite recruited largely by ascriptive criteria. This has placed special obstacles in the path of economic development and created prospects of ultimate political instability. The particular problems of modernization which Ethiopia faces because of the absence of political parties suggest the functions which parties usually perform in the political systems of developing states, and indicate the difficulty of finding suitable structures to substitute for them.

18. The organization of the state and social structures in Ethiopia

L. RICCI *Civilisations* Vol. 14, Nos. 1/2, 1964; pages 19–22 (In translation)

All Moslem political entities with a culture and social structure of their own, which are different from those of Europe but which have adopted European forms of social life and organization, have gone through a critical phase of a severity depending on their internal condition. The State of Ethiopia is a typical example, and the crisis it is undergoing merits close examination. Ethiopia is a special case: it is developing in the context of a very old Christian culture in which both the intellectual heritage and the fund of moral and practical knowledge have been built up through the use of written language, a fact which gives this culture a considerable and complex maturity. The all-pervasive influence of Christianity has meant that political authority which is completely vested in the sovereign draws its legitimacy and its justification from Divine Will. The Christian sovereign is thus the source of all public power; all forms of association of a public nature are sanctioned by his will. This is the fundamental principle which has governed and still governs the organization of traditional Ethiopian society, and it is upon this that all acts of civil and political life have been founded. It is true that in practice the absolute and exclusive power of the sovereign is limited by other sources of authority but these still derive from his unique sovereignty and remain subordinated to it. These sources of authority acquire however a degree of autonomy and themselves enact laws. Among the most important of them are the religious and ecclesiastical authorities, who are also the depositaries and initiators of all written knowledge. As a general rule they act alongside the supreme secular power and with its support; they remain subordinated to it in the political sphere and often in the religious sphere as well; sometimes they intervene in the exercise of the absolute authority of the sovereign, preventing or annulling certain of his acts. In the sector of private life, there is yet another set of laws which have grown up within local communities and which the local communities have kept alive, handed down, and even—through the ages—modified. This whole complex of institutions has never been written down (among the very rare exceptions the most ancient are the sovereign acts of granting feudal privileges). The oral tradition is sufficient to keep alive the organization of society, not only in the seat of government, that is to say in the royal household, but also within the community itself; custom confirms and crystallizes the institutions. The fact that there exists among Christian Ethiopians, the holders of supreme political power, a code of written laws is no exception. Ethiopians refer to it as their basic code, but it is scarcely more than a set of laws borrowed from eastern Christendom via the Coptic Christian Community of Egypt, and given a rough translation at a relatively late date. It is in fact merely a scholarly work like so many others introduced into Ethiopia in translation, but inapplicable in practice to the local Christian society. The provisions of private law, and to some extent those of public law, often reveal considerable variations and divergencies, resulting from the diversity of the ethnic groups making up the political system ruled over by the sovereign. Furthermore, the Amharic-speaking Christian society, to which this 'code' is applicable, is only a minority. The other sectors of the population are made up of peoples of extremely diverse origin, language, culture and religion. Very often each of them has its own social order, being subordinated to the authority of the Ethiopian monarch only by bonds of political sovereignty. It is in this political context that the State endeavoured to superimpose a European political and social order. The sovereign's decision to do so is made legitimate by his normative power.

The social and political orders are interdependent and indissolubly bound together. And so the new institutions introduced at the beginning of this century led to a slow *de facto* transformation which created the moral conditions required for the application of the foreign legal order. When it was opportune, the first fundamental step was taken (we shall disregard the ordinances promulgated from time to time to make provisions in particular spheres of public life, especially the economic sphere). The act which politically and juridically gave concrete form to the innovations was the promulgation of the State constitution. This was a somewhat rudimentary constitutional charter, because of the vague terminology and lacunae in its wording, in keeping with the still elementary degree of evolution towards new political and social forms, but it was an ineluctable first step towards the construction of a European State. The constitution was followed by an organic code of laws aimed at punishing breaches of the constituted order, that is to say, a penal code.

At this point in the process came a radical acceleration due to the occupation of Ethiopia by a European state (Italy) and the immediate setting up of a political and administrative organization of a European type, but drawn-up and administered by Europeans.

When the Ethiopian monarchy was restored shortly afterwards it found fully installed the instruments of the new legal order which it had timidly tried to introduce several years before. It maintained the structure of the state it thus inherited and tried to fill the vacuum in the juridical, caused by the departure of the European power, by a series of legislative acts drawn up on the advice, and with the collaboration, of foreign experts, in the absence of an Ethiopian ruling class trained for this work. These new regulations were put into operation as a matter of urgency, and the drawing up of a new formal order was pushed forward with haste; the climax of the process was reached in 1955 with the voting of a new, more complete and detailed constitution, followed by the promulgation between 1957 and 1961 of organic codes governing private, penal, commercial and maritime law. Thus the formal juridical order of the Ethiopian State could be considered as complete in its main outlines, and its framework seemed finally settled. It only remained to put it into practice. It was at this point that a crisis broke out which is now in its most severe phase. This crisis affects the whole of Ethiopian society in every sphere; the new formal order has met with resistance, not in the form of polemics or disobedience but rather in the form of a tension from the traditional structure of this society, which is still very much alive and which leads to endless friction. In fact certain elements of this structure have survived almost undamaged outside the urban area, that is to say outside the seat of sovereign authority—the capital which promulgated the reforms and put them into effect. Apart from this restricted area, in the rest of the country, which is far from being culturally homogeneous, the traditional juridical orders continue to prevail in 'spirit' as do traditional political and administrative orders.

The new constitution is already in operation, even in its fundamental principles. Basically, it is still too full of the old mentality which presided over the structure of the traditional Ethiopian state. In spite of the formal affirmation of the major principles which govern modern European society, in the final analysis it merely establishes the absolute and un-challenged authority of the sovereign.

Conceived as the first instrument of the new order, it remains paradoxically linked to the fundamental order on which the traditional social life of Ethiopia is based, and it bears the sign of the times—as the crisis shows.

The practical application of the provisions contained in the organic codes of laws presents difficult problems. Since they have been drafted by European jurists, these codes bear the stamp of the European legal conscience, and the way they have been conceived rules out any possibility of reciprocal influence or of hybrid fusion with traditional juridical principles. The notions that the Ethiopian has to assimilate are completely new to him, and this assimilation pre-supposes his acquiring juridical values which have been elaborated by the European tradition. Moreover the interpretation of the texts itself involves difficulties. For these rules to be translated into Ethiopian a vocabulary would have been needed which the language does not possess. It was therefore necessary to innovate, building on the experience acquired in translating particular ordinances and first drafted in a European language by foreign experts. The translators had not always the necessary competence in European law, and their interpretation of concepts contained in the original text is thus suspect. At a recent congress of Ethiopian studies an (Italian) expert in Amharic and also in law showed that translation of one of the codes, taken merely as an example, contained many inaccuracies, and even actual errors of interpretation of the European text (written in English). By coincidence the same kind of mistakes have been found in the text of the set of laws we referred to earlier, known in Ethiopian under the title of *Fétha Nagast*, and translated some centuries ago. One can imagine how much more difficult it will be for a future Ethiopian jurist to interpret the rules of the new codes. Up to the present, except for current acts, these codes also have remained a dead letter, at least as far as the Ethiopian population in its complex diversity is concerned. It has no doubt been different in the higher courts of the capital, the city of the king, where there are European consulates, and in certain other cases where the provisions have been applied to non-indigenous subjects, in commercial and maritime law, for instance.

Two vastly different worlds have thus been suddenly brought into contact by an act of government. The crisis is affecting the whole of Ethiopian culture; everything has been thrown into the melting pot, from conceptual processes of interpreting reality to attitudes towards religion considered as a social institution. The divergence between traditional Ethiopian conceptions and Western conceptions is the cause of extreme tension. This exists between those inhabitants immersed in the traditional culture and those others brought up and educated in a Western context who are already detached from the traditional culture and sometimes unable any longer to understand it; hence the uneasiness characteristic of the present crisis. On the one hand there is the great majority, tied to the realities of the past, on the other the new élite still restricted materially and morally to the towns. . . .

Translated by Dr S. I. Lockerbie

V. EAST AFRICA

19. Modern political movements in Somaliland

I. M. LEWIS *Africa* Vol. 28, 1958 Oxford University Press for International African Institute; pages 253–60

Political parties in Somaliland fall roughly into three categories (see chart). First there are those parties which are simply the modern political organ of a particular clan or group of clans and which, whatever lip-service they may pay to the ideal of Somali nationalism, are fundamentally committed to promote and safeguard the interests of the particular clan or group of clans which they represent. Secondly, there are those parties which are entirely opposed to the traditional values of agnation and to the distinction between Samaale and Sab. Their principal aim is to further a truly pan-Somali nationalism. The extent to which these ideals are promoted in practice is another matter. A third type of party, in a sense intermediate in composition between the clan party and the pan-Somali party, is that founded on common residence in a particular region. This type founded on regional or territorial (tribal) values occurs only in Somalia. Only in part of Somalia, as we have seen, have residential ties to some extent replaced agnation as a political principle in the traditional social organization.

TYPES OF PARTY[1]

A. Clan Parties

Mahlia Party	Formerly in the British Protectorate.
Ishaaqiya	Kenya, British East Africa.
Marrehaan Union	Somalia.
Hawiye Party	Somalia.

B. National Parties

The Somaliland National League British Protectorate mainly.
The National United Front   British Protectorate.

[1] Following Somali usage the word 'party' is used here in a broad sense to denote organizations not all of which are designed to contest elections and not all of which are at the same level of political development.

The Somali Youth League	French Somaliland, Ethiopia, British Protectorate, Somalia, Kenya, East Africa, &c.
The Somali Democratic Party	Somalia.
United Somali Association	Kenya, British East Africa.
Union Républicaine	French Somaliland.[1]

C. Regional (and Tribal) Parties

The Afgoi-Audegle Party	Somalia.
The Banadir Youth	Somalia.
The Hizbia Digil-Mirifleh[2]	Somalia.
Shidleh Party	Somalia.
Bajuni Fiqarini	Somalia.

A. Clan Parties

We take first those organizations which are founded on ties of clanship and whose aim is to promote the interests of a particular agnatic group. Parties of this type are less developed in the British Protectorate than they are in Somalia. This is to be ascribed to a feebler degree of political consciousness in the modern sense in the Protectorate, and not to a weakening of the ties of clanship, for it is, as we have seen, in Somalia that the tendency to overcome the bonds of kinship is most developed and associated in the south with an agricultural economy. The Habar Awal, 'Iise Muuse of the British Protectorate, had, however, from 1952 to 1954 a short-lived political party, the Malia, whose aims were principally the promotion of 'Iise Muuse interests. And at the moment there is a strong movement towards the formation of similar purely clan parties, although in 1957 no well-organized or clearly defined political party of this kind had made its appearance in the Protectorate. In British East Africa the interests of Somali immigrants (mainly Ishaaq) are served by the Ishaaqiya society, whose aims, despite some connexion with the Somaliland National League of the Protectorate, seem to be less political than simply those of an

---

[1] The constitution of this party, which is an alliance of Somali, Danakil, and Arabs, is discussed in the second part of this study.

[2] This party changed its name in 1950 to *Hizbia Dastuur Muustaqiil*, the Independent Constitutional Party.

association or club. The Ishaaqiya is, moreover, basically concerned with emphasizing Somali claims to Arabian descent in order that the Ishaaq settlers may be classed with the Asian section of the East African populations and in return for paying a higher tax[1] enjoy the advantages of Arabian education and other privileges. Africans regard this as typical Somali snobbery, and there is no doubt that whatever tangible benefits may result from their classification as 'non-natives', Ishaaq honour is at stake.[2]

The Marrehaan Union is the organ of the Marrehaan (Daarood) of the trans-Juban region of Somali. It is a splinter group of Daarood (Daarood in the main being S.Y.L.) and has some slight influence with one seat in the Somalia Legislative Assembly. The Hawiye Party represents some of the Hawiye of Somalia (other Hawiye support the S.Y.L.) but is of little importance and has no representative in the Legislative Assembly. Hawiye supporters were in 1956 estimated to comprise some 30 per cent. of the S.Y.L. following which indicates that, although there is a Hawiye Party frankly seeking support on clan lines, it has not yet achieved much success in its appeal to traditional kinship ties. To promote and encourage Hawiye support, however, the party was instrumental in organizing a memorial service (*siyaaro*) for the eponymous ancestor of the Hawiye clan-family at Mogadishu on 12 October 1956. This was an attempt to marry the traditional expression of Hawiye clan solidarity with modern political aims.

B. National Parties

Of the second class of political parties—those whose declared goal is the establishment of Somali nationalism and the destruction of the crippling ties of kinship and clan allegiance— the oldest is the Somaliland National League (S.N.L.) which has existed intermittently under various titles in the British Protectorate since 1935. This organization, with some connexion with the Ishaaqiya of Kenya, is principally confined

---

[1] Somali immigrants are not classed as 'natives' in Kenya and pay a 'non-native' tax graduated by income. The special tax paid by clansmen in the Northern (Frontier) Province is discussed in a succeeding article.

[2] The recently formed United Somali Association at Nairobi appears to have wider aims than the Ishaaqiya and to be more nationalistic in outlook.

to the Protectorate where it assumed its present form and title in 1951. It draws most of its support from the Isḥaaq clans although it includes also some Dir and Daarood amongst its members. The League has a central committee, local (or district) committees, and a general assembly. The composition of the central and local committees includes a president, secretary, treasurer, and other members. The League's head-quarters are at Burao and there are other branches at Hargeisa, Berbera, Borama, Erigavo, Sheikh, and Odweina. Admission to the League is by entrance fee (3s. E.A.) and a monthly subscription of 1s. 6d. is payable. Members wear a badge bear-ing the legend in Arabic, 'Be united in the name of God' and 'S.N.L.'[1] members are required to swear to sacrifice their lives for their country if necessary. The League is predominantly Muslim in outlook and aims, is in contact with Egypt, and has ties with the local Islamic Somali Association in Aden. The original programme was:

(a) to work for the unification of the Somali race and Somali territories;

(b) to work for the advancement of the Somali race by abolishing clan fanaticism and encouraging brotherly relations among Somalis;

(c) to encourage the spread of education[2] and the economic and political development of the country;

(d) to co-operate with the British Government or any other local body whose aims are the welfare of the inhabitants of the country.

With the return to Ethiopia, by an Anglo-Ethiopian Agree-ment of 29 November 1954, of the Haud and former Reserved Areas,[3] in fulfilment of the Anglo-Ethiopian Treaty of 1897,

---

[1] The badge also bears a replica of the Black Stone of Mecca, and costs 3s.

[2] Seventy-six Somali school boys who went for education to Egypt under the auspices of the S.N.L. and S.Y.L. have now applied for assistance from the British Government: *War Somali Sidihi*, No. 109, 9 March 1957, p. 9.

[3] This is the region of rich grazing, some 25,000 square miles in extent and occupied by a shifting nomadic population of some 200,000–300,000 persons which lies to the south of the British Protectorate. The region was incorpor-ated in Somalia by the Italians during their expansionist movement in East

a treaty which Somalis have never recognized,[1] and the independence which Somalia is destined to attain in 1960 (or 1959), the S.N.L. is now pressing for a grant of similar status to the Somaliland Protectorate. Recent (1956–7) events in the Middle East, the Egyptian seizure of the Suez Canal and Anglo-French intervention in Suez, have stimulated the pro-Egyptian and pro-Arab World tendencies of the League.

Another nationalist movement of importance in the British Protectorate is the National United Front (N.U.F.). This organization, which is entirely confined to the Protectorate, is a convention or congress rather than a party. It was founded in 1955 at a public conference with the aims of obtaining

Africa and Ethiopia, but with the exception of a few police posts, was hardly administered and in 1941 was placed under the British Military Administration. Under a British Civil Affairs Administration portions of the Haud and Reserved Areas were returned to Ethiopia over the years until 1954 there remained only two British Civil Affairs Officers. By the terms of the 1954 Anglo-Ethiopian Agreement these were withdrawn and replaced by a British Liaison staff with headquarters at Jigjiga. The duties of the British Liaison Officer and his assistants are to safeguard the grazing rights of British subjects from the Protectorate, whose rights to pasture in the former Reserved Areas were acknowledged by Ethiopia in the original Treaty of 1897 and reiterated in the Agreement of 1954. It is said to have been assumed by some of the British officials responsible for drawing up the terms of the Agreement that Ethiopia would not in fact actually go to the length of setting up a local administrative staff, and that, consequently, there would be little or no difficulty in the operation of the Agreement. As is well known, this prediction has proved to be very far from accurate and the difficulties which British Protected Somalis have experienced in their movements to and from the Reserved Areas (now known as 'the Territories') have given rise to repeated representations being made to the British Government to seek the return of the Territories, to Anglo-Ethiopian Conferences on the working of the Agreement in which both sides have alleged infringements, and to an abortive attempt on the part of the British Government in a mission in April 1956 led by Mr Dodds-Parker (then Joint Parliamentary Under-Secretary of State for Foreign Affairs) to return the administration of the Territories to Great Britain.

[1] Somalis consider that the terms of the previous treaties of the British Government with the Gadabuursi (1884) and with the Habar Awal (1884 and 1886) preclude Britain's right to cede territorial rights to Foreign Powers (Ethiopia) by any subsequent treaty (the Anglo-Ethiopian Treaty of 1897). Whatever the *prima facie* justness of the Somali view in alleging a transgression by Great Britain of prior treaties, it seems now to be generally accepted that in International Law the Treaty of 1897 with Ethiopia remains valid.

the return of the former Reserved Areas to the Protectorate,[1] and of working for the independence of the Protectorate within the British Commonwealth. A further aim now being given increasing prominence is that of federation to Somalia. Originally an alliance of the S.N.L. and S.Y.L. in the Protectorate and of other associations and private individuals and district representatives, it received wide support at the time of its inception.[2] Because of its character as a convention rather than a party and is failure hitherto in the first of its objectives—the return of the Haud and Reserved Areas—much S.Y.L. and S.N.L. support has been lost, and it now tends, although impressive in the calibre of its leaders, to lack any constant following in the country. Its force lies in its flexibility of organization, which is open to all and not bound by a party system, and in its extremely able administrative core. Unlike the S.N.L. and S.Y.L., the N.U.F. does not have local branches throughout the country, but that does not mean that it cannot on occasion receive support from all quarters. The amounts of

[1] A delegation consisting of Sultan 'Abdillahi ('Iidagale), Sultan 'Abdarahiim (Habar Awal), Dube 'Ali Maḥammad (Habar Tol Ja'lo), and Michael Mariano (Habar Tol Ja'lo) visited England in February 1955 to interview the Colonial Secretary and to arouse English public opinion and support against the transfer of the Reserved Areas to Ethiopia. This, of course, was a purely Isḥaaq delegation and received considerable publicity in the British Press. See *The Times*, 5, 8, 14, 15, and 23 Feb. 1955; *The Manchester Guardian*, 23 Feb. 1955. A second delegation consisting of Mr Mariano and Sultan Bihi (Ogaadeen), a refugee from Ethiopia, visited England in September of 1956 to discuss the Haud and Reserved Areas again with the British Colonial Secretary before proceeding to New York where it was intended to petition the United Nations Assembly and to seek their intervention or approval to put the Somali case to the International Court. The delegation's visit to the United Nations proved abortive and the dispute has still not been placed before the International Court.

[2] Conferences are periodically held at the N.U.F. Headquarters in Hargeisa attended by representatives of all districts and parties. At a Conference held on 15 May 1957, for instance, representatives of the following were present: Burao, Berbera, Borama, Las Anod, and Hargeisa Districts; S.N.L. and S.Y.L.; the Somali Officials Union (Hargeisa); the Somali Old Boys' Association (former pupils of Sheikh School); and the Somali Association, Aden. A report of the proceedings was circularized to all those mentioned and in addition to the Somali Brethren Society, England; the Somalis in Dahran (Saudi Arabia); the Somalis in Jiddah (Saudi Arabia); and the Somalis in Salalla (Aden). Financial contributions for the N.U.F. from Somalis in Saudi Arabia have been particularly generous.

donations and financial aid received from all sections of the Protectorate community, and not only in British Somaliland, are impressive. And in keeping with its mediatory character as an all-party convention the N.U.F. has on occasion successfully intervened in clan and lineage-group disputes.[1]

The Somali Youth League (S.Y.L.) was founded in Somalia in 1943.[2] From its inception it has championed the cause of a greater Somalia—of a linking together under one Somali government of all the Somali territories from French Somaliland to the Northern Province of Kenya. When the British Military Administration of Somalia (then ex-Italian Somaliland) was disbanded in 1949, the party campaigned strongly for the unification of all the Somali territories and this proposal was supported by Britain's Foreign Minister at the time (Ernest Bevin). This solution was not acceptable to the Great Powers who returned Italy to Somalia as administering authority of a United Nations Trusteeship Territory which was to attain independence in 1960. The S.Y.L. played a prominent part in the Mogadishu riots of 1949[3] which were held to demonstrate dissatisfaction at the return of Italian administration. Elections were held in Somalia during February 1956 for sixty seats in the newly created Legislative Assembly and voting took place both in the municipalities and the interior.[4] The S.Y.L. won a decisive majority of 43 seats.

[1] The leaders of the National United Front have recently (1957) returned from a visit to Mogadishu where they discussed with the Government of Somalia the possible future of the Somali territories. This mission seems to have given a fillip to the Party's influence.

[2] As its name implies, more than any of the other present nationalist organizations it depends for support upon the new élite—the educated younger generation most numerous in Somalia.

[3] The status of the U.N. Trusteeship Territory of Somalia in International Law was approved by the General Assembly of the United Nations on 2 December 1950 and ratified by an Agreement with Italy (Law No. 1301 of 4 Nov. 1951).

[4] Voting was confined to the masculine population, and candidates for the legislature were required to be over 30 years of age, literate in Italian and Arabic, and to have been resident at least one year in Somalia. In the municipalities voters were required to be registered on the municipal electoral lists. In the interior, where, in accordance with Somali custom, every sane male over 21 years of age could vote (as long as he had no grievous criminal record), voting took place through *ad hoc* councils or

QTCA

The headquarters organization of the party at Mogadishu includes a president, a deputy, a secretary, treasurer, comptrollers, and some twelve other members of council. District branches in Somalia and other Somali territories have a similar organization. Membership requires payment of an entrance fee and a small monthly subscription. A membership card is issued and a badge bearing the inscription 'S.Y.L.' As with the S.N.L. of the Protectorate, wherever there is a party branch weekly meetings are held in a building used as a meeting-place and club by the local party members. The proceedings at these meetings are generally formal. When the local party leaders enter the premises all present stand up as a sign of respect. Young members are appointed as ushers responsible for the discipline of the meeting. When the young members act as stewards at local meetings, and especially at public demonstrations, they wear a uniform consisting of white slacks and a white shirt crossed diagonally from shoulder to hip by a red and blue bandolier with the slogan 'S.Y.L.'[1] The introduction of a measure of formal discipline and of coloured uniforms and banners is a modern innovation foreign to traditional Somali clan life. Some precedent, however, exists in the organization (although less formal) of the Sufi Dervish Orders. The local weekly meetings are generally of much the same form. They are largely taken up with discussions and addresses on the aims of the party and with debates on matters of topical interest. A prominent feature common to all is the recitation and singing of patriotic verse (usually in the form of *gabay*)[2] and songs epitomizing the aims of the party. It is

gatherings (*shirs*, see above) at which representatives were appointed to carry votes to the recorders. It is alleged and generally recognized that a considerable amount of bribery and buying of votes took place. Out of a population represented at the time as twice as many, a total of 858,122 male adults are supposed to have voted. Either the election results had been very considerably exaggerated or the population of Somalia had been grossly underestimated. The most recent (1957) estimate of approximately 2 million for the population of Somalia is at least in better accord with the election figures.

[1] The S.N.L. wear a similar uniform but their sash is green and bears their own slogan. Proceedings at S.N.L. meetings are little different from those of the S.Y.L.

[2] *Gabay* is the traditional highly stylized Somali poem, the highest form of Somali verse.

particularly interesting that the *gabay*, which in the traditional social context is often an effective vehicle for clan and lineage-group enmity, should here be used to promote the extension of nationalist sentiments and unity. In the partly Bantu culture of southern Somalia the meetings, in which women also participate,[1] include entertainments and dancing.

The pan-Somali and non-kinship character of the S.Y.L. is illustrated in its membership in Somalia which was in 1956 estimated to comprise: Daarood 50 per cent., Hawiye 30 per cent., Digil-Mirifleh 10 per cent., and others 10 per cent. Its strength in Somalia is indicated by the overwhelming majority which the party gained in the elections for the Legislative Assembly. There are branches throughout Somalia. In the British Protectorate there are branches at Burao, Hargeisa, Borama, Las Anod, Erigavo, and along the Makhir coast in the east of the Protectorate. The central council for the Protectorate is established at Berbera. Although in close contact with the Somalia headquarters organization, the S.Y.L. in the Protectorate lacks the vitality of the movement in Somalia. Its leaders are not of the same calibre as those in the south. With a following in the Protectorate smaller than that of its rival the S.N.L., the party derives much of its support from the eastern Dulbahante and Warsangeli (Daaroof). The S.Y.L. exists also, necessarily under cover, in French Somaliland, Ethiopia, and the Northern Province of Kenya. In all these territories it is banned.[2] In every region of Somaliland its policy is nationalistic and pan-Somali, but the extent to which these ideals are promoted in practice should not be judged too harshly, for it should be compared with other mainly clan organizations such as the Hawiye Party and Marrehaan Union, discussed above.

Finally, among the present parties striving to overcome the bonds of clanship must be mentioned the Somali Democratic Party of Somalia, which although a small party, nevertheless managed to gain three seats in the legislature. It exists only in

[1] Among the northern nomads women do not attend local political meetings. At a mixed meeting which I attended in southern Somalia the dancers sang the refrain: 'We are Somali, what can the person who resists the cry "Somali" do?'

[2] Under the new régime in French Somaliland, established by the *loi cadre*, greater freedom will presumably be allowed to the S.Y.L.

Somalia and has an estimated following of: Daarood 50 per cent., Hawiye 40 per cent., others 10 per cent.

C. Regional (and Tribal) Parties

The final group of parties are those which represent territorial rather than clan interests. These existed in 1957 only in Somalia, where, as we have seen in the south, the traditional lineage structure has been superseded to a considerable extent. There are four small parties, none of which returned a candidate to the Assembly in the 1956 elections. The Young Banadir, representing the interests of some of the peoples of the Banadir coast and based on Mogadishu, is currently estimated to be composed of: Reer Ḥamar 80 per cent., Digil-Mirifleh 10 per cent., and others 10 per cent. The Afgoi-Audegle Party represents the cultivators (mainly Raḥanweyn) based in the region between the villages of Afgoi and Audegle on the Shebelle River to the south-west of Mogadishu. This party is much smaller than the Young Banadir which in the 1956 elections ranked fourth amongst the parties in the poll. It was primarily a combination of interests for the purpose of gaining seats in the elections and had almost completely collapsed in 1957. The remaining two small parties of this class and with little influence are the Bajuni-Fiqarini which caters for the interests of the coastal Bajuni of southern Somalia, and the Shidle Party which represents the Negroid Shidle cultivators of the Shebelle River.

The most important party of this type is the Digil-Mirifleh Party (Digil and Mirifleh, including Raḥanweyn 90 per cent.; Reer Baraawa 5 per cent.; others 5 per cent.), which represents the interests of the Digil and Raḥanweyn cultivators (or most of them) and associated tribes, and includes the support of the people of the town of Brava (Reer Baraawa). They gained 13 seats in the Assembly of Somalia in the 1956 elections, the largest number of seats held by any single party on the opposition benches, and with their good organization and vitality are the nucleus of an effective opposition. The existence of the Ḥizbia Digil-Mirifleh was in 1957 the nearest approach in Somalia to a modern political cleavage between Samaale and Sab and following traditional lineage principles. In classing the Ḥizbia Digil-Mirifleh with the regional parties, I have been guided by the fact that, although their name refers to the eponymous ancestors of the Digil and Raḥanweyn clan-families, their organization as a political party is not based on lineage affiliation. As was shown above, it is in this region that tribalism founded on territorial ties is taking the place of clanship, and it is the common cultural, economic, and territorial interests of the Digil and Raḥanweyn inhabiting the most fertile region of Somalia that their party represents. At times, indeed, the Digil-Mirifleh Party has gone so far in expressing the sense of independence and identity of the Digil and Raḥanweyn tribes as to advocate the creation in southern Somalia of a separate and autonomous Digil-Mirifleh state. This aim had not been achieved in 1957, nor can it command much support, for the riverine area occupied by the Sab is the richest and most capable of economic development in Somalia.

In this article I have examined the organization of modern Somali political movements in relation to the traditional political organization. I have argued that there are three principal types of party; clan, national, and regional or tribal. To some extent these three types reflect regional variations in the traditional social organization and traditional cleavages. Only in southern Somalia, where regional tribalism partly replaces agnation as a political principle, are regional and tribal political parties found.

20. The growth of nationalist parties in Uganda 1952–60

R. CRANFORD PRATT *Political Studies* Vol. 9, 1961 Clarendon Press, Oxford; pages 170–4

. . . Outside Buganda, Congress grew more slowly. Most of its leaders were Ganda and most of its energy from 1953 to 1955 was absorbed by the deportation crisis. Nevertheless it did tend for a time to attract a few educated non-Ganda who became interested in nationalist politics, while in most districts branches were established by the less educated but politically discontented who were already a disturbing element. But it produced no leader of wide popularity and real stature. Elaborate paper constitutions were drafted but never converted into working institutions. No mass membership was recruited, and regular fees were not collected. Registers of members and even of branches were not kept. The national officers did not keep in close regular communication with the branches, and the enthusiasm of the local district leaders soon waned.

The 'party' was nearly always a coterie of Kampala politicians. Even within this small group there was no machinery for resolving internal disputes. More assertive committee members could act in the name of the Congress without prior approval from any executive body. J. L. Zake, for example, issued in the name of the Congress a strongly worded attack on Sir Andrew Cohen's 1955 proposals without any prior consultation with fellow Congressmen. In the same year Joseph Kiwanuka announced, completely on his own, the names of a whole new executive for Congress. John Kale in 1958 established a Foreign Office of the Congress in Cairo without the prior approval of the central executive committee. Finally, in more recent years, when the Congress has had to sustain several serious splits in its leadership, the various leaders have assembled factions which they have claimed were competent to speak for Congress.

These splits were evidence of a further failure. Congress did not keep many of the important members it first attracted. Soon after its formation, Eridadi Mulira resigned to follow his own independent and unfruitful path. In 1955 an important group of Ganda resigned because leaders would not categorically reject constitutional discussions with the British until after the Kabaka's return. In 1956 a group of the younger and best-educated leaders attempted to seize control from Musazi and Kiwanuka. However, the rebels, though they included Zake, Binaisa, Luboga, Senteza-Kajubi, and Erisa Kironde, could not rival Musazi's or Kiwanuka's popularity, and had no organization, such as a youth movement or trade union, to provide them with wider and more general support. Nor were any of them professional politicians. They failed to dislodge Musazi and Kiwanuka, and finally they withdrew and formed a separate party, the United Congress Party.

In 1958 another split occurred, again with the object of ejecting Musazi. Although Kiwanuka went with the anti-Musazi faction this time, it was led by Milton Obote and Abu Mayanja[1] and it drew its support mainly from Acholi, Lango, Bukedi, and Bugishu rather than Buganda. Musazi attempted to insert an issue of principle into this controversy: he attacked his critics for the support they were receiving from the Afro-Asian Solidarity Committee in Cairo. Finally, in December 1958 and January 1959, Musazi and Obote each produced a large Congress meeting which dutifully expelled the leaders of the rival faction. Obote's meeting proved the more representative, and Musazi lost his control of the party he had founded.

Still another split occurred in the summer of 1959, with Kiwanuka and Kununka leading one faction and Obote and Mayanja the other. Again rival meetings expelled opposing leaders and again the Obote group proved to have the firmer hold on what remained of the organization. But Obote's and Mayanja's victory in this case was clouded by the fact that Kiwanuka succeeded in retaining control of the sizeable funds

[1] Obote is the elected member of the Legislative Council for Lango District. He is one of several new political figures outside Buganda who have had long periods of residence in Nairobi and whose initial political experience, and perhaps lasting political attitudes, were gained in the more embittering atmosphere of Nairobi in the early 1950s. Mayanja is a Muganda lawyer who returned to Uganda after eight years in the United Kingdom where he was at King's College, Cambridge, before reading for the Bar in London. Unlike almost all the other Ganda politicians he is of humble origin, and is a Muslim, not a Christian.

which had come to Congress from foreign, non-western sources.[1] Congress continued under Obote's leadership after January 1959, but with the focus of its power shifted to the Northern and Eastern Provinces. These internal controversies lost Congress five crucial years and it has recently had to face several important rival parties.

The first of these was the Progressive Party, formed in 1955 by E. M. K. Mulira. Its founder members were mainly educated Ganda Protestants, outside the dominant Palace Group. For a brief period immediately after the deportation of the Kabaka, Mulira and T. A. K. Makumbi, his most important supporter, won the ear of the Lukiiko, and both were chosen in 1954 to be members of the Namirembe Committee which considered the revision of the 1900 Agreement. Yet by 1955 both had lost ground to the more traditionally minded Kintu and the chiefs and ex-chiefs who had gathered about him. Although Mulira has since devoted all his time and energy to political activity and to the publication of his vernacular newspaper, neither he nor the Progressive Party has been important politically.

Much more important is the Democratic Party, founded in 1956 as a Catholic party. The intrusion of religion into politics is not new in Uganda. Rivalries between religious factions have been continuous and important in most districts. In Buganda from 1900 to the present day both ministries and chiefdoms have been divided between the adherents of the main religious groups. In these rivalries the Catholics have tended to be the less successful: in Buganda the Prime Minister, the Treasurer, and a majority of chiefs have always been Protestants. The Democratic Party in many ways merely expresses this older religious factionalism in more national and more political form,[2] and this explains why it has been more successful than Congress in maintaining itself against the hostile pressure of the

[1] Kiwanuka returned to Uganda in the summer of 1959 after a lengthy visit to Cairo and to Peking. He brought back with him a sum varyingly estimated to be from £45,000 to £50,000. Mayanja, who should know, gave me the £50,000 figure. In addition to this, a modern printing press followed his return and has since been under his control.

[2] The first President of the Democratic Party was Mathias Mugwanya, who as the Omulamuzi (Chief Judge) of the Buganda Government from 1951 to 1955, was the leading Catholic political figure in Buganda.

Palace Group. Catholics are used to being opposed by those in power in Buganda, and they are less easily moved from their loyalties and political attitudes. Mugwanya, for example, was easily able to win a by-election in the Lukiiko in 1956, although it was widely known that the Kabaka and his Government disapproved of him.[1] Benedicto Kiwanuka, the new President of the party, continues to be a severe and very unwelcome critic of the Buganda Government in the Lukiiko. Unlike Mulira, Joseph Kiwanaka, and Musazi, he did not lose his seat in the Lukiiko elections in 1958. Finally, when the Lukiiko re-elected the Katikiro in 1959, the Democratic Party won an impressive number of votes for their candidate, Y. K. Lule.

The Democratic Party is also very important outside Buganda. It is a strong minority in many districts and has been able to win an occasional majority in a few. In 1958 its candidate won the West Nile District election to the Legislative Council and, in the 1959 elections, the party won control of the Lango and the Acholi District Councils.

In the first direct elections to the Legislative Council in 1958, both the Congress and the Democratic Party lost in most districts to local politicians affiliated to neither party. After the election, seven of these formed the Uganda People's Union, which has been important as a parliamentary group. Its members formed a sizeable minority of the Wild Committee and can justly claim much of the credit for the radical nature of its recommendations. Individually they are important political figures in their districts. None of them, however, has any electoral appeal outside his district. Few of them are professional politicians, and they did not build up any national party organization. Moreover, the Union has no support in Buganda and, as it was formed by politicians elected in an election which Buganda boycotted, it is unlikely to win any.

More recently, in March 1960, the Union and the Obote wing of the Congress have united to form the Uganda People's Congress. This is a strong alliance, and although it is still without a powerful organization, it is, along with the Democratic Party, the most important political group in Uganda today. It is an entirely non-Ganda party and has become more and more

---

[1] He was never permitted to take this seat in the Lukiiko because the Kabaka refused to sign the formal appointment notice.

hostile to what it regards as the feudal tribalism of Buganda.[1]

From what has been said, some points of contrast between the present state of organized nationalism in Uganda and that in other territories are obvious. No party in Uganda has a monopoly of the slogans of nationalism. None has yet the leadership, organization, or political power needed before political control of the Protectorate Government could be handed over with any confidence. None has an aroused and well-disciplined mass following. Each would have to alter significantly before it could hope to be a genuine unifying political force. With the single exception of the Democratic Party, no party speaks for a stable and organized mass of Africans with common political values and objectives. Instead, the party leaders are involved in a constant search for the issue and the alliance that might touch the popular imagination and win lasting popular support. Politicians migrate from party to party and from principle to principle in a depressing search for political status. The parties themselves have shown a similar fluidity. I think it is true to say that there is no combination of parties that has not considered amalgamation at some recent date. Such constant intrigue and manoeuvring have made it all the harder for any party to reach the mass of the people and win their confidence. At this early stage in the development of nationalism, when one might expect unquestioning and uncritical support of one or a few leaders, there is, instead, a cynical and suspicious attitude towards 'the politician'.

This constant bargaining could, of course, result in a coalition of interests capable of winning a national majority. Such a coalition might well win a majority of the representative seats in the new Legislative Council. But it would not be a solid and centralized party, only a shrewdly balanced cluster of interests that would disperse when one of its leading members calculated that his interests were better served outside. The politics of Uganda are likely to continue to be those of intrigue rather than those of a monolithic and well-organized party.

[1] A political understanding between the Congress and the Kabaka, possibly in the form of Congress support for a federal constitution and an electoral alliance with the Uganda National party, would of course transform politics in Uganda. Although widely canvassed early in 1960, it has become less and less likely.

Again while there are in Uganda, as in almost all other African territories, the less-educated but important political activists, these men have not been the agents of nationalist parties; some of them on occasion have claimed to support one party or another, but no party has yet brought their activities under a purposeful discipline. The result is a political restlessness, a discontent, a tendency to violence, a general lack of political control which, in an independent Uganda, could prove as hard to overcome as the problems of tribalism. . . .

21. Developments in Kenya

COLIN LEGUM *Current History* Vol. 46, No. 271, March 1964; pages 142–5

. . . Kenya's struggle for independence divides naturally into three overlapping phases. In the first phase, roughly between the two world wars, the struggle was mainly between the British settlers—led by pioneer figures like Lord Delamere—and the British Colonial Office. The settlers aspired to achieve an élite white government as in South Africa and in the self-governing colony of Southern Rhodesia. But their strenuous, and at times rebellious, demands were defeated largely through the efforts of the Church missionary societies and radical British politicians. One of the effects of this conflict, however, was to arouse in the Kikuyu tribe the first flickerings of African nationalism.

This development shaped the second phase which became increasingly a conflict between the Kikuyu tribe and the settlers, with the Colonial Office at times holding the balance between them and at times siding with the settlers. This phase—which began with the formation of the Young Kikuyu Association by a government telephone operator, Harry Thuku, at the end of World War I—reached a climacteric in the violence of the Mau Mau rebellion (1952–1959).

During this period tribes other than the Kikuyu played only a tangential role in Kenya's political affairs. The central issue was one of land. White settlement in Kenya had taken place

mainly in the central province, the traditional home of the
Kikuyu and of nomadic Kalenjin tribes like the Masai. The new
capital, Nairobi, was right in the middle of the Kikuyu homeland, and the Christian missionaries concentrated their
activities, especially their schools, among the Kikuyu. Thus the
Kikuyu felt the impact of the West more sharply than any other
tribe. Many accepted Christianity and modernism; the
majority, however, clung tenaciously to their old ways. This
cleavage produced deep tensions among the Kikuyu themselves,
and sharpened the minds of a naturally gifted people.

The Kikuyu were energetic and ambitious, quick to learn,
but slow to give up their fierce ethnocentricity. Above all, they
were a people with a grievance. They believed that an
important part of their tribal lands had been "stolen" from
them by the settlers who had established themselves on 7·5
million acres in an area which came to be known as the White
Highlands because only whites were allowed to own land there.

The settlers, once established on their farms, quickly struck
deep roots in the country. They were as adamant in their
determination to hold on to the land (which they sincerely
believed was fairly theirs) as the Kikuyu were in their
determination to reclaim "the stolen lands". The White
Highlands came to be regarded as a symbol of white exclusivity
in a country predominantly black.

Two factors made land the touchstone of all Kenya politics,
and gave it a strongly racial overtone: the real land hunger felt
by the Kikuyu, and the sincere belief of both the Kikuyu and
the settlers that their respective claims to the White Highlands
were justified. Neither side could be dissuaded from this belief.
No discussion on the Highlands could be conducted rationally.
On this issue the Kikuyu sharpened their political consciousness, and African nationalism was forged.

The Mau Mau Influence

The Mau Mau rebellion, which started as a Kikuyu tribal
rebellion with strongly atavistic features, ended as a nationalist
movement. Even though the majority of the other ethnic
communities did not actively support Mau Mau, the tenacity
and audacity of the challenge to white rule that it represented
were widely respected. Even those bitterly opposed to Mau Mau

came to feel that the rebellion struck a decisive blow at the political dominance of the settlers.

There can be no doubt that Mau Mau succeeded in destroying the old Kenya. Even in the middle of the rebellion, white attitudes underwent radical changes. Colour bar practices began to fall away. The white community—hitherto strongly united on major issues—became divided between moderates and extremists; and the moderates came out on top. Britain, too, was alerted to the fact that Kenya could no longer be denied representative government. But perhaps the most important result of Mau Mau was the political awakening of Africans of all tribes.

Thus Mau Mau ushered in the third phase of the independence struggle. Now the issue was no longer between the settlers and the Kikuyu; it was no longer even a question of colonialism or independence. The issue had become a struggle for power among the various communities in Kenya. For although the first reaction to Mau Mau was to create a united African political leadership, this development did not last long. The African Elected Members' Organisation split into two wings: the Kenya African National Union (K.A.N.U.) and the Kenya African Democratic Union (K.A.D.U.).

Militant Nationalism

K.A.N.U. came to represent militant African nationalism. Although its activating force had been the Kikuyu, its appeal spread to include several of the other large tribes like the Luo, the Kamba and the Meru. And even though the Kikuyu and the Luo are the two pillars on which K.A.N.U. power mainly rests, there is almost no part of the country in which it has not come to enjoy a considerable measure of support. Its charismatic leader was and is Jomo Kenyatta whose authority remains almost unchallengeable as "the Father of the Nation" or, as he is simply called, "Mzee"—The Old Man. K.A.N.U.'s leadership as a whole, though concentrated largely in the hands of the Kikuyu and Luo, has been extended to make place for representatives of the other tribal and ethnic groups. But, although several prominent Europeans and Asians joined K.A.N.U., it failed, at first, to win substantial support from the immigrant communities.

These communities mostly preferred to support K.A.D.U., which emerged as the champion of the weaker ethnic groups that felt, or claimed to feel, threatened by the large tribes which were dominant in K.A.N.U. Thus K.A.D.U. saw itself as a defence political movement seeking to safeguard "the weak" against "the strong". It brought together not only many of the whites and the Asians but also a variety of other ethnic groups such as the Kalenjin people (the nomads of the Rift Valley), the people of the coastal strip, and the Baluhya. Under the leadership of Ronald Ngala (for a time Chief Minister of Kenya), Musinde Muliro, Arap Moi and Taita Towett, K.A.D.U. championed independence as vigorously as K.A.N.U.

Where the two movements disagreed was on the fundamental principles to be stated in an independence constitution. K.A.N.U. favoured a strong unitary form of government with elaborate safeguards for individual human rights. K.A.D.U. favoured a loose federal constitution, based on strongly entrenched regions and a comparatively weak central government. The settlers and many of the Asians tended, at first, to support this federalist idea.

The struggle between unitary government and federalism characterized the third phase of the independence struggle, which lasted from about 1960 to early 1963. But there is another important feature of this phase: the "forgiveness" preached by Jomo Kenyatta towards the settlers. He went out of his way to seek white and Asian support for K.A.N.U. Meeting white farmers in the Highlands, he asked forgiveness for mistakes on both sides. He firmly supported the policy of paying full compensation for all farms taken over in the Highlands, and came out in favour of a planned system of land resettlement.

Kenyatta's policy was made possible by the decision of the settlers' leaders to accept the agreement reached at the famous Lancaster House constitutional conference in London in 1960, when the then Colonial Secretary, Iain Macleod, came out in favour of African majority rule for Kenya. But even before this decisive step was taken, the settlers' leaders had themselves agreed to abandon the sacrosanctity of white settlement in the Highlands. This was a major retreat taken under pressure from the moderate white leaders who believed that this retreat was essential to encourage moderate policies in the African leadership. But three more bitter years of political rivalry had to be endured before a second Lancaster House conference adopted a constitution acceptable to K.A.N.U.—a policy decision which became inevitable after K.A.D.U. had gone down to a heavy electoral defeat in the early part of 1963.

Thus victory went to the militant nationalists, and K.A.N.U. emerged at the end of the long struggle for independence as the dominant political force. It controlled almost three-quarters of the membership of the legislature, and was entrusted with a constitution largely of its own making. As the inheritor of British power, Kenyatta's government was faced with a number of challenging problems, any one of which was capable of producing serious upheavals.

Nation-Building

The greatest of these problems is one that is common to all emergent states in tropical Africa: the task of nation-building. Whatever else colonialism might have achieved in Africa, nowhere has it been able to weld the numerous, diverse tribes into a single nation. Colonialism in Africa, in fact, has stood Europe's own history on its head by creating the nation-state before the nation. It has been left to the new leaders to build the nation.

So far, almost without exception, in the new states of Africa the difficulties encountered in trying to reconcile tribal and other particularist interests with the overriding needs of the new state have resulted in the setting up of a single-party state, at least as a temporary substitute for the homogeneous society.

What complicates this task of nation-building in Kenya is the presence of so many diverse racial as well as tribal communities. At the last census in 1962 there were 8,676,000 people of whom 178,000 were Asian, 66,000 were white, and 39,000 were Arab. The Africans were divided into 60 ethnic communities with five of these (the Kikuyu, Luo, Baluhya, Kamba and Meru) accounting for 65 per cent of the total.

The minority groups are all naturally fearful of their future. The smaller tribes are anxious about their land and local development. The Asians and Arabs are concerned about opportunities for work and trade, and for promotion on merit in the civil service. The whites are anxious about their place in the new society now that they have lost their political importance, and always fearful of the dangers of *revanchisme*.

22. The Somali-Kenya dispute

J. DRYSDALE *The Somali Dispute* Pall Mall and Praeger 1964; pages 35–8, 39

. . . The present frontier between the Somali Republic and Kenya was a historical accident, dating from Britain's treaty with Italy in 1891 which partitioned the Sudan and East Africa from Ethiopia and the Somali plateau into respective zones of British and Italian influence. The southern part of the boundary followed the Juba river northwards into Ethiopia across the Blue Nile to the shores of the Red Sea. Italy declared a Protectorate over the vast area to the east of this line as far as the French and British zones on the northern Somali coastline. To the west of this line, Britain declared her interest, safeguarding in particular the source of the White Nile which she had successfully secured from her German rivals by treaty the previous year. The port of Kismayu lay to the west of the mouth of the Juba and thus remained in the hands of the Imperial British East Africa Company which occupied the port for four disastrous years on a lease from the Sultan of Zanzibar.

In his history of the King's African Rifles, Moyse-Bartlett writes that "from the time when the administration of Kismayu was taken over by the Imperial British East Africa Company in August, 1891, to its conquest from the Italians fifty years later, Jubaland was the scene of frequent campaigns. . .".

From the beginning the Company ran into trouble. The Company's administrator, J. Ross Todd, was a young Scotsman of twenty-four with more burdens than he could carry. He had received no letters from home for two months and had to pay dearly for cables to his family seeking assurances that all was well. He was not in the best frame of mind to handle disputes with Somalis over the title deeds to plots in the town. Todd was adamant that all unoccupied plots belonged to the Company under its treaty with the Sultan of Zanzibar. The Somalis were already in a state of unrest over the division of blood-money which the administrator in Mombasa had sanctioned as a conciliatory gesture. The Somalis became increasingly suspicious, insolent and resentful. Todd finally called their elders to a meeting. He took the precaution, however, of arranging in advance for HMS *Widgeon*, lying off shore, to land a party of bluejackets and marines if the flag on the Residency was lowered.

Count Lovatelli, a Lieutenant in the Italian Navy who had recently arrived from Italy on a voyage of exploration, accompanied Todd to the meeting. Shortly after it had begun, the Somalis got wind of the proposal to land marines and showed signs of considerable agitation. As Todd rose to his feet, the Somalis did likewise. Thinking that they were about to attack Todd, Lovatelli fired his revolver. Pandemonium broke out. Todd was stabbed in the neck and fell to the ground. HMS *Widgeon* was signalled to carry out a bombardment and the Somalis ran from the town and occupied the surrounding country.

In the meantime, W. G. Hamilton, the superintendent in charge of fifty soldiers who had mutinied, established himself, with a few locally recruited ex-slaves, on Turki Hill at the mouth of the Juba. His stronghold was overrun at night by combined forces of Somalis, Indians and Arabs. Hamilton was wounded by a poisoned arrow and afterwards shot at close range. At dawn, the rebels swept into the town and attacked the Residency. After three hours' fighting they were repulsed by the local garrison under command of Count Lovatelli who was awarded the CMG for this action. The Somalis returned to the bush and all contact with them was lost. Todd resigned and in 1895 Jubaland was placed under British Government control and proclaimed a Protectorate.

With the transfer of the administration to the British Government a series of punitive expeditions into the interior were planned to secure tribute from the Somali chiefs.

War was declared against the Ogaden, [wrote Sir Charles Eliot, the Commissioner for East Africa] and a costly expedition was despatched. It gained no success proportionate to its size and expense, for it was unable to capture or force a battle on the light-footed

RTCA

nomads, who vanished before it in a scrubby wilderness, well known to them, though pathless to strangers, while it was on the other hand exposed to sudden attacks from fanatical desperados.

By assuming the responsibility for the 'protection' of these clans, the administration found itself increasingly involved in attempts to defend one clan from another and to protect them all against bands of armed marauders from Ethiopia. A forward policy was made all the more compelling by the action of the administration to disarm Somalis. Thus, between the years 1895–1912, the British administration reluctantly penetrated further into the Northern Frontier District for two reasons: to counter continuing Somali westward expansion against the Galla, and to prevent Ethiopian armed raids on the livestock and inhabitants of these regions.

It was not until 1909 that the Somalis reached the Tana river and drove the Boran Galla from Wajir.

In a period of some three centuries the wheel of fortune had turned full circle. The first Hamitic settlers in the north of Kenya had been the Somali Madanle and Dabarre; these had been ousted by the Warday Galla; and the latter were eventually beaten and harried by the Ajuran and Boran Galla and later Somali immigrants.

Wajir was occupied by British forces in 1912 but hastily evacuated four years later after eighty people had been killed following a surprise attack by Somalis on Lieutenant Elliott's Constabulary at Serenli in the upper Juba. The NFD came under effective administration for the first time when Moyale and Wajir were garrisoned by regular troops in 1919. . . .

The Treaty of London was signed in July 1924, but the cession of Jubaland to Italy did not in fact take place until June 29 the following year.

Kenyans today claim that Britain was morally wrong to have ceded Jubaland. Certainly Britain could only justify the action on the same principle that she applied to the conditional transfer of the Dodecanese Islands to Greece, in which case she should have made a clean breast of it and transferred the whole of Somali territory in Northern Kenya to Italian Somaliland. She seemed to be partially conscious of this when Mr Amery, in a statement to the House of Commons on December 18, 1924, said ". . . the reason for the cession of the territory as a whole is to keep these tribes together as a single unit, and give them the full use of their natural grazing ground . . .". In addition, the Earl of Onslow (Under Secretary of State for War) said in the House of Lords on March 5, 1925, "I may say that the whole of this country is inhabited by a small population of nomad Somalis, and the line has been drawn as closely as possible in accordance with racial divisions."

23. Asians in East Africa

G. DELF *Asians in East Africa* Oxford University Press for Institute of Race Relations 1963; pages 5–9

Any attempt to depict the peculiar quality and purpose of Indian settlement in East Africa must soon come to terms with religious beliefs which divide the entire community into mutually exclusive compartments. This basic fragmentation is difficult to explain to Westerners for whom only class consciousness suggests a somewhat remote parallel today. Ironically, the unity of the Indian community has been fostered as much by those who had little interest in it as from within its own ranks. By treating all Indians as a single group, Africans and Europeans have provided an incentive for greater cohesion than there was in India itself. Land laws, education acts, and immigration laws have presented the Indian community with common problems and the need for joint action.

After sixty years of colonial rule, however, religious divisions remain strong, though there are signs today that this is less true of the young and well-educated. But even in 1962 a remark by the Kenya African leader, Tom Mboya, about the place of intermarriage in an integrated society, excited widespread indignation. 'Shahs', said one leading Indian, 'will not give their daughters to Patels, and they will not give them to Africans.'

Muslims

Despite the fact that Arab influence might have been expected to favour Muslim Indians, at least in the early stages of Indian settlement, it is only in Tanganyika that they now outnumber the Hindus. In Kenya and Uganda they form less than one-third of the Indian population.

Within one hundred years of the death of Mohammed, his followers disagreed about the method of choosing the head of the Muslim community. Two groups formed as a result, the Sunnis, by far the larger, and the Shias. Most of the Muslims in East Africa belong to one of three sects of the Shias: the Ithna'ashri, the Bohra, and the Ismaili Khoja. The first of these is the largest, and is particularly strong in Iran, but in East Africa it is the Ismaili Khojas who predominate.

The Ismaili Khojas were originally Hindu traders living in the Upper Sind area of north-west India. The word Khoja means 'honourable disciple', and the first conversions are said to have taken place in the twelfth century. This sect does not go on pilgrimage to Mecca. Certain Hindu customs survive in its pattern of life, including that relating to testate and intestate succession. Gujerati is a language which they use in common with other non-Muslim groups whose original homes were in the same coastal belt in western India.

Most Westerners know of the Ismaili Khojas through the world-wide fame of their religious leader, the Aga Khan. The community owes much to the cosmopolitan interests of its leaders and has a justified reputation in East Africa for its progressive policies. Of the total membership of over 50,000 more than half live in Tanganyika, about 18,000 are in Kenya, and the remainder in Uganda. The local Khoja communities have a federal organisation controlled by a Supreme Council, and this body is responsible for administering the many schools, clinics, and welfare centres paid for out of an annual tithe. Housing schemes have also been carried out successfully in the main towns. Possibly more than any other Indian group in East Africa, the Ismaili Khojas produce an increasing number of well-educated young men and women who fit easily into a modern society. They have been urged repeatedly by the Aga Khan to ally themselves with African development, and their schools have been among the first to accept the principle of multi-racial education.

The Bohras, whose name is said to derive from a Gujerati word meaning 'to trade', form another part of the Ismaili sect, and owe their separate existence to another of the many Muslim disagreements surrounding Mohammed's succession. They have their own mosques and burial grounds, and offer three daily prayers instead of the orthodox five. In 1871 this community already numbered about 600 in East Africa, mainly centred on Zanzibar and Mombasa. Many of them are ironmongers, watchmakers, and tinsmiths. Perhaps the most successful Bohra family has given its name to the firm of Jivanjee, which has sisal estates in Tanganyika and branches in the main towns. In 1954, Sir Tayabali H. A. Jivanjee gave £62,500 towards the building of a hospital in Zanzibar, and his other contributions to charities are estimated to be worth £300,000.

The third of these Shia sects, the Ithna'ashri, has its own beliefs about 'the Hidden Imam', whereby their true leader will reappear one day to lead all mankind into the true Shia faith. Perhaps of more direct social relevance to the East African scene is another small Muslim sect which is on the fringes of the Sunnis. It is named Ahmadiya, and most of its members originate in the Punjab, where the sect was founded in 1889. The founder claimed that Jesus Christ did not die on the cross but lived to a great age in Kashmir. Apart from this unusual belief the sect is conservative in its customs. Recently it has proselytised vigorously among Africans in East and West Africa, with some success. Two million, or about 10 per cent, of the total population in East Africa are Muslims. Arab influence, too, has been important in winning conversions. Swahili translations of the Koran have been published, together with tracts in many vernacular languages.

Hindus

It is impossible in a short space even to sketch in outline the pattern of Hinduism in East Africa. The religion itself is as complex as one might expect from something which has developed over thousands of years in India, offering to the curious observer as many faces as its gods. Its teachings include the most subtle expressions of poetic insight and yet as a way of life Hinduism finds room for primitive animism and what to the West seems gross superstition, for mature tolerance as well as for a tough modernism.

In 1841 there were about 500 Hindus resident in East Africa.

Today there are about 150,000. Many originate from Cutch and belong to the Bhattia sect, one of the oldest branches of a trading caste. Most are strict vegetarians, and their customs governing eating and drinking habits make intercommunal mixing difficult. There is little intermarriage between members of different castes. Some of the leading Hindus, such as A. B. Patel and S. G. Amin of Kenya, have combined an effective interest in politics with deep religious conviction and learning.

The more modern face of the Hindu community is well represented by the Arya Samaj, a reformist society which originated in India in the nineteenth century. Its activities spread beyond sectarian boundaries. Many of the educated younger generation today pay scant attention to the minuter articles of their faith, and are often impatient with the traditional observances of their elders. In a recent survey of Indian society, H. S. Morris has indicated some of the problems which face the higher ranks of the caste system when transferred to East Africa. He writes:

Since only fragments and isolated groups from many districts in India established themselves in Africa, the immigrants were not able to use their wealth in gaining prestige in a local African caste hierarchy, and could make sense of themselves and their success only by referring to the caste system at home in India. Everybody would hope eventually to take his wealth home to India and begin the long task of raising his status and that of the caste there. In the meantime, they lived in an environment which did not encourage orthodox Brahmin practices, partly because large numbers of the other Indians were not even Hindu, and social contact in a trading world could not be avoided, and partly because the need for dealing with the Europeans and Africans forced everybody who could to enter an elaborate system of entertainment, in which drinking and dinner parties broke all orthodox Brahmin rules.

The Sikhs, about 20,000, who are to be found mainly in Kenya, and the Jains, about 12,000, nearly all of whom also live in Kenya, account for most of the rest of the non-Muslim community. The former are particularly assertive and have many of their own institutions. Apart from being renowned for their adventurous driving habits, the 'Singhs', as they are popularly known, have won a secure niche for themselves as mechanics, carpenters, and railwaymen.

Goans

The Goans form a community of about 10,000, and are Roman Catholic. They come from the tiny former Portuguese colony of Goa, south of Bombay, and normally dislike being classified as Indians, being often of mixed blood. Many of their most common names, such as D'Souza, indicate their ancestry. They have earned a high reputation for reliability, and many hold responsible clerical jobs in banks. Most speak fluent English, as well as the Indian vernacular, Konkarim. Despite their small numbers they run their own schools. The young men often return to Goa to find wives, and caste-consciousness among them is still strong.

24. Malagasy: patterns and prospects

W. J. FOLTZ *Current History* Vol. 46, No. 271, March 1964; pages 164–8

. . . The origins of the Malagasy people are only approximately known, though scholars agree that they are basically Malayo-Polynesian people, and they retain many cultural features common to Southeast Asia. The fortunes of world trade and conquest, abetted by Madagascar's strategic position on both the European and Arab routes to the Indies, have mixed in other racial strains, particularly Africans of the Bantu stock, many of whom were brought over originally as slaves. While the different Malagasy peoples are racially mixed, the proportions of African and Malayo-Polynesian blood vary considerably over the island. Near the coast, among peoples like the Bara, Sakalava, and Tsimehety, dark skin and Negroid features are most common. On the central plateau, among the Merina and particularly those Merina of upper and middle caste (Hova), the Malayo-Polynesian strain is most prominent. This racial difference by itself would be of little importance were it not allied to a history of Merina military and political dominance over the darker coastal peoples.

In the latter part of the eighteenth century, the Merina king, Andrianampoinimerina, established an efficient state organization—initially for the extension of a complex irrigation system for rice culture. With this organizational resource and the added wealth from agricultural abundance, Andrianampoinimerina began systematic raids against his neighbours to extend his plateau kingdom to the sea. His successors continued the work and, to strengthen their forces, actively sought instruction for their people from European nations. British officers helped train the Merina army in 1820; British, and later American, Protestant missionaries were encouraged to proselytize and to develop an education system. French Catholic missionary activity was less successful among the Merina where it was confined principally to the lower social orders, in part because long-standing French missions on the coast had allied the Catholics with many of the Merina's opponents and subject peoples there.

By the middle of the century, the great majority of upper-caste Merina were members of the official Protestant church, and in 1869 the Merina queen, Ranavalona II, broke definitively with traditional religion by receiving Protestant baptism. Under missionary auspices, education in the Malagasy language made rapid progress. In 1895 there were some 155,000 Merina students in missionary schools, and the capital city, Tananarive, boasted a secondary school, a technical institute, a normal school, and a medical academy.

Against such a dynamic people, the coastal peoples could offer little resistance except in port areas where outside commercial interests, principally French, could back up the local populations with money and arms. By the 1890s, the Merina kingdom covered two-thirds of the island and held outposts in the remaining territories. To govern these vast holdings, which covered an area almost the size of France, the Merina monarchy relied on a regular state bureaucracy with regional governors and administrators for some of the conquered lands, augmented by relationships of vassalage and tribute for the less docile peoples. The Merina actively set out to teach Merina customs and techniques to the coastal peoples. The very name of the city they established in Betsileo territory, Fianarantsoa, means "good teaching".

"La Politique des Races"

It was thus a dynamic civilization in full expansion that confronted the French when, in 1895, their army defeated the Merina at the battle of Tananarive. Once the French had gained control of the island, they saw two alternative means of governing it: taking the Merina kingdom under French protection, which would have completed the "Merinization" of the island, or annexation pure and simple with destruction of the Merina hegemony. Despite pleas to the contrary from many Frenchmen on the scene, the French government decided on the latter course and sent out one of its most brilliant colonial officers, General Gallieni, to apply what came to be called *"la politique des races"*. This policy abolished the Merina monarchy, encouraged the coastal peoples to assert their independence from the Merina by naming local headmen, extended French language schooling to the coastal peoples and sought to develop the economy of the coastal regions to the level of the Imerina plateau.

Despite initial success under Gallieni, the new policy and the development of national unity suffered greatly under the less expert guidance of the General's successors who applied little of the policy beyond its "divide and rule" aspect. In fact, little was done to promote serious economic development among the coastal populations; World War I and, later, the depression of the 1930s put an end to most of what had been started.

With limited fiscal and human resources, the French fell back on their tradition of centralized administration and concentrated on Tananarive, by then the capital of the Madagascar colony. It was the political, administrative, and commercial centre of the colony. Encouraged by the presence of a large market for consumer goods, and by the necessary social and physical substructure, the economy of the Tananarive province (essentially the Merina homeland) developed far faster than that of the coast. By the end of the French colonial period in Madagascar, the economic discrepancies between the central plateau and the coast were accentuated and the social discrepancies between Merina and costal peoples were little changed.

From the purely political point of view, French policy was

equally undistinguished. Through *la politique des races* the French accentuated all the disadvantages of continued Merina pre-eminence, but failed to gain the advantage of a single Merina-led Malagasy political unit. The lower ranks of the colonial administration throughout the island were staffed primarily by Merina, who thereby continued to enjoy high status compared to the coastal peoples. At the same time, many upper-caste Merina resented the fact that the French denied them access to the positions of higher administrative responsibility they would have enjoyed under the pre-colonial Merina regime.

The first political reactions to the French policy were not long in coming. In 1915, a group of some 300 upper-caste Merina intellectuals and students formed a secret society, the V.V.S. (from the Malagasy words for Iron, Stone, Branches), which talked of an uprising against the colonial power. The group was discovered and the young men were punished by severe prison terms. While the extent of the "plot" was undoubtedly greatly exaggerated by the French, the disaffection felt by many Merina for their colonial overlords was none the less real. The interwar period saw continued evidence of occasionally violent political disaffection.

The establishment of territorial representative political institutions under the French following World War II brought the Malagasies their first real participation in the government of the island since 1895. Political dominance on the island was quickly gained by the *Mouvement Démocratique de la Renovation Malgache* (M.D.R.M.), among whose leaders were some who had participated in the V.V.S. years before. The M.D.R.M., which enjoyed support from the French Communist party, appealed particularly to the Hova and other young nationalist intellectuals. Many of the latter saw a radical nationalist party with Hova backing as the best way of breaking the influence of the traditional conservative coastal élites. The major opposition group, named significantly the *Parti des Déshérités de Madagascar* (P.A.D.E.S.M.), found its major strength among the coastal peoples and was openly backed by the colonial administration. Other smaller parties reflected primarily religious, caste, and ethnic divisions on the island.

For reasons that remain to be fully explained, sections of the M.D.R.M. launched a full-scale armed revolt against the

French regime on March 29, 1947. Armed only with ancient flintlocks and spears, the rebels had no chance, despite a prophecy that French bullets would turn to water when they were fired. But the French were not able to restore peace to the island for a year and a half. By that time, well over 12,000 people had been killed in the terrorist attacks and in the bloody repression by the colonial army aided by civilian vigilantes. Brought to trial in October, 1948, most of the M.D.R.M. leaders were sentenced to prison or exiled and the party dissolved. The P.A.D.E.S.M., however, proved completely incapable of developing any national cohesion, and rapidly dissolved into competitive local sections. In this political vacuum, the small Malagasy section of the French Communist party made notable progress, primarily in the trade union movement. Malagasies owe their freedom from a serious Communist problem to the missions (primarily the Catholics, who succeeded in splitting the Communist-led labour movement) rather than to the colonial authorities, who lacked political finesse and popular trust.

The Parti Social Démocrate

It was not until 1956, when, under a Socialist Minister of Overseas France, France granted substantial internal autonomy to its overseas possessions, that political life was resumed and a serious political movement based on something other than Hova leadership emerged. With the direct help of the French Socialist party, the Tsimehety schoolmaster, Philibert Tsiranana, founded the *Parti Social Démocrate* (P.S.D.) which today rules the Malagasy Republic. Under Tsiranana's leadership, the P.S.D. has followed a conscious policy of national reconciliation and unification.

The French Socialists' greater emphasis on "equality and independence of the individual" as opposed to the idea of sacrificing all for immediate national independence, appealed particularly to Madagascar's disadvantaged population groups. To the party's primarily coastal base of support, Tsiranana has added members of the Merina middle and lower castes and some of the Hova intellectuals. After the Republic's independence in 1960, President Tsiranana declared a general amnesty for political prisoners and permitted the exiles to return to

Madagascar. Today the P.S.D. and its affiliates control some 90 of the 107 seats in the Malagasy National Assembly.

Against the P.S.D., the major opposition party, the A.K.F.M. (the initials stand for Madagascar Congress and Independence Party in the Malagasy language), represents primarily the Hova-intellectual liaison that earlier led the opposition to colonial rule. The A.K.F.M.'s support comes primarily from Tananarive. Where the P.S.D. has sought close cooperation with the French and has encouraged private enterprise, the A.K.F.M. has advocated a more independent and neutralist foreign policy and has demanded rapid nationalization and collectivization of the economy. The opposition between the two parties recalls similar conflict in other former French colonies where the party backed by the colonial regime remained in power after independence.

Domestic Politics

In addition to the range of difficulties common to under-developed countries, President Tsiranana's government has had to deal with the problems of reinforcing unity at home and establishing an independent national identity in world affairs. In the domestic sphere, the government has sought to promote rapid economic development while maintaining the political status quo. So far its success has been more apparent in the second than in the first of these goals. President Tsiranana's political abilities and the support he has enjoyed from the French government have allowed the P.S.D. to put together a skilfully balanced cabinet that includes representatives from all important interests on the island. Crucial to Tsiranana's success has been his appointment of Jacques Rabemananjara, one of the most prestigious of the M.D.R.M. leaders exiled after the 1947 revolt, as Minister for the National Economy. Although of Betsimisaraka origin, his past activities and his fame as a poet and historian have won him wide support among the Hova and other Merina. The balance of interests is so finely calculated within the government that President Tsira-nana has avoided making significant personnel shifts since independence.

The P.S.D.'s dominant position has been strengthened by division and bickering in the opposition parties. Most recently, in March, 1963, Joseph Raseta, one of the former exiles, broke with the A.K.F.M. to found his own splinter party. When opposition activity seems serious, the government has on occasion taken firm steps. The combined opposition lists presented for the September, 1963, senatorial elections in Tananarive and Tulear were outlawed for "irregularities".

The apparent political stability of the Malagasy Republic does not mean that the old social and economic divisions have been completely submerged. Many of the most bitter disputes within the government concern the conflicting interests of the plateau and the coast. The deputy who announced to the national assembly that the appointment of additional Tananarive representatives to the finance commission would "continue the historic subjection of the coastal peoples" was not just indulging in empty political hyperbole. However, the mere fact that such discussions go on *within* the governing party, and not only among parties, is a promising sign for continued political stability.

Economic Disparities

The P.S.D. officially gives "primacy to the economic over the political realm" as a focus for governmental concern and action. The government has explicitly sought to submerge the economic and social discrepancies between the Merina plateau and the coastal regions in a programme of rapid economic development. While it is as yet too early to judge the programme's success, a few statistics give some appreciation of the advantages the Merina plateau enjoys at present. Although it covers only about 9 per cent of the island, the province of Tananarive (essentially Imerina) produces about one-third of Madagascar's gross national product and contains some 23 per cent of the population. With an intensive system of rice cultivation producing two crops a year, the province is exceptionally well-nourished. Despite this agricultural abundance, only some 43 per cent of the population engage in agriculture, while almost as high a proportion are in white collar or service professions.

Almost three-quarters of school-age children are in school in the Tananarive province. Over 60 per cent of the population are literate in Malagasy and nearly half understand French. This contrasts with a school attendance rate for the island as a whole of 48 per cent, while only 41 per cent are literate in Malagasy and 18 per cent understand French. The vast majority of Madagascar's professionals are Merina from Tananarive. As a result of both the province's prosperity and the dynamism of Merina society, the Merina population is growing at a rate of 3 per cent per annum as against 2 per cent for all the Malagasies.

At the other extreme, the Bara, a herding people from the southern coastal area, live in a food-deficit economy, send fewer than 10 per cent of their children to school, and are increasing in number at a mere ·7 per cent per annum.

In attacking these regional disparities, the government has given priority to agricultural development in the less favoured coastal areas and has promoted rapid expansion of the export sector of the economy, since about 95 per cent of Madagascar's exports come from non-Merina areas. Despite some encouraging starts and a few local successes, the agricultural development programme has made only limited headway on the coast. Major impediments have been the lack of internal communication lines which hinders the extension of the market economy, and, above all, the persistence of economically irrational social and religious customs. Chief among these latter are a prevalence of religious celebrations connected with the cult of the dead which, like the celebrations in some Latin countries, are frequent enough to reduce the work effort to a minimum necessary for subsistence. Other culturally induced uneconomic practices like indiscriminate cattle breeding and overgrazing, and the use of brush fires to clear land, continue to destroy productive lands faster than they can be reclaimed or improved. Finally, despite some earnest attempts at decentralization, the administration of agricultural development has continued to make the Tananarive bureaucracy the source and partially the beneficiary of agricultural development funds.

Expansion of exports, particularly coffee, vanilla, and cloves, has been more successful; their yearly value has increased from some 64 million in 1957 to some 93 million in 1962. Until now the effects of increased export prosperity have not been greatly felt by the coastal peoples because most export production and virtually all export-import commerce are still owned and controlled by foreign groups. Some 85 per cent of Madagascar's private employers are drawn from the country's foreign community of 52,000 Europeans, 12,000 Indians, and 9,000 Chinese, and most of the Malagasy employers are Merina. Virtually all the marketing arrangements for Madagascar's exports are in the hands of a few closely linked French trading, banking, and transportation organizations.

Because of the Malagasy economy's need for foreign earnings and the country's lack of indigenous commercial élites, the Malagasy government has not attempted to change the commercial structure. As President Tsiranana declared in September, 1963, "I do not believe in destroying anything without knowing how, and with what, one can reconstruct." . . .

VI. POLICIES AND IDEOLOGIES IN SOUTH AFRICA

25. The eighth Kafir war: Nongqause

EDWARD ROUX *Time Longer than Rope* University of Wisconsin Press 1964; pages 35–9

. . . Further wars were inevitable. In less than two years came the Eighth Kafir War, "the longest and most costly in blood and treasure that the Cape Colony had ever engaged in". The chief significance of this war for the historian is the part played by the Hottentots. It had been hitherto the custom of the Government to employ them as soldiers against the Bantu. But on this occasion large numbers of Hottentot soldiers mutinied and joined the Bantu. This did not affect the issue of the war. At the end of it large tracts of land previously occupied by the Temblu tribe were given to the colonists.

Not only was a considerable part of the Xhosa people now reduced to the status of an internal proletariat, but the external proletariat across the Kei River also felt the increasing pressure of the white advance. Many of them must have felt that as an independent people they were doomed and that only a miracle could save them. It was as though the Bantu, beaten by the guns, horsemen and superior organisation of the Europeans, turned to the spiritual world for help. As some thirty years earlier they had listened to the prophet Makana, so now they were willing to listen and find hope in the leadership of a new prophet, the girl Nongqause.

The story of Nongqause[1] and the great cattle-killing of 1856 is still the subject of controversy. In some ways this Xhosa girl of sixteen resembled the French Joan of Arc. She was the prophet of Xhosa nationalism as Joan was of French. Like Joan, she heard voices telling her to come forward and save her country. Like Joan she was called to her great mission when she was but in her teens. Unlike Joan, she was not burnt as a heretic nor did it fall to her lot to be canonised as a saint: she lived to be an old woman.

[1]Pronounce it *Non-kah-oo-seh* if you cannot achieve the click.

Her story begins on the morning in May, 1856, when she went to draw water at the Gxara, a small river east of the Kei. On her return she said she had met the spirits of the dead. The "eternal enemies of the white man, they announce themselves as having come from battlefields beyond the sea to aid the Xhosas with their invincible power in driving the English from the land." Nongqause's uncle, Mhlakaza, took the message to the paramount chief, Kreli. The spirits had given orders that all the cattle were to be killed and eaten and no one was to cultivate the land. Then, on a certain day, millions of fat cattle would spring out of the earth and great fields of corn would appear ready for eating. At the same time the sky would fall and crush the white people and with them all the blacks who had not obeyed the commands of the spirits.

There are a number of variants of this story. One has it that Nongqause was working in the fields when she met ten young men who gave her the message. She went to fetch her uncle, who was able to communicate with the young men through her, though he could not see them. Some reports said that they were Russians! This story undoubtedly owed its origin to the fact that more or less distorted accounts of the Crimean War, which ended in 1856, had penetrated to Xhosaland; to the Xhosas the Russians were the enemies of the English.

The cattle-killing was begun almost immediately. It had the full support of Kreli, who set an example by destroying his favourite horse. Mhlakaza himself destroyed all his own cattle. The people became divided into believers and non-believers, but the former steadily gained ground. Many of the Ciskeian tribes also became infected. A traveller between Peddie and East London in December, 1856, reported that he hardly saw a single beast or a single acre under cultivation over a distance of eighty miles. "The Kafir women are, in their adherence to the Prophet (Mhlakaza), far more stubborn than the men. These have a tale among them to the effect that a Kafir man attempted, in opposition to the mandate of the Prophet, to turn up the ground, but that he had no sooner struck his hoe into the land than he became paralysed, could not move from the spot, and it was only after great difficulty that the charm was broken and the offender liberated."

Another writer in a colonial newspaper said that the proceedings of the Kafirs were the most extraordinary ever known. They were perfectly reckless in making away with their cattle; a cow or a calf might be bought for a few shillings which a short time before would not be parted with at any price. The trade in hides was enormous. The notorious witch doctor had predicted that very shortly two suns would be seen at one time, that a desperate battle or collision would take place between them and that then would ensue a time of profound darkness. After that "all, whether black or white, who wore *trousers* would be swept away by a whirlwind, the lucky *sansculottes* being left in undisturbed possession of the whole country."

Of the non-believers the most numerous and consistent were the Fingoes. Refugees from the wars of Dingaan and Tshaka, Zulu chiefs, they had fled to the Cape, only to come under the domination of the Xhosas. The Cape Government had made them its allies, giving them land taken from the Xhosas. They were often "trouser" people and more Westernised than the majority of the Bantu in the Eastern Cape. They steadfastly refused to kill their cattle, but were quite prepared to buy cattle from the prophet-ridden Xhosas. As one reporter put it, "the wild stories so freely circulated had no effect on them; they stood their ground, ready for bargain or battle."

The general feeling among the colonists as they witnessed this spectacle of a nation's suicide was that the cattle-killing was merely the prelude to an armed attack on the Colony. It was believed by many that behind the whole mad business was a plot on the part of the chiefs to throw the whole Xhosa people, fully armed and in a famished state, upon the Colony. It was reported in a Grahamstown paper in August, 1856, that scores of farmers had abandoned their homesteads and that many missionaries had removed their furniture to King William's Town. On the other hand, it was said that adequate military preparations had been made to stop any armed breakthrough on the frontier.

Resurrection Day was originally fixed for Friday, August 15, 1856. Nothing unusual happened on that day. It was said that the date had been postponed. There was a comparative lull in the cattle-killing. It was said that Kreli had begun to get tired of the game he was playing and had ordered his people to cease from destroying their cattle. According to another story, he had asked the Prophet for three months' extension, his herds being so immense that it would be impossible to sacrifice the whole in a shorter time.

But the slaughter of the animals was soon revived. Charles Brownlee said in January, 1857: "I think not less than three or four hundred thousand cattle have been killed or wasted." It became impossible for Mhlakaza, or whoever was at the back of it all, to delay any longer. Starvation was already staring the people in the face. The day of the full moon in February, 18, was finally decided on. "At length," says Theal, "the morning dawned of the day so long and ardently looked for. All night long the Xhosa had watched, expecting to see two blood-red suns arise over the eastern hill." At length the sun rose looking much as usual and with no supernatural companion. "But perhaps after all it might be midday that was meant. And when the shadows began to lengthen towards the east, perhaps, they thought, the setting of the sun is the time. The sun went down, as it often does in that fair land, behind clouds of crimson and gold, and the Xhosas awoke to the reality of their dreadful position."

If it had been the intention of the instigators of the cattle-killing to lead a hungry army in a final assault on the Colony, they had bungled badly. The warriors had not been collected at a single point on the border ready to burst through. Now it was too late to collect them. "The only chance of life was to reach the Colony, but it was as suppliants, not as warriors, that the famished people must now go." It was estimated that between 25,000 and 50,000 people died as a result of the cattle-killing, out of a total population of possibly 150,000. Thousands managed to reach the Colony, where they were given food and work. Nongqause and Mhlakaza had indeed effectively solved the labour problems of the colonists! But the military might of the Bantu was broken and it was a generation before they were able to fight again. . . .

26. Sources of apartheid

L. M. THOMPSON *Historians in Tropical Africa* University College, Salisbury, Rhodesia 1960; pages 381–6

V

. . . After twelve years of rule by a Nationalist party which proclaims that its policy is apartheid, the basic facts of life in South Africa are as far from Cronje's blueprint as ever. Black and White, Coloured and Asian, continue to form parts of a single but stratified society. *Gleichschaltung* rather than the separation of the races into autonomous territories has been the dominant feature of the period.

Reputable Afrikaner historians have refrained from producing large-scale apologia for the theory and practice of apartheid, but other Afrikaner academicians have not hesitated to do so. The most recent work of this sort is *Apartheid: a socio-economic exposition of the origin and development of the apartheid idea*, by N. J. Rhoodie and H. J. Venter. It is a publication of the departments of sociology and criminology of the University of Pretoria, in which H. J. Venter holds the chair of criminology.

The central thesis of the book may be stated as follows:[1] From an early stage the founders of the Afrikaner nation, the free burghers of the Cape Colony, learnt from experience that the differences between Whites and non-Whites are fundamental. Though they used slave, Hottentot and, later, Bantu labour, they were determined to preserve their racial identity, so they spontaneously applied a policy of "differentiation" based on colour. A "colour morality" was the core of their social philosophy. In the seventeenth and eighteenth centuries government officials and soldiers, sailors and other visitors to the Cape had a different outlook because they lacked a local patriotism. They were more lax in their relations with the non-Whites, with the result that Coloured people were produced from their unions with slaves and Hottentots. In the nineteenth century British negrophilism, commercialism and imperialism caused a breakdown of legal differentiation in the Cape Colony

---

[1] The book contains many inconsistencies. In this summary I have tried my best to present the central thesis as coherently and logically as possible, and for the most part I have done so in the words of the text.

and of territorial segregation between White and Bantu; and
initiated a deliberate policy of assimilation. The Great Trek
was an organized revolt against racial equality and assimilation, and in their republics the Afrikaners tried to enforce
differentiation in all spheres of life; but they did not achieve
territorial segregation, because they themselves used Bantu
labourers on their farms and imperialistic factors also prevented
it. The foundation of the Union in 1910 created the means
whereby a uniform colour policy could be applied. Until 1924,
however, the government adopted a weak compromise between
the pre-Union policies of the north and the south—differentiation and assimilation. Thereafter, Hertzog's segregation policy
was a great improvement, but it did not go far enough and it
was largely ignored by the succeeding Smuts government. The
result was that by the end of the Second World War the Bantu
were gaining a stranglehold on the Whites in the towns and the
future of the White race in South Africa was in jeopardy. By
that time, too, the Afrikaner had come to realize that it was
necessary to come to terms with Bantu nationalism, and to
believe that this could be done by preparing the Bantu for
independence in their own areas. So the apartheid idea crystal-
lized in the Afrikaner mind, as "the Afrikaner's formula for the
solution of conflicting racial interests and the peaceful regulation of human relations". It is a synthesis of the Afrikaner's
traditional conviction that "Assimilation will mean the . . .
suicide of the Whites" and "a revolutionary . . . programme for
the complete emancipation of the Bantu". Since 1948 the
Afrikaner Nationalist government has been giving expression
to apartheid. The Promotion of Bantu Self-Government Act,
1959, provides for the peaceful and healthy development of the
different Bantu national units in their own national homelands
in a Bantu-centric way, building on the traditional tribal
democracy; and for their eventual national independence,
preferably within a system like that of the British Commonwealth. In the rest of the Union the interests of the Whites will
always be paramount: the Whites will be protected against
Bantu competition; the Bantu will be treated as temporary
visitors. The ultimate end is "the comparatively permanent
and complete separation of White and Black in South Africa".

In some respects this thesis is suppler and more accurate than the pre-1948 theses of Coetzee, van Biljon and Cronje. Even so, the historical part of the thesis is riddled with errors and distortions. The origin of the Afrikaner tradition of discrimination on the ground of colour is taken beyond the bounds of accuracy, when the authors imply that the official, the soldier, the sailor and the casual visitor to South Africa were virtually the only White progenitors of the Cape Coloured people, and that the free burgher, and more particularly the trekboer, abstained from miscegenation. In fact, the so-called Bastards of the Cape Colony, some of whom later became known as Griquas, were the product of miscegenation between trekboers and Hottentot women. Trekboer society usually refrained from assuming responsibility for its mixed progeny, it is true; but it did not refrain from generating such offspring. The authors say, on the authority of Professor N. J. Olivier, that "It is a complete fallacy to state that the Bantu in South Africa have a stronger aboriginal claim to this country than the Whites". This is an evasion of the truth. Bantu tribes occupied most of the eastern and better-watered half of the present Union of South Africa long before White people settled there—in some cases for several centuries. The assertion that it was negrophilism, commercialism and imperialism which caused the breakdown of territorial separation between Black and White on the eastern frontier of the Cape Colony is a serious oversimplification. When trekboers and Africans began to meet in the neighbourhood of the Bushman and the Fish rivers in the late eighteenth century, they began to intermingle without the aid of any external-isms. The trekboer had the habit of expansion; he bartered with Africans for cattle and ivory; and he took Africans into his service. Successive governments tried to check this process. They failed. It was the trekboers themselves who were responsible for the first stages in the collapse of a line of division between Black and White on the eastern frontier of the Cape Colony. The old story, which was concocted by Theal, that Landdrost Maynier, whom trekboers drove out of the district of Graaf-Reinet in 1793, was a naïve negrophilist of the eighteenth-century French school, is repeated, though it has been demolished in detail by J. S. Marais. Dr Philip and other missionaries are castigated with adjectives and quotations in the traditional manner, without any attempt being made to present the facts fairly and draw valid deductions from them. Their influence is sweepingly labelled "iniquitous and demoralising"; they are said to have been provokers of native wars and Anglo-Boer hostility; their reputation is a byword in South Africa. What specific crimes are listed against these dreadful men? The crime of having sponsored the "notorious" 50th Ordinance of 1838, which relieved Hottentots and other non-Whites who were not slaves of severe disabilities, which amounted to a form of legalized serfdom; and the crime of having wished to protect Africans from exploitation by Whites by—paradoxically—creating a system of territorial separation between them. Then the Glen Grey Act of 1894 is said to have contained the "seed" of the Promotion of Bantu Self-Government Act of 1959, whereas it was based on the principle of elected district councils, which is almost completely absent from the recent law. It is also asserted that in their republics "The Boer-Afrikaners never tried to emulate the arbitrary annexation policy of the British authorities". This is in flat contradiction with the facts of the expansion of the Orange Free State against the Basuto, and of the South African Republic against the African tribes to the east and the west of the original area of white settlement.

The account of the present position in the Union and its future prospects is vitiated by five cardinal weaknesses. The present area of the "Bantu territories" is about 13% of the total area of the Union, and according to Rhoodie and Venter their ultimate area will be about 13·7% of the total. After explaining that most of this land has a moderately good rainfall, they assert that: "These territories should therefore be more than adequate to ensure their Bantu populations a decent existence". However, the territories in question are at present economic backwaters and, even if their development were promoted by the most lavish financial aid from the Union government,[1] they would never be likely to become economically viable, or capable of supporting more than a fraction of the African population of the Union.[2]

[1] This is not in fact the policy of the Union government, which rejected the somewhat moderate recommendations of the Tomlinson Commission on this subject.

[2] At the time of the 1951 census the total 'Bantu' population of the Union was 8,560,083, of whom 3,307,234 were in the 'Bantu areas' and 5,252,849

Secondly, it is misleading to assert that the Promotion of Bantu Self-Government Act of 1959 is a significant step towards autonomy for the Bantu territories. It does not even provide for a true restoration of traditional tribal authority, since the chiefs and councillors are strictly subordinated to the central government of the Union, which may veto their appointments, override their decisions, and dismiss them at any time. These facts are not stated. Until the authorities in the Bantu territories hold office by virtue of some sort of local sanction and have the final say in at least some fields, the first step towards genuine autonomy will not have been taken. Thirdly, the only reason which is advanced for withholding political and other rights from all the Africans in the 'White territory' is at variance, not only with present facts, but also future probabilities as admitted in the book itself. The reason is set out in two quotations, one from Dr W. M. M. Eiselen, the former Secretary of the Department of Bantu Administration and Development, the other from H. F. Verwoerd, the present prime minister. According to Dr Eiselen:

All the Bantu have their permanent homes in the reserves and their entry into other areas . . . is merely of a temporary nature and for economic reasons. In other words, they are admitted as work-seekers, not as settlers.

And according to Dr Verwoerd:

There (in the Bantu territories) the Whites have no permanent rights of any sort whatsoever. The case in the White territory is just the opposite . . . there the Bantu is the temporary dweller and the guest, for whatever purposes he may remain.

Yet it is admitted elsewhere that there will always be a large number of Africans permanently resident in the 'White territory'. True, one passage reads:

The recogition of a permanent Bantu population in the cities was another principle which cannot be reconciled with the apartheid idea.

But in another place we find:

---

were outside them (*Union Statistics for Fifty Years* (1960), p. A–10). It is probable that the number of Africans in the Union, but outside the 'Bantu' areas', is now larger than it was in 1951.

Supporters of apartheid all admit that the Whites will make use of Bantu labour for the foreseeable future—although to a gradually lessening degree.

And elsewhere it is said bluntly (and realistically):

South Africa will have to reconcile herself to the fact that she will always have large concentrations of Bantu living in her metropolitan areas.

The last quotation explodes the only justification that is offered for discrimination against Africans. Fourthly, the account of the present condition and future prospects of the Union ignores the existence of the Coloured and Asian inhabitants. Even if there were genuine self-government in the "Bantu territories", and even if no African people lived in the "White territory", the protagonist of apartheid should still justify the multifarious forms of discrimination practised against the million and a half Coloured people and the half million Asian people in the Union.[1] Fifthly, the book is written exclusively from the Afrikaner point of view. Apartheid, we are told, is "the spiritual possession of the Afrikaner people". The Afrikaner "decided . . . that separate development was in the best interests of the Bantu". He "grants the Bantu . . . a national home where they can live and develop their own particular qualities unimpeded". And the "details" of the practical application of apartheid today are said to "have significance" only for the observer who is "able to identify himself mentally with the Whites in South Africa". There is no suggestion that the observer should also identify himself with the non-Whites. Presumably, therefore, the "details" have no "significance" for the very people who are their victims. Indeed, nowhere in the book is it so much as hinted that there may be wisdom in considering the feelings and the wishes of the other inhabitants of South Africa, least of all the feelings and wishes of the more than five million Africans who are declared to be "visitors" in the territory which is declared to be "White". The Afrikaner Nationalist has decided what is good for them: they must comply. These weaknesses destroy the validity of the very core of this apologia for apartheid.

[1] The official estimate of the population of the Union of South Africa on 30 June 1960 is: Whites 3,123,000; Coloureds 1,450,000; Asiatics 459,000; Bantu 9,896,000: Total 14,928,000 (*Union Statistics for Fifty Years*, p. A–8).

VI

One element in the Afrikaner national mythology was determined by the fact that South Africa was incorporated in the British Empire at the beginning of the last century and bore the main brunt of British imperialism at its close. It is an anglophobic mythology, like the French Canadian and the Irish. During the last fifty years, however, the Afrikaner has advanced to a dominant position in the power structure of South Africa, and as he was doing so he became aware that his gains were being challenged, not by the old imperial authority, but by the new force of African nationalism. Consequently the negrophobic element which was present in the mythology from the first gradually became its principal element.

For the most part it is a hard and humourless mythology of an anxious, embattled people, who have never been assured of a continued national existence—a mythology of bitter grievances and solemn heroics. Intellectuals and churchmen were the first to give effective literary expression to it. It has been perpetuated, in varying degrees of intensity, in some of the principal works of Afrikaner historical writing. It is strongly entrenched in the text-books and the teaching in the schools. And it is taken extremely seriously.

So potent is it, that it has moulded the political outlook of a majority of the Afrikaners, creating an intellectual and emotional climate in which it was easy for them to accept apartheid as though it were a morally and rationally credible policy, whereas in sober truth it has always been an escape from reality. And in the latest exposition of apartheid, with its obsessive group-centredness and its semantic illusions, the distinction between myth and fact is as elusive as ever.

27. Apartheid legislation

c. m. tatz *Shadow and Substance in South Africa* University of Natal Press 1962; pages 137–45

(i) *Social* apartheid

In the field of "social" *apartheid*, important legislation has been passed with the purpose of "preserving and safeguarding the racial identity of the White population" of the country. The Prohibition of Mixed Marriages Act, 55/1949, made marriages between Whites and non-Whites illegal. It may be mentioned that in 1943 there were 92 such "mixed" marriages in South Africa; in 1944, there were 99, in 1945, 92 and in 1946, 77. The Immorality Act 1927 Amendment Act, 21/1950, extends to non-Whites generally the provisions of the original Act which prohibited illicit carnal intercourse between Africans and Whites. The sequence of these Acts is important, for the former Act prohibits mixed marriages and this Act prohibits couples from living together. In South Africa, sex, in the sense of marriage and physical relations, can hardly be said to be the concern of the individual. In 1949 when the Bechuanaland chief, Seretse Khama, married a White woman, the Nationalist press expressed strong disapproval and the Dutch Reformed Churches passed a resolution that Khama should not be recognized as a chief. One paper called on the British Government to "honour the principle of *apartheid*". A further amendment, Act 23/1957, increases the maximum penalty for "immorality" from five to seven years and makes the "soliciting" for immoral purposes an offence. In order to facilitate the administration of these two Acts, the Population Registration Act, 30/1950, was passed. It provides for the classification of the population into Whites, Coloured people and Africans—the two latter groups to be classified further into ethnological groups. The racial group of an individual is determined by his appearance and by general acceptance and repute. A person who objects to his classification may appeal to a classification board on payment of £10—which he forfeits if his complaint is "vexatious and unfounded". (The South African Institute of Race Relations has published a fact paper: *Race Classification in South Africa—Its Effect on Human Beings*, which deals with the provisions of the Act and with the great hardships which result from race classification by officials.) The idea of race classification is not a new one: in 1935 a Select Committee considered the question but rejected the scheme on the grounds that it was impracticable, expensive and the personal liberty of the individual should "not be curtailed without important reasons".

(ii) *Social-security* apartheid

In the field of social-security *apartheid*, the Workmen's Compensation Act 1941 Amendment Act, 27/1945, made provision for compensation of disabled workmen. The definition of "workmen" excludes those people in domestic service, agriculture and mining. Thus large groups of Africans were excluded from the benefits of the Act. The Unemployment Insurance Acts, 53/1946 and 41/1949, extended unemployment insurance benefits to certain workers. The provisions did not apply to any racial groups in domestic service, agriculture, the public service, provincial administrations and to persons who earned above a certain income. Africans employed in coal and gold mines who had board and lodging were excluded, as were Africans employed in rural areas, except those employed in factories and industries. The 1949 amendment excluded from benefits all those Africans whose earnings were less than £182 per annum, *all* "seasonal" workers and *all* migratory labourers irrespective of income. The Silicosis Amendment Acts, 42/1950 and 63/1952, increased the rates of grants and pensions payable to White miners, but there was no corresponding increase for African sufferers. Whites have always been paid on the basis of a monthly pension and Africans in the form of a lump sum benefit—in spite of the strong criticisms of this latter form of payment since the inception of social-security legislation.

(iii) *Public amenities* apartheid

The first Act as regards public amenities *apartheid* was passed in 1916; since then a number of Railways and Harbours Acts, notably Act 49/1949, have been passed which empower the Government to reserve train accommodation for the exclusive use of persons belonging to a particular racial group: the Government has the power to reserve separately, railway premises, wharves, docks and airports. The Merchant Shipping Act, 57/1951, contains a clause which specifies that separate crew accommodation be provided for White and non-White seamen. Sections two and three of the Reservation of Separate Amenities Act, 49/1953, provide, *inter alia*, that if there is only one waiting-room on a railway station, the station-master may lawfully set aside that room for the exclusive use of Whites: any non-White who enters such a reserved place is liable to a fine of not more than £50 or to imprisonment for not more than three months, or to both penalties. A Government proclamation provides in effect that it is unlawful for a White person and a non-White person to drink a cup of tea together in a tea-room anywhere in South Africa unless they have obtained a special permit to do so.

After the passing of the Reservation of Separate Amenities Act in 1953, it was found that the Act did not empower local authorities to enforce *apartheid* on beaches; they could reserve public premises or land or portions thereof for the exclusive use of particular racial groups, but the term "land" did not include land below the high-water mark. The Reservation of Separate Amenities Act, 10/1960, contains a new definition of land: it includes the sea and sea-shore as defined in the Sea-Shore Act of 1935. This Act states that the sea is "the sea and the bed of the sea within the three miles limit" and that the sea-shore is "the land situated between low-water mark and high-water mark".

(iv) *Labour* apartheid

As regards labour *apartheid*, the Native Labour Regulation Act, 15/1911, assisted White employers by making a breach of contract by African labourers a criminal offence. Section four of the Mines and Works Act, 12/1911, gave the Governor-General the power to make regulations for, *inter alia*, the issuing of certificates of competency in the skilled occupations in mining and engineering. In terms of these regulations certificates were not to be granted to "Coloured persons" in the Transvaal and Orange Free State. In 1923 these regulations were declared *ultra vires* by the courts. The "Colour Bar Act", the Mines and Works Amendment Act, 25/1926, limited the granting of certificates of competency for engine driving, blasting and many other skilled occupations to "Europeans, Cape Coloureds, Mauritius Creoles and St Helena persons". The Wage Act, 27/1925, was the basis of the "civilized labour" policy. Section three (3) distinguished between employees who were paid a wage upon which they could support themselves "in accordance with civilized habits of life" and other employees who were "uncivilized". The Prime Minister's Circular, 5/1924, defined "civilized labour":

Civilized labour: the labour rendered by persons whose standard of living conforms to the standard generally recognized as tolerable from the European standpoint.
Uncivilized labour: that rendered by persons whose aim is restricted to the bare requirements of the necessities of life as understood among barbarians and undeveloped peoples.

Of the Industrial Conciliation Act, 36/1937, the Report of the Industrial Legislation Commission of Enquiry, 1951, said:

The Act, by virtue of the definition of "employee", excludes the vast majority of African workers . . . . Native trade union organizations are not recognized and consequently Natives cannot participate in collective bargaining, while workers of other races have adequate means not only of stating their views but of enforcing their demands. Native workers are in a weak position *vis-à-vis* their employers.

In 1947 the United Party introduced an Industrial Conciliation Bill in reply to persistent demands for the recognition of African trade unions. The Bill aimed at racial separation in industrial legislation: it excluded *all* Africans from the operation of the 1937 Act. Separate machinery was to be created for African workers. It would be illegal for Africans to be members of trade unions registered under the 1937 Act and to be associated with other racial groups in unregistered trade unions. It was obligatory for all African trade unions to be registered. The Bill not only excluded domestic servants and agricultural employees, as had the 1937 Act, but also African employees in mining all minerals except natural oil, stone, gravel, earth and water. If the Bill had become law the preponderant number of African mine workers in the coal and gold industries would have been excluded.

In 1949 the new Government issued a circular through the Prime Minister's Department which reaffirmed the "civilized labour" policy of 1924. In all Government departments, except Native Affairs and the Railways, "civilized labour" was to be substituted for that which might be regarded as "uncivilized". When the Minister of Labour, Mr B. Schoeman, introduced the Native Building Workers Act, 27/1951, he said that the Bill was for the protection of White workers and Coloured workers against the undermining of their wage standards by "cheap Native labour". Sections 15 and 19 of the Act, for example, stated that a White person living in a town who employs an African to do any carpentry, bricklaying or other skilled work in his home, commits a criminal offence unless special exemption has been granted by the Minister of Labour. Any African who performs such skilled work in a town elsewhere than in an area set aside exclusively for African occupation also commits an offence. In each case the penalty is a fine of not more than £100, or imprisonment for not more than one year, or both penalties. The Native Labour (Settlement of Disputes) Act, 48/1953, re-defined the definition of "employee" in the 1937 Industrial Conciliation Act to exclude all Africans, for whom separate industrial machinery was now created. Strikes by African employees were prohibited. African trade unions were not prohibited but were denied recognition and registration.

In accordance with its policy of protecting "the interests of White workers in White areas", the National Party enacted the Industrial Conciliation Act, 27/1956, which, *inter alia*, gave the Minister of Labour the power to direct an industrial tribunal to investigate the desirability of job reservation if he considered it necessary "in order to safeguard the economic welfare of employees of any race in any undertaking, industry, trade or occupation". As a result of Supreme Court decisions which invalidated a job reservation proclamation of 1957, the Government passed the Industrial Conciliation Amendment Act, 41/1959, which gave industrial tribunals wider powers in determining jobs for reservation. The wording of Section 77, quoted above, was amended: the Minister said that job reservation should not be applied merely to safeguard the economic welfare of employees, but

. . . because it is perhaps more desirable to reserve work for, say, White workers, on social grounds, because White workers are often squeezed out not only as a result of a lower wage structure, *but mostly as the result of undesirable contact with others while employed on the same work.* The Whites get out and lose this type of employment. This tendency will be combated by job reservation, wholly or partly.

The principal Act, he said, only enabled a determination to be made for a specified undertaking, industry, trade or profession and it was desirable "that any investigation in terms of section 77 into such general avenues of employment should take place on a general basis, and should not be confined to a particular industry only".

The Act of 1956 excluded from its operation any occupations covered by the Mines and Works Act; the Amendment omitted this provision, thus making it possible for job reservation to be applied to certain classes of work in the mining industry. A penalty clause provides that anyone, unless exempt, who employs a person on work which has been reserved for members of some other race or class, or who performs such work, will be guilty of an offence and liable, on conviction, to a fine of not more than £100, or imprisonment without the option of a fine, or to both penalties. Two examples will serve to show the nature of job reservation: Determination No. 5, operative from 4 January, 1960, states that the operating of passenger lifts in the municipal areas of Johannesburg, Bloemfontein and Pretoria is reserved for Whites only in estate agencies, building societies, insurance, banking, finance and investment companies, the commercial distributive trade, hospitals and nursing homes, educational establishments, the printing, newspaper and mining industries, municipal and electric supply undertakings, employers' undertakings and trade unions. There were two exceptions: non-White employees may operate passenger lifts for the conveyance of people of their own group only, and they may continue to operate lifts used for goods only, or goods and personnel employed by the firm owning the lift. Determination No. 7, dated 30 October, 1959, relates to a section of the iron, steel, engineering and metallurgical industries that is concerned with the manufacture, for domestic uses, of metal cupboards, shelves, sinks, refrigerators, electric stoves, electric geysers and other similar articles. It reserves for Whites only 27 listed categories of work in this section of the industry (except in the Western Cape, where 23 instead of 27 types of work may be performed by Whites only).

(v) *Property and residential* apartheid

In the sphere of property, residential and freedom-of-movement *apartheid*, legislation applicable to Africans, which controls or prohibits residence in certain areas, began with the Natives Land Act in 1913. The Native Administration Act, 38/1927, empowered the Governor-General to order the transfer of an African or of an African tribe from any place to any other place "whenever he deems it expedient in the public interest". On the same basis he could order the removal of any tribe from one place to another within the Union upon "such conditions as he may determine". Any African who "neglected" or "refused" to comply with any of these provisions or conditions was guilty of an offence and liable to a fine of not more than £10 or to imprisonment for any period not exceeding three months. Thus Africans no longer had any *right* to personal freedom but a *privilege* of that freedom until the Governor-General "deems it expedient in the public interest". This is one of many examples where the freedom of movement of Africans is at official discretion. The main intention of the Native (Urban Areas) Consolidation Act, 25/1945, is to prevent Africans from settling in large numbers in urban areas or in the vicinity of those areas. The Governor-General is empowered "whenever he deems it expedient" by proclamation to declare that after a specified date all Africans in an urban area shall reside in a location, village or hostel. Any African who, after three days' notice, fails to comply is guilty of an offence. Power is given to a local authority to demand from any African entering a proclaimed area that he report his arrival and obtain a document—which must be produced on demand—that he has permission to be in the areas. The Govenor-General, after consultation with the Minister of Native Affairs, can, on being satisfied that the number of Africans in a particular area is "redundant", require the local authority to compile a list of those who ought to be removed and make provision for their removal. The Act provides for the removal from any urban area of Africans who are "habitually unemployed, have no sufficient means of livelihood, leading idle, disorderly or dissolute lives" or who have committed certain specified offences. After an enquiry by a Native Commissioner or

TTCA

Magistrate, an African who fails to give a satisfactory account of himself may be sent to his home and ordered not to return to the urban area for a specified period or sent to a work colony for not more than two years.

The present Government has amended this Act from time to time: some of the provisions, notably those contained in Section 10, should be mentioned. An African who was born in a town and lived there continuously for fifty years, but then left to reside elsewhere for any time, is not entitled, as of right, to return to the town where he was born and to remain there for more than 72 hours: should he do so, he is guilty of a criminal offence. An African who, although not born there, has lived continuously in a town for fifty years and is still living there, loses his right to remain there for more than 72 hours if he commits a criminal offence for which he is sentenced to a fine exceeding £50. An African who has, since birth, resided continuously in a town is not entitled, as of right, to have living with him in that town for more than 72 hours, a married daughter, a son of 18 or more, a niece, a nephew or a grandchild. No African, lawfully residing in a town by virtue of a permit issued to him, is entitled, as of right, to have his wife and children residing with him. An amendment to Section Nine (7)(b) states that the Minister of Native Affairs may, provided that the urban local authority concurs, by notice in the *Gazette*, prohibit the attendance of Africans at a Church service in a town, if it is, in his opinion, undesirable that Africans should be present in the Church in the numbers in which they ordinarily attend that service.

During the second reading debate on the Group Areas Bill, Dr Malan acclaimed the measure as heralding a fresh start and a new period in South Africa. From the Government's point of view, he said, this Bill was the most important of all *apartheid* measures: "What we have in this Bill before us is *apartheid*. It is the essence of the *apartheid* policy which is embodied in this Bill". Dr A. J. R. van Rhijn described the "logic" of the Government's *apartheid* legislation. One could not maintain a law against mixed marriages, or a law against illicit intercourse between Black and White while people still lived in mixed residential areas. Mr M. D. C. de Wet Nel told the House that the Zulu did not feel happy among the Sotho, and the Sotho was unhappy amongst the Xhosa. Each group wanted to live among his own group: there the individual could find "rest for the soul and happiness for which each human being yearns". Dr Dönges, who had charge of the Bill, declared that there was sufficient evidence to show the dangers of racial juxtaposition and the necessity for establishing separate areas for the different racial groups. Since 1909 it had been hoped that the problem would be solved by voluntary segregation: as this had failed, the Government now felt called upon to provide a new solution. The desire to live among one's own people, he said, was not limited to Whites—it was a desire shared by other sections in the community. There was a "natural, if slow, gravitation towards this end" by all members of the same group: "it is the natural feeling of oneness and of group awareness which makes members of the same group desire to live in the same area". There were three fundamental reasons which justified the enactment of this measure: first, the various racial groups were still in such widely differing and often conflicting stages of cultural and political development that it was impossible to treat them all alike; secondly, it was essential to both Whites and Blacks that western civilization be maintained in South Africa, and a policy of racial differentiation was better calculated to achieve this aim than a policy of racial assimilation; thirdly, it was proven that race conflicts and tensions resulted when different racial groups lived together in juxtaposition, and thus it was in the interests of racial peace that focal points of contact should be eliminated as far as possible. The National Party was adamant that there should be no amendments to the Bill: it was necessary, said J. G. Strijdom, "to end friction and its source in contact", otherwise he foresaw "a bloodbath". It was important to maintain "the colour sense which is the basis of the purity of the race".

The title of the Act is: "To provide for the establishment of group areas, for the control of the acquisition of immovable property and the occupation of land and premises and for matters incidental thereto". The basic concepts are "groups" and "areas", for the object of the Act is to segregate different racial groups into separate areas set aside for each. Provision is made for the classification of groups into White, Coloured and Native, and such classification is at, and by, official discretion.

As regards "areas", one provision, for example, is that in a "full group area" the acquisition, ownership and occupation of land and premises will be confined almost exclusively to members of a certain racial group. Certain classes of persons— domestic servants, *bona fide* hospital patients, people in work colonies, etc.—are allowed to occupy land or premises in a group area proclaimed for a group other than their own if they have obtained the necessary permit to do so. The Act provides for a complex system of classification of "areas".

A measure of local self-government is provided for in some group areas. The Government has allowed for the institution of a measure of self-government by persons belonging to a particular group for the persons belonging to that particular group. The relevant section places no obligation on the Government to introduce this self-government, but the Minister may, with the concurrence of the Administrator, establish a governing body for any non-White group area. This body may consist wholly or mainly of the members of the group for which the group area has been established and it shall have powers and functions as may be prescribed by regulation. Professor Kirkwood has remarked that it was made plain that the granting of local self-government will depend upon the capacity of the particular group to exercise such powers and functions satisfactorily. It would seem, he says, that "local opinion", presumably White opinion, is to be allowed to indicate whether or not a particular group is "ripe" for a measure of self-government.

(vi) *Education* apartheid

In January 1949, the Government appointed a Commission under the chairmanship of Dr W. W. M. Eiselen to consider, *inter alia*, the formulation of the principles and aims of education for Africans as an independent race "in which their past and present, their inherent racial qualities, their distinctive characteristics and aptitude, and their needs under ever-changing social conditions are taken into consideration"; the extent to which present syllabuses should be modified "in order to conform to the proposed principles and aims" and to prepare Africans more effectively for their future occupations. The Commission issued its report in April, 1951. In Chapter VII—

"A Critical Appraisal of the Present System of Bantu Education"—the Commission concluded that the four most important criticisms of the present system were:

(a) Bantu education is not an integral part of a plan of socio-economic development;

(b) Bantu education in itself has no organic unity; it is split into a bewildering number of different agencies and is not planned;

(c) Bantu education is conducted without the active participation of the Bantu as a people, either locally or on a wider basis;

(d) Bantu education is financed in such a way that it achieves a minimum of educational effect on the Bantu community and planning is made virtually impossible.

The Commission stated the fundamental premises of African education: first, from the point of view of the whole of society, African education is the development of a "modern, progressive culture, with social institutions which will be in harmony with one another and with the evolving conditions of life to be met in South Africa"; secondly, from the point of view of the individual, the aims are the development of "character and intellect, and the equipage of the child for his future work and surroundings". Certain guiding principles were laid down by the Commission for the achievement of these aims:

(a) education must be so organized to provide both adequate schools "with a definite Christian character" and social institutions to "harmonize" with these Christian-orientated schools;

(b) to achieve this, African education should be entrusted to a department of the Union Government, with Union-wide jurisdiction, that is, the central government should take over the control of African education from the provinces;

(c) there must be more emphasis on the education of the mass of Africans "to enable them to co-operate in the evolution of new social patterns and institutions", that is, there should be a new emphasis on education for all, both in the "social" and in the "school" sense;

(d) the mother-tongue should be the medium of instruction, at least during the primary school stage;

(e) African parents should as far as is practicable have a "share in the control and life of the schools"; in this way children would realize that parents and schools "are not competitors but that they are complementary"; similarly, the schools will educate the parents "in certain social values". To achieve this ideal, Bantu Local Authorities should be established in the reserves and in the urban areas; the intention is that these bodies should in the course of time "evolve into local government units charged with the administration of all local services, including education";

(*f*) the responsibility for the financing of African education should be shared by the State and the Bantu Local Authorities: as the development plan takes effect "it is expected that Bantu Local Authorities will be able to shoulder a proportionately heavier share";

(*g*) "the schools should provide for the maximum development of the Bantu individual, mentally, morally and spiritually".

From the debates on the Bantu Education Bill, which clearly embodied the principles and recommendations of the Eiselen Report, it is plain that the Bill was linked directly with the Government's *apartheid* policy. The Minister of Native Affairs, Dr H. F. Verwoerd, said:

Racial relations cannot improve if the wrong type of education is given to the Natives. They cannot improve if the result of Native education is the creation of frustrated people, who, as a result of the education they received, have expectations in life which circumstances in South Africa do not allow to be fulfilled immediately, when it creates people who are trained for professions not open to them, when there are people who have received a form of cultural training which strengthens their desire for the white-collar occupations to such an extent that there are more such people than openings available . . .

Above all, good racial relations cannot exist when the education is given under the control of people who create wrong expectations on the part of the Native himself, if such people believe in a policy of equality, let me say for example . . . . It is therefore necessary that Native education should be controlled in such a way that it should be in accord with the policy of the State.

Education, he said, must train and teach people in "accordance with their opportunities in life, according to the sphere in which they lived". In a policy statement to the Senate in 1954, Dr Verwoerd deplored the fact that African education had not been placed under the control of the Native Affairs Department in the past: in 1936 legislation had been prepared to implement such control but owing to difficulties, "such as provincial objections against loss of prestige", the legislation was not introduced. In his summary of the reasons for the failure of the (then) present system, the Minister stated that mission schools had failed because, amongst other things, "they were strangers to the country's policy". Another defect was that the curriculum (to a certain extent) and the teaching methods "by ignoring the segregation or *apartheid* policy, could not offer preparation for service within the Bantu community": by blindly producing students on the White model, "the idle hope was created that they (the Natives) could occupy positions in the European community in spite of the country's policy". This, he concluded, was what he meant by "the creation of unhealthy 'white-collar ideals' and the creation of widespread frustration among the so-called educated Natives". There is little doubt that the Government intended that African education should equip the African people for their role in life which Nationalist policy prescribed. . . .

28. The Bantustans

GOVAN MBEKI *South Africa: The Peasants' Revolt* Penguin Books 1964; pages 15–17, 18, 19–22, 39–42

. . . The establishment in South Africa of Bantustans is based on the apartheid supposition that certain areas of the country belong to the Whites, and others, generally known as the reserves, to the Africans, with neither people able to enjoy rights in the areas belonging to the other.

Which are these two South Africas, one for Whites and the other for Africans? In Dr Verwoerd's 'European' territory live 6,000,000 Africans, 1,500,000 Coloured (those of mixed descent), 500,000 Indians, and 3,000,000 Whites. The total area of South Africa is 472,359 square miles. The area of the 'European territory' is 416,130 square miles. The remainder, some 56,000 square miles, or less than 12 per cent of the total, is the land comprising the 'Bantu homelands'. Here live 5,000,000 Africans.

The so-called White state is a contiguous land area, containing practically all the natural resources and advanced development secured by the labour and skill of all South Africans—the majority of whom, of course, are Africans. This territory includes all the large cities, the seaports, the harbours, the airfields, the areas served well by railways, main roads, power lines, and major irrigation schemes. It contains the enormously rich gold mines, the diamond mines, the coal mines. It includes all the main industries, maintained largely by African labour, in this industrially advanced country. It includes the best and most fertile farmlands.

The Bantu 'homelands' consist of 260 small and separate areas scattered throughout the country. They are South Africa's backwaters, primitive rural slums, soil-eroded and underdeveloped, lacking power resources and without developed communication systems. They have no cities, no industries, and few sources of employment. They are congested and permanently distressed areas where the inhabitants live on a narrow ledge of starvation, where a drought, as experienced recently in the northern areas, leads inevitably to famine. They are areas drained of their menfolk, for their chief export is labour, and while the men work on white-owned farms and in mines and industry, their women-folk and old people pursue a primitive agriculture incapable of providing even subsistence. The 'homelands' are mere reserves of labour, with a population not even self-sustaining, supplying no more than a supplement to the low wages paid on the mines and farms.

Dr Dönges, South Africa's Minister of Finance, speaking at Burgersdorp on 26 July 1962, proclaimed that this arrangement of territory into Black and White areas was the final division. His words were:

It is history that has drawn the boundaries, and not the government, for the Bantu Homelands are the area which Non-Whites originally occupied. Therefore they have no moral claim to more land.

History is a record of events, not a *deus ex machina*. People, and not the record, drew the boundaries of the reserves, enacted the land laws and the Group Areas Act, enclosed black and brown communities in segregated ghettoes, with all the land beyond denied to them, and prohibited them from obtaining rights in land.

Historical arguments that justify the White claim to exclusive rights in 88 per cent of the country are absurd. The true record is that brown and black people were spread throughout the sub-continent long before the first Whites arrived. Van Riebeeck found the Nama at the Cape when he landed in Table Bay. Boers found and fought the Khoikhoi and Batwa when they trekked into Namaqualand—an area which still bears the name of its original inhabitants. Xhosa lived on the banks of the Buffalo River in 1686 and settled at what is now Somerset East in 1702. Whites fought Xhosas in the 1770s on the fringes of the Tsitsikama forest, and drove them back from the Gamtoos to the Fish River in 1778. Zulu tribes once occupied the whole of Natal, down to the borders of Pondoland. Whites drove deep into tribal territories in the Orange Free State and the Trans-vaal before their expansion was halted at last late in the nine-teenth century. The White man's claims to rights of first occupancy are false. But, true or false, they are plainly irrele-vant. It is the existing distribution of the population that should decide South Africa's future—and present. . . .

Here is the extent of dependence of White upon Black, and this state of dependence has only grown greater over the years. There were 2,328,534 Africans living in urban areas during 1951; by 1960 the total was 3,443,950, or 1,115,000 more. There are 280 black and brown workers to every 100 Whites in the five major employment sectors: mining, manufacturing, construc-tion, railways, and postal service. The proportion was much the same in 1951. Of the total African population of South Africa less than one third lives in, or comes from, the 'homelands'. The great majority live, were born, and work either in the cities or on the farms of 'White' South Africa. South Africa is a single multi-national society, integrated and inter-dependent. This is the reality which the apostles of apartheid seek to disclaim. . . .

What of these Bantustans and the compensation they offer? The African reserves are made up of 260 separate areas, patches and pieces scattered over the face of South Africa. Clearly there cannot be 260 independent homeland states, and a glance at the map shows that the majority of these isolated areas cannot be incorporated into larger units. The Tomlinson Report, which investigated Bantustan planning, wrote that—save for a few blocks such as the Transkei and Vendaland—the Bantu areas were too scattered to form any foundation for community growth.[1] The Transkei, covering 16,000 square miles and containing between 1,500,000 and 2,000,000 people, is the only African reserve that constitutes a coherent and substantial area of land. The Transkei is thus crucial to the whole Bantustan programme. If apartheid cannot succeed here, it cannot succeed anywhere. The Transkei is the South African government's Bantustan shop-window. Already the goods displayed are fly-specked and faded, but the government tries to disguise their appearance with gaudy advertising material. A government booklet proclaims that there are 64 secondary industries in the Transkei with a gross output of £795,000 a year. This is a *per capita* output of about 10s. a year, which is in any event negligible. But further analysis reveals that these units are in fact services rather than industries, such as dry cleaners, bakeries, and smithies: and, in addition, that they are almost all white-owned. The picture is as dreary in the field of agriculture, where crop yields, according to official figures, produce the equivalent in gross annual income of £4 5s. a person; livestock income, the second largest source, gives an additional gross annual income for each inhabitant of less than 2s. 6d. The Transkei's largest source of income is migrant labour. Every year the government bureaux recruit 160,000 Africans from the Transkei—or 11·5 per cent of the total population—to work in mines and industries.

The Tomlinson Commission stressed that the development of the reserves in the primary sector alone—agriculture, forestry, and mining—would not meet the needs of the Transkei, for the reserve would then support only one fifth of its present population in a backward subsistence and peasant economy. For the other four fifths there would be no livelihood in the reserve. There would have to be, stressed the Commission, the rapid establishment of secondary industry in the reserve. Since the Commission deliberated and made known its findings, the government has arrived at policy decisions. No private investment in the reserves is to be permitted, and the government has limited its own investment in these areas to agricultural development.

So the Transkei will remain dependent on the proceeds of its

[1] Page 181, section 13 of the Report.

migrant labour, while there will be no attempt to provide industrial employment in the reserves. The policy of separate development, far from being an instrument to bring Africans back to their homelands, is in effect a compulsion on them to leave it.

The Transkei Constitution Act passed by the all-White South African parliament recognizes the facts. It supplies a dual type of citizenship for Transkeians, who are citizens of the Transkei but not aliens within the Republic of South Africa. The Act says:

The Republic [of South Africa] shall not regard a citizen of the Transkei as an alien in the Republic and shall by virtue of his citizenship of a territory forming part of the Republic of South Africa regard him for all external purposes in terms of international law as a citizen of the Republic and afford him full protection according to international law.

What are the rights of this Transkeian citizen, the man who is no alien and yet is treated as an alien, without the privileges granted to the immigrant settling from abroad in the Republic? The Transkeian citizen may live in White territory, if he works for the White man and if he pays taxes, but he may have no say whatsoever in the government that rules him. In the Transkei he can vote for a Legislative Assembly in which 64 appointed chiefs over-rule the wishes of the 45 elected members. The chiefs can generally be relied upon to toe the government line because they are officials of the Republic's government, responsible to that government and not to the Transkeian citizen.

Back home in the Transkei, the African may dream of some future economic and political well-being, but the dream shows little signs of ever turning into reality. The Transkei is as firmly subject to the demands of white supremacy as ever it was. The people of the Transkei had no say in the drafting of their constitution. The elections held in 1963 took place under a state of emergency which imposed a ban on all meetings of more than ten persons, laid down severe penalties for 'statements disrespectful to chiefs', and permitted the indefinite detention, without warrant or trial, of political opponents.

A reign of terror had succeeded in temporarily crippling the African National Congress, the best organized and most influential of the banned national liberatory organizations. An observer of the Transkei election wrote:

It is impossible to describe fully to anyone who was not there to sense it the atmosphere of distrust and suspicion that lay thickly over the whole of these election proceedings. There was an oppressive condition of fear everywhere—fear of government action, fear of police action, fear of the action of the chiefs. The campaign had taken place in conditions of secrecy and wariness—if candidates did run election campaigns, it must have been through whispers.

Women dominated the election queues, women and elderly men, providing their own comment on the possibilities of the Transkei becoming an economically viable territory. For they were the visible demonstration of the fact that most of the able-bodied men between 18 and 50 are out of the Transkei—earning their livings in mines and farms. The sight of an electorate consisting of women and elderly men was in itself a quiet human protest against a deprived society.[1]

Yet, despite all the repressive measures of officials and police, despite the deliberately complicated electoral procedure, the voters of the Transkei succeeded in inflicting a significant political defeat on Dr Verwoerd and his government. In a surprisingly high poll (70 per cent in some areas), the voters routed the pro-government candidates and proved conclusively that the people of the Transkei, despite all blandishments, are overwhelmingly opposed to apartheid and the newly evolved theory of separate territorial development.

Of the 45 elected members, 38 are known to be strong opponents of the Nationalist régime. But the members nominated by the central all-White government enjoy an automatic majority over the representatives elected by the people. And the South African government has the power of veto and the right of supervision over every act of the Transkeian Legislative Assembly. This is the face of 'self-government' or 'independence' for the Transkei.

The decision to give the Transkei its own Legislative Assembly was taken by the South African government at a time when world pressures and protests at the policy of apartheid were particularly severe. By advertising its gift of self-government to Africans in certain areas, even if those areas were strictly limited, and the self-government effectively handcuffed, it hoped to silence world censure. The opposite has happened. The Transkei scheme has revealed the fraud of apartheid in theory and practice.

[1] Alistair Sparks in the *Rand Daily Mail*.

Dr Verwoerd had another reason for attempting to build an apartheid state for Africans in the Transkei. It was, he hoped, a way of slowing down the surge of African nationalism in South Africa. The whole Bantustan policy is based on the calculation that white supremacy cannot hope to defeat African nationalism unless the force of that nationalism is first diverted into manageable channels. But the channels have proved too devious. The carefully plastered structure of apartheid remains makeshift and rickety. Economic facts visibly wear away the Bantustan fantasies. And far from being a South African plan to meet the challenges of today and tomorrow, the Bantustan scheme is a slide back into the South African past. . . .

South Africa, the Nationalist Party proclaimed of a country in which Blacks outnumber Whites four to one, had to be *'kept white'*. The doctrines and ordinances of apartheid were, of course, sacred; yet the Africans could not be denied even an illusion. The substitute for African parliamentary representation was to be the *Bantu Authorities* system. No new general, district, or local councils of the Rhodes variety were created in the reserves. The two general councils of the Transkei (with its 26 district councils) and of the Ciskei remained for the moment, while besides these there were three further local councils in the Cape, three in Natal, and 13 in the Transvaal. But under the 1951 Bantu Authorities Act new-look Bantu Tribal Authorities were established, mostly in the northern provinces, by proclamation of the Governor-General (in fact, the Minister of Bantu Affairs). He designated chiefs to head these Authorities—and could at any time depose them; he also fixed the minimum and maximum number of councillors to serve on each Authority. The Bantu Commissioner had the right to veto any appointment. The system entirely excluded the elective principle. The Minister and his officials had strict control over the membership of the Authorities; and members of the general public could be excluded from their meetings.

The aims of the Bantu Authorities Act were to abolish the Native Representative Council as an elected 'umbrella organization' representing all Africans, and to substitute councils—based upon tribal and ethnic groups—whose members would be largely selected by the government. It was these councils or Bantu Authorities through which later apartheid and Bantustan measures would be forced on the African people in the guise of consultation and consent. The government would ensure for itself an easy passage in advance by rigging up a network of non-elected councils around nominated chiefs for the expression of 'popular will'.

In 1955 the Bantu Authority system reached the Transkei, and the Bunga, with its 26 District Councils, was erased—after it had accepted the Bantu Authorities Act in principle. At the base of the new administrative pyramid are the Tribal Authorities, composed of the chiefs and headmen. All chiefs owe their office to appointment by the government. They are government officials. The State President (the Department of Bantu Administration and Development, in effect) decides the size of the Tribal Authority and its composition. Chiefs may appoint a number of councillors—the number is decided by the State President—and of the remainder the Bantu Commissioner nominates one-third and the taxpayers, with the chief's approval, two-thirds. The administration has the right to veto any nomination.

The District Authority is the next stage in the pyramid. Its head is the chief of the dominant tribe in the district, and it includes at least eight other members—nominated by the head, the Bantu Commissioner, and the taxpayers—all of them drawn from the Tribal Authorities. All appointed chiefs in the district are members *ex officio*. It is a method of indirect selection by the traditional chiefs and White bureaucrats.

Still higher come the Regional Authorities—of which there are nine in the Transkei—each embracing two or more District Authorities. The head of the Regional Authority is a Paramount Chief, if there is one; if not, the leading chief in the area; and members are drawn from the District Authorities by the indirect method previously described. The Regional Authority includes all chiefs *ex officio* while most of the other members are appointed by the Paramount Chief and the Bantu Commissioner.

Finally, for the Transkei at least, comes the Territorial Authority, consisting of all the members of all the Regional Authorities. They nominate a presiding head with the approval of the State President.

The Minister may veto the appointment of a councillor to the

Territorial Authority, as indeed he may at all lower levels of the pyramid.

It is clear from the composition of these bodies that they represent merely the messengers of government will; the elected element is so small and so remote from the voters that it can hardly be held even to contribute popular participation. The thesis of government policy is clear—Africans are still in the tribal stage, chiefs are the natural rulers, and the people neither want nor should have elected representatives.

By 1959 the government had set up 324 of these Tribal Authorities throughout South Africa (123 in the Transkei); 26 District Authorities (all in the 26 districts of the Transkei); 16 Regional Authorities; and one Territorial Authority (the old Bunga, converted).

The stage was now set for further legislation. The Promotion of Self Government Bill was introduced in 1959. As with so many other South African laws, the title is of course misleading. For the real object of the Act was to abolish the representation of Africans in Parliament.

As a substitute for depriving the Africans of this small share in the supreme law-making body of the country, the Territorial Authorities created for each ethnic group were to be given greater powers, and the Prime Minister, Dr Verwoerd, even declared: 'If the various Bantu national units show the ability to attain the required stage of self-sufficiency, they will eventually form a South African Commonwealth, together with White South Africa, which will serve as its core and as guardian of the emerging Bantu states.'

In all, there were to be eight Territorial Authorities topping the pyramids of Tribal, District, and Regional Bantu Authorities: for the North-Sotho; the South-Sotho; the Swazi; the Tsonga; the Tswana; the Venda; the Xhosa; and the Zulu 'national units'. At the time that the national units were announced, the extent of the territories they would compose were not specified, and they have not been specified since. White Commissioners-General were to be appointed by the government to the areas of these 'national units'.

The chiefs had long had their duties outlined to them, but again these were stressed as the maintenance of law and order, the reporting to the Bantu Commissioner of any unrest, the enforcement of all government laws and orders, and the dispersal of unlawful assemblies.

The new Authorities had to maintain contact with the Commissioners-General for their areas; and could have assigned to them 'such powers, functions, and duties relating to the conduct of African Affairs as might be specified by the Governor-General'. The Authorities had power to provide for the establishment of markets and pounds, and to allocate trading and other sites to Africans. They could make enactments on matters assigned to them by the Governor-General; but this would not divest the latter, or the Minister of Bantu Affairs, of any powers. All enactments had to be approved by the Governor-General and published in the government gazette. The powers extended to these bodies would be mainly administrative: the Bantu Authorities would play no part in the framing of education, health, employment, or any other policy, except in so far as the Territorial Authorities could influence the government through the Commissioners-General.

The system thus provided nothing like a genuine system of African self-government. (For that matter one half of the African people—those living in the towns or on White-owned farms—were to be excluded altogether from its scope.)

These legislatures for self-government, however dressed and decorated, were meant to be—and are—only advisory boards. If they possess any independence at all, it is on minor matters of administration, *inside the patterns imposed on them and unalterable by them.* . . .

29. Industrialization

G. V. DOXEY *Industrial Colour Bar in South Africa* Oxford University Press, Cape Town 1961; pages 43–6, 179–82, 187–8

The Determining Factors in the Labour Market

Many of the permanent features of the South African labour market were conceived and nurtured in the development of the gold-mining industry—the institution of the recruiting system; the encouragement and permanent establishment of the migratory system; the struggle for power between different groups of workers, the outcome of which was to be the colour bar in industry.

To some extent, the unemployment which resulted from the contraction of mining activities in Kimberley following the amalgamations helped the recruitment of labour for the gold-mines, but the right men were not always forthcoming. Indeed, some of the people who went to the Transvaal from Kimberley were of an undesirable type and included a number of agitators. The new fields also provided a useful hide-out for diamond smugglers.

Suitable labour was, therefore, hard to come by and, as in the case of Kimberley, the European artisan was placed in a position of advantage vis-à-vis the unskilled African worker. In a situation where the need for low costs was paramount, and in which labour constituted the major item in the cost structure, the European skilled worker, by virtue of his scarcity value, was able to divert the attention of economy-conscious mine-owners to the African. It has been estimated that in the 1890s African wages amounted to between 40 per cent and 45 per cent of the total mining costs, whereas the wages of white labour accounted for between 20 per cent and 25 per cent and explosives for between 12 per cent and 20 per cent. At this time (1894) about 40,000 Africans were employed at an average wage of 61s. a month, while the cost of feeding was in the region of 10s. per month. Europeans employed numbered approximately 5,400 and their average wage was about £21 per month.

Once again, as in Kimberley, the stage was set for an unequal struggle for paramountcy in the labour market, with conflicting groups competing for the lion's share of what could only, of necessity, be a limited reward. Presiding over the scene were to be the mine-owners, ever mindful that it would be necessary to maintain a reasonably attractive level of profits if investors were to continue to take a healthy part in the development of the industry, while outside the struggle were to stand the authorities: first the Transvaal Government, then the British administration, followed by the Government of the Crown Colony, and finally, the Union Government: though not always as strictly impartial observers.

The three determining factors which moulded the permanent

UTCA

pattern of the labour market in the gold-mining industry were
the relative strength of the European, as opposed to the relative
weakness of the African, the importance of keeping costs at the
lowest possible level, and the firmly established official colour
prejudice. The fact that the mining companies were unable to
reduce effectively the cost of supply of other factors of production ensured the reliance of the industry upon cheap African
labour. Furthermore, the climate of opinion in the Transvaal
was not unfavourable for the development of rigidities in the
labour market based on colour, for whereas in the Cape the
force of authority was weighted in favour of a more liberal
approach to the indigenous inhabitants, the Transvaal was
founded firmly upon principles of racial inequality. The Voor-
trekkers, in leaving the Cape Colony, had clearly stated their
attitude in this respect, in the famous Retief manifesto, while
the Transvaal's *Grondwet* (constitution) totally excluded the
black man from any participation in the government of the
country, and relegated him to a subservient position. Therefore,
whereas the structure of the labour market in Kimberley was
being moulded chiefly by the force and strength of white labour,
in the Transvaal the whites were also able to draw support from
official quarters. Furthermore, the attitude of the authorities in
the Transvaal could hardly be described as having at any time
been favourable to the mining companies, even though the
revenue from the goldfields had saved the Republic from certain
bankruptcy.

The Problems of Labour

Faced with the fixed price of gold and the consequent need to
minimize costs, it was natural that the mine companies should,
from the first, have turned their attention to the problem of
assuring a steady supply of basic labour, at the lowest possible
outlay. The only possible source of supply of this type of labour
was, of course, the African section of the population and there
were several factors at work during the 1880s and 1890s which
influenced the conditions of supply and demand with regard to
African workers. In the first place, the huge demand of the
goldfields for labour came at a time when there were other
competing demands; secondly, the African had not reached the
stage where his material wants were sufficient to induce him to

enter the exchange economy readily and willingly, and, thirdly, the Rand soon earned a bad reputation among Africans as a place of employment.

Competing Demands for Labour

At Kimberley and elsewhere on the diamond-fields, there remained a steady demand for African labour, and many Africans, especially those from the Cape, chose to seek employment in these areas. Furthermore, the opening up of the diamond diggings had initiated a boom in the general economic life of the Colony, which was given added impetus by the discoveries of gold on the Witwatersrand. There followed a spate of railway construction, accompanied by a general stimulus to farming. A healthy competition for all grades of labour was engendered which naturally encouraged an upward movement in wage-rates, and although the rise in the wages of non-whites was not spectacular, it was sufficient to worry mine-owners who were concerned not only because of the cost factor, but also because they feared that higher wages would reduce the supply of African workers, on account of the limited range of their wants. In the 1880s and 1890s, few Africans could be described as being more than slightly acquainted with the exchange economy. Even fewer knew what to do with their money earnings, and there was a tendency, as they earned more, to work for shorter periods. In the absence of compulsion, the process of transition from the narrowly based indigenous subsistence economy to one based upon a more advanced system of monetary exchange is slow, particularly where it was, and still is, the case that the people concerned were not wholly forsaking the one environment for the other. From the earliest times, in South Africa, the exchange economy has constituted a supplement to the subsistence economy rather than a substitute. This has been due partly to the peculiar requirements of the mining industry and partly to the pressures exerted by white opinion, which, in spite of economic considerations, showed itself from the first to be against the total absorption of the African into urban society. With the growth of constructive and secondary industry, as opposed to purely extractive industry, this problem was to develop into one of the most crucial affecting the labour market. . . .

The Advent of Apartheid

The decade following the declaration of war in 1939 saw the consolidation of the industrial economy, and the return to political power of the champions of traditional white prejudice. In 1948, Dr D. F. Malan, the leader of the National Party, was able to form a government in coalition with the small Afrikaner Party led by Mr N. C. Havenga.[1] The new government had as its main platform the policy of apartheid, which could be broadly regarded as an extension of the Hertzog-Cresswell seg-regationist platform of a generation earlier. Henceforth, as has been shown in the last three chapters, the labour market was to become more rigid and the inequalities between white and non-white more blatant. While traditional attitudes remained largely unchanged, the economic scene had become vastly different; expanding industrialism had enveloped the Poor White problem and had provided new and wider opportunities for non-whites.

Yet the economic progress which took place was constantly bedevilled by the conflict of views on the permanent role of the African in the industrial sphere. Even before the advent to power of the Nationalist Government, and in spite of colour bar relaxations to meet the exigencies of war, there remained a clash between the needs of industrial development, which called for a stable and settled labour force, and those influences stemming from the traditional prejudice which refused to allow African townward migration to follow the same pattern as that of the whites. The need for additional African labour for war-time industries forced a lessening of control over African townward movement and settlement, but once hostilities ended, there were growing calls for a tightening up of influx control. The Natives (Urban Areas) Act of 1945 was largely a concession to these pressures.

On the other hand, throughout the years from 1936 until 1948 little was done to relate the problem of the Native Reserves to the over-all economic pattern.

---

[1] In May 1948, the Malan-Havenga coalition had an over-all majority of 5 in the House of Assembly. The two parties soon merged and in the 1953 General Election the National Party majority was increased to 29. In 1958, their majority was increased to 47. By this time Mr J. G. Strydom had succeeded Dr Malan as Prime Minister and upon the former's death, Dr H. F. Verwoerd assumed this office in August 1958.

The Impact of War

With the outbreak of hostilities in September 1939, it was necessary to organize South Africa to meet the requirements of a war economy and to offset as far as possible the curtailment of overseas sources of supply. Before the war the country was greatly dependent upon imports, and the wartime shortage of shipping, with consequent shipping priority ratings, meant that it was doubly necessary to encourage local industries. Production generally underwent considerable expansion. Steel output, for example, increased from 344,700 tons in 1939 to 520,000 in 1945, while clothing output almost trebled in value from £8,160,000 in 1938–9 to £22,530,000 in 1944–5, with an increase in the number of employees of all races from 22,222 to 31,077.

Similar advances were recorded in other branches of secondary industry, as well as in mining.

In the labour market the most pressing problem was soon to become the shortage of skilled labour; the armed forces made considerable inroads into the country's manpower, while the colour bar made it difficult to utilize fully the reserve of non-white labour. Nevertheless, some 'dilution' did take place, particularly by using Coloured and Indian males as skilled workers.

The Post-War Expansion

The accelerated growth of the economy continued in the years immediately following the war, and this can be largely attributed to the following factors: a very high level of investment; increased exploitation of mineral reserves; an accelerated shift to more intensive agricultural methods with more advanced techniques; improved entrepreneurship; improved ancillary services; and a wider utilization of manpower.

The real national income increased in the decade 1946–56 at an average annual rate of 4·8 per cent, while the number of persons employed in secondary industry doubled in the same period and the value of industrial output more than trebled. Investment averaged 26 per cent of gross national production during the same period.

Secondary industry was, of course, afforded a sheltered position during the war years because of the cutting off of traditional overseas sources of supply, and after the imposition of import control in 1948 there was the added factor of artificial protection; in addition to the stimulant this gave to local enterprises, many overseas exporters found it expedient to establish factories in the Union itself. Overseas investors were also influenced to some degree by the uncertain immediate post-war conditions in Europe and elsewhere, while the particularly attractive prospects of the new Orange Free State gold discoveries acted as an added inducement to new investment.

Favourable export markets were a further influence: the high world prices of primary produce not only meant that the terms of trade shifted in the Union's favour but farmers, in consequence, were encouraged to improve their farming methods and engage in more intensive cultivation. The index of the physical volume of agricultural production rose from a 1937–8 base of 106 to 176 in 1956–7.

The Effect on the Labour Market

All these developments were not to leave the labour market untouched. Conditions of full employment were experienced, while serious shortages of administrative and clerical workers, technicians and artisans became evident. It was estimated that by May 1956 the shortage of European artisans was 7·4 per cent; the shortage of apprentices 11·5 per cent; and the shortage of clerical workers 5·5 per cent males and 4·1 per cent females.

The expanding requirements of secondary industry also led to an acceleration of the shift of population from primary to secondary and tertiary industry and there was a general widening of opportunities for all races, with a vertical movement of whites from semi-skilled and labouring jobs to more responsible positions.

The shortage of skilled artisans and 'white-collar' workers could not be alleviated by the wider use of non-whites owing to the erection of legal barriers to their advancement. Nor has white immigration proved adequate to meet these needs, largely because of the absence of positive official policies in this direction. . . .

African Migration and the Rural Areas

The rapid expansion of manufacturing industry since 1939 meant that Africans were drawn into the exchange economy in increasing numbers. It was thus imperative that some long-term plan should be devised to cope with the situation.

It was evident that the new industrialism would be better served by a stable and permanently settled labour force than by a continuation of the migratory system under which male workers continued at regular intervals between the urban and rural areas.

If stabilization and urbanization had been allowed to continue unhindered, it would have represented a radical departure from what was now generally considered the natural and traditional order of things and would have required not only a drastic change in policy, but also a fundamental reorientation of the outlook of most whites. The crux of the problem was whether the African was to be looked upon as an essential and permanent element in the urban industrial society, in which he could be encouraged and helped to develop away from primitivism towards modernity, or whether he was to be forced to retain or to revert to tribalism and have contact with the advanced economy only through intermittent periods of migratory work.

The emergence of a truly urban African population, sophisticated and unhindered by archaic tribalism, would have constituted a serious affront to traditional prejudices which refused to admit the need to encourage advance on these lines or (which is of greater consequence) refused to believe that the African was capable of such advance, at least within the foreseeable future.

The fact that, prior to 1948, official policy did little positively to encourage or prevent the process of change was important, in that it permitted the expansion of the urbanized African *élite* who had no ties with the rural areas, who were to become increasingly restive in the role allotted to them, and upon whom, with the Coloured and Indian peoples, the brunt of the colour bar inequalities was to fall.

The problem did not, of course, escape official attention. The Smuts Government appointed a commission under a distinguished jurist (the Hon. H. A. Fagan) to inquire into the operation of laws relating to Africans in urban areas, the Pass laws and the employment in mines and other industries of migratory labour. In its Report, published in 1948, it took the firm view that the Reserves must be regarded as an integral part of the South African economy and advocated a policy of encouraging stabilization of Africans in urban areas. It stated that 'the conclusions to be drawn from the facts . . . cannot be otherwise than that legal provisions or an administrative policy calculated to perpetuate migratory labour and put obstacles in the way of the stabilisation of labour are wrong, and have a detrimental effect'. Furthermore, the Commission went into great detail to show that 'in South Africa's industries, Europeans and non-Europeans are not in each other's way but complement each other' and that total segregation, or separate, self-contained areas for whites and blacks was virtually impossible to achieve.

Nevertheless, these forward-looking ideas were not destined to be implemented as shortly afterwards the concept of apartheid was accepted by the South African white electorate and the country saw once again a return to the expedient of separate development as a solution of the race problem.

Inevitably, the new government repudiated the opinions of the Fagan Commission and in 1950 it appointed a new commission, under an agricultural economist, Dr F. R. Tomlinson, to 'conduct an exhaustive enquiry into and to report on a comprehensive scheme for the rehabilitation of the Native areas with a view to developing within them a social structure in keeping with the culture of the Native, and based on effective socio-economic planning'. The Commission's terms of reference thus presupposed two basic aims: (1) the setting up of separate areas for white and African, and (2) the development of the African on the basis of tribal culture as opposed to western culture.

30. The African National Congress 1961–3

MARY BENSON *African Patriots* Faber & Faber 1963; pages 285–95

Outlawed—but momentarily triumphant—at the Treason Trial Court in Pretoria on March 29, 1961, the vindicated A.N.C. leaders with their allies and followers joyfully sang *Nkosi Sikelel' i-Afrika*—Lord Bless Africa. They swept their tall senior counsel—Israel Maisels Q.C.—high on to their shoulders as people cheered and danced and hugged each other and wept.

Outlawed, but honoured: in Oslo on December 10, 1961, Chief Lutuli, in the presence of King Olaf of Norway, was presented with the Nobel Peace Prize for 1960—a symbol of the world's respect. He accepted the Prize in the name of the 'true patriots of South Africa', giving credit for the Africans' policy of non-violence and non-racialism to the leaders of the A.N.C. who, over fifty years, had set the organization 'steadfastly against racial vaingloriousness'. In his rich baritone he led the distinguished gathering in singing *Nkosi Sikelel' i-Afrika*. The A.N.C.'s anthem had indeed become the anthem of Africa.

Outlawed, but abroad its representatives travel more widely than ever before—Tambo, Nokwe, Kotane and Resha lead a small team with bases in East Africa, North Africa and London. Also they regularly attend the United Nations, propagating Lutuli's call for economic sanctions to bring the South African Government and white electorate to their senses before too late.

One advance was achieved in 1961 at the Commonwealth Prime Minister's Conference. The United Front in exile (the A.N.C., the S.A. Indian Congress and the P.A.C.) lobbied against the projected South African Republic being re-admitted to the Commonwealth so long as the policy of white supremacy prevailed. A strategic cable in the London *Times* from Chief Lutuli, a powerful article in *The Observer* from Julius Nyerere in Tanganyika, together with contributions from Bishop Reeves and others, paved the way for the Commonwealth Prime Ministers' demand that apartheid be abandoned. The South African Government chose rather to leave the Commonwealth. At the subsequent annual debate on its racial policy at the United

Nations, the delegates for Britain and Australia for the first time voted against South Africa. The South African Government, feeling the cold draught of isolation, clung desperately to its membership of the United Nations and accepted ever fiercer condemnation rather than walk out.

Meanwhile in South Africa former members of the banned A.N.C. continue to be subjected to relentless persecution. For instance Canon Calata—although he had not had a Congress membership card since 1956—was imprisoned for twelve days in 1961 (under a new law enabling the Government thus to hold people without charge or trial), and was charged with furthering the aims of the unlawful A.N.C. The grounds? Two pictures of A.N.C. deputations, hanging on his wall as they had done since they were taken some twenty years before. One was of the 1942 deputation to the Deputy Prime Minister. For this 'offence' Canon Calata was sentenced to six months' imprisonment, suspended for two years. His appeal to the Supreme Court of Grahamstown was dismissed. The Bishop of Grahamstown commented that a sentence on such grounds 'makes our laws appear ridiculous in the eyes of the civilized world. If it was not for the suffering and the indignity, it would be very amusing that such a sentence had been passed on a highly respectable citizen'. Calata, sixty-six years old now, his strong thin face heavily lined but his deep, hoarse laugh as much of a tonic to hear as ever, remarked: 'I feel no breach of my conscience . . . I have become used to persecution and I am leaving it to God who can turn it to some good.'

It is in the nature of many Africans to believe in good overcoming evil in the end. They have another consolation—they are able to laugh at the whites.

Leaders of the women are among those placed under the most rigorous restrictions—Lilian Ngoyi and Florence Matomela are two who for five years have been confined to the townships in which they live. Something of their spirit is shown by Annie Silinga. A policeman weary of having to pursue her reproved her: 'No, Mrs Silinga, you are too old, you can't go on with this.' But she does go on. In between the restrictions clamped down on her, she returns to her family and to her obstreperously painted little house, done in lemon, pink, blue and green.

A singular case—barely reported in South Africa—was the

trial of Duma Nokwe and eleven other men, charged with helping to achieve the objects of the banned A.N.C. The State
seemed unaware of the irony of thus charging members of the
Liberal Party, the Progressive Party and even the former
P.A.C., who were among the eleven. On the very day of the
Parliamentary election in 1961, when white voters were freely
expressing their political views, these men were being sentenced
to a year's imprisonment for advocating one man one vote,
abolition of the pass laws, no taxation without representation
and compulsory education. However on appeal they won the
case—a decisive victory.

Another small victory, achieved through internal protest
combined with overseas pressure, came with the Government's
ignominious admission that its police had violated the Basutoland frontier and kidnapped Anderson Ganyile, an A.N.C.
member who had been active in Pondoland. (Though certain
members of Congress sought refuge in the High Commission
Territories, by far the majority of leaders remained. One of
them, asked why he did not go abroad, replied: 'It is so exciting
here.')

In 1960, it had seemed that the movement for liberation must
surely be numbed by the outlawing of the A.N.C. and P.A.C. and
by the long imprisonments of the Emergency. At this critical
moment Nelson Mandela was freed from successive bans for
the first time in nine years. After the long imposed silence his
magnetic forcefulness came as a revelation when he addressed
the All-African Conference held in Pietermaritzburg early in
1961. The conference, which included a remarkable attendance
from Pondoland and Zululand, elected him leader of a National
Action Council of African leaders, and renewed the demand for
a 'truly' National Convention to establish a new Union of *all*
South Africans. If the Government did not comply, there should
be a three-day stay-at-home; thus also African opinion would
be felt at the time of the establishment of a Republic of white
South Africans.

In May 1961 Mandela called the three-day strike. Whereupon the Government called out police, army, commandos,
citizen forces and Saracen armoured cars. As white civilians
were sworn in to be special constables and gun shops sold out
their stocks of revolvers to whites, police arrested thousands of

Africans throughout the country and pursued their leaders, imprisoning many under the twelve days' provision. Some, including Mandela, eluded them. From underground he renewed the call. He toured the country, organizing, seeing both supporters and opponents. He even wrote to the leader of the United Party, Sir de Villiers Graaff, pointing out that the Africans' call for a National Convention had achieved the support of the newly formed Coloured Peoples' Convention, and that many of the English language newspapers and several churches as well as prominent academics and white citizens were suggesting such a Convention. Where, he asked, did the United Party stand? Graaff did not reply.

As May 29 drew near, the English language Press suddenly swung from the objective reporting of the call, into warnings against it. The *Rand Daily Mail* reported a secret plan for the non-whites to invade cities. Mandela's denial was rejected. But the greatest blow at this time, when African feeling was strong, when the Coloured people were promising to give support as never before, was the decision of the former P.A.C. to oppose the stay-at-home.

On the eve of the stay-at-home, authorities warned that strikers would be sacked from their jobs or endorsed out of towns; police would move into the townships in force to drive residents to work. During the night helicopters flew low over townships flashing searchlights down on the matchbox houses and rough roads. Police and army were ready. A sudden undeclared state of emergency again took hold of the country.

Yet, despite this massive intimidation, on Monday, May 29, 1961, hundreds of thousands of Africans risked jobs and homes to respond to the call. In Durban Indian workers and in Cape Town many Coloured workers also stayed away. (The South African Broadcasting Corporation, which had deteriorated over the years into a Government mouthpiece, repeatedly announced all was 'normal'. On May 30 it announced that all had 'returned to normal'.) And on May 30 in Port Elizabeth—after night-long organizing in the townships—there was a 75% strike. In several areas a significant response came from African schools which struck in a chain reaction to the call. However in terms of world-wide impact it was not a success and on the second day Mandela called it off. In secret interviews with overseas journalists he conceded partial failure; but, he said, the massive mobilization of armed forces by the State had been a 'striking testimony of our own strength and a measure of the weakness of the Government'.

This was a turning point in South Africa's history. In face of the naked force with which the Government thus crushed their peaceful demonstrations, Africans were coming to consider it futile to rely on non-violent methods. The violence of the State was about to provoke counter-violence. It was symbolic that in October 1961, at the very time when the award of the Nobel Peace Prize to Chief Lutuli was announced, sabotage broke out. This was 'a political demonstration of a formidable kind', one leader said, from people 'unshakeably determined' to win freedom whatever the cost. (During 1962 and 1963 the sabotage grew more efficient and evidently its organizers were trying not to harm *people*.)

And symbolic of closer ties with African states was the tour made by Nelson Mandela. His natural authority enhanced by his years of political and legal experience and by his militant leadership from underground, he conferred with heads of State throughout the continent, and went on to London, where he met the leaders of the Opposition—Hugh Gaitskell and Jo Grimond. For the first time in his life he was free from white oppression and arrogance. In Addis Ababa, early in 1962, he addressed the conference of the Pan-African Freedom Movement for East, Central and Southern Africa. He reinforced the demand for economic sanctions, and affirmed: 'The centre and cornerstone of the struggle for freedom and democracy in South Africa lies in South Africa itself. . . . It is first and foremost by our own struggle and sacrifice inside South Africa itself that victory over white domination and apartheid can be won.' Secretly he returned to South Africa to continue his work underground, brilliantly evading the nation-wide police net. But in August 1962 they at last succeeded in capturing him. His blazing courage was shared by his wife Winnie who, undeterred by the long separations and by police raids on her home, went on addressing meetings, inspiriting people, until the Government confined her to Johannesburg.

For nearly twenty years Mandela, Sisulu, Tambo and others had worked tirelessly. In October 1962 Mandela was sentenced to five years' imprisonment: for inviting the people to stay-at-home and for leaving the country illegally. In its report on his self-conducted defence *Die Transvaler* placed on record his belief that later generations would believe him guiltless and not a criminal. He told the court: 'When my sentence has been completed I will still be moved by my conscience to resist race discrimination.' Meanwhile Sisulu, with Kotane, was among the first to be placed under house arrest, the Nationalist Government's latest barbarity; then in March 1963 he was sentenced to three years' imprisonment. And, though the new Minister of Justice, Balthazar Johannes Vorster, with his vicious far-reaching 'Sabotage' Act was outbidding his predecessors in imprisoning, banning and restricting, the protests continued: J. B. Marks, who for ten years had been banned from addressing meetings, joined in the 'Free Mandela' protests the moment his latest ban ran out, while in the Bechuanaland Protectorate leaders of the former A.N.C. based in London and African capitals met with others from inside South Africa to plan the next stage in the freedom struggle.

Fifty years earlier, in Bloemfontein in 1912—responding to Pixley Seme's call—frock-coated chiefs, intellectuals and tribesmen had first come together in the humble location hall and as a symbol of their new unity and their aspirations they had first sung *Nkosi Sikelel' i-Afrika*.

They had been hopeful. What has come of their hopes?

There was the Land Act—restricting millions of African peasants to small tight reserves. These, during the fifty years, have grown ever more crowded, denuded, struck by famine; until recently they were shaken by the worse disaster—the Government's travesty of Bantu's 'self-government' which drives asunder tribes and clans and families as those willing to capitulate to Government tyranny clash with those who refuse.

There were the pass laws—the hated 'verdomde pass'—which deny a man's personal freedom as a right, and turn him into a criminal; far from being relaxed over the years, they came to be extended to youths and women. From 1951 to 1960 more than $3\frac{1}{2}$ million Africans were convicted under these laws.[1] They still take their daily toll, draining humanity of its self-respect.

[1] Statement by Minister of Justice, February 1962.

There were Hertzog's Segregation Acts—accomplished only with the collaboration of General Smuts and United Party M.P.s who represented many African voters—which entrenched the separation of man from man, robbed the few Africans who had them of their votes and introduced a travesty of representation as a sop to the white conscience.

African progress which was made despite every obstacle—whether in education, commerce, industry or political organization—was met by white resistance; the more advanced the Africans became, the harsher the restrictions against them.

The A.N.C. had to face forces they had not conceived of: racial fear was one. Yet history shows that the black man has had far more to fear, has suffered far more at the hands of the white man, than the contrary. Perhaps the whites subconsciously feared retribution?

As powerful a force was greed: an elemental force that economists might dress up in other terms when it came to the mining industry maintaining cheap migrant labour, and the crushing of the African mine strike of 1946. Dr Moroka's poignant wish—to understand how Smuts, after all he had done in the world 'for humanity', could 'return to his own country and say that freedom cannot be given to the black people'—could have no fulfilment. In 1946 Smuts had advanced not one step from 1906 when he had shifted 'the intolerable burden of solving that sphinx problem to the ampler shoulders and stronger brains of the future'. Thus he seemed blind to the new era brought about by the war, with its extension of self-determination to Asia and Africa, the rejection of racialism, and the surge of nationalism. The Africans, however, were not blind, with their 'Claims' based on the Atlantic Charter, their appeals to the United Nations, and their contacts with the Pan-African movement. The Indians were not blind. And the Afrikaner Nationalists and sinister Broederbond were not blind. They glimpsed the new era and they dreaded it. And the inevitable happened for which the Act of Union had surely paved the way in 1910: the Afrikaner Nationalists came into power in 1948.

Then to financial greed was added a more terrible force: racial pride. Hitler willed *'Deutschland uber alles'*. The Afrikaner Nationalists will *'die Volk sonder alles'*.[1]

[1] The Afrikaner people without all the rest—alone.

From these forces flowed the persecution, the poverty, the malnutrition, the violence that beset the everyday lives of the majority of South Africans; so wasteful, so *unnecessary* in a country so rich and beautiful. The A.N.C. had to contend with these forces and these effects; as well as further effects—the activities of informers and *agents provocateurs*, the escapism of many Africans who turned to strange religions, to the selfish pursuits of middle-class society in the townships, or simply to drink.

In assessing the A.N.C. certain conclusions are clear. During five years in the Treason Trial the organization was subjected to an exhaustive scrutiny by the finest legal minds in South Africa. Its minor weakness was obvious: inefficiency—the ramshackle office where time and energy were spent in wrangling about what happened to that £5 13s. od. (not that they found any hint of peculation). A major weakness—exemplified in the campaign against the Western Areas Removals—was its tendency to work on slogans rather than through real analysis. And, unlike the S.A. Indian Congress which coped with some success with the bread and butter problems of the people, the A.N.C. was not always alive to the ordinary people's desires.

But if some of its leaders were not close enough to the people others, like Sibande, were right in amongst them—when not severely restricted. One strength of Congress was its range—from the peasant Sibande to the professor Matthews—men with every political viewpoint and with wide contacts. Courage and continuity—these were assets. Its further strength lay in the men of first-rate calibre who led it and whose characters and ability were brought to light during the Treason Trial. This strength could be a weakness however, for while it drew the best educated and better-off members of the community, men who had much to give, they also had much to lose; more than the ordinary worker. And this meant that some of them lacked militancy. Such men, in any decent society, would have fulfilled themselves in quiet academic or religious fields—Dr Dube was one, Dr Xuma another. Yet they did not, as they might so easily have done, settle for the comparatively prosperous life that their professions could ensure for them. For them there could be no satisfaction without dignity and no dignity without a struggle for freedom. The Rev. Zaccheus Mahabane, now eighty years old, white haired and alert, is busy in the role for which he was cut out—leadership of church councils. Professor Z. K. Matthews, active as ever, became in 1962 a representative of the World Council of Churches in Geneva, paying frequent visits to Africa.

Running through the story of the A.N.C. is the reminder that in human relations people with strong personalities can seldom 'serve' without dominating. The human struggle thus becomes a battle of personalities. Dr Seme almost brought the A.N.C. to grief through his egotism. Yet among several examples more than adjusting the balance were Father Calata and Albert Lutuli; they kept above personal conflicts, often seeming to respond to the supernatural force by which they sought to be guided. Lutuli grew with the toughening situation. His maturing was visible—his face became noble, his bearing commanding. The quality of selflessness was also apparent among the left-wing: Walter Sisulu, for instance—heavier in middle age, with a blunt black beard—regularly arrested and imprisoned on one doubtful charge after another, steeled by each new attack to a harder resolve to overcome the forces of the racial myth.

In the face of the dread evil of racialism, the A.N.C.'s greatest strength and achievement is clear—its refusal to be driven by the racialism of a society based on white supremacy to an equally damaging racialism. To the end it contained a creative quality. And if Dr Seme failed personally in the 'thirties, his earlier achievement is what matters more. The founding of the A.N.C. was a positive act of unification rare in South Africa's history. It was sad that he did not live to see its finest moment but, almost blind, he died shortly before the great non-violent Defiance Campaign in 1952.

Under the South African sun sportsmen play golf and tennis and swim. The mines make great profits—to the satisfaction not only of Johannesburg commercial houses but of the City of London and Wall Street. The Nationalists have been quick to make inroads into big business and commerce. The servant problem is more troublesome than before, but still less troublesome than in most countries in the world. It is indeed a delightful place to live in.

For the oppressed peoples and the handful of the white dissenters the future looks blacker than ever. Many are imprisoned, banned, banished or under house arrest. The 'Sabotage' Act, with its death sentence and heavy penalties for almost every

WTCA

known kind of political activity, hangs threatening over an anxious people. It has successfully intimidated the Press and bookshops from publishing or circulating the words of Chief Lutuli or others of the banned. Only in the outside world can their diminishing voices still be heard. The South African Defence Force, according to the Minister of Defence, has been increased to twenty times its size of two years ago; by 1965 its fully trained specialist troops will be more than trebled. The police have been reorganized to greater efficiency, the Special Branch reinforced.

It is not only in these overt ways that the Nationalist Government is creating a forcing house of violence. The social disruption caused by apartheid has ensured an upsurge of ugly gangsterism, menacing to black and white alike; taking terrible form in the Western Cape of POQO—'we go it alone'. Then through the Bantu education system generations of frustrated children are being produced, their minds stunted by the perversion of education imposed upon them. Under the bright sun Dr Verwoerd is producing a nation of tsotsis.

Britain too bears a heavy responsibility. Her misconceived act of liberal generosity in 1910 has not been forgotten; nor have her long years of voting with the South African Government at the United Nations. But worst of all in the eyes of Africans and white dissenters were the British Government's continued sales of military aircraft and other arms to the Nationalists.

When will the United States act upon their declared beliefs? In 1961 their delegate to the United Nations announced 'in unmistakable terms' that 'the United States abhors and actively opposes apartheid'. What form will that *active* opposition take? It is not only modern Congress leaders such as Lutuli and Mandela who have called for sanctions: Dr Xuma, before his sudden death in 1962, disclosed that he had recently lobbied in several African capitals and at the United Nations for economic sanctions. The alternative to this comparatively peaceful application of force is to allow South Africa to disintegrate into inevitable racial chaos, which, as the American delegate warned, could 'rock the entire continent'. African and Asian states are ready to act but lack the necessary power. Time is short if those with the economic means are to prove their civilization by putting an end to the 'ghastly aberration' of apartheid, as Christopher Gell saw it. Such intervention, as Tolstoy saw it, would be the 'most important activity' the world could take part in. The United Nations have paved the way sixteen years after the A.N.C.'s first appeal to them: in November 1962 by sixty-seven votes to sixteen the Assembly called for sanctions to end apartheid and by ninety-six votes to none called for a U.N. presence in South-West Africa.

Meanwhile ahead in South Africa lies the 'long and greater suffering' that Gandhi foretold, the suffering, even to death, that Lutuli and Matthews could forsee. But, as Mandela said on being sentenced to five years' imprisonment, 'If I had my time over I would do the same again, as would any man who dares call himself a man.'

The South African Government could outlaw the *organization* of the African National Congress—its uniforms, its thumbs-up sign, its slogans. It cannot outlaw its spirit. Whatever the failures and the startling brief successes of Congress; its amorphous nature; and the paradox at its heart, between muddle and division and strength and vision; its great spirit lives on. One leader, on being asked what it felt like to be in Congress, explained: 'I became so much a part of it, the question should be, how does it feel to be yourself? It is the group feeling and the feeling you are living for some future—it is very exciting and a tremendous inspiration.'

Over the years the Congress leaders maintained an extraordinary level of humane action. In face of their civilization the Nationalist Government appears dangerous and stupid in turn; at once pathetic and terrifying in its self-chosen isolation from international society and civilized standards. Communication with it on normal terms becomes increasingly impossible.

Albert Lutuli has said: 'South Africa is a heroic country.' In it the A.N.C. and its associates symbolized all the conflicting forces in the world today: black, white, brown, Christian, Jew, Hindu, Muslim, pagan, communist, capitalist, liberal. Although it was the negative force of opposition to apartheid that brought them together, nevertheless they came together as nowhere else in the world. Pixley Seme saw the Native National Congress in 1912 as a force to unite the African tribes. We have seen it, as the African National Congress, however imperfect, uniting people of all races. This has been the A.N.C.'s contribution to humanity.

31. South West Africa: Mandate in trust

MARGARET ROBERTS *Mandate in Trust* Africa 1960 Committee, London 1961; pages 5–6, 21–4 (additional material specially commissioned 1967)

These people have a long history of conflict with their European rulers. Originally colonised by Germany, they suffered a conscious and concerted policy of repression and extermination, during which 65,000 out of 80,000 Hereros were killed. The exposure of these abuses was partly responsible for the solemn, if not unctuous, spirit in which the Mandates System was established. Article 22 of the Covenant of the League of Nations is as follows:

To those colonies which . . . are inhabited by peoples not yet able to stand by themselves under the strenuous conditions of the modern world, there should be applied the principle that the well-being and development of such peoples form a sacred trust of civilisation, and that securities for the performance of this trust should be embodied in this Covenant.

These intentions reflect the League's determination not to allow a repetition of the abuses and atrocities of the German administration. In accepting the Mandate, South Africa implicitly agreed that the wrongs of the previous administration should be righted. She agreed to administer it in accordance with several provisions, of which the most important are:

Article 2. The Mandatory shall promote to the utmost the moral well-being and social progress of the inhabitants of the territory.
Article 3. The Mandatory shall see that the slave trade is prohibited and no forced labour is permitted, except for essential public works, and then only for adequate remuneration.
Article 4. No military or naval bases shall be established or fortifications erected in the territory.

The Mandate was conferred by the Principal Allied and Associated Powers—Britain, France, the United States, Italy and Japan. At that time the British Crown acted for the British Empire as a whole, since the Statute of Westminster was still to come. The Mandate was therefore conferred "upon His Britannic Majesty to be exercised on his behalf by the Union of South Africa".

Now the problem can no longer be shelved. South West Africa is the only territory which is still administered under the Mandates System of the League of Nations. She is also the only one of these territories in Africa not to have achieved or been promised independence; and the only one in which no representative institutions have been established to give the indigenous peoples a voice in their own government. South Africa has eighteen times refused to obey an annual resolution of the General Assembly calling on it to submit a Trusteeship Agreement for South West Africa. . . .

International Status under the United Nations

The International Trusteeship System superseded the Mandates Commission as a means of supervising the administration of former Mandated Territories. Authority over these Territories now lies with the General Assembly which may adopt binding resolutions by a two-thirds majority. In a sense, therefore, the administering powers are now at a comparative disadvantage, since the Mandate Commission was a non-political body composed of specialists, and its decisions required a unanimous vote. Nevertheless, all the Mandatory Powers except South Africa voluntarily submitted a Trusteeship Agreement for those of their Mandates which were not given independence.

A resolution of the General Assembly in 1959 drew the attention of member states to the legal steps open to them to ensure that the terms of the Mandate are carried out in South West Africa.

A brief diversion will be useful at this stage to clarify the relationship between the International Court of Justice at the Hague and the other organs of the United Nations.

First, any organ of the United Nations, such as the General Assembly, is entitled to seek from the Court an advisory opinion on any point of international law in much the same way as a private individual might consult his lawyers. In such circumstances, the decision of the Court is not binding, though its pronouncements carry strong moral weight.

Second, an individual member of the United Nations may, in certain special circumstances, invoke the compulsory jurisdiction of the Court by instituting contentious proceedings against another member. This course of action is *not* open to organs of the United Nations acting as corporate bodies. It is a very much more complicated process than the delivery of an advisory opinion, since it involves an initial decision by the Court as to whether it has jurisdiction or not. In theory the Courts' judgment in these circumstances is binding upon both parties. But since the Court has no police force of its own, the enforcement of its decisions rests with the Security Council of the United Nations, and can only result, in the last resort, from a political decision by members of that body.

At the request of the General Assembly, the International Court has already given an advisory opinion and two subsidiary opinions on the international status of South West Africa. In the course of these opinions, given in 1950, 1955 and 1956, the Court has found that:

The Union of South Africa is obliged to accept international supervision of South West Africa; and the General Assembly of the United Nations is qualified to exercise such supervision in such a way as would correspond most closely to the Mandates Commission. This includes the examination of petitions and annual reports, which the Union Government is obliged to transmit, as well as the hearing of oral evidence.

Nevertheless, South Africa is not legally obliged to place the territory under the International Trusteeship System.

South Africa, acting unilaterally, is not competent to modify the international status of the Mandated territory.

South Africa is obliged to accept the compulsory jurisdiction of the International Court of Justice relating to the territory, in terms of Article 7 of the Mandate and Article 37 of the Statute of the International Court.[1]

These opinions of the Court are summarised as follows in the sixth report of the Committee on South West Africa, which was accepted by the General Assembly:

The International Court reiterated in 1956 that the obligations of the Mandatory continue unimpaired with this difference, that the supervisory functions exercised by the Council of the League of Nations are now to be exercised by the United Nations.

This is an unambiguous definition of the status of South West Africa in international law, and of South Africa's obligations to the United Nations General Assembly.

[1] See below.

What can the United Nations do about it? A special Committee on South West Africa was asked in 1957 to examine what steps were open to individual members of the United Nations or to the organization acting as a whole to ensure South Africa's fulfillment of the Mandate. They concluded that there were two possible courses of action.

The first arises from Article 7 of the Mandate which reads:

The Mandatory agrees that if any dispute whatever shall arise between the Mandatory and another member of the League of Nations relating to the interpretation or the application of the terms of the Mandate, such dispute, if it cannot be settled by negotiation, shall be submitted to the Permanent Court of International Justice.

This would imply that certain members of the international community[1] could invoke the compulsory jurisdiction of the International Court. The rôle of the Court was made clear by Sir Arnold McNair, a British judge, in the course of the 1950 opinion of the Court:

The judicial supervision (of the Mandate) has been expressly preserved by means of Article 37 of the Statute of the International Court of Justice:

'Whenever a treaty or convention in force provides for reference of a matter to a tribunal to have been instituted by the League of Nations, or to the Permanent Court of International Justice, the matter shall, as between the parties to the present Statute, be referred to the International Court of Justice.'

If therefore any qualified member of the United Nations brought before the Court a dispute with South Africa relating to the interpretation or application of the provisions of the Mandate, South Africa would be obliged to abide by its judgment. . . .

Accordingly, in 1960 Ethiopia and Liberia, the only two independent African States which had been members of the League of Nations, instituted contentious proceedings against South Africa before the International Court of Justice under Article 7 of the Mandate (see this page). They were given the

---

[1] While there is some doubt as to the right of members of the United Nations who were not members of the League of Nations to invoke the compulsory jurisdiction of the Court in a contentious proceeding, there seems to be no doubt that a former member of the League is vested with such a right under Article 7 of the Mandate.

explicit backing of the 1959 Conference of Independent African States. They asked the Court to declare that the Mandate was still in force; that South Africa continues to have duties thereunder; that the United Nations is the proper supervisory authority to which annual reports and petitions should be submitted by South Africa, and whose consent is a legal prerequisite to modification of the terms of the Mandate; and that South Africa is in breach of Article 22 of the Covenant of the League and Articles 2, 4, 6 and 7 of the Mandate. They also asked for a declaration that the practice of race discrimination, as embodied in the policy of *apartheid*, is contrary to internationally accepted standards of political conduct and therefore to the conduct of a Mandate; and that the policy must therefore be abandoned.

South Africa first questioned the jurisdiction of the Court, arguing that Ethiopia and Liberia did not have a legal interest in the issues they raised, and that the Court was not qualified to adjudge those issues. In 1962, the Court gave its judgement upon this jurisdictional point. By a majority of one—eight to seven—it rejected the South African contentions; and proceeded to examine the merits of the case. South Africa argued that the Mandate was not still in force; and, alternatively, that the policies of *apartheid* did not constitute a violation of the terms of the Mandate. It contended that the methods used to promote the well-being of the inhabitants had been left to the Mandatories by the League, that it was known at the time the mandates were given that South Africa's policies were based on discrimination, and that there was no intention to interfere with those policies. Ethiopia and Liberia responded with the argument that the precise perspectives of the League at the time are less relevant than the duty of the Mandatory to move with current standards of welfare, promoting them according to modern standards.

The Court's final judgement in 1966 caused widespread surprise and consternation. It declared that it would not pronounce upon the merits of the case, since Ethiopia and Liberia had not established a legal interest in bringing the case on the issues raised. It justified this apparent return to the issues assumed to have been despatched in 1962 on the grounds that, although a prima facia case for legal interest had then been established, no final assessment of the issue could be made until the merits had been argued. This judgement was reached only after the Court had deadlocked on the issue, dividing six to six, and necessitating the use of the casting vote by the President of the Court. This situation had arisen because of the death of one of the judges between the 1962 and 1966 judgement. During the latter part of the case, no argument was heard, or called for, on the issue of legal interest, which formed the basis of the judgement.

In effect, then, the matter of South West Africa has reverted to the political arena. In any case, even had the Court made a firm judgement on the merits of the case, its enforcement would have been a matter for the Security Council, a political body. In theory there remains the possibility that some State or States other than Ethiopia and Liberia might be able to establish a legal interest for the purposes of a new Court action; but there is presently no serious inclination to initiate new, inevitably lengthy contentious proceedings before the International Court.

Indeed the chief effect of the Court's judgement was to strengthen the demands from U.N. members, especially its African members, for rapid political action to end South Africa's rule in South West Africa. Once before—in 1961—a U.N. resolution had been passed calling for the establishment of a U.N. 'presence' in South West Africa; but it came to nothing. The resolution passed by the General Assembly in October 1966 went even further. It began with a declaration that since South Africa had persistently flouted the Mandate with which it had been entrusted, the Mandate was thenceforth terminated. A fourteen-nation *ad hoc* committee was set up to examine and make recommendations upon 'practical means by which South West Africa should be administered, so as to enable the people of the territory to exercise the right of self-determination and to achieve independence'. The resolution was passed with two votes against (South Africa and Portugal), and three abstentions (Britain, France and Malawi).

The *ad hoc* committee consisted of representatives of the following countries: Canada; Chile; Czechoslovakia; Ethiopia; Finland; Italy; Japan; Mexico; Nigeria; Pakistan; Senegal; the Soviet Union; United Arab Republic; United States. Its report was presented in April 1967. Its members were unable to reach agreement; and three separate proposals were advanced: one, calling for immediate Security Council action if South Africa refused to comply with the October resolution, put forward by the African members of the committee; another, advanced by the Latin-American States, allowing for a delay before Security Council action was implemented; and the third, put forward by Canada, Italy and the United States, proposing a time-table for installing a U.N. administration through negotiations with South Africa.

The report was debated at a special session of the General Assembly. On 19 May 1967 a resolution was adopted by a vote of 85 to 2. Under it the Assembly decided, *inter alia*: to establish a U.N. Council for South West Africa to administer the territory until its independence, and to arrange elections with universal franchise under a new constitution; to entrust executive and administrative tasks to a U.N. Commissioner for South West Africa; to enter into negotiations with South Africa to arrange for its orderly withdrawal from the territory, together with its police and armed forces, these to be replaced by the Council; to instruct the Council to consult the people of the territory about the date of their independence, and to do everything in its power to enable independence to be achieved by June 1968.

This resolution received the support of almost all African and Asian members. Only South Africa and Portugal voted against. The thirty abstentions included countries of Western Europe and north America, the Scandanavian nations, as well as most of the communist states. The Council established under the resolution was instructed to report to the Assembly at its next session.

VII. THE EMERGENCE OF SOUTHERN RHODESIA

32. Rhodes and the making of Rhodesia

W. M. MACMILLAN *The Road to Self-Rule* Faber & Faber 1959;
pages 166–73

In a phrase of Sir Robert Ensor's, the guiding star of the new
imperialism was not in the east but in the south: and there, for
years, it stayed.

Cecil Rhodes, the invalid son of an English rector, was dream-
ing dreams of Africa as a field for development and planning
ahead long before any 'scramble' began. His dreams were all
his own; they came of his imagination being fired by his first big
African journey, a leisurely, 300-mile trek in 1871 from a
brother's Natal farm, over the Drakensbergen and across the
fine pasture lands of the sparsely peopled High Veld, to the
dusty turmoil of the newly opened diamond fields—I have
heard many good judges who happened to get their first impression at the right season go into rhapsody over the lush grass
of this country. But Rhodes was original; surely no one since
Francis Bacon has seen so clearly the conditions of successful
development, and its capital cost. Finding himself in the diamond industry, 'on the ground floor', he put dreams aside and
worked to build a fortune, not for the wealth's sake but always
as the means to an ever more clearly defined end. By 1881, at
the age of 28, he had built the de Beers Company (partly by
buying up claims fallen to ruin, one over another, in the great
open hole that is the Kimberley mine), and was commanding an
income of about £1 million a year: then, having completed a
course of summer terms at Oxford and taken his degree, he was
elected to the Cape Parliament. . . . The founding of the de
Beers Company was only a rehearsal for the dramatic moves
that outmanoeuvred the financial genius of Barney Barnato and
virtually unified the diamond industry in de Beers Consolidated.
The motive force of this great combine was Rhodes's magnetic
personality; when Sir Alfred (Lord) Milner, another man of the
first rank, took over the governorship of the Cape in 1897, his

first recorded impression of Rhodes was of 'a really *big* man . . . among dwarfs'; his own circle occasionally spoke of him as the *Colossus*, but more normally used the full formal title, *Mr* Rhodes! His extraordinary powers of cajolery and persuasion ruled even the directors of de Beers; they actually empowered him to use the company's resources for any purpose he thought fit. This bigger de Beers was born in March 1889; by October of the same year H.M.G. had granted the charter of the British South Africa Company. The resources even of de Beers would not quite suffice; but when Rhodes commended African development to the City of London as an opportunity for 'philanthropy at 5 per cent', he was speaking a language the men of the '90s well understood. Thereafter shares in 'Charter-eds' alternately boomed and slumped on world stock exchanges; though investors drew no dividend till after 1924 faith in Rhodes's venture never really died.

Twenty years of active life, 1881–1902, went whole-heartedly to the 'big idea' that came to Rhodes in the early '70s—to his mission, the development of Africa. His own liberal Cape must take the lead and this required that South Africa, the base, stand strong and united. At once he found South African divisions obstructing the only road to the north, the 'Missionaries' Road' blazed by Livingstone and Moffat through Bechuana-land—'the Suez Canal to the North', as he called it; in 1882 Boers from the newly freed Transvaal streamed over their loosely defined western border and planted themselves in two new republics, Stellaland (Vryburg) and Goshen (Mafeking), leaving Kuruman, the old headquarters of the L.M.S. and the starting point of his road, virtually isolated. In 1883 the German occupation of South-West Africa threatened to cut off the Cape altogether from his 'North'; a link-up between Boers and Germans was to be expected, in spite of the difficulty of crossing the Kalahari. Rhodes at once stepped in as champion of Cape interests. A campaign conducted by telegram with Cape Town was followed by his famous pronouncement in the Cape Parliament in August 1883:

'We want to get rid of the Imperial Factor in this question and to deal with it ourselves, jointly with the Transvaal.'

It was a hard saying. The appeal successfully rallied the Cape

Dutch to his side, and the alliance with the first J. H. Hofmeyr, Leader of the Dutch party known as the Afrikaner Bond, carried Rhodes to the Prime Ministership in 1890. . . . Joseph Chamberlain, the rising apostle of pure Empire, was profoundly shocked and never really trusted Rhodes, less than ever when— Commonwealth man as he was and Federal Home Ruler—he made a princely contribution to Irish Party funds! But Rhodes, the Englishman, never dreamt of giving up the flag; there were German claims to be countered and the Imperial Factor could be helpful, or even necessary. The Boer Republicans, on the other hand, have rarely appreciated the advantages of a broad-based unity. To them Rhodes's ideal meant accepting the British flag, and it was the flag, of all things, they most affected to abhor. They therefore refused even the 'Commonwealth' bait and stood moodily aloof—or were actively obstructive, as in Bechuanaland.

Rhodes himself made one serious miscalculation by never allowing for what might be called the African (or 'Native') Factor. His all-African policy was strong in its economic grasp, strong too in assuming the well-tried Cape policy of equal law as its basis; but it took little account of social consequences. Africans as he knew them at Kimberley might be useful but, being inefficient, were often a hindrance to a man in such a hurry; and since African politics were not yet born, any necessary safeguarding of African interests must inevitably fall to 'the Imperial Factor'. At the very outset, when he found Boer farmers in occupation (with Transvaal titles) of tribal lands they had cut up into farms, his instinct was to leave them to it; there was room for all, and the Boers were the better farmers; the North road alone mattered. John MacKenzie, the missionary at Kuruman, thought otherwise, and from 1883 to 1886 struggled on behalf of the dispossessed tribes for an alliance with the Governor in his capacity of High Commissioner and local representative of the Imperial Government. The issue was apparently more purely local than those that engaged Philip before him; MacKenzie has had his detractors as yet another interfering missionary;[1] but the outcome of two or three years of confusing comings and

---

[1] Shortly after I had acquired his private papers, and before they had been exhaustively studied, the collection went up in the same University fire of 1931 that consumed the Philip MSS.

goings is not in question. British control of the Road was finally asserted by imperialists of the older school; in 1886 a strong expedition under Sir Charles Warren went in and annexed most of the two republics as British Bechuanaland, and this, instead of being incorporated in Rhodes's Cape, was made a directly ruled Crown Colony. At the same time a Crown Protectorate was proclaimed over as much more of the Bechuana country as marched with the Transvaal, up to 22° S. Ten years later Rhodes so far prevailed as to get the Crown Colony annexed to the Cape; but Chamberlain, and the Crown, yielded to the appeal of the Bamangwato Chief Khama and retained direct control of an enlarged Bechuanaland Protectorate, expressly excluding it from his company's field of operations. The success of a visit by Khama to London did much to consolidate the tradition, which has lived on, that 'native' interests are the special responsibility of the 'Imperial Factor'.

The dealings in Bechuanaland were unlooked for and preparatory only. Bechuanaland was a vast, barren expanse of country which no one coveted; only the road to the North must not be blocked by tolls or customs houses, or by the active obstruction of Boers or Germans; for evidence of mineral wealth had come, it will be remembered, from faraway Mashonaland. The way there lay past Matabeleland where Moselekatze's successor, Lobengula, was now the great power. At the very moment the road was finally cleared, in 1885, the Berlin Conference announced the rules of the game and the 'scramble' was on; rights must be based on occupancy. Rhodes was well ahead of his rivals with his ideas, but found himself once again forestalled by the quietly expansionist Boers of the Transvaal; in 1887 one Grobler persuaded Lobengula to accept a Transvaal consul and to concede privileges. President Kruger and his advisers were becoming conscious that a seaport was desirable and they badly wanted Swaziland as a step seawards; but they had mines enough to be going on with and Grobler was probably concerned only about grazing rights and shooting. Rhodes quickly set out to make sure. His emissary, J. S. Moffat, son of Robert, was well equipped to speak to the son of Moselekatze, and in February of the next year Lobengula agreed to make no treaties except as should be approved by Queen Victoria's Government; this in itself was at least some protection against the wiles of concession-hunters. Then, in October 1888, Moffat himself helped Rhodes's business representative (C. T. Rudd) to conclude the agreement that availed to convince H.M.G. that a charter was warranted; later it became the basis of the Company's operations. The terms of the Rudd Concession suggest how essential it was that even the most responsible of these African dealings with foreigners be under the eye of such foreigners' own law and government. The exclusive mining rights now granted were the main and not unreasonable objective; a single mining authority is a necessity in any conditions and certainly was in Lobengula's country; but a time limit was desirable—this and other safeguards were imposed by a Rhodesian Government some seventy years later and are now a normal accompaniment of the exclusive rights which any government that wants mining started will recognize as an inducement it must be prepared to offer.

It remained for Rudd and company, two or three Europeans negotiating in wild country a thousand miles from anywhere, to put a value on mineral rights whose worth was not yet proven. They had in the first place to satisfy the African seller: the 1,000 Martini rifles and 100,000 rounds to shoot with were the form of wealth most Africans in those days coveted. The £1,200 to be paid annually was at any rate something solid, and not inconsiderable. A third item was surely an attempt to meet the expectations aroused by the talk that went on—a steamer on the Zambesi! These treaty-makers, however, had their minds so set on distant objectives that they made no mention of rights in land—even in the land to be worked for minerals—and another sharp concession-hunter saw his opportunity, approached Lobengula two years later, in 1891, when he was still well away from company control, and secured the land rights for himself. Rhodes solved this problem (in the way the speculator must have hoped for) by buying the so-called 'Lippert Concession'. Meantime de Beers Consolidated was good for initial capital needs, and the Rudd Concession was something definite for Rhodes's company to go to work on. In effect (as the Courts explicitly ruled many years later) the B.S.A. Company became from October 1889 H.M.G.'s agent, responsible as such for *good* government and for the advancement of civilization. The Company's powers were as wide as its jurisdictional functions made

necessary—a few pre-existing rights were safeguarded and there
were provisions that trade be reasonably free, except in liquor
which was to be kept under control—but all its actions were
subject to the distant, yet never-to-be-disregarded, overruling
authority of one of H.M.'s Principal Secretaries of State.

The sphere of the Company's operations was, and could be,
only vaguely specified and had yet to be determined. By 1890
the scramble for Africa was at its height and if this had to be done
it were best done quickly. Only the white men 'scrambled'—
African interests suffered little damage; but Rhodes wasted no
time. A carefully picked pioneer column of some 200 men which
set out in June 1890 had by September planted the flag at Fort
Salisbury in the uplands of Mashonaland. It is characteristic of
this adventure that the offer of fifteen mining claims was more of
a magnet than the promise of a 5,000-acre farm. The claims
proved to be of little worth and farming got going only slowly;
but there was enough to keep all hands busy establishing a base
—and the Company had rivals. The great hunter, F. C. Selous,
had been called in to guide the pioneer column by a new route
avoiding Matabeleland, ostensibly in order not to disturb Lobengula; but the Salisbury stance, as the promoters also knew,
left them better placed to make a bid for delectable country to
the east, against Portuguese claimants who had suddenly become aware of their 'hinterland'. Rhodes's ambition was to
acquire Beira, in spite of its pestilential climate, to serve as his
seaport, but Portuguese claims were strong. Empty land was
never the quest—Colonel Grogan, a pioneer still active in
Kenya in 1956, wrote in the late '90s deploring the loss not only
of Beira but of Tongaland, Shangaan country and a great
reservoir of African labour. The Company was able at least to
secure Umtali and the fine highland country in its neighbourhood, where there were also some useful gold-mines.

Farther north the Company had successes, and one major
disappointment. In 1890 the Home Government was unwillingly making itself responsible for the mission zone of Nyasaland
—so unwillingly that Sir Harry Johnston, its representative, was
kept going at all only by Rhodes surreptitiously subsidizing him
with a grant of £10,000 a year. East and south the Nyasaland
boundaries were fixed by H.M.G. with the Portuguese; on the
other side, with the Shire country as a 'jumping-off' ground, the

Company made good a claim to what became 'North-Eastern' Rhodesia (Fort Jameson). In the far north-west the Barotse king in the well-favoured upper valley of the Zambesi was prevailed on, with help from a well-known French Protestant missionary, François Coillard, to choose British suzerainty. The Company's agents also improved their boundary with German Tanganyika by making sure of what is now Abercorn. But they lost the highly mineralized region of Katanga; the story goes that Rhodes's men were beaten to it, by days, by an English officer in the service of the Congo Free State—they were held up by Luapula, a mighty river even before it becomes first the Lualaba, then the Congo. Shorn thus of the coveted Katanga, known as the Congo 'pedicle', which breaks into the rough right-angle made by the Rhodesian border near the modern Copper Belt, the limits of the Company's sphere were now set; but its representative in North-West Rhodesia (Barotseland) was delayed by more pressing business and took up his duties only in 1897. There remained Lobengula, a thorn in the Company's flesh nearer headquarters. The Company's officers clearly went on the assumption that the Matabele private military despotism could only and must be broken. Lacking the patience and perhaps the means to build the administrative system needed for civilized government, they allowed an accumulation of 'incidents' to become the occasion for a Matabele War. A sharp campaign in 1893 ended tragically; the Matabele were broken and Lobengula died miserably of smallpox, a fugitive in the bush.

Rhodes meanwhile, as Prime Minister of the Cape, was caught up in the chain of events finally responsible—by way of a South African railway 'war' and the Jameson Raid of 1896—for the disatrous political fixation which made the troubles of southern Africa turn entirely on the feud of Boers and Britons. The new poor relations of the prosperous Transvaal were desperate to get what share they could at least of the carrying trade to the Rand hive of industry—the South African railway system grew up, not as a network carefully planned to help local development, but rather as a straggle of lines all making as directly as possible from the five principal seaports to the goldfields. President Kruger and his advisers, foiled in their effort to get a seaport of their own, favoured a Delagoa Bay line which, besides being the shortest route to the sea, ran most of its length through the Transvaal. Their obstinacy in vetoing a direct line from the Cape and refusing to permit even the fifty miles of line needed to link the Free State terminus with Johannesburg reached a peak in August 1895 when the President went so far as to close the 'drifts' or Vaal River crossings used by wagons carrying goods from railheads to the Rand. It then came so near open war that Kruger alienated sympathy throughout the country, making it likely that, even if he ran at all, a younger and less conservative candidate would win the election due in 1897 and make a comprehensive settlement on a broadly South African basis. It was not to be. The 'drifts' crisis dragged on till November. In December Rhodes lost patience and decided to strike (or to stand aside and let his second-in-command in Rhodesia strike) into the Transvaal with a sketchy force of 500 men. Rhodes, who knew little of the Rand, deceived himself, or was deceived, into supposing that the grievances of its British and other *uitlanders* had them on the verge of revolt. In fact, busily prosperous in spite of political handicaps, they were disinclined to risk what they held by launching a revolution. The Jameson Raid was a bid to stimulate incipient revolt and bring the Transvaal into a United South Africa—the forlorn hope of a man, conscious that his time was short, who died only six years later lamenting, 'so much to do, so little done'. . . .

33. Rhodesian dilemma

PHILIP MASON *Birth of a Dilemma* Oxford University Press 1959; pages 190–6, 312–17

Section 2: The Reasons for the Matabele Rising

On the surface, then, all was well. It was the general belief among Europeans that though a few had regrets—the Indunas who had once ruled the country, the Amatjaha who had so often washed their spears in innocent blood—most of the people were glad to be released from tyranny. When it became necessary to account for the rebellion, many theories were put forward; it is easy to list the factors that one observer or another believed were decisive, much harder to assign a relative importance between them. A man's own temperament and experience will guide him, one putting first the grievances about land, cattle, and labour, another the deep injuries to self-esteem—to more than self-esteem, to all that complex system of emotional involvement with the world that is built up from custom and past history, a system from which man is no more severed without a shock than the unborn child from the *placenta*.

There was the land, there were the cattle, there was the labour question. This had been touched on in Jameson's interviews with those who surrendered; 'the people were now to settle down and till their ground and the Indunas were advised to induce them to work for the white people on their lands and in the mines, for which they should all be paid. . . .' This is the language in which Jameson reports what he said to the High Commissioner; it is guarded language, because Jameson knew very well the sharp reaction he might expect if any newspaper in England caught a sniff of anything that smacked of slavery or forced labour. But Selous was not a diplomat; aware that things looked different under grey English skies, he yet described them as he saw them in the harsh African sunlight.

They found themselves treated [he wrote of the Matabele] as a conquered people . . . who had only been permitted to return to the country from which they had been driven . . . under certain conditions, of which one was that the indunas should, through the medium of the native commissioners, supply miners and farmers with native labour—all the able-bodied young men in the country being required to work for a certain number of months per annum at a fixed rate of pay.

He goes on to say that he thinks 'the boys' were usually well treated, cruelty being a rare exception; but 'owing to the excessive indolence of the people, there can be no doubt that the labour regulations were most irksome to them'. There were not exactly official 'regulations' enforcing paid labour; but Selous, who was managing a large estate in Matabeleland when the rebellion broke out, thought there were, and that they were not all of them committed to writing made no difference to the Matabele. They found it just as hard to see why they should

leave their homes and live under discipline in alien surroundings, toiling all day for what seemed altogether someone else's
good.

There was a reluctance among the Victorians to discuss another element in the situation, but there is good evidence of its
importance in Dr Jameson's account of his interview with the
Matabele who came in to surrender. They were assured that
their wives and daughters would be protected—and the point
was specially emphasized because of their dread of interference.
Three years later, Rhodes himself admitted by implication that
this protection had not always been given. And 'it was
very widely said in South Africa that the Native rebellion had,
as one of its causes, the treatment of the Native young women
by white men and also by Native police'.

Selous probably spoke for the great majority of his fellows
when he wrote:

the Matabele broke out in rebellion because they disliked their
position as a conquered people and imagined they were strong
enough to throw off the yoke of their conquerors. . . .

And he goes on:

We Europeans make the mistake of thinking that, when we free a
tribe of savages from what we consider a most oppressive and tyran-
nical form of government . . . we ought to earn their gratitude; . . .
we invariably fail to do so. . . .

What 'the savage' says, Selous writes elsewhere, is:

hang your Pax Britannica; give me the good old times of superstition and bloodshed; then, even if I did not know the . . . hour
when I might be smelt out as a witch and forthwith knocked on the
head, . . . I could have basked in the sun till my time came; and
then, too, when the *impi* went forth, what glorious times I had and
how I revelled in blood and loot!

It was not a rising against intolerable injustice or cruelty, he
believed, but a very understandable attempt to go back to the
old days by a people who did not perceive the true strength of
the conquerors.

This was the general view; the Matabele had not been dealt
with severely enough in 1893; half their regiments had never

been in action and they had not been so thoroughly disarmed as they should have been—due, of course, to interference from Whitehall. The opportunity had been provided—so the farmer or miner would say—when Dr Jameson withdrew every armed man he could and stationed his police on the Transvaal border; when the Jameson Raid took place and ended ignominiously in defeat by the Transvaalers, then the leaders of the Matabele knew that the time had come. And they brought the rank and file, discontented already, to the point of rising, by working the oracle, inspiring the priests of the Mlimo, the Makalanga spirit of fertility, to prophesy success.

There is much in this, the view of common sense; it is true that no very elaborate explanation is needed for the desire of a conquered people to be free, that the police had been taken away and Jameson defeated and disgraced. Yet one may wonder—and the answer can only be conjecture, an opinion that can never be tested—whether the rebellion would have occurred if personal humiliation and uncertainty about the future had not been added to these more tangible grievances regarding land, labour, cattle, and women. On one aspect of the humiliation there would be general agreement; Selous, Colin Harding, Marshall Hole, all speak of the bullying and insolence of the black police, recruited immediately after the war and, naturally, not recruited from those who had been fighting, therefore from the despised Maholi. Selous speaks of a visit to him at his home in Essexvale by Umlugulu, an important Induna under Lobengula, who 'complained bitterly of the high-handed manner in which the "Ama-Policey-Minyama" behaved. I have no complaints,' he said, 'against the white policemen; but the black police, *wa duba, wa duba sebele*, they give me trouble, they really give me trouble.' The same cry was raised again and again. It was the recruiting of labour more than anything else that gave them their chance; they would arrive in a village and until they had taken their pick of the young men and led them away, would—so the complaints ran —take their toll of the daughters and the wealth of the homestead. To this active oppression the inexperience and sometimes indifference of their officers must have contributed. It is not easy for an administrator to encourage the confidence and pride of his police without licensing brutality; he must walk a tight-rope between a suspiciousness, a meddlesomeness that will paralyse initiative and a trustfulness that will encourage oppression. In those first three years, the Company's earliest administrators in Matabeleland would have been more than human if they had always kept their footing.

After the rebellion, when Rhodes went alone into the Matopo Hills to parley with those who still held out, they told him their grievances and one of the Indunas told how he had come in with his advisers and young men, as befits a chief, to pay his respects to the Chief Magistrate in Bulawayo. He had waited all day; towards evening he had sent a polite message. He did not wish to hurry the great man but his people had not eaten all day; when a white man came to visit him, he killed a beast and gave him a meal. The answer came: there were stray dogs in the town; he might kill those and eat. That answer must have come from a policeman or a messenger, not from the Magistrate, but the insult would not have been given to a man whom the Magistrate delighted to honour. It grew from a soil of indifference.

Uncertainty contributed perhaps almost as much as humiliation. The Matabele had been defeated; if Rhodes himself had come to live among them—and a Rhodes unhampered by either voters or shareholders, either in England or in the Cape—perhaps they would have been quiescent, if not content, with a rule that was direct and personal. It was for this they asked him in those long talks in the Matopo Hills: 'We want one, not half a dozen heads,' Somabulana said to him. And Faku added: 'Give us a head and we are satisfied.' But the leaders they had been given were divided among themselves; and within themselves; they were partly controlled from a distance by a will alien to their own, so that they must draw back as soon as they had stepped forward; they alternated between the firmly paternal and the mildly trusting. And there were differences between one Native Commissioner and the next; even a rule that is both strange and harsh can be borne if it is certain in its operation; a man becomes reconciled to what he knows is inevitable. But when the new order is unpredictable, every manifestation of it strikes home with the impact of the first.

On top of all this came natural disasters. Locusts and drought had come when the Pioneers entered Mashonaland and never gone; next came rinderpest and the cattle died; those the rinderpest did not kill the Company's veterinary officers shot to prevent its spread. Cattle were the life-blood of the country, providing transport as well as milk and meat; it is not surprising that the Mlimo, the Makalanga godling of the Matopo hills, began to prophesy that nothing would go right so long as the white men were in the country.

The Mlimo was one of many spirits who were in the country before the Matabele came. There are many kinds of spirits at work among the Mashona, having in common the attribute of seeking from time to time a human host or medium, the *svikiro*, in whom the spirit chooses to dwell. This spirit may take up residence permanently in one human host; this is what happens in the case of a *mhondoro* or tribal spirit, when the man too is called the *mhondoro*, as well as being the *svikiro* of the spirit; when the human host dies, the *mhondoro* spirit will after a time take a new residence, who will be recognized by various signs, rather as a new Dalai Lama is recognized. There are other spirits[1] which possess a man or a woman for a few hours at a time and who again are recognizable by the strange behaviour of the host.

The Mlimo was a god of harvests and ferility who spoke from a cave; Selous says his chief priest was also called the Mlimo and that there were other human Mlimos in other parts of Rhodesia; others say that in this case the distinction between the invisible spirit and the host was always clear. Charles Bullock describes him as a god whose jurisdiction extended over the whole of Mashonaland and Matabeleland, called Mwari as well as Mlimo, not interested in individuals or even tribes, being too far above them, 'a god of the Cosmos, ordering it in its course'. This does not agree with what others say and may be a confusion, but all are agreed that Mlimo was a god of this country before the Matabele came; perhaps just because he did not concern himself (until 1895) with war or politics, but only with the course of nature, Lobengula consulted the Mlimo and he had a following among the Matabele. Now, when natural disaster piled itself upon political, he turned to a new role and began to prophesy that nothing would go well until the Europeans were driven out of the country.

[1] These are called Shave spirits and are very like the voodoo gods of Haiti; see *Divine Horsemen of Haiti*, Maya Deren: Thames and Hudson, 1953.

Faced with a grain famine, robbed of their newly-acquired cattle, importuned in season and out of season to provide unaccustomed labour, bullied by their former tribesmen and slaves who had enlisted in the Police Force . . . what wonder if the Matabele Indunas began to seek a short cut out of their troubles. . . .

The words are not those of some theorist from Whitehall but of Marshall Hole, who for a quarter of a century was the Company's servant in Rhodesia. The short cut was a conspiracy of a kind not very carefully co-ordinated or thought out, a mere determination to rise and kill every European in the country; it arose from and linked itself to the prophecies of the oracle, the one feeding the other. It was in October of 1895 that Jameson moved his police to the Transvaal border; it was on 2 January 1896 that they surrendered to the Transvaalers at Doornkop. The first steps in the short cut took place in March, a little more than two months later.

Section 3: The Nature of the Matabele Rising

There is little need to dwell on what happened. A determination to kill—that certainly was wide-spread. But there was little more planning to it than that. As a military operation, it was hardly planned at all; the Matabele never grasped the dependence of the Europeans on lines of communications; their policy, if they had thought one out, should have been to cut the roads, particularly to the south, to avoid battle, to cut off stragglers, to starve out the Europeans. In fact they ambushed an occasional wagon but made no determined attempt to keep the roads shut; there was even talk of their having deliberately left the road to the south open so that the Europeans might have the opportunity of escaping. They let themselves be brought to battle, were defeated, and from then on were simply hunted. All they could do was to hold out in the tangle of granite kopjes that is the Matopo Hills. . . .

The conqueror faces a dilemma as soon as the last battle is won. He cannot for ever maintain the high mood of the paean and the feast; he will wake, with victory sour in the mouth, to a colder light in which he must make peace. And if he is a realist, the kind of peace open to him is never wholly to his liking. This is true of any conqueror; the dilemma is the more poignant if the victor proposes to live in the country of the vanquished.

There are two kinds of peace open to him. Of this he is seldom aware; he does not, as a rule, sit down to think them over, deliberately choose one and reject the other; indeed, historical decisions are taken in that way far less often than most historians appear to suppose. No, to the conqueror, as a rule, one kind of peace alone presents itself as possible; he endeavours to impose it; gradually it is borne in upon him that the nature of the peace is changing, that it is turning into the other kind of peace; he may on reflection welcome the change, he may accept it with resignation, he may resist it, but it will come, and he will in the end find himself living side by side with the vanquished on new terms, that will largely depend on his attitude to this change.

Rhodesia was the geographical meeting-place of two peoples who had been separated by immense distances in culture and achievement, by immense possibilities of misunderstanding; one conquered the other and was faced with the problem of what kind of peace they wanted. The conquest was not complete until after the rebellions; it took place in three stages—the march of the Pioneers in 1890, the Matabele War in 1893, the rebellions in 1896. And the peace, too, was made by driblets; a beginning of an accommodation, a way of living together, was made before 1893, another after; only after the rebellions did the form of the peace begin to settle and harden into shape; it was still far from rigid by 1918.

And there can be no question which kind of peace it was originally meant to be. It was to be one in which victors and vanquished should remain separate from each other and all power should be in the hands of the conquerors. It was imposed by a people who set a high value on kindliness; those on the spot were themselves professing Christians and were directed from afar by statesmen officially Christian and responsible to a public opinion which admired Christian virtues and found them much easier to exercise at a distance than at home. It was a settlement which was intended in the end to bring both enlightenment and material progress to the vanquished. But it was not such a settlement as was made with the French Canadians, nor again with the Afrikaners in 1910, both deliberately designed to enable two peoples to live together in unity and equality; it was not such a settlement as Sebituane and his Makololo had made with the Barotse, nor such as Warren Hastings had dreamed of in India, by which the influence and teaching of the military victors would have pervaded a nexus of self-governing states; nor such as Lugard made with the Emirs in Nigeria. It could not be expected to be like any of these, because historical circumstances are never exactly repeated; indeed, a settlement envisaging a future of equality would not at the time have seemed possible, could hardly have occurred even as a flight of fancy to the most imaginative.

Yet very soon a trend displayed itself to which such an outcome was the logical development. It was not possible to think in terms of equality, but as soon as Wilson Fox set himself to the consideration of broad problems of development and policy, he saw at once that the aims must be unity and integration rather than separation and permanent domination.

The native population of Rhodesia [he wrote] under good government will certainly increase. It must be dealt with as a permanent element of the body politic and neither its existence nor its welfare can be ignored in any schemes for future development. It would be both wrong and short-sighted to ignore them and the real problem for the statesman is to make the native play his part in that development under conditions that will best conduce to his welfare and advancement. . . .

Thus the official Doctrine was born, that the right course for Rhodesia lay along the road of assimilation. That is a word and an idea which may mask an intolerable arrogance, the assumption that one culture, one religion or one system of national standards alone is valid. But it need not be so; it is possible for a people to be assimilated into a new economic system and a new tradition in art, education, and religion, yet mould all these into shapes of their own, as is happening in the West Indies and in Brazil. Such possibilities were however still far from the minds of Wilson Fox and the Directors of the British South Africa Company in the period before 1914; to them the problem was 'how best to elevate and utilize the indigenous inhabitants' and the Doctrine at this stage confined itself to economic integration. The object should be to increase the natives' wants; 'only contact with civilization will do this and the branch of civilization most needed is commerce, in the shape of the trader, farmer and pioneer'.

The Doctrine then involved taxes, meant not so much to bring in revenue as to force the native out to work, and make him meet the trader and the farmer, make him learn new wants and decide to work longer in order to satisfy them; taxes would provide not only labour but a market for goods. But the Doctrine implied much more than taxes; it meant a new kind of peace and a slightly different approach to every point of contact between the races. It involved for instance the idea that reserves of land were a temporary expedient, to last only while the native needed protection; they would gradually give way to open areas in which anyone might own land. Tribalism was a decaying force and its decay should be encouraged; chieftainship as an institution would wither away; superstition would melt; the Africans of Rhodesia would gradually become a working class, and would grow more and more like the British working class—and perhaps, though this was not stated in so many words, there would be men in Rhodesia as in Britain who would rise from the ranks of the working class to positions of wealth and power.

This was the detached upper-class form of the Doctrine, which was acceptable to the directors of the Company, in which the Attorney-General, the Judges, and the Chief Native Commissioners would have concurred. It appears in a form basically the same but subtly and slightly transmuted in the report of the Native Affairs Committee, which included members responsible to electors in Southern Rhodesia; here the progress and well-being of the native is still the aim but there is also a readiness to perceive the value of native institutions and an inclination to preserve the best of them, a touch of the Museum Attitude. This is an attitude which may arise from concern for the native, but also from a concern that he shall stay as he is and not be a rival to anyone else. The Commission on Reserves preached in general the sincere milk of the Doctrine, but they showed also that it might be used to support what was contrary to its basic intention; that reserves would one day be merged in open areas could for instance become an argument for driving through the Sabi reserve a ten mile strip which would carry the railway, an act justifiable if this strip was really to be an open area, not if it was to be used for white farmers and if it meant moving Africans back into tribal reserves.

The Doctrine of assimilation was accepted, then, by the reasoning and directing party of the community, though even in their hands it might be distorted or modified, and particularly by those whose upper-class detachment was shaken by responsibility to voters with a sectional interest. It was by no means accepted by every Rhodesian. One may guess that in most conquests it has been easier to show a tolerance for the vanquished from the top; a Norman baron, secure in possession of half a county, could see that the interest of the countryside lay in Norman and Saxon working together; he could afford to dispense impartial justice. The man-at-arms who had come with him, with not much but his Normanness to show his superiority, would be the one who was reluctant to give up privilege. So even today the barrister and the doctor do not fear African competition; they are a trained aristocracy of the intellect used to sharp competition, and from any quarter; not so the manual worker who knows African muscles are no weaker than his and that his own skill can be learnt. He begins very soon to feel uneasy about the dangers of rivalry; his voice begins to be heard in the first decade of the century; he has little but his whiteness to rely on for a position much better than he would enjoy in England. He therefore stays faithful to the original idea of a settlement after conquest, of which it is the essence that dominion by one race over the other shall be maintained indefinitely. This applies not only to the artisan but to the clerk and the lower grades of civil servant. They will be the first to be displaced when there is a flow of Africans from the secondary schools; to them the policy of 'elevating the native' may be for the good of the territory as a whole but is likely to be a personal disaster.

This is the first basic dilemma that confronts every conqueror; maintain the position by force and make certain of hatred in the end, or aim from the start at an equality which involves an immediate sacrifice of power. From that first dilemma another develops. That part of the community which is in power—and likely to be more intelligent and more detached in outlook—soon perceives that the second of these choices is in the long run the lesser evil; how are they to convince their followers, to whom that second choice is likely to mean an immediate personal loss? Are they to sacrifice the support of their own people in order to win the co-operation of the vanquished? Or must they abandon the policy they believe to be morally right and from their own point of view in the highest degree prudent? If they abandon it, they do so for the sake of the least intelligent and the least energetic of their own community, and at the expense of the most intelligent and the most energetic of the vanquished. That is the second pair of horns.

And there is a third, as sharp as the other two if more delicate, a pair which present themselves with particular menace to conquerors nursed in the tradition of English freedom. Their history rings with the cries of men determined to be free; it has been a long struggle against despotism, against the irresponsible rule of kings, barons, and borough-mongers within, against absolute monarchy and the dictatorial empires of Spain, France, and Germany without; their songs, plays, poetry, the speeches of their great leaders—all they are taught at school tells the same tale. They come of a stock that has refused to be humbled, mainly perhaps from a fierce awareness of their own selfhood, but partly from a belief that freedom is something good in itself. They are proud of their stock and of its tradition, even though they may express its basic ideals incoherently in terms of cricket and fair play. They may spend most of their working hours in pursuit of gold but the fact of their own freedom is important to them, and among themselves they display the methods of freedom—consultation and persuasion, compromise, willing co-operation. Are they to belie all they stand for by denying freedom to others? Or must they forfeit their heritage by losing their identity among an alien and defeated people? Shall they teach freedom and provoke revolt? Or shall they suppress the lesson of their own history and themselves become as miserable and as leaden-eyed as is usually the fate of conquerors who are slaves to their own fears? . . .

34. Rival philosophies

RICHARD GRAY *The Two Nations* Oxford University Press for
Institute of Race Relations 1960; pages 3–10

The upheaval of the First World War was followed in Britain by
a decade of intense examination of her imperial role in Africa
and especially in the mixed communities of East and Central
Africa. 'Trusteeship' and 'the paramountcy of native interests'
inspired the pronouncements, and to a lesser extent the practice,
of the Colonial Office. These ideas, going back through Johnston
and Livingstone to the Abolitionists and Burke, now provided
the nearest approach to a coherent theory of British imperialism.
This theory of trusteeship encountered, however, another and
yet older colonial theme. In the twenties it was still possible, and
indeed common, to regard the highlands of Eastern Africa,
extending in an unbroken belt hundreds of miles broad from
Kenya to South Africa, as the last great area in the world ready
and waiting for European settlement. For the first time, following the fall of German rule in East Africa, the map was virtually
coloured red from Cairo to Cape Town; and, deep in the centre,
copper promised to rival the revolutions brought about previously by gold and diamonds. There was little to show that the
great impulse of European migration, which so recently and
spectacularly had transformed the Transvaal, would slacken
and fall away. Yet these high hopes of settlement were accompanied by uneasiness and fears which brought with them the
practice, and, to a lesser extent, the theory of 'segregation'—the
idea that European and African were best left each to develop
on his own lines.

The clash and mingling of these two philosophies distinguishes
the inter-war years. Though drawn from such opposite sources,
the concepts of 'trusteeship' and 'segregation' shared two basic
assumptions which marked them out from the previous and the
following periods. The introspective questioning of Western
civilization, induced by the catastrophe of the war, made men
more ready to appreciate the new values and worlds which
social anthropologists were beginning to reveal in African cultures. The period of the 'manifest' superiority of the European's
way of life contrasted with the 'primitive savagery' of the

African was passing. The doubts and questionings, and the new awareness of African potentialities, were reflected not only in the readiness of colonial administrators to delegate power to Native Authorities, but also in the positive, protectionist element in the thought of some advocates of segregation. It was partly this that led many men, including Smuts and Lord Lugard, to support elements of both theories simultaneously. Both theories also shared a confident expectation of long life. Their exponents were concerned with a very gradual development of relatively intact societies, with the progress and status of peoples rather than the aspirations and achievements of individuals and an emergent class. They envisaged decades of undisputed European control. They thought in terms of centuries rather than five-year plans.

Both philosophies also assumed an unavoidable, and at times an almost complete, clash of interests between 'settlers' and 'natives'. The harmonious and increasingly integrated development hoped for by Livingstone was on the whole replaced by the suspicious, somewhat negative, watchfulness traditionally represented by the Aborigines Protection Society. The exponents of Colonial Office 'trusteeship' felt that the essential role of the Imperial Government should be to preserve a balance of interests by acting as an 'impartial arbiter'. And although the advocates of European settlement maintained that their leadership was the only sure means of bringing lasting benefits—and thus an element of trusteeship—to all the inhabitants of Africa, it is evident that the concept of segregation presupposed at least a temporary, and generally a permanent, incompatibility between the races.

Neither of these two approaches was defined or developed primarily for the territories of Central Africa. The practice of British colonial administrators of delegating power to Native Authorities—or 'indirect rule'—based partly on Lugard's experience in Nyasaland, Uganda, and Nigeria, was developed by Sir Donald Cameron in Tanganyika and was only later introduced in Northern Rhodesia and Nyasaland. The definitions of trusteeship were also occasioned by events elsewhere. The League of Nations' Mandate for Tanganyika, by accepting a 'sacred trust' for 'peoples not yet able to stand by themselves under the strenuous conditions of the modern world', was soon held to have prominently reaffirmed an 'axiom of British policy'. Lugard's looser use of the term 'mandate' gave it a wider circulation. For him the Mandate—dual in its obligation to foster the welfare of the colonial inhabitants and to develop for the world the potentialities of a dependency—was universal in application and economic in emphasis; and in the British conception of it as a slow continuous process there was little emphasis on the advance to self-government already implied in the phrase 'not yet able to stand . . .'

The policy of trusteeship was brought into focus by the situation in Kenya. Here the small group of European settlers, with their numbers augmented by a settlement scheme for ex-soldiers, claimed an increasing share in the government of the Colony. Indian immigrants, however, originally encouraged with a disregard for political complications, now heavily outnumbered the Europeans and it was realized in Whitehall that any attempt to discriminate against them might have serious repercussions in India. The declaration of 1923 issued by the Secretary of State, the Duke of Devonshire, sought to counter these claims by the assertion of imperial responsibility.

Primarily Kenya is an African territory, and His Majesty's Government think it necessary definitely to record their considered opinion that the interests of the African natives must be paramount, and that if, and when, those interests and the interests of the immigrant races should conflict, the former should prevail. Obviously, the interests of the other communities, European, Indian or Arab, must severally be safeguarded. . . . But in the administration of Kenya His Majesty's Government regard themselves as exercising a trust on behalf of the African population, and they are unable to delegate or share this trust, the object of which may be defined as the protection and advancement of the native races.

Partly as a result of this declaration, the Kenya settlers concentrated their hopes on achieving power through a closer union of the East and Central African territories, and in response to their agitation a Commission was appointed in 1927 to examine the problem. Under the chairmanship of Sir Edward Hilton Young, its members included Sir George Schuster and Mr J. H. Oldham, secretary of the International Missionary Council. The report was of major importance not only for its recommendations on the subject of closer union, but also for its comprehensive and authoritative discussion of the implications of trusteeship. It provided also a striking example of the difference in viewpoint between Parliament and the man on the spot. Immigrant communities, with their initiative, knowledge, and material resources, were regarded by the Commission as 'necessary instruments' in the fulfilment of the dual mandate; their importance was rigorously confined to this function. Economically their main contribution would be the stimulus they could give 'to the vast potentialities of native production'; politically the leadership claimed by the European community would 'never be secure until it rests on consent and not on privilege'. The argument that strong white settlement was essential to ensure the permanence of 'white civilization in Eastern Africa' was repudiated. The strongest foundation of Western civilization and British rule was seen to lie not 'in the size of the white community, which must always remain a relatively small island in the midst of a greatly preponderant black population, but in the establishment of a rule of justice which will enlist the loyalty of the native people, and strengthen their confidence in British rule'.

With the Imperial Government alone capable of creating this atmosphere of 'disinterested justice', a parallel form of political development was envisaged. Both immigrants and natives would be encouraged to develop local self-governing institutions in their own areas, while power at the centre would be retained by the representative of the Secretary of State. The native areas were seen as 'a first charge on the territory', where Africans would be able to 'develop on their own lines in a process of continuous evolution'. If this Dual Policy was followed honestly, it was felt that it was 'only a question of time before the natives will have to be admitted to a share in the whole government which fairly balances that accorded to the immigrant communities', and the Commission 'would not close the door' to the ideal ('though many would consider it visionary') that 'if white and black can some day meet on equal terms, intellectually, socially and economically, the racial and economic antagonisms may be merged in a community of interests which will admit of some form of free representative government'. Since, however, there might remain even in that far-distant future 'fundamental differences of outlook', and since the dangers of a premature or wrongly directed advance for Africans were manifest, the whole emphasis of the Report was on parallel development of the different communities within their own areas under the control of the 'impartial arbiter'. The benefits of closer union, it was suggested, could be better obtained by the institution of a central authority in East Africa to provide for a more effective exercise of the Imperial Government's powers, than by delegating these powers to a settler-dominated Assembly. The immediate practical implications of this policy of parallel political development would be similar in some respects to those of segregation as conceived south of the Zambesi, but the assumptions and ultimate objectives of trusteeship were vastly different.

Segregation, as slogan and theory, had become widely accepted by 1918 and not only in Africa. Across the Atlantic, in the Southern States, the compromise of 1877, by which Southerners regained control of their affairs after the brief upheaval of Reconstruction and the reign of the Carpet-baggers, was followed by a period in which Southern Conservatives and their opponents, the Populists, alike advocated programmes which were by no means Negrophobe. Paternal Conservatives, to whom class distinctions were sometimes more important than those of race, defended the Negro franchise and wooed the Negro voter. Radical Populists strove to establish an alliance based on an 'egalitarianism of want and poverty'. By the end of the century, however, both these alternatives were rejected: Northern liberalism, already on the retreat and keen to seek reconciliation with the South, fell back before the doctrines of Anglo-Saxon superiority which were used to justify imperialism in Cuba, Hawaii, and the Philippines; in the South the economic discontent caused by agrarian depression vented itself in hostility to the Negroes and white supremacy became a rallying cry. Virtual disfranchisement of the Negro was accompanied by segregation in public institutions and employment, in residential areas, in parks and trams. By 1907 segregation was regarded as the immutable foundation of the 'folkways' of the South, a way of life manifestly appropriate to a white man's country. During the First World War a visitor from South Africa to the United States found that 'the separation of the races in all social matters is as distinct in South Africa as in the Southern States' and saw separation as the solution of the common problems of both countries. After the First World War racial violence intensified and racial hostility began to spread throughout the United States. Labour in the North resented Negro competition, and Negroes were excluded from unions; the Ku Klux Klan, which reached its peak of activity in the mid-twenties, had a larger following outside the South than within. In the North there was uncertainty, guilt, and anxiety; segregation could never be accepted whole-heartedly because the contrast with egalitarian, democratic, and Christian ideals was too sharp. But it seemed probable that a hesitant enforcement of segregation would continue to be the American response to the problems of race relations.

In South Africa, segregation had a longer and more complex history. In the early nineteenth century missionaries had supported measures of segregation to protect the Hottentots. In Natal, Sir Theophilus Shepstone, recognizing the need for a special treatment inconsistent with full citizenship, attempted to carry out a protective policy towards the Zulu, and Cape Colony policy in the Transkei was based on the same principle. Ultimate objectives were not fully stated, but segregation was regarded as a temporary measure designed to aid an inevitable and beneficial transition. In the twentieth century the will to protect persisted among some officials and missionaries, but doubts about the beneficence of the transition became common. Segregation came to be thought of as a necessary, permanent institution, even among those South Africans who were primarily concerned to protect the Bantu. The first descriptions of tribal life by anthropologists, continental theories of 'primitive mentality' and the 'group mind', as much as ideas embodied in Lugard's concept of indirect rule—initially designed for territories where there were virtually no immigrant European communities—all seemed to suggest the permanent necessity of different institutions for the Bantu; the destructive effects of contact with Western materialism were only too evident, and Western institutions themselves were under criticism. Segregation came to be thought of as a permanent protection, a means of preserving cultural roots, a provision for a full and free existence, and a panacea against racial tension. In this form it would involve, it was realized, sacrifices by all communities. And it was still not clear to many in the twenties that these sacrifices were impossible or unacceptable.

Others were concerned to protect white rather than black. In the Orange Free State and Transvaal segregation came to be regarded as something designed to defend the Voortrekker principle of not 'creating equality' in Church and State: the sources of power were to be closely guarded. It became linked with the growth and survival of an Afrikaans nation. This defensive aspect was powerfully reinforced by the demands of European labour, led by trade unionists on the Rand, that the inflated wage structure of 'civilized labour' should be protected by a colour bar. The intercolonial commission of 1903–5 recommended segregation in the franchise and in land-ownership. The Native Land Act of 1913 prohibited the African from purchasing land in European areas, and postulated somewhat vaguely that other areas would be provided in return. The Mines and Works Act of 1911 consolidated the colour bar. The defences were going up, and now they seemed to be protecting privilege alone.

Besides segregation and trusteeship a third theme, at first faint but of increasing importance, was beginning to influence Central Africa. The ideas of popular sovereignty, propagated with increasing success in Europe in the nineteenth century—and particularly among the English with their memories of Byron and their support of Garibaldi—won their greatest recognition in the Allies' settlement of the Balkans after the First World War. The twenties witnessed an extension of these ideas to the peoples of Asia and also to those of African descent. In India the Congress under the leadership of Mahatma Gandhi developed into a mass movement, and in America Negro and African race-consciousness emerged. This took two widely differing forms, but both rejected the pre-war spirit of co-operative acquiescence in the programme of discrimination and the meek acceptance of an inferior status. The fierce, flamboyant, yet defensive pride in 'a pure black race' proclaimed by a Jamaican Negro, Marcus Garvey, with slogans such as 'Africa for the Africans at home and abroad' and 'Wake up, Ethiopia! Wake up Africa!', was enthusiastically received. Garvey's pre-eminence in the States was brief and his 'Back to Africa' movement foundered ignominiously; but his conventions, his church, his newspaper, his bombastic self-confidence, and his delegations to the League of Nations produced a revolutionary stirring of the imagination, a vision of a future power which eclipsed past and present degradation. The philosophy and approach of Dr Du Bois and the National Association for the Advancement of Coloured People (N.A.A.C.P.) were entirely different. A university professor, Du Bois attacked the racial ideologies of Gobineau and based his case on a thorough application of American democratic ideals. As chief publicist for the N.A.A.C.P., Du Bois deeply influenced thought and action in the United States, and his Pan-African Congress movements, started in the twenties, were a training-ground for West African nationalists.

Signs of this stirring were present in South Africa. The Native Land Act of 1913 led to the formation of the African National Congress, then composed principally of intelligentsia with a moderate outlook. But a few years later the Industrial and Commercial Workers' Union was founded and it proved to be the first forward-looking movement to appeal to the masses. Founded in 1919 by Clements Kadalie, a missionary-educated Tonga from Nyasaland, it gathered in the twenties a membership of a quarter of a million. Combining political agitation with industrial activities, it paralleled the rapid impact of Garvey's movement, until it too declined at the end of the decade, weakened by internal dissensions. There remained, however, the vision, hopes and ideas that it had produced and these reappeared elsewhere.

35. Politics in Southern Rhodesia

COLIN LEYS *European Politics in Southern Rhodesia* Clarendon Press, Oxford 1961; pages 290–3

The key to Southern Rhodesian politics is the basis on which the European population has come to be there. The first Europeans came to seek fortunes from gold; a second influx came to live by farming the land. Both resources were seriously over-valued, and not even a virtual monopoly of them both was sufficient in itself to provide the European population with the standard of living that had been expected. Moreover, large sums had been invested, in railways and other forms of capital, on the basis of expectations which proved to be unjustified.

In the first forty years of this century, therefore, every available artificial means was employed, from taxes and pass laws to the Industrial Conciliation Act and the Grain Marketing Act, to squeeze from the country a standard of life which would increase the European population and make it secure. The African population was cleared from the bulk of the best land; by the recruitment of African labour from a very wide area beyond the country's borders, wages were kept to a minimum which made possible enterprises which would not otherwise have paid; the European economy was insulated in every way possible from African competition, skilled employment being reserved for European artisans, paying markets for European farmers.

This apparatus was created to overcome insecurity; but the apparatus itself created a new and chronic type of insecurity. By all these means it endeavoured to divert growth in the national wealth in directions which would attract more European immigration. The larger the European population became, the better its chance of preserving its economic and political position against the challenge which, sooner or later, it would inevitably meet from the Africans. But this meant that the new immigrants, even more than the old, entered the country on terms which could only be made secure by making the protective apparatus permanent. Before 1934 the artisan was already partly protected from African competition by convention; but he would have been to some extent entitled to feel that his job was his, and not an African's, because there was no African who could do it. The real significance of the Industrial Conciliation Act was that in the 1930s the European artisan did not feel this; and immigrant workers entering the country since then have rightly regarded that Act as fundamental to their security.

The same circularity is inherent in land apportionment, in the pass laws, in agricultural marketing, in the Native Labour Boards, and above all in the electoral law. Each of these measures is a plank in the structure which shores up the European standard of living, and so attracts immigrants; and each of them in turn becomes a vital and permanent interest for some section of the European population as it grows.[1]

[1] There is, moreover, no point at which immigration solves this kind of insecurity. In 1953 Welensky campaigned on the theme of a target of

The structure of the European population reflects this apparatus on which it depends, and this in turn determines the composition of the electorate; the 'average voter' is an artisan, and one who has come relatively recently into the country, not a man with a degree or a company directorship, a house without a mortgage and a substantial bank balance. The average voter over-spends his income, even though his wife works; and although his consumption is among the world's highest, he does not necessarily feel economically secure. The protective apparatus of law and convention seems important to him, and the ideas and attitudes current in European society offer a rationalization of it which social segregation and other 'homogenizing' factors make it hard to resist, and which he is often glad to accept.

The political mechanism has evolved from this situation and mirrors European needs. There is a strong element of 'direct democracy' in it, as there is in the local politics of any town in Europe with a population of the same size. People in office, public or private, know each other, and informal procedures are important. While the Native Commissioners and Directors of Native Administration govern the bulk of the population directly, as proconsuls in the provinces and African towns, the interest organizations which represent the main European interests have established a particularly close and influential relationship with the government, which reflects the absence of the Africans whose trade unions are not recognized and on whose votes the government does not depend. Economic growth, by diversifying these interests and enlarging the European population, has strained and stretched this relationship in the years since 1940; but the history of the Native Industrial Workers' Unions Bill of 1954, and the Industrial Conciliation Bill of 1957, showed how closely these groups are bound together, and how the apparatus which regulates the place of Africans in the economy is an interest which they generally recognize to be common to them all.

The party system expresses the Rhodesian political situation most poignantly. Throughout the years covered by this book

500,000 immigrants; in 1955 Mr Wightwick thought that from 1 to 2 million Europeans would be a number too large to be 'eliminated'; in 1957 the Dominion Party called for numerical equality of Europeans and Africans, with 20–30 million Europeans by the end of the century.

control of the government was, in effect, in the hands of only one party, closely interlocked with the major European interest organizations, and reflecting in its organization and policies the social and economic solidarity of the European electorate. A multitude of opposition parties have challenged it; but because the electorate has been confined to Europeans the real opposition has been excluded from the system. The identity of interests of the Europeans being much stronger than their diversity, the only electoral tactic which offers any prospect of success is to fight to be accepted as the most effective champion of these interests against the 'real', though suppressed, opposition of the Africans. The Opposition Party has thus been an institution as essentially stable and permanent as the Government Party, in that its electoral significance has invariably consisted in the same appeal to racial fear and the same call for strengthened defences of European supremacy.

It seems at first sight puzzling that the party which has consistently gone furthest in championing European interests should have remained in opposition; the logic of the system suggests that the party which best exploits this appeal should win office and keep it. The explanation seems to lie in a variety of factors, some of which—such as the voting-habits of newly-registered immigrants—are extremely obscure. But the most important seem to have been fear of Afrikaner nationalism, and the associated hope of union with the territories to the north; the former helped to keep the Rhodesia Party and its successors in office, while the latter tempered the racialism of their electoral appeal. It was mainly owing to these factors, and the advent of the war, that repeated challenges by the Opposition Party were repulsed. Nevertheless, the opposition did gain office with a segregationist programme within ten years of the establishment of Responsible Government; and after federation it grew much more likely that, with essentially the same electoral appeal, it would not only gain office for a second time but be able to establish itself permanently in control. When Sir Edgar Whitehead lost his by-election in April 1958 this was not a result to be seen in isolation, but an instance of what one is tempted to call the 'inner law' of European politics in Southern Rhodesia.

In federation the Government Party gained an objective

which had tied its hands in the party contest for many years. Federation gave Southern Rhodesia independence from the Union of South Africa, and guarantees against the threat to her way of life which was contained in the rapid pace of African advance in countries to the north. European political institutions were quick to respond to this enlargement of their sphere of influence. Interest organizations and parties both reorganized themselves on a federal basis, and fresh constitutional aspirations quickly found expression, including the demand that the constitutions of the two Northern Territories—especially Northern Rhodesia—should be placed on a footing which would guarantee some security for European predominance in territorial as well as in federal government. The forces which had produced the demand for 'Dominion status' for Southern Rhodesia—the Opposition Party's call for a free hand in native policy—continued to operate after federation, and the British Government was confronted with these realities in a series of demands—for extensive constitutional concessions before the earliest date envisaged for a constitutional review, for holding that review at the earliest date, and for independence on that date; and by conceding the first two of these demands it went a long way towards limiting its freedom of action in respect of the last. . . .

VIII. ZAMBIA AND MALAWI

36. The modern emergence of Malawi and Zambia

ROBERT I. ROTBERG *The Transformation of East Africa* (eds. Stanley Diamond and Fred G. Burke) Basic Books, New York 1966; pages 340–5 (all footnotes present in original have been deleted; paper written 1964)

... Europe intruded into trans-Zambezia during the last years of the nineteenth century. The British government gave that region the unity of colonial rule and the integrity of artificial borders. It offered a focus for the loyalties of disparate peoples, channelled the aspirations of a subject population along new paths, and provided a necessary framework within which "nationalism" could eventually transform itself into African self-government.

The explorations of David Livingstone and the presence of English-speaking missionaries provided an historical excuse for the British diplomatic and military conquest of what became Nyasaland and Northern Rhodesia. At the same time, successive British foreign ministers at first refused to interest themselves in the affairs of such distant peoples. About 1887, however, the agitation of the missions and their influential supporters coincided with an imperial attempt to prevent either Portugal or the Transvaal from occupying Matabeleland and Mashonaland.

The alliance of Cecil John Rhodes and Henry Hamilton (later Sir Harry) Johnston finally persuaded Lord Salisbury, the then British prime minister, to act decisively in Central Africa. In 1889 Rhodes, a thirty-six-year-old imperialist personally worth millions, came to London from South Africa. He requested the support and the sanction of Her Majesty's Government for the annexation of Matabeleland. In return, he offered to pay for the colonization and administration of Matabeleland and the Bechuanaland Protectorate, to extend the existing rail and telegraph lines to the Zambezi River, and to obtain for the Crown all of trans-Zambezia. With that abundant resolution of which Livingstone would have approved, Rhodes simply proposed to paint the heart of Africa British red without cost to the imperial exchequer. By a few, swift strokes of Salisbury's pen, Rhodes promised to forestall the Transvaal and Portugal, to obviate any disastrous entanglements with African warriors, and to discharge all the responsibilities of a government.

The British government authorized the British South Africa Company, a creation of Rhodes, to rule and administer lands lying between the Limpopo and Zambesi Rivers. In addition, Salisbury declared that the Northern Rhodesian portion of trans-Zambezia, in which the Prime Minister was essentially uninterested, and which he purposely excluded from the first draft of the charter, would—probably because Rhodes suspected the existence of copper there—henceforth form a part of the British sphere. In concert with Johnston, Rhodes also made possible the inclusion of Nyasaland within this domain. He offered at once to provide funds for future treaty-making expeditions and promised to absorb the expenses of other activities in the future. For more than three decades, practical sovereignty in much of Central Africa thereby passed to a chartered undertaking, the activities of which remained effectively beyond the control of the British government.

Johnston became Queen Victoria's representative in the Nyasa regions. He quickly forestalled the forceful assertion of Portuguese sovereignty over trans-Zambezia by unilaterally declaring the protectorate over the Shire Highlands that Salisbury, in his turn, secured by threatening the Portuguese with war in Europe. At the same time, Johnston's representatives concluded a series of agreements with indigenous chiefs throughout a vast un-partitioned land stretching from the Ruo River west to Lake Mweru and north toward Lake Tanganyika. These treaties simply bound the chiefs in question to seek British approval before ceding any territory or sovereignty to another European power. They testified to the existence of peace between a tribe and the Queen of England, and promised to accord Her Majesty's representatives consular jurisdiction over all disputes that arose between the indigenous inhabitants and Britons. These treaties did not, however, confer or promise protection and, when Johnston later "protected" the environs of Lake Nyasa, his action bore no juridical similarity to the original understandings between the Queen's consuls and the chiefs. Nevertheless, in May 1891, after the British government and Rhodes had settled on a financial allowance for the new protectorates, the Foreign Office formally declared that "under and by virtue of Agreements with the native Chiefs, and by other lawful means, the territories in Africa, hereinafter referred to as the Nyasaland Districts, are under the Protectorate of Her Majesty the Queen."

In western trans-Zambezia, Rhodes sought minerals and territory. There, with the help of the French missionary François Coillard, a representative of his chartered company persuaded Lewanika, chief of the Lozi, to sign away his lands and subsoil rights. This treaty, however unscrupulously obtained, later proved the basis for the British South Africa Company's assumption of direct rule in north-western Rhodesia and, perhaps wrongly, for its rights to the lucrative ores that have since allowed Northern Rhodesia to become the world's second largest producer of copper. In 1891, it and the treaties obtained by Johnston and his representatives also permitted the chartered company formally to include these regions within its sphere.

But treaties really meant little. During the next eight years, soldiers forcibly imposed British rule, throughout what became Nyasaland and North-eastern Rhodesia. They deposed difficult or troublesome chiefs, and fought a number of bloody wars with Africans. "The history of Sir Harry Johnston's Administration," a colleague later wrote, ". . . while it records many notable civil achievements, is yet in its more salient features a history of successive military expeditions." Indeed, Johnston and his compatriots destroyed the power of the principal Yao, Cewa, and Arab rulers, and then turned their attentions first to the Ngoni and the Eastern Lunda, both of whom fought unsuccessfully to forestall a British conquest.

Nyasas and Northern Rhodesians henceforth found themselves "protected". In practice, however, Her Majesty's Government and its local representatives tended to ignore the legal limitations presumably inherent in a "protectorate" and treated these new dependencies of the Crown as conquered colonies. Johnston and later commissioners, administrators, and governors thus derived their legal authority to rule Africans not from the consent of their subjects, but from the British Order-in-Council of 1889, as amended. Empowered thereby, they made so-called Queen's Regulations in order to promote "peace, order, and good government". They established courts wherein Africans could be tried and sentenced for transgressing the Queen's Regulations. Thus, after 1891 in Nyasaland and after about 1901 in Northern Rhodesia, the subordinate imperial pro-consuls (variously styled Collectors of Revenue, Resident Magistrates, and Native Commissioners) each supervised particularly circumscribed districts. They became super-chiefs and, as agents of the governor or administrator, their word constituted local law. They settled disputes between chiefs, decided where roads should be constructed, conscripted labour, organized a postal service, raised revenue, and acted as a combination of overseer of, and handyman for, the public weal.

Under such a system, the authority of the chiefs in Nyasaland soon became merely nominal. By 1904, they played "no real part in the affairs of their country". Eight years later, the government once again congratulated itself on the success of its policy of direct rule.

The decay of the power of native chiefs and the tendency all over the Protectorate to the splitting up of villages into small family groups continues: this tendency is to some extent gratifying in that it originates in the native's sense of his complete security under the existing Government. . . .

Across the territorial boundary, the two separate protectorates of North-eastern and North-western Rhodesia led separate administrative lives until 1911. In that year, the British South Africa Company fused them in order to form a united Northern Rhodesia. Most of the few thousand settlers who had been attracted to the territory after the Boer War then lived on either side of the single railway. Some farmed, others mined lead and zinc at Broken Hill, and, in a small way, copper at Bwana Mkuba and a number of smaller centres.

These settlers exerted an influence out of all proportion to their number (in 1921, only four thousand whites resided in Northern Rhodesia) and the Company listened carefully to their grievances. The white farmers and miners of Northern Rhodesia grew increasingly more powerful than their counterparts in the neighbouring Protectorate. As a result, the government of Northern Rhodesia never really attempted to safeguard African rights to the same extent as the government in Nyasaland. Northern Rhodesia, as its name implied, furthermore was ideologically no more than an extension of the commercially controlled colonial system of Southern Rhodesia.

In both Nyasaland and Northern Rhodesia, the character of white rule disillusioned Africans. Sanctioned by their governments, settlers occupied choice terrain in the productive Shire Highlands, along the Rhodesian railway, or in the eastern districts of Northern Rhodesia. In Nyasaland, admittedly, whites early purchased a proportion of their large estates. But Africans knew nothing of Western ideas about property. They sold much of what later became the municipality of Blantyre-Limbo for trifling amounts; a coffee planter purchased more than three thousand acres for a gun, thirty-two yards of calico, two red caps, "and several other things". A missionary obtained more than twenty-six thousand acres for seven trusses of calico measuring about 1,750 yards. No more than Lewanika of the Lozi, the Africans who signed away much of the land of Nyasaland hardly knew what they were doing. A district officer later analysed the problem:

> They could not possibly have understood the meaning or functions of a commercial firm and they could not have realized that the agreement they made was a sale, and that by this act they disinherited their tribe and deprived posterity of the right to their lands. I submit that this is tantamount to false pretence. . . .

Nevertheless, by 1900, the ownership of more than half of the best part of the densely populated Shire Highlands had passed into European hands. Overall, whites controlled about fifteen per cent of the total land and water area of the Protectorate.

On these large estates, Africans became tenants at will *without* security of tenure. Other abuses followed. White planters monopolized the labour of their tenants, paid Africans only nominally for their labour, and prevented them from selling the produce of their own gardens without first offering it to the estate. Moreover, despite the claims advanced by the local Chamber of Agriculture and Commerce, Africans had no option. Cultivatable acreage for gardens was available only on the vast European-owned estates. Near Blantyre, the government earmarked all unused Crown land for railway developments or official construction. Then too, Africans saw that the more important land holding companies refused to develop the bulk of their extensive holdings. By 1903, Europeans had developed less than one per cent of the total alienated acreage of the country. On the British Central Africa Company estate, for example, the owners had cultivated only 5,000 of its 367,000 acres. On the Bruce estates, against which John Chilembwe later directed his ire, all but 500 of its 160,000 acres lay fallow.

The lack of rights of Africans on alienated estates in Nyasaland remained a source of indigenous grievance for fifty years. Settlers successfully opposed administrative attempts to alleviate some of the main causes of African distress. The European planter simply wanted cheap labour and disliked policies that tended to raise Africans above the level "at which they would be content to work for him at a pittance". In 1928, an ordinance even enshrined custom. Thereafter, the government officially excused Africans residing on tea and coffee plantations from the obligation to pay rent so long as they worked for their proprietor whenever he called. If Africans refused to work, they either paid rent in cash or subjected themselves to eviction. Further, landlords told their tenants what and when they should plant, and purchased the resultant crops from them at arbitrarily contrived prices. From the settler's point of view, the estates were private property that had been purchased with hard-earned money. Africans, on the other hand, claimed that they had been arbitrarily deprived of their lands and, in the process, unconscionably abused. When they exhausted one patch of land, estate owners refused to allot them new ones. If they moved onto fallow land, the owner uprooted their crops. They could not cut down trees in order to build huts in the traditional manner. In an area where the customary pattern of settlement was matrilocal, Europeans forbade young men to settle on the lands of the family of their prospective spouse. Proprietors often compelled youths to leave the estates when they came of age. In short, if Africans distrusted white rule, they need only to have resided on a European-owned plantation for all their worst fears to be confirmed.

To add to the African burden, the governments of Nyasaland and Northern Rhodesia imposed taxes. Protectorates had simply to support themselves. As early as 1892, an African living in the

Shire Highlands found that Johnston's Administration demanded 3s. from him for each of his huts—that is, for each of his
wives. By 1894, Johnston raised more than £1,100 a year from
this source. In 1901, the British South Africa Company began
to collect taxes in North-eastern Rhodesia. "The natives",
wrote the Administrator, "consider the tax inevitable."

The pacification of trans-Zambezia attracted increasing
numbers of immigrants and imposed new responsibilities upon
the respective administrative staffs. The immigrants—most of
whom had obtained some experience in South Africa—wanted
the services of African labour in order to assist the development
of newly alienated lands. They early demanded that their
governments should—by any one of a number of means—
encourage Africans to forsake their tribal chores for employment
on white-owned estates. The administrators themselves sought
to obtain labour for a variety of routine tasks; they always
needed head porters. Both the Foreign and Colonial Offices
frowned upon methods of recruitment that approximated im-
pressment. As a result, the governments of Nyasaland and
Northern Rhodesia used the tax as an instrument with which
to induce Africans to offer their labour to whites in return for
artificial rates of pay that were geared entirely to the level of
the prevailing tax assessment. The Administrator of North-
eastern Rhodesia explained that

... the natives are able ... to pay the three shilling hut tax. It would
prove, as ... in the British Central Africa Protectorate [Nyasaland],
a means of getting a certain amount of work out of the natives, and
would in this manner greatly assist transport difficulties.

Taxation became the main reason behind a new wave of migration that transformed the Central African countryside and
destroyed a traditional way of life. . . .

37. King Copper 1923–30

L. H. GANN *A History of Northern Rhodesia* Chatto & Windus 1964; pages 204–8

When the new Governor took over at Livingstone, Northern Rhodesia was a poverty stricken backveld Protectorate which only few people could have identified on the map. But at this time a group of financiers came together in London whose deliberations were to usher in the most far-reaching economic changes ever to have come over Central Africa. In 1923 world demand for copper revived; prices rose as the scrap supplies dating from the Great War were gradually used up. In addition there was a new industrial revolution, for electrical, automobile and light industries were coming into their own overseas, with the result that more orders went out for wire, pipes and a host of other products made of copper, a metal both malleable and possessing excellent conductive properties. The second change occurred in the realm of technology. Investors for long would rarely look at the Northern Rhodesian deposits where oxide ores only contained an average of 3 to 5 per cent as compared with the rich reserves of 15 per cent ores available on the Belgian side of the border, where even 6 to 7 per cent oxides were thrown away with contempt, being too poor for profitable treatment. In the Katanga, however, ore bodies did not alter to workable secondary sulphides at depth, but suddenly changed into lean primary ores of no value. Mining engineers at first assumed that the same thing would happen in Northern Rhodesia, where shaft sinking down to water level gave poor results; their reasoning, however, overlooked the different geological structure of the Copper Belt, where drills ultimately struck enormous deposits of valuable sulphide ores, once work was continued to a sufficient depth. In earlier times miners did not know how to work these low grade ores profitably, but then experts discovered the so-called 'flotation method' of concentration which allowed them to exploit sulphides successfully.

The first phase in Northern Rhodesia's copper revolution began in 1922 with the reconstruction of the Bwana Mkubwa mining company which had carried on a little intermittent mining during the war. Bwana Mkubwa, formerly a small concern, was now launched with an impressive authorized capital of £1,500,000, its new board containing some of the most powerful mining magnates to be found in Southern Africa. Edmund Davis with his extensive Rhodesian base mineral and coal connexions was chairman, whilst Dougal O. Malcolm provided the link with the British South Africa Company. Equally important was Alfred Chester Beatty, an American-born financier who had started off in life as a consulting engineer in the U.S.A. where he made his name in the search for low grade copper deposits. Beatty, unlike most other experts, possessed enormous financial and administrative ability as well as technical knowledge, and gradually worked his way on to the directorates of several important American copper companies. In 1913 he settled in London where a year later he founded the Selection Trust Ltd, an investment corporation which later also bought its way into Bwana Mkubwa. The South African Mining industry was represented on the Board by Sir Ernest Oppenheimer, one of South Africa's most influential mining men. Oppenheimer's career provides a vital link between the pioneering period of Southern Africa's mining history and its subsequent consolidation and is therefore worth mentioning at some length. Oppenheimer was born in 1880 in Friedberg near Frankfurt-on-Main in Western Germany. The Oppenheimers, by a strange twist of fortune, came from the same region as the Hochschilds, American metal magnates who later also heavily invested in Northern Rhodesian copper, with the difference that the Hochschilds were already well established in the German metal trade before they took their upper class Frankfurt Jewish liberal tradition across the Atlantic, whilst Oppenheimer, the eighth son of a small-town merchant, started off with little. At the age of sixteen Oppenheimer went to London in order to learn English and modern methods of commerce at the hub of world trade. The young apprentice began his business career on a salary of £1 a week in a dingy room in Camden Town, but London proved a stepping stone to South Africa; and when Oppenheimer was only twenty-one, his employer, a diamond merchant, sent him as representative to Kimberley, Oppenheimer's career thus affording a parallel to that of Alfred Beit, Rhodes's great financial ally. Things went well with the young immigrant who soon became a successful and highly respected diamond dealer, and became Mayor of Kimberley. During the First World War, however, anti-German feelings ran high; his house was stoned and he had to be given protection, with the result that the Oppenheimers had to leave town. Misfortune, however, turned out to be the high road to success; Oppenheimer subsequently settled in Johannesburg, became greatly interested in gold mining, and got to know an American mining engineer by the name of W. L. Honnold who was convinced that the Rand's mineral content had not yet been fully gauged. Oppenheimer, in one of his famous 'hunches', believed that the American must be right, and between them the two in 1917 formed the Anglo American Corporation which managed to secure big American credits and soon became a great power in the South African gold industry. Later on, Oppenheimer bought out extensive German diamond interests in South-West Africa as a prelude to an attack on De Beers, Rhodes's old firm, where he captured a directorship in 1927 and the chairmanship two years later, his position being further strengthened by a seat on the Board of Barclays Bank, one of the 'Big Five' of British banking.

The next step in the development of Rhodesian copper was taken in 1923 when the British South Africa Company decided on a new policy of giving out vast concessions to strongly capitalized concerns. This decision was made easier for the Chartered Board by the fact that in Northern Rhodesia the Directors did not have to contend with organized opposition from small European prospectors who formed a powerful pressure group south of the Zambezi and bitterly opposed large monopolistic grants. In addition Britain was now conscious of her war-time dependence on American copper and became anxious to remedy this state of affairs at a time when she was still trying to maintain parity with the U.S.A. as the world's leading naval power. In February 1923 Beatty and Oppenheimer, assisted by some other financiers, floated the Rhodesian Congo Border Concession Ltd which received an exclusive grant of 50,000 square miles; the Chartered Company then made a number of further concessions and within a few years the whole of the Protectorate outside Barotseland and the north-eastern region was parcelled out into six vast areas, each bigger than a European principality.

Prospecting proceeded and in 1926 Beatty reconstituted the Selection Trust with American backing and holdings in the

Balkans as well as Northern Rhodesia. During the same year, at a time when Northern Rhodesia copper was still regarded as a speculative kind of investment to be avoided by the cautious, Oppenheimer laid his plans for the setting up of a Rhodesian Branch of Anglo American with headquarters at Broken Hill, the influence of his company having already been vastly expanded by the fact that it served as consulting engineers to several prospecting concerns. Two years later, in 1928, Rhodesian Anglo American was incorporated with a capital of £3,500,000 much of which was provided by co-operation between Davis and Oppenheimer, whose financial power still exceeded that of the rival Selection Trust. Work then proceeded on such a scale that the supply of British capital became inadequate, the London market being less receptive to copper shares than the American markets because of earlier disappointments in Rhodesia. In 1927 Dr Otto Sussman, a German-Jewish mining engineer and at that time Vice President of the American Metal Company, visited Southern Africa, and immediately recognized the potentialities of the Rhodesian deposits. He quickly cabled to New York that Roan promised to become a major producer and advised American Metal to acquire an interest. The first share acquisitions took place in 1927, and two years later arrangements were made to advance £1,500,000 to the Rhodesian Selection Trust, the American Metal Company committing itself to by far the largest portion of this amount. In 1930 the American Metal Company vastly extended its holdings by acquiring 800,000 shares of Roan and 1,000,000 shares of R.S.T. against which it issued 350,000 new shares of its own common stock and paid $1,000,000 in cash to an affiliated company of Selection Trust Ltd in London. Apart from its financial advantages, the transatlantic connexion helped the Rhodesian copper industry to secure the services of American metallurgists, the best known experts in the field at a time when the U.S.A. was dominating the world's copper production. There followed further financial consolidations for the purpose of facilitating marketing, cutting down over-production, assuring a more efficient utilization of technical services, and more effective representations to the Northern Rhodesia Government. The details of these negotiations would be tedious to relate, but in the end two powerful, partially inter-connected combines controlled the entire Copper Belt. The first centred on the Rhodesian Anglo American Corporation, linked in turn to the Broken Hill Mine, the South African gold and diamond industries and the British South Africa Company. This group owned Nkana, Bwana Mkubwa and Nchanga. Sir Ernest Oppenheimer himself would have liked a financial union between the two copper-producing groups, paralleling comparable arrangements in the diamond industry, but could not achieve this aim. He did, however, help in keeping the Copper Belt primarily an 'Imperial' interest. In 1928 he prevented Bwana Mkubwa from largely falling into the hands of the American Metal Company. A year later a powerful British financial alliance, comprising Rhodesian Anglo American, the Rio Tinto Company, the Rothschilds and other interests, stopped Nchanga from being bought by transatlantic investors, Nchanga becoming definitely part of the Anglo American empire, whilst Americans only held a minority share in the Northern Rhodesian copper industry.

The Selection Trust for its part controlled Roan Antelope and Mufulira mines, Beatty himself receiving a seat on the American Metal Company's Board, his transatlantic connexions rendering his policies much more independent of local South African considerations than those of his rival Oppenheimer.

Financial combinations on this scale raised vast problems and left the Governor practically powerless with regard to the mining policies which decided the country's future. But without these imposing concentrations of capital the Copper Belt could never have come into its own. Individual prospectors and white 'small workers' who took the lead in creating Southern Rhodesia's gold industry, and exerted such a strong influence on the country's social policies, were excluded from vast areas, which were thus 'locked up' and probably still present great opportunities for future prospectors. But from the copper industry's point of view, this restrictive policy was sound, for base mineral prospectors looking for copper found themselves gravely handicapped in a country where intense leaching made surface indications of the red metal rather scanty. 'When I was working on the Roan Antelope', related a well-known German geologist who now occupies a Chair at Göttingen University, 'I remember that out of twenty rock samples as big as my fist, I noticed just one tiny speck of copper . . . this one being only as big as the point of a pin'. Distances moreover were great; labour not easy to get, difficult to feed, and harder to keep healthy; transport alone posed a major problem, and drilling below the water level, often at a depth of several hundred feet below the ground, exceeded the resources of small investors. Work on a really big scale began with an aerial survey over the 52,000 square miles alloted to the Rhodesian Congo Border Concession, and landing grounds were established at 20-mile intervals. Surveying by plane, however, met with difficulties; in the rainy season heavy layers of clouds obscured the view, whilst in the dry months photographers could not see through the heavy palls of smoke from veld fires, which still show up on early photographic maps as grey blotches; clearing the landing fields taxed the tempers of the most patient, for meadows would flood during the rains, whilst the huge termite hills characteristic of the northern bush could not be blasted by dynamite. Worse still, aerial surveying failed to show up those 'blind dambo' clearings in the vlei characteristic of the Katanga fields where acid solutions from surface copper ores interfered with growth. The main burden of work thus fell on teams of first-class young geologists, who were only too glad to find a job during the years of depression and came from many different countries, including Britain, Germany, South Africa, Canada and the U.S.A. These teams systematically slogged through the bush, covering some 20 miles a day, armed with a couple of yards of graph paper, a compass, and the front wheel of a bicycle which counted the number of miles traversed. . . .

38. African administration and politics

L. H. GANN *A History of Northern Rhodesia* Chatto & Windus 1964; pages 379–88

The rise of the 'new men' in African trade and agriculture found a parallel in the field of local administration, where tribal chiefs gradually became more dependent on village 'progressives'. In the early 'forties the process had not gone very far, and in 1943 the Provincial Commissioner for the Northern Province for instance still bitterly complained of the large number of petty, ineffective and jealous chiefs, who were rapidly losing the respect and obedience of the younger generation, a further weakness of the existing system being found in the fact that some of the Superior Native Authorities were not created in accordance with native customs, and that councillors and clerks were so inadequately paid that well-educated people would not enter the chiefs' service. A Provincial Commissioner's Conference, held in the same year, arrived at similar conclusions, and agreed that Government in future should vest power in the Chief-in-Council rather than the chiefs in person, that more 'progressives' should be appointed to the Native Authorities; which ought to meet regularly, and should be paid in a more adequate fashion. The Native Authorities gradually ought to take over social services like primary education, sanitation and roads, whilst the number of petty rulers must be reduced; at the same time the demarcation between Native Authorities, that is to say Chiefs and Councillors on the one hand, and Native Courts, Chiefs and Assessors on the other, should be emphasized; the importance of Superior Native Authorities as law-making bodies must be stressed, and Native Authorities in time should collect all taxes, returning a proportion to the Central Government, whose share should be progressively decreased. A year later the Legislature voted an extra £25,000 to improve salaries, the remainder being paid into Native Treasury Funds as the Provincial Commissioner might advise, whilst the Secretary for Native Affairs had to busy himself more with political duties occasioned by his membership of the Legislative Council. In 1945 the Administration thus announced the abolition of 79 redundant Native Authorities, mostly in the Kaonde-Lunda and Eastern Provinces. In 1948 Government went one step further, and began to build up stronger African tribal councils on which existing chiefs and traditional councillors were joined by more progressive Africans; in addition departmental councillors began to be elected, each responsible for one particular function of government, reorganization of government proceeding so quickly that by the end of the following year the great majority of Native Authorities were operating in the new fashion.

At the same time the Administration attempted to provide a better education for chiefs who were now forced to deal with problems of ever-growing complexity. A beginning was made in 1939, when courses started at the Jeanes Training School, Chalimbana, under the auspices of the African Education Department. In 1943 these courses were extended, but it was only in 1946 that Government first began to give a specific training in local government, as opposed to more general subjects like history, geography, civics, agriculture, hygiene and village improvement which used to form the bulk of the curriculum. In 1948 the Administration agreed that a separate African Local Government School should be established at Chalimbana and the first course opened in 1951, lectures being given on all kinds of administrative questions, native courts, elementary accounting and so forth. Finally Government tried to tighten up the financial supervision of the Native Authorities, where peculation was rife, administrative integrity as understood by Western civil servants not perhaps being easily compatible with far-flung kinship obligations of a traditional kind, and in any case difficult to enforce amongst poorly paid officials to whom even small sums presented a great temptation.

Whatever the merits of administrative devolution, the process was inherent in the whole theory of Indirect Rule, and soon speeded up under its own momentum, even though some district officers disliked the rate of change. 'Formerly we did things ourselves' said a disgusted 'D.C.' 'and then we told them [the Africans] what we did. Now we tell them what to do, and we still do it!' But senior civil servants soon found that in fact they could no longer do it all themselves; they became more and more concerned with technical questions, with war and postwar problems, and supervision of native courts; whilst the Secretary for Native Affairs found more and more of his working hours taken up with political duties which were inescapably linked to membership of the Legislative Council. At the same time more educated Africans were leaving the Mission schools, and demanding new kinds of services which could only be supplied by a more efficient type of local government. Indirect Rule was therefore bound to expand, and from 1945 the process met with even stronger encouragement from the British Labour Government, which regarded local bodies as a means—not only of administrative, but also of social and economic change—as instruments peculiarly well suited to its own mood of cautious reform. In 1947 Creech Jones sent round an important circular despatch in which he urged that local authorities must become 'efficient, democratic and local'—sufficiently close to the common people to command their confidence, but also sufficiently effective so as to manage local services and raise the general standard of living. The Labour Government was thinking both in terms of its own democratic ideals, and of promoting long-term development plans for the colonies, arguing that Africans would not derive full benefit from the monies voted for their benefit from the Imperial Parliament and the local Legislature, unless local government developed in a more adequate fashion. The building up of local authorities was also considered important for political reasons, as a step towards giving the African masses a greater say in the running of their country. At the moment—Creech Jones felt—the more responsible jobs were largely filled by members of an educated black minority. This was inevitable for the time being; but Government did not want a class of professional African politicians absorbed in work at the centre, but out of touch with the people. The answer was a chain of councils, rising from local institutions to the Legislative Council, the rate of progress being bound to be rapid because of the force of world opinion, local pressures and the stimulus provided by Government's own development programme. Creech Jones thought that conditions in the various African territories differed too widely to lay down hard and fast rules, but that there should be a common objective and a common manner of approach. The Colonial Secretary therefore proposed to hold a Summer School at Cambridge—itself a move characteristic of post-war England, where Summer Schools were becoming an important cultural institution, taking over in some ways the functions of intellectual upper-class *salons* and the great Whig Houses of old. The Summer School would study the various questions involved in local government, the view of African Governors being subsequently obtained on the subject. Under the new dispensation 'D.C.s' were to become primarily agents for putting the new policy into effect, the development of African local government being regarded as the District Commissioner's primary task, whilst their routine work should be made easier by the installation of more mechanical office aids and by professional office managers. The Summer School recommended that Native Authorities should receive a sufficiently large share of direct revenue to defray recurrent administrative expenditure and expand existing services, whilst Central Government grants should be provided mainly for specific local developments, particular stress being placed on the importance of local taxes to develop local services. The Northern Rhodesian Administration professed itself in fundamental agreement with these principles, but urged a somewhat more cautious approach. Traditional chiefs were still highly respected by all classes, including the intelligentsia, and their authority should not be undermined, even if their rule involved some departure from democratic principles as understood in Western Europe. The Administration was already strengthening Native Authorities by amalgamating smaller units, pensioning off redundant chiefs, and building up councils containing both progressives and tribal elders. Reform was of course essential, but was impeded by the fact that the best men were leaving the country-side for the towns, and that the Native Authorities often depended on part-time workers who preferred easy work with little supervision and low pay, provided they could work near their homes. The answer was to build up larger Native Authorities; and Government therefore made a determined effort to get rid of smaller Native Authorities and accept them, where possible, as members of the Council of Superior Native Authorities, the new administrative units becoming economically stronger, and better able to afford a full-time staff. At the same time the Administration encouraged specialization by pushing for the appointment of 'Departmental Councillors' in charge of particular functions. From 1949 administrative differentiation became more widespread, the resultant division of labour further encouraging the recruitment of 'new men' to the local authorities, with the result that chiefs became more dependent on their 'progressives' whom they could soon no longer afford to alienate.

The Administration promoted similar changes in Barotseland, where the old order continued with the greatest vigour, and where British Administrators were probably exaggerating the extent of the abuses believed to exist under the traditional system. Reform began on the *katengo* council, a body which at one time used to give representation to minor chiefs, headmen, stewards and lesser members of the royal family, who between them wielded considerable power by their numbers, though they might not possess much influence as individuals. British officials used to regard the *katengo* as Barotseland's 'House of Commons', and the *katengo* thus seemed to lend itself naturally to 'Parliamentary reform'. In 1946 the Barotse—under persuasion from above—agreed to make a number of important innovations, which were subsequently defended as forming a return to traditional ways. In future, members from each district *kuta* (*Khotla*) would combine with older members of the *katengo* to meet twice a year, subsequently joining the full National Council, a special stipulation providing that none of the *katengo* members should be office-holders under the Barotse Native Government. In 1947 the Provincial Commissioner received instructions to choose members from each district for the new *katengo*, the new members being selected after consultation between the District Commissioners and district *kutas*. The new appointees were to consist of commoners, and also comprised members of the subject tribes who thus achieved a greater say in government.

In 1948 the Administration followed up its success by introducing the elective principle, even though the new procedure was not at first always fully understood. In Mongu-Lealui and Senanga literate people wrote the names of their candidate on a piece of paper, whilst voters who could neither read nor write told the Cadet-in-charge of their choice, some stating that they did not know the candidates and would leave the decision to the returning officer! In the Kalabo district the headmen voted for their villages, a procedure well adapted to a backward area, but in Sesheke the electors used ballot boxes according to the approved Western fashion. The reform movement also affected the native administration, which 'N.R.G.' considered to be cluttered up with obsolete posts and sinecures, as the functions of government continued to alter and many of the older posts became obsolete. During the War Dr Max Gluckman investigated the problem, and in a closely reasoned paper argued that the territorial division had come to stay on the grounds that the modern functions of government could be exercized on no other basis. But at the same time Gluckman stressed the need for historical continuity, and stressed the value of the older non-territorial divisions, recommending, amongst other things, that the old system of storehouses should be revived, so as to provide travellers with food. The Administration, however, remained wedded solely to the territorial concept of government, and put all its trust into the *silalo indunas* whom it regarded as 'the backbone of government'. These dignitaries now received direct access to the *kuta*, even though they could not fully share in its deliberations. At the same time the number of indunas was reduced, some losing their posts though being compensated by a gratuity, whilst the remaining dignitaries received better salaries, reorganization aiming at a more rational system, so that the Barotse system became more assimilated to the patterns of a European bureaucracy. The Secretary for Native Affairs expressed thorough satisfaction with these reforms, which, in his view, introduced a democratic element into the stronghold of a well-entrenched aristocracy.

Nevertheless there was some discontent, opposition being aroused in several ways. A number of indunas in the neighbourhood of Lealui supported a 'back to Lewanika' movement, and there was an outbreak of arson directed against the house and person of the Ngambela, discontent apparently being made worse by a food shortage. In addition, the constitutional changes provided a new mouthpiece for dissatisfied people, including some younger members of the intelligentsia. The position was made worse by the death of Imwiko, the Paramount chief, whose demise in 1948 temporarily unsettled the country. Imwiko's successor, Mwanawina III (later knighted as Sir Mwanawina Lewanika), was himself anything but a radical. An elderly man, some sixty years old at the time of his accession, he was educated at Lovedale, and professed the Christian faith. During the Great War he made a name for himself by personally leading 2,000 carriers and taking them as far as the Luapula, his loyalty to the Imperial cause never remaining in doubt. In 1937 he was appointed to head the Mankoya district; when hostilities broke out against the Germans, Mwanawina again did his share towards the Imperial war effort by collecting funds, encouraging the collection of wild rubber, and assisting with the recruiting campaign. But conservative as he might be, the Paramount shared the intelligentsia's fears of the European

Unofficials' growing power. The Barotse Native Government moreover regarded the African Representative Council with some suspicion, and whilst not actually boycotting the Council, their delegates confined themselves to a watching brief, the Barotse remaining determined not to integrate their interests too closely with those of the remainder, even in such important measures as the control of natural resources. Isolationism derived further strength from literate and articulate Barotse who disliked the influx of educated strangers from the east, especially members of other tribes who belonged to the African Civil Service or were employed as Government artisans. The chiefs also complained that the Barotse Native Authority and Barotse Native Courts legislation, issued after the signing of new agreements, conflicted with the spirit—if not the letter—of the Lewanika treaties which guaranteed the Barotse against interference in their internal affairs, an additional source of discontent being found in the vast loss of territory by the Barotse since they put themselves under British protection. Government, however, refused to give way, and explained that Barotseland should not cut adrift from the rest of Northern Rhodesia, at a time when the Territory was entering a period of unparalleled prosperity, an argument sufficiently well founded to carry conviction.

In the townships, power remained with the Europeans, and African progress remained confined to a limited number of institutions. First of all there were African townships which owed their origin to settlements of self-employed Africans; these people included carpenters, bicycle repairers, hawkers and the like, who did not fit into the locations run by local authorities, and who faced housing problems of particular severity, having no claim against any employer for accommodation. In addition the better paid Africans wished in some cases to avoid the disciplined atmosphere of locations, and Government therefore decided to institute African townships near the bigger centres. By 1943 sites were chosen near all the Copper Belt settlements, and three years later African Townships came into being at Ndola, Mufulira, Kitwe, Chingola and Luanshya. Houses in these townships were built either by the owners themselves according to approved standards, or by Government for disposal to Africans. In 1947 all these five settlements were gazetted as such, and Management Boards consisting of African householders were set up under the chairmanship of District Commissioners, the Central Government making *bloc* grants available to these new local authorities, which could also raise local rates. Africans also gained a greater measure of control over their own affairs through the setting up of Urban Courts whose members were drawn from the tribes having the largest number of followers in the area, the members of the Urban Courts being appointed after consultation with the Native Authorities and receiving their pay from Government. The new courts tried civil cases between Africans in the first instance, as well as some minor criminal offences, the urban councillors facing a vast range of new problems in the exacting task of try-ing cases between members of different tribes, with different customs, coming together in the new environment of a city.

Africans lastly achieved some measure of representation through Urban Advisory Councils. Once again Government began to propagate the elective principle, even though its efforts at first met with only limited success. In Fort Jameson, for instance, the District Commissioner divided the township into six wards, one for independent traders and artisans, others for employees of general dealers, for skilled and semi-skilled workers, for personal servants, for unskilled labourers, and for housewives—both inside and outside the location. The 'D.C.' then proudly reported that 756 persons registered their votes, though he failed to add that Fort Jameson township during this period comprised some 2,812 Africans in employment, so that representation remained a minority affair. All the same, election results provided a good indication of the way in which political consciousness was spreading through the various layers of Afri-can society. The unskilled labourers showed so little interest in the affair, that only six people turned up to vote, and elections had to be abandoned. The clerks and storemen, on the other hand, took a more active part, and so did personal servants. But astonishingly enough, the housewives turned out to be the most numerous voting group of all, making up more than half of the registered voters, a remarkable new departure in the field of African politics.[1]

[1] The total number of Africans in employment according to the 1946 census was 2,821. The independent traders and artisans had a turnout of 55,

Urban Advisory Councils of the type elected at Fort Jameson, rural Native Authorities, and Welfare Societies between them made up the African Provincial Councils, which joined in 1946 to form the African Representative Council, Northern Rhodesia's first instrument of black representation on a national scale. The Council owed its existence to Government which was anxious to channel the intelligentsia's political ambitions away from Welfare Societies, and to create a common link between the 'new men' and chiefs. The Council consisted of 29 members, of whom the four members from Barotseland owed their appointment to the Paramount Chief, whilst the remainder were elected from the African Provincial Councils. The new body met under the chairmanship of the Secretary for Native Affairs, procedure being modelled as far as possible on that of the Legislative Council. Government undertook to submit to the Council all Bills affecting black people, and the standard of debate was fairly high, the Council at first confining itself to proposals for specific reform, particularly those affecting the 'new men'. One motion demanded that Africans be allowed to sell their maize anywhere they wished; another proposed the establishment of a War Memorial College; a third asked that trading by Indians and white men should be restricted to townships. A further important move dealt with the question of wills, an overwhelming majority voting in favour of a motion that Africans should be able to make wills like Europeans, enabling them to dispose freely of their property to their immediate descendants, a practice not possible under the customary law of the matrilineal tribes, where the absence of legal wills most probably prevented the accumulation of rural capital. The Rev. Henry Kasokolo, a Bemba, thus urged that people with money, anxious to leave their property to their wife and children, should put their funds into a Savings Bank in their child's name. Otherwise the tribesmen would insist on the traditional manner of disposing of his inheritance, and the dead man's wife and children would be subjected to so many threats from their numerous relatives that

employees of general dealers 105, skilled and semi-skilled 15, personal servants 152, unskilled labourers nil, housewives in locations 282, housewives outside locations 147. The new council consisted of an artisan, a literate head capitao of a firm, a head clerk, a cook, a rubbish-disposal worker, the wife of a clerk and a medical orderly's wife.

the beneficiaries would be forced to hand over all they had. In addition the more advanced Africans were becoming resentful of the wide disparity between their own wages and the white man's; and whilst there was widespread agreement that 'equal pay for equal work' would simply cut out the skilled African from the labour market, all felt convinced that black incomes should approximate more closely to those received by Europeans.

Right from the start the African Representative Council thus became the mouthpiece of 'progressive' Africans, an outcome not specifically intended by Government, but perhaps inherent in the whole structure of an assembly which was wholly based on the European model. But in addition to the Council the new men acquired an even more effective organ of expression through a Federation of Welfare Societies which in time developed into an African nationalist movement of great power. The origins of the movement were extremely modest. In 1946 Dauti Lawton Yamba, a schoolmaster born at Mbereshi mission, George Kaluwa, a trader and farmer from Mazabuka, and a veteran politician, as well as various other sympathizers, mostly with a background of elementary teaching, managed to combine various traders', shop assistants' and farmers' associations, as well as Welfare Societies and a body known as the African Christian Council. The new Federation specifically expressed the objects of the new African petty bourgeoisie and minor 'salariat' which was still unsure of itself, and groping for Government support. The Society thus began with an extremely moderate programme and asked for administrative backing to strengthen its position. In 1946 a deputation called on the Assistant Chief Secretary, asking that Government should officially recognize the new body, that the Secretary for Native Affairs should preside over its meetings, and that the Federation should be authorized to raise the sum of £1,000. In addition the delegates demanded that the Society should be allotted five members on the African Representative Council, stressing the wide support which they enjoyed amongst African traders, shop assistants, 'boss boys' and the more advanced farmers, the Society having branches in the Copper Belt as well as at Broken Hill and the Tonga country. Government made no attempt to interfere with the new body, though some officials regarded the new society as nothing more than a bunch of disgruntled intellectuals, but the Administration refused to be in any way officially associated with the movement, and denied them any special representation on the African Representative Council.

The Federation soon became more radical in temper, as its members worried increasingly about European agitation for self-government and amalgamation with Southern Rhodesia. Apart from that, a much vaster tide of anti-colonialism was gathering momentum abroad. In the Metropolitan countries anti-Imperial sentiments became linked with demands for reforms at home; at the same time European working-class movements often identified their own cause with that of the colonial races. Many intellectuals moreover were deeply influenced by the mechanized carnage of Auschwitz and the nuclear holocaust of Hiroshima, which led many Europeans to question the values of a civilization which, they thought, had produced such horrors, and which some began to contrast with the real and supposed virtues of 'pre-literate' man, untouched by the soul-destroying influence of advertising, mass entertainment and militarism. Britain's social conscience moreover became much more alive to African issues, though local Rhodesians like Welensky argued that all British Progressives were doing was to shift the blame for past British exploitation on to the shoulders of the local white settlers who profited least from colonialism! In Asia the tide of independence seemed irresistible; Indonesia cast off Dutch rule; the British voluntarily handed over power in India, and subsequently evacuated Palestine, where they had been unable to solve the Jewish-Arab problem. The Western colonial powers moreover could not agree amongst themselves, with regard to their Imperial policies, and the French were forced out of the Middle East where their influence had been strong for centuries. In Africa itself the process of decolonization began with the collapse of Mussolini's East African Empire under the blows of white South African and British multi-racial forces; and later on the Italians lost Libya to the valour of the British 8th Army. On the West Coast the British began to make concessions to local nationalists, and in 1946 a more liberal constitution came into force on the Gold Coast. Besides, the Allies' own war propaganda affected their subject races, and even in faraway Northern Rhodesia, Welfare Societies began to speak

AITCA

of freedom from want, freedom from fear, and the peoples' right of self-government. The Indian Congress Party in particular acquired particular prestige in the eyes of politically conscious Africans, who as yet put their trust in peaceful persuasion rather than violence, and in 1948 an Annual General Meeting, held by the Federation of Welfare Societies, decided to form the Northern Rhodesia African Congress. The new organization aimed at breaking down tribal barriers, fostering African unity and promoting African advancement in co-operation with Government. Congress was financed by small annual subscriptions from its members, and run by an Executive Committee, composed of a President, Secretary, Treasurer and four other members, who were all annually elected. Godwin A. M. Lewanika, an aristocrat from Barotseland who led the Kitwe African Society, and took an active part in founding the Federation, became the first President. The new movement retained a strong Protestant and missionary flavour, so much so that its General Meeting at Munali in 1948 opened with prayers by the Rev. Edward G. Nightingale, one of the Specially Nominated Members for African Interests in the Legislative Council. Nevertheless, Congress now aimed at much wider political objectives. The immigration of Afrikaners was to be restricted, whilst any kind of association with Southern Rhodesia was to be prevented at all costs. African interests should remain paramount—a reversion to the older Passfield doctrine—and the Colonial Office ought to carry out past promises for African self-government until Northern Rhodesia would join UNO. Congress argued that African interests clearly ought to over-ride all others because Africans predominated in numbers, because they were the sons of the soil, because of Imperial trusteeship obligations, and because Northern Rhodesia had never been conquered. Any policy not designed from the start to promote the interests and welfare of Africans ought to be rejected, never mind how much they might benefit the Europeans. In order to differentiate the Protectorate from Southern Rhodesia—the detested white-occupied country beyond the Zambezi—a further resolution suggested that Northern Rhodesia should become known as the 'Queen Victoria Protectorate'. Congress speakers, in other words, now turned round older trusteeship doctrines, originally designed to justify British Imperial rule to white critics, and reshaped this ideology into a weapon to serve the aims of African nationalism. In addition, Congress came out with a number of limited constitutional demands. Two African Members of the Legislative Council ought to join the Executive Council to balance the Unofficials' growing influence in Government. Congress also reiterated the former request for special representation on the African Representative Council on the grounds that, at the moment, elections depended on the number of friends a man could muster, instead of personal ability! The Society's economic objects at first largely confined themselves to the needs of the 'new men', particularly the schoolmasters, and Congress thus put forward suggestions for improved secondary education, a more generous programme of scholarships for bright youngsters, reduced fees for school children, and also demanded more pay for educated men serving on the chiefs' councils, as well as better railway facilities for African farmers. . . .

39. The significance of Chilembwe

GEORGE SHEPPERSON and T. PRICE *Independent African* Edinburgh University Press 1958; pages 404–9, 411–13

. . . It was his weakness that the only positive emotional bond that he could provide for his supporters was that of personal friendship; and that was prepotent only for those who lacked other social ties. This weakness might have been deduced from the relative isolation of the Providence Industrial Mission before 1915; but it only became apparent when tested by the demands of the Rising; and when it was recognized by the Europeans, it could be employed deliberately in their activities of suppression. Chilembwe perhaps failed to assess realistically the general condition of Nyasaland, and took the concurrent views of other sufferers from European discourtesy, and other seekers in vain for a hearing for native protests and native points of view, as implying acceptance of his attack on the situation. The unstable alliance of such interests, which he was able to assemble out of the heterogeneous population which resorted or drifted to his independent settlement, broke up when he was compelled to go into concealment as a fugitive, and was finally killed. When the personal centre of the association was removed, it could no longer exist.

It will be seen, then, in these reasons for the failure of the Rising, that it marked the emergence of the spokesman for the angry discontent of those who had no longer a tribe to give them an effective voice; but neither those detribalized by entry into civilized activities and ambitions, nor the immigrant or mobile manual labourers, were as yet able to see any ground for perseverance or indeed for acceptance of direction and discipline, beyond the luck of the leader. The leader himself was sensitive enough to realize what an accumulation of discontent existed, as it were, in parallel with his own increasing sense of outrage; but he did not allow sufficiently for the underlying sense of the compensating benefits of European rule, in spite of all its drawbacks, that was present in the minds of many whose support he needed. Probably, like any sensitive person, Chilembwe was incapable of estimating the deadening force of sheer inertia on most people; and he certainly assumed too readily that African suspicion was concentrated on non-Africans: so far, at least, Hetherwick was justified in denying that Chilembwe's movement was a 'Native Rising', in the sense that the Europeans feared and Chilembwe initially hoped. But it did mark the beginning of a stage at which the native population would realize that the future offered more possibilities than the alternatives of helplessly accepting whatever, good or bad, the Europeans might offer, or of returning to tribal allegiances. It provided the 'new men' with an example of action, a pattern of practicability, and a martyr; and it shocked a thoughtless group of the Europeans into considering their ways, and into recognizing that the Africans could not simply be taken for granted.

Some aspects of this reassessment of African feeling deserve more detailed examination. While the independent African churches were regarded with distrust, it was not because they were thought of as centres where tribal antagonisms would be sunk and common supra-tribal aspirations developed. It was felt, rather, that such a dangerous role would be played by Islam. Throughout the nineteenth century Great Britain had been learning in its social laboratory of imperialism, India, that Islam was a revolutionary faith. The attempt to restore the Mogul Empire through the great Mutiny of 1857–8 was simply the most notable of a series of outbreaks, of which the Moplah risings from 1836 to 1896 in Malabar are typical. At the end of the century the Islamic messiah, the Mahdi, Mohammed Ahmed, had given the Sudanese tribesmen 'the enthusiasm they lacked' to make common cause against Egyptian domination, and had cost Britain, as Egypt's guardian, over thirteen million pounds in money, the lives of two thousand officers and men, and seven thousand invalids, to overthrow the movement. General Gordon's death at Khartoum, publicized as that of a Christain hero, had reawakened in Protestants the traditional Catholic sense of the eternal enmity of Cross and Crescent. Gordon himself had drawn attention to the social revolutionary aspect of Islam when he wrote of Mahdism that it was 'a question of property, and is more like Communism under the flag of religion'. Africa offered the most promising field for this threatening infection of militant religion. Sudanese Mahdism was the most virulent case, but there were others. In Nyasaland the Muslim Arab and Yao slavers had fought stubborn wars to repel the imposition of British rule; though it was not to be forgotten that the Arab Jumbe of Kota-Kota, obedient, as his co-religionists were not, to the Sultan of Zanzibar, by his alliance with the British had helped considerably to bring about their victory. In the early twentieth century a new Mahdi in Somaliland, the so-called 'Mad Mullah', was able to maintain forces of fierce nomads in long and successful campaigns which painfully embarrassed the British Empire—and supplied the 2nd (Nyasaland) Battalion of the King's African Rifles with its historic tragedy, when one of its companies was ambushed and completely wiped out. The British apprehensiveness that Islam might inspire and unite the separate tribes in her colonial territories was so apparent that Germany had no hesitation in encouraging the pan-Islamic movement, and in using agents to stir up trouble wherever a basis of Islam could be discovered.

In Nyasaland this Islamic basis went back to the pre-European days of the slave trade, and it was reasonable for the Europeans to expect that their power would be challenged from that quarter, anti-European and insubordinate by religious prescription, and smarting from the overthrow of a way of life satisfactory and profitable in its time. The Nyasaland Government might naturally consider that the ferment of reformism and sectarianism which was stirring so much else of the Islamic world would spread to Nyasaland. Indeed, as has already been noted, it may have been that which for so long prevented officials, and influential and informed missionary-statesmen like Hetherwick, from noticing the real threat to European government that was growing in the work of John Chilembwe and the African independent churches.

Warnings about Islamic aggression were common in the territory's missionary literature. In 1900 the Livingstonia missionaries, working in the area of the last stubborn stand of the Arabs, concluded that a general native rising in the Protectorate under the Muslim banner was possible. The Anglicans working at the permanent Muslim centres of Kota-Kota and Mponda's spoke constantly of this possibility, and were particularly explicit in 1905, perhaps in view of the Muslim elements in the unexpected and staggering Maji-Maji revolt in the German territory between them and their mother diocese of Zanzibar. Two years later the Blantyre missionaries noted the social factors which might inspire such a rising, in discussing *Chinasala*, a term which might denote either the Swahili language, or 'a spurious kind of Mohammedanism' which would pander to the aspiring Africans' ego by giving him a quickly obtained status higher than that possessed by 'the common run of the natives'. But what they did not take into account was that, although the Turkish Revolution and Egyptian independence movements were in the air and promised modern types of Islamic culture, yet, for aspiring Africans of the Chilembwe type, Islam was identified with a non-technical civilization which offered none of the power and comforts to be had from acquiring the civilization of the Christian West. Nevertheless, in Central African history, Islam had first offered a way of advance beyond rigid tribalism, and still provided a possible alternative for the African who sought some status or dignity *vis-à-vis* the European. It is impossible to say how many of Chilembwe's fellow Yao had found in Islamic profession a mode of asserting that discontent with the European order which others found in membership of separatist churches. Yet the traditional Yao association with the Coast and the Islamic outposts there clearly supplies another reason, in addition to sectionalism and jealousy, for the lack of support for Chilembwe from his father's tribe.

On the eve of the War, all the colonial Powers were apprehensive of Muslim risings, and lay and clerical observers of Nyasaland's affairs agreed in pointing to the danger. But Chilembwe's movement, the agency which did, in fact, realize to some extent the Islamic threat of uniting tribesmen in revolt, was one which, though troublesome, had been in the eyes of most Europeans a much less potent danger to their dominion. From their own angle the Germans seem to have shared the common expectation, for the letter to Chilembwe from the 'judge' at Tunduru addresses him as 'sultan', as if assuming him to be a Muslim. And from another angle one of the strange consequences of the Rising was, on the witness of the Blantyre Mission's paper, that 'it made many natives take up Islam, lest the faintest suspicion of having been influenced by [Christian] missions might lead to the same difficulties as the rioters'. How far this apparent increase in the number of even nominal Muslims suited the German policy is hard to say; but there is evidence that in pursuance of the design of directing Islam against the Allies the Germans had infiltrated African agents into Nyasaland. Non-officials, as well as Government, were concerned about this, and the *Beira Post* of 16 February 1915 put the point as part of its criticism of the local character of the Commission of Inquiry into the Chilembwe Rising, when it linked that incident with the question of a Muslim 'fifth column' working against European rule in Central and East Africa:

. . . the general seriousness of the affair in its inception at this juncture . . . and the underlying question of the Jehad [the Muslim Holy War against unbelievers] renders a more general inquiry than one of local origin essential.

Towards the end of 1915 there were scares, the more readily entertained in view of the recent Chilembwe affair, of Islamic risings in both southern and northern Nyasaland; and in July of that year a missionary of the U.M.C.A. reported 'much talk of the coming of Mzilima [a sort of Mohammedan messiah-mahdi]'. In 1916, when the outcome of the Inquiry into the Rising was being debated, the discovery of a letter from Count Falkenstein, commander of the German forces on the Nyasaland borders, 'to a certain Mwalimu Isa who exercised great influence on the large Mohammedan population living on both sides of the British Portuguese border near Lake Nyasa', raised uneasiness to a new height. The letter asked for the names of Ngoni who, like Chimtunga of Mombera's district, or the few who followed Chilembwe, refused to support the British war effort. The scare was apparently over by August of 1916; but until the end of the war and later the missionaries, at least, continued to point to Islamic dangers. Yet their apprehensions were ideological rather than political, for by the end of 1916 the local tide of war had clearly turned against the Germans, and the subversive adherents of Islam had lost all hope of effective support. The divisions of Nyasaland's African society which derived from diverse origins and traditions, and from complicated and internally conflicting patterns of alliances with and against the European order, had overcome another potential unifying factor in opposition to that order.

But though it is now apparent that Chilembwe's movement is not unique as an attempt to work on a supra-tribal level, this must not obscure its importance as a stage in that development. There had been earlier alliances in British Central Africa between tribal units and the heterogeneous bands of henchmen who followed the Coast slavers, in the latter years of the nineteenth century: for example the 'concerted plan' of the three Yao chiefs Zarafi, Kawinga, and Matipwiri, who controlled the slave road which rounded the south end of Lake Nyasa and passed the bottlenecks at either end of the precipices of Mount Mlanje. They allied themselves with Nguru from beyond Mlanje to drive out the British and open the road again. The last stand of Mlozi's Arabs in 1895 had been in alliance with the Bemba of what is now Northern Rhodesia. But such alliances were purely matters of convenience, with no intention or prospect of enduring beyond their immediate purpose. It is not misleading, then, to say that Chilembwe's was the first Central African resistance to European control which looked to the future, not to the past, and which did not assume that tribal potentates, whether by inheritance or by usurpation, would head the new state. He did not propose to reject or destroy the traditional order, since he sought the support of the headmen who were his neighbours at Zomba and Mlanje, and of certain sections of the nearly monarchial Ngoni—though, if he had succeeded, he would probably have had the usual experience of combining new wine and old wine-skins. Nevertheless, the prospect for which Chilembwe began to fight was one of founding a nation rather than of restoring the fortunes of the tribes. It is true that Kamwana's movement, though relying mainly on the Lake-shore Tonga, included other tribesmen, and this deserves more attention than it has been given as a link between the old resistance and the new, and as an important incident in the growth of Ethiopianism in Africa. But, on the whole, Kamwana's effort was akin to the tribal reactions of the past. It lacked the secrecy and sense of wide purpose which marked the movement that grew out of the first Providence Industrial Mission; and it was of John Chilembwe, not Elliott Kamwana, that an African informant said: 'He was not of one tribe, but for all tribes.' . . .

It was this basis of conviction, derived from deep and long consideration, that marked Chilembwe's movement as something new in Central African resistance. All former movements of African resistance to European rule had aimed at recovering old conditions rather than at creating new ways of life. The Arabs had sought to preserve free hunting-grounds for slavers and their Yao satellites to continue in enjoyment of the irresponsible profits and prestige of middlemen in the business. The Ngoni, whose commoners were a motley crew of diverse origins, looked to the Zulu ancestors of their chiefs, the robber-kings Shaka and Zongendaba, as patterns for their ideal future. The handful of Makololo chiefs thought nostalgically of the days when, as 'friends of the British' who appeared only on occasional expeditions, and as sophisticated gun-men, they had lorded it over the tribes of the lower Shire Valley. Kamwana's glimpse into the future, as he sought to inspire his first Watch Tower adherents, did not look beyond destruction: 'The Government will go . . . we shall build our own ships [ships on the Lake were gun-boats or potential gun-boats.—AUTHORS], make our own powder; import our own guns'. Chilembwe's ideas may have been utopian; they may have sprung up in a soil of insecurity, and have grown in the atmosphere of the African independent church movement which is fitly expressed in the slogan *Kairos*, 'the due season [is here]'; and they may have borne their fruit in action dictated by despairing frustration. But, at their heart, there was a solid matter-of-fact element that was constructively forward-looking, and kept for the most part within the bounds of practical, even if remote, possibility. This detached Chilembwe from vain dreams of the past, and set him in a central position in the new, non-tribal way of life which was developing.

African strivings towards this new way of life were already taking three forms in Nyasaland. First, there was the purely individual reaction, open to capable and adventurous spirits: escaping from the home situation, temporarily or permanently. Mostly, this took the line of trekking overland to the Rhodesias or South Africa, though it had been extended by some to making their way as far afield as America. Among the numerous Nyasaland expatriates there were individuals who rose to considerable prominence: Daniel Malekebu, who grew up in Chilembwe's fold, left it in 1907, secured medical qualifications at Selma University in Alabama and Meharry Medical College, and was able to return to Nyasaland in 1926 to re-establish the Providence Industrial Mission; Clements Kadalie, the Tonga teacher of the Livingstonia Mission who went away from the Protectorate in 1915, and by 1919 had founded in the Cape the Industrial and Commercial Workers' Union, the first modern labour union amongst South African native workers, which convulsed the whole labour scene between 1919 and 1926 and caused a Cabinet crisis; Hastings K. Banda, a Livingstonia pupil who left home in 1915, worked his way through South Africa to America, took one medical qualification, came on to Britain and took another (which made him the first Nyasaland African to hold full British medical qualifications), and played a leading part in the agitation against Central African Federation in the early 1950s; Peter Nyambo, Booth's follower, who had taken the 1914 anti-war petition to Britain, and remained out of Nyasaland for twenty-seven years; and J. G. Phillips, who founded the 'Holy Catholic Apostolic Church in Zion', one of the main African secessionist churches in South Africa. The many expatriates who made no such mark in history are simply, to those with whom they work, 'the Nyasas' or 'Blantyres', of good reputation among employers. But in the country which they have left they are *machona*, 'the lost legion', many of whom never return.

Chilembwe, with his independent stay in America, pioneered the way and its possibilities for all of them.

Secondly, African organization in Nyasaland has assumed the form of religious separatism, often with a distinctly political air: the new Providence Industrial Mission, the African Church of Christ, the African Methodist Episcopal Church, the African Presbyterian Church, the Watch Tower congregations both regular and independent, and many others. Several of these bodies have been objects of official and unofficial suspicion. Some have broken the bounds of permitted self-expression and have caused 'disturbances', like Wilfred Good and the 'Sons of God' in Cholo, and the African Seventh Day Baptists at Mlanje in 1938. Others have had a transcendental kind of air about them; for example, the universalist type of church which Peter Nyambo founded when, as an old man, he returned to Nyasaland in 1943, preaching, in the spirit of the teachings of Sri Ramakrishna, a conception of the best that is to be found in all religions. Some endeavours which have not taken the title of 'church' seem to have affinities with independent African religious movements in general; for example, the *mcapi* movement of the mid-1930s, which professed to control the witchcraft which, it was asserted, found fresh room to flourish in European-regulated Africa. In general, as the Nyasaland disturbances of 1953 indicated, all forms of African political organization in the Protectorate tend to express themselves in Christian forms: Bible quotation, prayer at meetings, and a general pulpiteering structure of activities to secure effective action. Here too Chilembwe, from the time in 1895–6 when he was helping Booth to organize the first independent church in the country, to the day when Government forces blew up his brick church at Mbombwe as a measure of suppression, was laying foundations which have endured.

In the third type of organization adopted by disquieted Nyasaland Africans the religious element is not prominent. These organizations are bodies which have modelled themselves on the more secular sort of European association. . . .

IX. NATIONALISM AND PAN-AFRICANISM

40. The contribution of tribalism to nationalism

RICHARD L. SKLAR *Journal of Human Relations* Vol. 8, 1960; pages 407–18

Tribalism is the red devil of contemporary Africa. It was condemned by nationalists at the first All-African Peoples Conference as "an evil practice" and "a serious obstacle" to "the unity . . . the political evolution . . . [and] the rapid liberation of Africa".[1] The case against tribalism rests mainly on the premise that tribal movements thrive on ethnic group loyalties which undermine wider loyalties to emerging national states. Moreover, tribal loyalties are supposed to entail implicit attachments to traditional values and institutions which are thought to be incompatible with the requirements of social reconstruction.

These assumptions are questioned in this article which is limited to the discussion of two manisfestations of tribalism in south-western Nigeria. The first, pan-tribalism, is a vigorous offspring of modern urbanization and the distinctive expression of ethnic group activity for the most politically conscious members of a new and rising class. The second, communal partisanship, is endemic to rural areas and old towns where traditional values are paramount and the socially cohesive ties of traditional authority are binding upon the people. Both manifestations of tribalism have given impetus to the growth of mass political parties and the movement for national independence.

. . . Nigeria is a Federation of three political Regions, each of which has a Legislature and an Executive Council headed by a Premier. In every Region a single "nationality" group of culturally related tribes[2] is numerically preponderant: The Yoruba in

[1] These strictures were applied to religious separatism as well as to tribalism. See the Resolution on Tribalism, Religious Separatism, and Traditional Institutions, adopted by the All-African Peoples Conference held at Accra, Ghana, December 5–13 1958.

[2] James S. Coleman has defined the concepts of "tribe" and "nationality" as follows: A tribe is "a relatively small group of people who share a

the Western Region, the Ibo in the Eastern Region and the Hausa in the Northern Region. There are three major political parties: the Action Group, the National Council of Nigeria and the Cameroons (N.C.N.C.), and the Northern People's Congress; they control the Governments of the Western, Eastern, and Northern Regions respectively. The Action Group is the official Opposition in the East and in the North; the N.C.N.C. is the official Opposition in the West and operates through an ally in the North; the Northern Peoples Congress is restricted to persons of Northern origin. The Northern Region, however, contains about 54 per cent of the population of Nigeria, and the Northern Peoples Congress emerged from the federal election of December 1959 with 142 of the 312 seats in the Federal House of Representatives, followed by the N.C.N.C. with 89, the Action Group with 73, and 8 members who are independent of the major parties. Presently the Federal Government consists of an N.P.C.—N.C.N.C. coalition with an N.P.C. Prime Minister, while the Action Group forms the Federal Opposition. Nigeria is destined to achieve independence within the British Commonwealth on October 1 1960.

Pan-Tribalism

The Yoruba People, or "nationality", of Western Nigeria comprise a number of tribal sections that have a long history of conflict with one another attributable largely to pre-colonial effects of the slave trade. Pan-Yoruba unity was an ideal fostered by a twentieth-century elite of educated men and women who followed entrepreneural, professional, managerial, and clerical vocations in new urban areas, principally in the commercial centres of Lagos and Ibadan. In 1944 a group of Yoruba students and professional men in London organized a Pan-Yoruba cultural society called *Egbe Omo Oduduwa*[1] (Sons of the

common culture and who are descended from a common ancestor. The tribe is the largest social group defined primarily in terms of kinship, and is normally an aggregation of clans." "A nationality is the largest traditional African group above a tribe which can be distinguished from other groups by one or more objective criteria (normally language)." *Nigeria: Background in Nationalism* (Berkeley and Los Angeles: University of California Press, 1958), pp. 423–4.

[1] *Oduduwa* is a culture hero and mythical progenitor of the Yoruba people. The principal founder of the society, who later became Premier of the

Descendants of Oduduwa). Four years later the society was inaugurated in Western Nigeria at a conference attended by illustrious Yoruba personalities who claimed to follow the example of pan-tribal organization set by other tribes and nationalities, in particular the Ibo people of Eastern Nigeria. It is not improbable that the founders of the *Egbe Omo Oduduwa* were motivated by interests that were political as well as cultural. Most of them were politically oriented men of the new and rising class-lawyers, doctors, businessmen, civil servants, and certain far-sighted chiefs—who perceived that the locus of economic and political power was not local but Regional and national. In 1950, leaders of the *Egbe Omo Oduduwa* were among the principal organizers of a new political party called the Action Group, which came to power in the Western Region as a result of a general election held the following year. It was the chief aim of the founders of the Action Group to overcome the ingrained particularism of the Yoruba tribes and weld them together behind a political party that would serve their common interests. In the rural areas and in traditional towns of Western Nigeria, chiefs are among the most influential leaders of opinion, and the fate of a political party may hinge on the extension of their support. The Action Group applied that principle and reared its mass organization largely upon the foundation of support by traditional authorities. Two powerful inducements attracted various chiefs into the fold of the Action Group: some of the chiefs were non-parochial in outlook and responded to the cultural appeal of Pan-Yoruba unity; others were impressed by the political and economic power of the pan-tribal elite and embraced the new party with enthusiasm or with resignation to the new facts of political life.

The rise of the Action Group in the city of Lagos attested to the efficacy of collaboration between a traditional authority and the pan-tribal elite. Lagos, the capital of the Federation, is a Yoruba town that burgeoned into the principal port and main commercial centre of Nigeria. Prior to 1954 it was administered under the Western Regional Government. The population of

Western Region and is now leader of the Opposition in the Federal Government, expounded a theory of nationalism based on pan-tribal integration under the auspices of educated elites. See Obafemi Awolowo, *Path to Nigerian Freedom* (London: Faber & Faber, 1947).

Lagos may be said to comprise three main ethnic categories: the indigenous Yorubas, the non-indigenous Yoruba settlers, and other settlers who are non-Yoruba. Traditional values weigh heavily upon the indigenous community while the values and social perspectives of the settler groups are primarily non-traditional. For about 25 years prior to 1950, Lagos local politics pivoted on the rivalry between a majority of the Yoruba indigenous community and the main body of Yoruba settlers. When the Action Group was organized in 1950, it derived its following in Lagos mainly from the Yoruba elite, most of whom were settlers. The vast majority of indigenous Yorubas and most of the non-Yoruba settlers favoured an older party, the National Council of Nigeria and the Cameroons (N.C.N.C.). Within a few years of the inauguration of its Lagos branch, the Action Group managed to obtain the support of a majority of the Yoruba indigenes, an achievement that was due largely to the efforts of the *Oba* (Paramount Chief) of Lagos. The latter was an enthusiastic proponent of pan-Yoruba unity and he applied his influence among the indigenes effectively on behalf of the Action Group.

Everywhere in the Western Region, leaders of the Action Group solicited the active co-operation of traditional chiefs. Those few chiefs who were hostile to the party or obstructed the implementation of its policies courted jeopardy. A celebrated case of opposition by one paramount chief, the ex-*Alafin* (king) of Oyo, created a general impression throughout the Western Region that no chief could stand against the Government Party and survive. Oyo was once the capital of an extensive Yoruba empire, and the *Alafin* is one of the most exalted of the Yoruba chiefs. However, the ex-*Alafin* was a conservative chief of the old order whose relationship with the Action Group deteriorated rapidly soon after that party came to power. Supporters of the *Alafin*, including non-traditionalists who opposed the Action Group for political reasons, formed an Oyo Peoples Party and decided to affiliate with the N.C.N.C. In September 1954, there was an outbreak of partisan violence at Oyo in the course of which several people were killed. The Regional Government held the *Alafin* to blame and suspended him from office; eventually he was deposed. In this context the substance of the issue at Oyo is irrelevant. What matters to us is the fact that a powerful chief was suspended by the Government and banished from his domain upon the recommendation of a committee of *Obas* (Paramount Chiefs) at a joint meeting with the leaders of the *Egbe Omo Oduduwa*. The Action Group may have resolved to banish the *Alafin* in any case, but the Egbe, technically a pan-tribal cultural organization, supplied a moral sanction from the most respectable elements in Yoruba-land, including the *Alafin*'s traditional peers.

It must be emphasized that the Action Group as a political party, and the *Egbe Omo Oduduwa* as a cultural organization, are technically distinct organizations. In theory the *Egbe* is non-partisan and its relationship to the Action Group is beyond compare. The two associations are virtually inseparable in certain rural areas where the traditional chiefs bless them both in the name of the cultural and political interests of the people. Frequently the pan-tribal organization is employed to settle disputes between Yoruba personalities, in particular among chiefs, that might otherwise embarrass the Action Group. Occasionally, it has been utilized by the pan-tribal elite, as in the extreme case of the ex-*Alafin* of Oyo, to coerce a recalcitrant chief. In general, the *Egbe Omo Oduduwa* functions as a crucial link between the Action Group, the chiefs, and other men of influence to facilitate the implementation of party policies (including policies affecting the position of chiefs) with a minimum of difficulty or resistance.

Communal Partisanship

Communal partisanship, unlike pan-tribalism, implies the affirmation of traditional values. Yet the nationalistic parties have relied upon it for mass support in areas of traditional habitation. The Government Party of the Western Region has enlisted communal partisanship by means of a systematic programme involving the co-operation of chiefs. However, there are examples of communal partisanship emerging in opposition to the Government Party and persisting in defiance of the communal chief. Two such cases, at Benin and Ibadan, are examined here.

Benin, the capital city of the Edo people, provides an example of conflict between a traditional community and a rising class. The Edo are a minority group in the predominately Yoruba Western Region. Some years ago, Edo men of wealth and high social status formed a Benin branch of the Reformed *Ogboni* Fraternity,[1] an exclusive society founded at Lagos by rising class Yorubas who were inspired by the example of European freemasonry. At first, membership in the Lodge was restricted to the town elite, i.e., professionals, businessmen, employees of firms, and leading chiefs. Subsequently, the Lodge was transformed by its leadership into a political machine and opened to all administrative and business officials, both high and petty. From 1948 to 1951 the *Ogbonis*, under a dynamic leader, dominated the administration of the Benin Division to the chagram of its traditional ruler, the *Oba* of Benin, and the distress of the people. *Ogbonis* are reported to have controlled the tax system, the markets, the police, the courts, access to the firms, etc. It is said that the members of the Lodge could violate the law with impunity, and that they enjoyed special privileges in most spheres of political and economic activity. By 1950 *Ogbonism* had become synonymous with oppression. Moreover, the people of Benin identified it with the bugbear of Yoruba domination, and their anxieties mounted in 1951 when the principal *Ogboni* leaders affiliated with the Action Group, a new political party under Yoruba control. Meanwhile, non-*Ogbonis* formed a popular party, known as the *Otu Edo* (Benin Community), dedicated to defend tradition and the sacred institution of *Oba-ship* against the alleged encroachments of usurpers. In 1951 the popular party swept the *Ogbonis* from office in local government elections and defeated them soundly in contests for the Regional Legislature.

However, the vindication of traditional values by the electorate did not restore the political supremacy of the *Oba*. His attempts to control the *Otu Edo* were frustrated by progressive leaders of that party for whom the cause of tradition had been an expedient means to further nationalistic and other political ends. Since *Ogbonis* were partisan to the Action Group, the leaders of the *Otu Edo* resolved to affiliate with the N.C.N.C. The *Oba* spurned the thought of affiliation with either national

---

[1] The traditional *Ogboni* was a politico-religious institution in certain historic Yoruba states. See W. R. Bascom, "The Sociological Role of the Yoruba Cult Group", *American Anthropologist*, 56, No. 1, Part 2, Memoir 63 (January, 1944), pp. 64–73; and Saburi O. Biobaku, *The Egba and Their Neighbours 1842–1872* (Oxford: Clarendon Press, 1957), p. 6.

party. His primary interest was the creation of a new state in the non-Yoruba provinces of the Western Region, where *Edo* influence would be dominant, and he organized an independent party to attain that objective. But it is perilous for any chief to stand against the party in power. In the words of an official report, commenting on the case of the ex-*Alafin* of Oyo, to which we have referred: "The shadow of one great Chief, now deposed and in exile, lies across the foreground of every Chief's outlook today."[1] In 1955 the *Oba* made his peace with the Western Regional Government; the Government endorsed the idea of a non-Yoruba state in principle, and the *Oba*, in turn, agreed to join the Government as a Minister without portfolio. A small minority of the Benin people who supported him against the *Ogboni* menace to his authority now followed him into the Action Group; but the vast majority remained loyal to their communal party, the *Otu Edo*. Their reverence for Benin tradition and the institution of *Oba*-ship (Chieftaincy) persisted, but they condemned the incumbent *Oba* (Paramount Chief) for his switch to the party that was associated in Benin with *Ogbonism* and class interest.

Our second case of communal partisanship, at Ibadan, capital of the Western Region, reflects an underlying conflict between urban settlers and sons of the soil. Ibadan, with a population of nearly 500,000, is the largest African city on the African continent. Urbanization at Ibadan exemplifies the two-sector pattern of development that is typical of traditional towns. A vast majority of the people dwell in the teeming indigenous sector; they live in family "compounds" of more than one hundred people in most cases, subject to the traditional authority of a family head. An average Ibadan man divides his time between the town and the rural districts, where he cultivates cocoa on family land. Men of initiative from other towns and villages have settled in the new sectors of Ibadan for commercial and occupational reasons. Among them, the Ijebu people are the most numerous. The Ibadan and the Ijebu are neighbouring Yoruba tribes; traditionally they were rivals and in recent years the historic antipathy between them has been revived by economic competition. In 1950 the indigene-

[1] Colonial Office, *Report of the Commission appointed to enquire into the fears of Minorities and the means of allaying them* (London: H.M.S.O., 1958), p. 11.

settler conflict reached a climax over issues involving land ownership and local representation. The non-Ibadan group formed a Native Settlers Union to press for the rights of settlers both to acquire landed property in Ibadan on a freehold basis and to stand for election to the Ibadan local government. These demands were supported by the pan-Yoruba tribal association.

We have observed that in 1951 the Action Group triumphed in the Western election and became the Regional Government Party. It is pertinent to this discussion of Ibadan politics that the Action Group leader, an Ijebu Yoruba, was the General Secretary of the pan-Yoruba tribal union and a highly successful barrister resident of Ibadan where he was a legal adviser to the Native Settlers Union. Six Ibadan indigenes were elected to the Western House of Assembly on the platform of an Ibadan Peoples Party. Following the election, five of them declared for the Action Group and one was appointed as a Minister in the new Western Regional Government. The Ibadan chiefs and people reacted sharply. For several years the trend of events had run against their perceived interests; Ibadan chiefs had been shorn of their traditional prerogatives by a number of administrative reforms; acres of cocoa plants belonging to Ibadan farmers had been destroyed by the Government in a well-intentioned but costly and unpopular attempt to check the spread of a contagious blight; Ibadan lands were acquired by settlers who supported various objectionable reforms; and a settler personality had suddenly become the leader of the Government. In 1954 the single elected member who did not join the Action Group organized an Ibadan tribal party with the support of the chiefs and the leaders of an Ibadan farmers' movement. The new party, called the *Mabolaje*, which means in Yoruba, "Do not reduce the dignity of Chiefs", affiliated with the N.C.N.C. Swiftly the *Mabolaje* established its supremacy in Ibadan; eventually its leader became the First Vice President of the N.C.N.C. and Leader of the Opposition in the Western House of Assembly. Only a small minority of the indigenous rising class embraced the populist *Mabolaje*. The great majority of entrepreneural, professional, and educated men of Ibadan gravitated to the Government Party. Furthermore, in 1955, an Action Group supporter was elevated to the head chiefship of

Ibadan, whereupon most of the chiefs and aspirants to chieftaincy, who require the endorsement of the Head Chief for promotion or recognition by the Government, transferred their support from the party named in their honour to the party in power. As at Benin, the loss of the citadel of chieftaincy did not weaken the party of traditional value, and the dominance of the *Mabolaje* of Ibadan has been evinced at every election of recent years.

At Benin and Ibadan, communal partisanship emerged as a reaction to the political drives of a rising class. In Benin the new class was wholly indigenous; in Ibadan it was mainly a settler class with an indigenous component. In both cases the outlook of the indigenous rising class was supra-tribal, which led it to embrace a political party that the people at large identified with interests which they regarded as being inimical to the values of their communal traditions. The tribal parties affiliated with a rival national party, in both cases the N.C.N.C. They are properly termed tribal party affiliates because their respective memberships are confined to the indigenous communal groups of Benin and Ibadan. Non-indigenous supporters are considered to be partisans of the N.C.N.C. at Benin or the N.C.N.C.-*Mabolaje* Grand Alliance at Ibadan, but not of the *Otu Edo* or the *Mabolaje* per se.

The ordinary follower or member of a tribal party in an area of traditional habitation is likely to regard it as an extension of the social order to which he is spiritually, sentimentally, and spontaneously attached. In his mind, and in the minds of others with whom he habitually associates, the party is endowed with the values of the traditional order. Partisanship of this nature is communal in the classical sense.[1] It implies the ideal of an integrated system of values involving the combination or synthesis of political, spiritual, and cultural values into a unified moral universe similar to the symbolic universe or traditional society.[2]

[1] Ferdinand Tonnies, *Fundamental Concepts of Sociology* (Gemeinschaft und Gesellschaft), translated and supplemented by Charles P. Loomis (New York: American Book Company, 1940), pp. 37–9; 67–70.

[2] Cf. M. Fortes and E. E. Evans-Pritchard, *African Political Systems* (London: Oxford University Press, 1940), pp. 16–18. S. F. Nadel drew attention to the cohesive value systems of sub-tribal groups that we find operative in the case of tribal parties. *A Black Byzantium* (London: Oxford University Press, 1942), pp. 22–6.

Consequently, supporters of a communal membership party are apt to view opposition to that party by a member of the community with moral indignation and to punish it as anti-social conduct. Of course, the concept of communal partisanship does not correspond exactly to the psychology of any particular individual. It does not apply at all to the leadership of the tribal parties of Benin or Ibadan which was drawn primarily from the rising class, mainly from those populist and radically disposed individuals who rallied to the popular cause in principle or in consequence of a perceived advantage. The nature of their partisanship is properly termed associational rather than communal; it implies rational, deliberate affiliation without ritual significance in affirmation of a political belief or in pursuit of a personal goal.[1] Owing to the influence of radical leaders, communal participation parties have assimilated nationalistic principles within their codes of traditional values. A prime example is the *Mabolaje* of Ibadan, which was conservative with respect to administrative reform but radical with respect to political nationalism, i.e., the movement for independence. . . .

Progressive chiefs and other culturally conscious members of the enlightened minority required an ideological nexus of their ethnic and class values that would supply a rationale for their non-traditional and supra-tribal interests. That need was admirably satisfied by the theory of pan-tribalism.

Within its defined cultural sphere, pan-tribalism is cosmopolitan and consistent with the affirmation of non-traditional interests or the negation of traditional interests that obstruct the policies of the pan-tribal elite. Pan-tribalism, like Jewish Zionism, is innately secular, and produces a sense of "national" identity among peoples who are ethnically or tribally diverse but culturally related. The pan-tribal spirit was ardent in the breasts of those who felt the most urgent need for unity beyond the parochial confines of their tribes. These

---

[1] Maurice Duverger utilized the concepts of Community and Association to distinguish between ideal types of participation. He observed " . . . the nature of participation can be very different according to the categories of members: especially does it seem probable that electors and members are not joined to the party by links of the same nature and that it is the Community type party that is predominant among electors, even in parties where members and militants belong rather to the Association type." *Political Parties* (London: Methuen, 1954), pp. 128–9.

were typically men of the rising class to whom the conditions of colonial rule were least tolerable. When their perspectives rise above the stage of ethnic "nationalith", pan-tribalism may be expected to lose its class distinction and the magic of its political appeal.

Communal partisanship is a social and psychological form of party-type tribal movement in areas of traditional habitation where the integral values of traditional society have not been transformed by the process of social change. In many cases local parties based on communal partisanship have been brought into existence deliberately by nationalists and rising class elements with the co-operation of chiefs. Occasionally, as at Benin and Ibadan, the emergence of communal partisanship has reflected the repudiation of a rising class by the people of a traditional community in transition where class structure is incipient and a lower class of psychology has not evolved. Most chiefs have a leading foot in the rising class, especially if it supports a governing party, and they are likely to disavow communal parties that are associated with the Opposition. At Benin and Ibadan, the nature of conflict was class versus community, rather than modern elements versus traditional elements or higher class against lower class.[1] However, rising classes herald the decline of old orders, and the transformation of classless communities into class societies is perceptible in the tendency of communal partisans to shed their traditional values and to adopt lower class perspectives.[2]

[1] Needless to say, party division never corresponds exactly to sociological differentiation, but it is significant of most of the rising class and most chiefs who affiliate with a particular party in areas where popular sentiment is to the contrary. In this paper competition between rising class and communal membership parties is not regarded as a manifestation of class conflict inasmuch as the tribal societies involved are not structured in terms of class. Anthropological studies of them generally describe communal societies of a corporate nature, segmented vertically by lineages and stratified by age grades and title associations. Chieftaincies may be vested in particular families; but the families of kings, chiefs, elders, and titled men have not been differentiated in terms of social class.

[2] This kind of change in perspective is evident at Ibadan and elsewhere, as at Enugu in Eastern Region, where many of the communal partisans are employed as industrial labourers. In the Emirate states of Northern Nigeria, class structures are traditional and the class factor is fundamental to the analysis of competition between parties in that section. Rising classes in

Throughout Nigeria, millions of tradition-bound people were drawn through the medium of communal partisanship into the mainstream of political activity where they accepted the leadership of progressive nationalists. Therein lies its historic significance. No nationalist movement or political party could have achieved independence for Nigeria without the massive support of the people, especially the rural masses and those millions who live in traditional urban communities. The British Government would not, in principle, have agreed to transfer power to a leadership group that was not broadly based. On the other hand, Britain could not, in principle or in fact, deny independence to popularly elected leaders who enjoyed the confidence of a decisive majority of the people and insisted upon the termination of colonial rule. Communal partisanship, based on psychological commitments to the traditional values of tribal groups, was utilized by nationalist leaders to mobilize mass support in rural areas and old towns.

These observations will not restore tribalism to grace in Africa. But the devil deserves his due; and in Nigeria, at least, the contribution of tribalism to nationalism has been crucial.

41. Islam and nationalism

w. h. lewis *The Arab, Middle East and Muslim Africa* Thames & Hudson and Praeger 1961; pages 65–80

Speaking before South Africa's Parliament [in 1960], the Prime Minister of the United Kingdom, Harold Macmillan, indicated that the most striking impression he had formed during his peregrinations through the "Dark Continent" was of the strength of African national consciousness. The Prime Minister pointed out that: "In different places, it may take different forms, but it is happening everywhere. The wind of change is

Northern Nigeria emerge within an existing class structure which they alter; rising classes in the part of Nigeria with which this paper is concerned emerge from classless communities which they transform into class societies. Since the new classes do not rise relative to other classes it might be preferable to term them emerging or emergent classes.

blowing through the continent." Since African national consciousness is a political reality, Macmillan remonstrated: "Our
national policies must take account of it." The Prime Minister
went on to conclude: "Of course, you understand this as well as
anyone. You are sprung from Europe, the home of nationalism.
And here in Africa you have yourselves created a full nation—a
new nation. Indeed, in the history of our times yours will be
recorded as the first of the African nationalisms."

The winds of change are indeed pouring through the continent, and even the political and racial nationalism of the original
white settlers of South Africa now is being overshadowed by the
political awakening of Africa's people of colour. The Africans'
drive for independence, equality, and status has been cloaked in
many forms—such as messianic movements, tribal revivalism,
and modern-based nationalist organizations—as well as assumed
many modes of expression—including Mau Mau barbarism,
passive resistance, boycotts, and agitational strife. Whatever the
form or the mode of expression, however, the tide of independence is rising, and 1960 has truly become the "year of Africa".
Over the course of the next seven months alone, Mali, the Malagasy Republic, the Belgian Congo, Somalia, and Nigeria are
scheduled to gain their independence, bringing to seventeen the
number of independent African nations. Even more significantly, perhaps, almost two-thirds of Africa's peoples will have
unshackled themselves from the colonial imperium by the
declining days of 1960.

Overshadowed in this dramatic welter of political change has
been the somewhat less publicized but equally significant spread
of Islam through the northern half of tropical Africa. Unlike its
nationalist counterpart, however, Islam has deep historical roots
in the *Bilād as-Sūdān*. The contact of tropical Africa with Islam
was achieved soon after the death of the Prophet Muhammad
in A.D. 632. However, this zealously evangelical faith first came
to the region in full tide in the eleventh century when Ibn Yasin,
a Muslim missionary, established himself as religious proconsul
among the southern Berber communities of present-day Mauritania. His followers, known as Almoravids, created a vast empire
extending from the Senegal River in the south to Castile in the
north. The Almoravids' most important contribution, however,
was to anchor Islam in the western Sudanic belt through the

conversion of powerful neighbouring tribal chieftains. With the subsequent decline of the Almoravids, more powerful Sudanic kingdoms sprang into existence under the Islamic banner. The Mali Empire, which endured from 1050, when its ruling monarch apostasized to Islam, until the fifteenth century, was perhaps the greatest Negro polity to grace the world stage during this period. It was succeeded by another West African kingdom, the Songhai (1468–1591), which provided yet additional impetus to the spread of Islam.

In East Africa, Islamicized tribes have been carrying their religion down the Red Sea coastline and into the Nile Valley since the seventh century. While the Coptic Christian kingdom of Aksum (or Ethiopia) stood as a mountain-locked barrier, the tide of Islam soon swirled past this isolated civilization. In the sixteenth century, a combined Arab-Somali army actually marched almost to the outskirts of Ethiopia's capital only to be defeated and forced back towards the coastal littoral of the Gulf of Aden. Farther to the south, an Arab force established itself at Mombasa in 1696. Subsequently, in 1784, Zanzibar was conquered and subjugated by the Imam of Muscat and, in 1832, the ruling Imam, Sayyid Sa'id, transferred his capital from the Arabian Peninsula to this gossamer island kingdom. From Zanzibar, Islamic influence penetrated along the coastal reaches of Kenya and Tanganyika, reinforced at the beginning of the twentieth century by the arrival of large numbers of Indian Muslims.

The greatest impetus to Islamic propagation, however, has come from a wholly unanticipated quarter. The European, through the implantation of his political dominion over Africa for more than fifty years, through the seduction of his material culture, the quaint conceits born of his feelings of cultural superiority, the excellence of his bush schools, and by sheer force, has placed in doubt many of the traditional institutions of tribal Africa. He also created out of whole cloth new cities and towns, mining and industrial complexes, and the sinews of new African classes, elites, and leadership. Concomitantly, Africa has spawned a new breed of man, the disinherited rural proletariat, the town wage earner *cum* political agitator, and the cultural entrepreneur, who serves as a middleman between tribalist and Westerner, interpreting the demands of the modern world to his illiterate brethren. Accompanying the inroads of the West in Africa have been new ideals of progress, unique modes of political expression, shifting loyalties, and value constellations totally divorced from the lore of the past.

Under the European impact, especially in those areas most accessible to Western material influence, the African's traditional religion has often proved of limited value in supplying meaningful solutions for the ubiquitous problems posed by the modern world. While generalization concerning the pantheon of animistic beliefs and rituals which prevailed among Africans at the moment of European interlopement is hazardous, a brief excursus is necessary. As Dr Trimingham has underlined in his recent West African survey, most Africans have tended to believe that the world about them was created in balance or harmony. Within this universe—which was both harsh and menacing—the role of religion was primarily ritual involving "the action of man to maintain power in equilibrium" and to preserve the "harmony" of the dynamic cosmos. Within this cosmos, the African was "wielded through birth and initiation into a holy community" *in which religion and society were one. Ritual and belief tended to reflect the degree of social integration.* With the widening Western impact, however, traditional religion and African society tended to come unhinged, and the individual African increasingly felt compelled to seek his salvation elsewhere.

In spiritual matters, the African increasingly has turned to Islam, transforming his new religion at the same time that he embraces it into a peculiarly African confession. In areas of more secular urgency, political nationalism, albeit also in transmogrified indigenous raiment, has been eagerly adopted to cover the African's temporal nakedness. When one considers that many Africans are drinking deeply of the wines of Western materialism and nationalism, the limited tapping of the spiritual cask of Christianity seems anomalous, at least upon first glance.

Colonial policy, at least in part, also has played a significant role in the rapid spread of Islam in tropical Africa. In northern Nigeria, for example, the British system of "indirect rule" helped to bolster the flagging fortunes of the Muslim Emirs. By according political preferences to the Fulani rulers of the north, the British reinforced the existing socio-political hierarchy, one which was founded on the *jihad* and the holy writ of *Sharī'a* Law. S. F. Nadel has demonstrated that, as a direct result of British colonial support, Islamic law within recent years has gradually been superseding the customary precepts of tribal animism in the Nupe area of Nigeria. At the same time, the ruling Muslim Emirates have tended to take on an "almost fictitious orthodoxy and rigidity in the face of any unwelcome demands or innovations, while the Protecting Power has almost invariably respected this attitude for the willing cooperation" of the Muslim rulers. Thus:

The policy of indirect rule as interpreted in Nigeria shackled its peoples with the existing ruling class, tied down both Muslims and pagans to the *status quo*, and isolated them from the rest of the world; and although this policy failed since it did not take into account the inevitable encroachments of new forces, it succeeded in so retarding the northern Emirates that they remained stagnant and undeveloped until recent years.

For the bulk of animists, consequently, all hope of salvation before the power of the Emirs has reposed in conversion to Islam. Nadel has shown how in the Nupe tribal community conversion has become almost mandatory due to the application of *Sharī'a* Law to cases involving customary rights. In addition, apostasy to Islam offers the hope of identification with the Fulani ruling class, with the "social elite, and, by extension, with the power which has become apparent in the Nupe capital" where the bulk of the Fulani overlords reside. In the process, however, Islam has added to the unification of the northern Nigerian conquest-states, "extending the area of a common culture over a population otherwise unified only by political means". Islam, thus, has transformed a binding of peoples together by military coercion in the nineteenth century, into a belonging together— the "conscious belonging together that goes with" a shared religious creed.

Of course, other factors can be adduced for the growing and most singular success of Islam throughout West African regions bordering on Nigeria. This dynamic, extremely plastic religious confession is propagated by Africans among people of colour. Thus, it has popular appeal as a fundamentally African religion. In addition, its dogma, while fixed, is nevertheless susceptible to external influences, permitting local beliefs and other accretions to be baptized into the new religion. In its folk manifestations, Islam does not challenge the underlying beliefs of Africans; rather it frequently reinforces them. Conversion to Islam also is made attractive as a consequence of: (1) the cultural prestige which it brings—as witnessed by opportunity Islam affords for at least a rudimentary education in remote rural areas; (2) the social integration it offers—in a world increasingly fragmented by the Western impact Islam extends the individual African an opportunity to anchor himself to new corporate institutions; and (3) the comforting religious values it embraces—in that Islam purports to provide assured solutions to the problems both of this world and the next. Apropos this question, Christian evangelism probably has contributed as much impetus to the processes of Islamization through its rigidity, internal contradictions, and perpetuation of inferiority-superiority complexes, as it has provided illumination of the Christian way.

While no accurate data are available relating to the number and rate of conversions in Africa south of the Sahara, some consensus obtains among qualified observers that Islam has burst out of the Sahara hinterland and the savannah regions of West Africa and is now making rapid inroads in the central and coastal rain-forest belt. In the Belgian Congo, for example, the number of Muslims has ballooned to more than 100,000. In former French West Africa, over eight million Muslims have been counted, while in excess of twelve million populate both northern and southern Nigeria. To the East, over six million Muslims inhabit what is commonly accepted as the Horn area, and more than three million are presently residing in Kenya, Uganda, Tanganyika, and Mozambique. In more meaningful terms, perhaps, it might be noted that, by the declining days of 1960, the affairs of at least ten of Africa's seventeen independent nations will be presided over by Muslim statesmen.

The political ramifications of Islam's spread have been viewed by some Western "Africanists" over the past several years with grave concern. Many profess to see serious international power problems in the possible emergence of a Muslim African "bloc" which would enhance Afro-Asian neutralist voting strength before the United Nations, as well as at general international conferences. Some observers also express consider-

able perturbation over the possibility of an extension of dispro-
portionate UAR throughout the African continent. Others
simply experience and manifest varying degrees of traumatic
shock at the prospect of growing Muslim power in world councils at the seeming expense of the once much-heralded Western
monopoly of power.

Such an approach subsumes a degree of political, social, and
cultural unity among African Muslims which is more apparent
than real. Numerous deep-seated cleavages exist within the
Islamic community which, *inter alia*, are predicated upon: (1)
traditional tribal and ethnic rivalries; (2) diverse racial backgrounds; (3) differences in degree of religiosity, as well as in
ritual practices; (4) clashing class and special economic interests
—as between Syrian-Lebanese traders and local African merchants; (5) membership in competing religious confraternities
(*turuq*); and (6) marked variations in degree of Westernization. In
addition, European colonial regimes have erected trans-territorial
barriers of their own which deeply impede efforts to create
broad political groupings. One might mention at this juncture some of the more obvious impedimenta: (1) differing
official languages and administrative operational procedures;
(2) fundamental dichotomies in outlook with regard to the
responsibilities and needs of government; and (3) different
currencies, marketing systems, and patterns of trade and commerce. These barriers are not easily overcome by the unifying
influences which may exist in African Islam.

Nor, for that matter, is Islam so firmly entrenched in most
territories that it has become the "national religion" of emergent
states. The complex situation obtaining in West Africa probably
best illustrates this point. In the Western region, European
empire-builders erected states in the nineteenth and early twentieth centuries at right-angles to major African culture zones.
The culture zones extend horizontally on an east-west axis,
while the European colonial powers tended to create new national entities on a north-south orbit. As a result, each emergent
West African state today contains a "cross-section of very
different cultural patterns, ranging from the predominantly
Negroid groups in the tropical forest on the coast to the predominantly Sudanic groups in the open savannah in the north".
Only in Mauritania, and possibly Niger—among the territories

of the former French West African Federation—has Islam become sufficiently entrenched to be accepted as the "national religion". Even in Mauritania, profound ethnic and cultural cleavages between the Arabic-speaking northern Moors and the riverain Negro Toucouleurs (*Takrur*) in the south have not been completely submerged by the Islamic veil which curtains the entire Mauritanian population. (Apropos this point, it is interesting to note that the Toucouleurs themselves have a low regard for their Negro Wolof co-religionists inhabiting the region across the Senegal River because of the laxity of the latter's religious practices and beliefs.)

In Mali (Soudan and Senegal), as well as Guinea, Islam has become the predominant faith of numerous Africans. However, it is not a universally accepted faith. Consequently, heavy reliance upon Islam, "in party ideologies or propaganda, as a basis for political solidarity, could have the effect of dividing people more than it united them". Probably nowhere in Africa is this fact more clearly portrayed than in the Chad, where ethno-religious cleavages between the Muslim communities of the north and the Christian-animist-Bantu south pose serious problems for national unity and political stability.

The north is relatively more backward and given to the perpetuation of tribal traditionalism, as well as religious conservatism. In the past, its leadership has been relatively weak and divided by personality clashes which impeded sustained, united action. However, on February 1, 1960, the north's five heterogeneous political formations amalgamated into the *Parti National Africain* (PNA) under the leadership of Ahmad Koulamallah. Its essential goals are the maintenance of "Muslim tradition" in educational and social matters and the loosening of political ties with France concomitant with the strengthening of relations with adjacent Muslim territories. The relatively advanced and politically sophisticated south, however, is more inclined to challenge tribal conservatism and to adopt programmes favouring secularization of education and social advance. The present government is controlled by the *Parti Progressiste Tchadien* (PPT-RDA) which represents the interests of the more progressive south, a region unalterably opposed to national unification with neighbouring Muslim states. As issues such as these become joined in the very near future, considerable political effervescence and disabling intercommunal strife can be anticipated, to the likely detriment of the Chad's national stability.

On the other hand, the situation in the Cameroun Republic, a former French trust territory which acquired its independence on January 1, 1960, is somewhat anomalous. Here, the seeming political homogeneity of the Islamic northern region, the moderate outlook of its Muslim leadership, and the profound cleavages and incompatibilities of the more advanced Christian-animist southern coastal communities, have produced a remarkable situation in which the nation's most conservative elements are primarily responsible for the preservation of the Republic's unity and stability. At the time of independence, the Cameroun's Prime Minister, Ahmadu Ahidjo, inherited a litany of serious difficulties highlighted by widespread civil strife inspired by the outlawed *Union des Populations Camerounaise* (UPC), as well as economic and social unrest among the Bamileke tribesmen of the south-west, and spasmodic feuding among local politicians in Douala and Yaounde. In the intervening period, Prime Minister Ahidjo has been able to maintain a delicate balance between his Muslim supporters in the north—who account for one-third of the total population—and the relatively more advanced coastal communities. A Fulani by birth, Ahidjo was educated in Yaounde and entered political life by joining a southern party which numbered among its leaders many of the nation's Catholic intellectuals. In 1958, however, Ahidjo formed his own party, *l'Union Camerounaise* (UC), an organization having basic roots in the north but which is making strenuous efforts to extend its influence into the coastal regions.

At present, the Prime Minister of the Cameroun Republic is serving as a political hyphen between Muslim north and Christian-animist south. With patience and considerable forbearance, he is attempting to establish a meaningful universe of discourse in a deeply divided West African land, one in which disagreements will be acted out and resolved in legislative assemblies rather than in the accidental, bloody encounters of army patrols and terrorist bands. In the process, Ahmadu Ahidjo is seeking to demonstrate that the conservative Muslim north can serve as a leavening political influence as the Republic searches for the correct path to an awakening "national consciousness" and eventual unity of effort.

It is not entirely inconceivable that a comparable situation might arise in Nigeria, where major political dichotomies in the more advanced Yoruba and Ibo south (between the NCNC and the Action Group) could afford the Muslim north an opportunity to assume a similar lodestar role. Thus, here too, positions would be reversed and conservative Islamic groups—willing to make some concessions to modernism—may ultimately be compelled to moderate differences between the followers of Azikiwe and Awolowo and, at the same time, seek to consolidate the bonds of an embryonic Nigerian national federation.

For much of Africa, however, the representatives of conservative Islamic groups are unlikely to encounter numerous opportunities for the assumption of such profitable, reassuring roles. Under the Western colonial impact, a new political geography has been imposed, the sacredness of old tribal cultures has been partially despoiled, and new African political elites have emerged in the crucible of colonial dominion. These new elites do not depend upon genealogical ties for ascriptive status, but emphasize instead achievements engendered by education, as well as inborn organizational ability. They seek to channel political activity outside the rules and procedures instituted by traditional society over the centuries to guide and to limit political action. Thus, in essence, the newly emergent political elites are changing the rules of the game—at least as it has been played in the past. Their goal is to mobilize African society behind efforts to fashion new institutions—as well as to disentangle the old—to formulate a more meaningful ideology with which to meet the problems of the twentieth century, and to marshal national resources, both physical and human, for a frontal assault upon the existing barriers to modernism.

The new religion of these elites is African nationalism, the appeal of which rests upon common experience with Western value systems, however variant. The strength, character, and appeal of this new secular religion often rest upon the charismatic qualities of leaders such as Kwame Nkrumah, Felix Houphouet-Boigny, Sékou Touré, Julius Nyerere, and Mamadou Dia. If there is a messianic quality in the appeal of these Africans, it is in their ability to inculcate overwhelming numbers of their fellow Africans and to secure mass support for essentially temporal goals. As one recent observer has noted: "The situation has been right for the emergence of such charismatic leaders; the assertion of African aspirations has required symbols which these men and their movements have provided."

Mass movements, a new phenomenon in Africa, are of particular significance for the evolution of nationalism in the continent since they have developed into the handmaidens of the emerging political elite. It is through these movements that policy decisions ultimately affecting the orientation of national governments are struck, territorial support elicited, and that the largest numbers of Africans gain experience in the building of a sense of "membership in an African state". The aim of these nationalist movements is to cut across diverse loyalties whether they are tribal, racial, or religious. In the case of Islam, they seek to reduce its far-reaching influence upon political loyalties to as negligible a level as possible. Recently in Ghana, for example, the formation and perpetuation of a Muslim Association Party provoked strong hostility from Prime Minister Nkrumah and his Convention People's Party. The CPP has vigorously sought to sublimate religious differences for the sake of political unity. As a result, the Muslim Association Party is a moribund organization today.

Thus, nationalism in contemporary tropical Africa confronts Islam with a challenge which is almost as old as the history of religion. As invoked by modern secularists, nationalism is anathema to orthodox Muslim theology since it questions what is at the very core of Islam. For example, African nationalism raises the fundamental issue of Islam's role as a political as well as a religious formative influence and questions whether or not it is capable of rapid adjustment to the dictates and exigencies of the "modern world". Indeed, can religious authoritarianism be subordinated to the authoritarianism of temporal nationalism? Is Islam capable of accepting an almost Augustinian opposition of the heavenly and the earthly? Can nationalist absolutism, with its principle of mass inclusion and its preferred role as custodian of the past and master of Africa's destiny, compromise with Muslim reformists? More crucially, perhaps, can Islam's reformers compromise with leaders who are more concerned with the meeting of today's material needs than with the geography of human souls on the morrow?

Guinea serves as an excellent illustration of the relationship of
CITCA

the points at issue. Nationalism as an expression of the African's search for identity, new status, and dignity is in full flood in contemporary Guinea. Under the leadership of Sékou Touré, himself a Muslim, Guinea opted for independence during the September, 1958, referendum held throughout French Africa on President Charles de Gaulle's Constitution of the Fifth Republic. In essence, Guinea voted against membership in the rapidly evolving French Community. Having severed its former colonial umbilical cord, the leaders of this small African state have sought to establish new roots for themselves in the international community. Dilatoriness and hesitation on the part of the Western world in affording Guinea diplomatic recognition permitted the Soviet bloc to hasten to fill a dreaded vacuum—that of isolation and lack of international status. In need of recognition, technical aid, and large-scale assistance in creating necessary administrative services, Guinea accepted Soviet blandishments with alacrity. However, to counter the impact of this action upon the West, as well as to underscore Guinea's neutralist foreign policy, loose ties were established with Ghana in a vaguely defined, embryonic political "union". Despite the overwhelmingly Islamic confession of its indigenous population, the Guinea government also has hastened to establish diplomatic and other ties with Israel from which it is hoped that some inspiration for the economic advance of an undeveloped society will be gleaned.

The basic fact of life for the existing Guinean leadership is the impoverishment of the bulk of the country's more than two million people. As Sékou Touré has understood, there is no Western nation which has found itself in recent years in the same human condition as is encountered in most African states.

Populations which include more than 80 per cent . . . illiterate peasants, with an annual individual income of less than $100, and therefore, with the most precarious conditons of life—these are the harsh realities of Africa, when it is no longer masked behind the ridiculous veil of exoticism which hides from unaware eyes the colossal misery of our vast underdeveloped countries at present sparsely populated because of centuries of slavery.

Within this harsh environment, the Guinean leader is not without hope:

And yet in this poverty, of which humanity should be ashamed, there is man with his invincible faith in the destiny of humanity; there is his hope, his determination to win and to grow; his immense thirst for brotherhood and harmony, his kindness still in its purest form; and, at the same time, his extraordinary energy and sharp sense of responsibility. . . .

In an apparent effort to harness the drives and ambitions of Guineans, political life has been focused upon the country's primary nationalist organization, the *Parti Démocratique de Guinée* (PDG), whose *leitmotiv* is complete independence combined with popular action. As the so-called brain of the state, the PDG serves as the medium through which the "general will" of Guineans is to seek expression. Indeed, no important governmental decision may be taken without the prior approval of the PDG, or more properly, its National Political Bureau. Once consensus is attained, however, all sectors of the national population are expected to cooperate in the implementation of PDG policy decisions.

The present-day action goals of the PDG are essentially revolutionary. The Party clearly seeks an early termination of all former colonial connections, profound social and economic reforms directed from the centre, the transformation of tribal communities into modern political societies as quickly as possible, and the creation of a strong, socialist-oriented central government. The existing leadership, as exemplified by President Touré himself, accepts Marxist ideology only in so far as it "applies to present conditions in Africa"—i.e., to the struggle against colonialism and the process of decolonization. Illustrative of the PDG's distinctively African approach to Marxist doctrine is its tendency to reject the concept of class warfare. While recognizing that some marked differences obtain between social classes, these differences are held to be insignificant when compared with those prevailing between colonized peoples and the colonizers. The PDG's main concern is the mobilization of *all* classes in the struggle against colonialism and poverty.

While the PDG tends to respect divergent social, cultural, and religious customs—and it should be remembered that over twenty tribal languages are spoken in Guinea today—it seeks, at the same time, to level all existing barriers to modernization. Thus, while it may organize festivities on the occasion of a Muslim holiday, the PDG concomitantly will seek to eliminate those tribal and religious obstacles which impede the advancement of Muslim women. For example, within recent months it has been pursuing an active campaign against polygamy, marriages before religious clerics, and divorce without satisfactory manifest cause. To those preservers of custom and religious guardians of Muslim tradition in the Futa Jalon region who vibrantly oppose the toppling of the lore of the past, the PDG offers only ultimate capitulation or banishment. Where orthodox and folk Islam interpose spiritual reservations to the secular road selected for material progress, they are likely to be received as the obscurantist remnants of a decadent civilization. On the other hand, where African Islam proves malleable and plastic, no longer anxious simply to underpin regional ethnocentricities, it may well serve as a leavening influence and force making for unity of action.

Elsewhere in Africa the struggle against Islamic obscurantism is not yet entirely joined. However, the issues are becoming increasingly, almost painfully, evident. They are most apparent, perhaps, in Senegal where the present debate between African nationalism and traditional Islam is most intense. Led by religious holy men (*marabouts*) *cum* politicians, traditional Islam has found its strongest expression under the inspiration of the *Parti de la Solidarité Senegalaise* (PSS). In a state where tribal chieftains have wielded little power, the influence of the *marabouts* upon the political affairs of local communities has been extensive—occasionally, all-pervasive. Under the leadership of the Grand Marabout of Kaolack, El Hadj Ibrahim Niasse, Senegal's religious elite has jealously sought to safeguard its political privileges and spiritual prerogatives. In particular, it has cast a baleful eye upon the territory's leading nationalist organization, the *Union Progressiste Senegalaise* (UPS), which has espoused a programme of extensive social and economic reforms. In the past, the UPS has been publicly branded as an enemy of Islam and, as recently as June, 1959, the *maraboutical* elite under Cheikh Tidjani Sy provoked grave demonstrations in the region of Tivaouane against the government headed by the UPS nationalists.

For Senegal's Prime Minister, Mamadou Dia, himself a Muslim who has recently returned from a pilgrimage to Mecca, the opposition of the conservative *marabouts* has been a cause for some substantial perturbation. He remains convinced, however, that his belief in secular progress for the "masses" is the only means of raising Senegal to higher status in the community of nations. The tenacity with which Mamadou Dia and his colleagues cling to their programmes of action appears, finally, to be producing some success. On January 13, 1960, the PSS extended the olive branch of reconciliation, thus terminating for the present a major skirmish between the defenders of conservative Islam and the proponents of modern nationalism. Despite this detente, however, the fundamental issue involving the proper role to be assigned Islam in the modern nation remains to be more fully debated and resolved.

Until the confrontation between Islam and nationalism is finally acted out, it would appear that religion in Africa south of the Sahara may prove as much a divisive factor as a unifying influence. If Islam is to serve as a positive force for greater African unity, at least in the near future, its greatest appeal is likely to be predicated upon the emotional appeal it conjures up from the history of the great Islamic empires and states which abided in Africa in centuries past. . . .

42. Christianity and African political development

NDABANINGI SITHOLE *Historians in Tropical Africa* University College, Salisbury, Rhodesia 1960; pages 354–7, 359–61

. . . The Christian Church has contributed to African political development through its contribution to the following areas:

1 African Literacy and Literature.
2 African Education.
3 African Religion.
4 African Health.

We shall put a little more flesh on the above skeleton so that we may be able, at the end of this section, to breathe more life into these dry bones.

1 African Literacy and Literature

Prior to the coming of the missionaries to Africa, there were, according to Lord Hailey, only four African languages, with the exception of Arabic, with a native script of their own out of more than 700 languages. Since the missionaries needed to translate the Bible into some of these languages, they were the first to reduce most of the present written African languages to a written form. Now 36 complete Bibles and 82 New Testaments exist in the various African languages. In other words, the Holy Bible which has a socially and politically redemptive theology is now available to many Africans, and Bible reading has greatly stimulated the African, not only religiously, but also politically. In my *African Nationalism* I pointed out that:

One of the unique teachings of the Bible, especially the New Testament, is the worth and dignity of the individual in the sight of God. There is a relation between this teaching and the present African nationalism. According to African tradition, at least in some parts of Africa, if not in the whole of Africa, the individual counted in so far as he was part and parcel of the group outside of which he lost his real worth. In actual practice this meant that no individual could follow his natural bent beyond the group. All new schemes, new adventures, new thoughts, and new outlooks on life were subject to the approval or disapproval of the group. The individual, to all practical intent, was dominated by the fear of the group; let alone the fear that comes from ignorance, superstitious beliefs, and belief in the existence of evil spirits. The individual socially, spiritually, and mentally, moved in shackles, and this was certainly not conducive to progress. Individual initiative was crippled. But now the African individual is being delivered from these fetters. The individual is being invested with a new status, and so today we find individuals venturing beyond the confines of the group, and in many cases the group now looks upon this new individual as its real saviour. The Bible is redeeming the African individual from the power of superstition, individuality-crushing tradition, witchcraft, and other forces that do not make for progress. The same Bible is helping the African individual to reassert himself above colonial powers! It is inconceivable to a logical mind that the Bible could deliver the African from traditional domination without at the same time redeeming him from colonial domination. If the Bible teaches that the individual is unique, of infinite worth before God, colonialism, in many respects, says just the opposite; so that, in actual practice, Biblical teachings are at variance with colonialism, and it becomes only a matter of time before one ousts the other. The Bible-liberated African is now reasserting himself not only over tribal but also over colonial authority, since these two are fundamentally the same.

According to various experts, about 300 African languages have now been reduced to writing. African literacy has been estimated continent-wise as ranging from 10 to 15 per cent. The importance of literacy cannot be over-emphasized. This Christianity-introduced literacy has brought to the African many powerful and stimulating ideas without which national organization of the masses remains an impossible task. It has linked the African with the rest of the literate world. It has placed Africa in step with the rest of the civilized world.

The introduction of literacy to Africa has resulted in the creation of African literature not only by European but also by African authors. In South Africa Xhosa, Zulu, Tsonga Venda, Shangaan and Sotho writers are increasing in quantity as well as in quality. In the Federation of Rhodesia and Nyasaland, Shona, Ndebele, Lozi, Nyanja and Bemba writers are also on the increase. This is also true in East and West Africa. The number of African vernacular authors is increasing. African authors have not only confined themselves to the vernaculars, but also to writing in English, French and Portuguese.

But what is important at this point is the trend of this African writing. It is unfortunate that I cannot go into any detail in a paper of this nature, but the following are the usual characteristics of African writing by African authors:

1 The authors usually play up the heroic aspects of African warriors and play down their shortcomings. This is intended to correct European authors who play up the villainous qualities of African warriors, but play down their heroic and noble qualities. As one African author once said, "Every hero is white, and every villain is black. It's about high time we created our own literature and introduced black heroes."

2 African authors usually satirize some of the vices of the Western world under the compelling desire to discredit the philosophy of the assumed natural superiority of the white man over the black man.

3 African authors often urge African tribes to sink their

individual identities in the interest of what has come to be known as the African Personality.

4 African authors often write to inspire, inform, enlighten, educate and uplift their fellowmen.

5 African literature by Africans serves as a mirror in which the Africans see themselves as people capable of any achievement if given opportunity, and they see in it the lie that an African is incapable of notable achievements in the various fields.

2 African Education

We now turn to the second field in which Christianity has played a very important part, and that is African education. Education in the Western sense of the word was introduced to most parts of Africa by the Christian Church. The study of such European languages as English, French and Portuguese, the study of such school subjects as arithmetic, history, geography, physiology and hygiene, biology, agriculture and animal husbandry, the training of African boys and girls in brickmaking, forestry, woodwork, sewing, laundry and housekeeping were introduced by the Christian Church.

It is impossible to assess fully the influence of these school subjects on the general development of the African peoples. In Africa, as already indicated, there are over 700 languages. This linguistic medley has been responsible for the lack of communication between the various tribal or ethnic groups, and it has also been accountable for social and political barriers between these groups. The study of the three European languages has established continent-wide communication among the 240,000 peoples of Africa, and many of the disadvantages of lacking a common language have been overcome. The study of French, for instance, has established effective communication in the vast areas of what used to be French West and Equatorial Africa. The English language in Central, East and West Africa has also established effective communication among the peoples of Africa. In the acquisition of these European languages by African students European habits of thought, European attitudes and outlook have unconsciously transferred themselves to the African, and these in turn have transformed, stimulated and fertilized his imagination. The study of these European languages has had a direct bearing on African political development.

It is noteworthy that when Pan-African Conferences are convened, the deliberations are conducted not in African but in European languages.

I should be forgiven to quote once more from my *African Nationalism* in which I summarize as follows the influence of missionary schools:

The study of European, English, and American, as well as African history in African schools, has had a profound influence upon the African people. The European struggle for liberty, for religious toleration, for freedom of thought and expression, and European resistance against tyranny, thrill the African students to the core. How often have my history students requested me to tell them about certain historical figures! 'Please, Sir, tell us about that tenacious English Bulldog (Sir Winston Churchill).' 'Please, Sir, tell us more about Martin Luther and his ninety-five theses. Oh, that man! He was a man!' 'Mahatma Gandhi whose soul was more powerful than the British Navy and Royal Air Force put together.' 'Tell us, please, about the Boston Tea Party.' 'David Livingstone the man who stopped the slave trade in Central Africa.' 'Please tell us about Mr Government-of-the-People-by-the-People-and-for-the-People (Abraham Lincoln).' European, American, and Indian heroism thrills African students. They admire the firm stand against tyranny. But sooner or later the African admirer seeks to overthrow the tyranny of his European hero so long as the latter appears the dictator in relation to the former.

3 African Religion

In the field of African religion, Christianity has also played a very important part. One of the major contributions of Christianity to African political development is the destruction, where it has been accepted, of ancestor worship which tended to divide religiously the African people. There is no such thing as African religion in the sense of Christianity, Islam, Buddhism or Hinduism in point of organization, method and content. Each family or clan worshipped its ancestors to the exclusion of those of other families. People belonging to different families or clans were not allowed to worship together. There were as many religious divisions as there were different families or clans. The introduction of Christianity has tended to give the African families, clans and tribes one common ancestor universally worshippable. Hence the 25,000,000 African Christians, drawn from hundreds of tribes and tens of ethnic groups, can now physically and spiritually worship together. In the pre-Christian era this would have been next to impossible. The religious unification of the otherwise religiously divided African families, clans and tribes was a necessary forerunner of African political unification. In a sense a religiously divided people are also politically divided. Religious unity strengthens, in many cases, political unity. Political development among a people with a common religious consciousness takes place more easily than in an atmosphere of great religious diversity.

To sum up the second section of this paper, it should be noted that if literacy contributes to the general enlightenment of a people; if the introduction of three common languages in place of 700 tends to bring such people together; if literature tends to inspire them, widen their horizons, deepen their sympathies and clear their vision; if education tends to encourage improved social, cultural and economic conditions; and if Christianity places above everything else the love of God, the love of our neighbour, the infinite worth and dignity of the individual, and if all these things have appealed to the African, it follows that the activities of the Christian Church have been most beneficial to African political development.

I am not, however, unaware that some anthropologists have seriously accused the Christian Church of ignoring and even discouraging African institutions. I am conscious that the Christian Church has greatly interfered with the ancestral beliefs and practices of the African people, and in turn this has culturally and emotionally uprooted the African. I am aware that it is contended that the study of European languages has tended to cause Africans to neglect their own languages with the result that they have become second-rate thinkers in that they have to do most of their thinking, not in their mother tongue, but in a foreign language. I am also aware that the cry has been to keep African customs, culture and languages pure. But of course to talk of cultural and linguistic purity in an era of inter-tribalism, internationalism and inter-racialism or multi-racialism is in itself quite unrealistic. The cry for the preservation of African institutions is often coloured, to use Philip Mason's phrase, by "a touch of the Museum Attitude". What I am trying to say here is that the three European languages had to be superimposed upon African languages to break down the numerous linguistic barriers. African political organization has been made easier by adopting a foreign language as the official language since the elevation of one African language to that status would have unleashed old tribal rivalries and could have made political organization extremely difficult. African ancestral worship had to give way to a larger religious unity. The African had to be uprooted first in order to find his roots in the latter half of the twentieth century. . . .

IV. THE EMERGENCE OF THE INDEPENDENT AFRICAN CHURCHES

Before we can account for the emergence of the independent African Church, it is important to outline briefly the unwritten pact between Christianity and European governments. The African observer has noted that the imperialistic, colonial pattern has its ecclesiastical counterpart in most of the European-controlled Christian churches, as the following statements show:

1 Both in political and religious spheres Africans were dominated by Europeans.

2 In politics and in church life the key positions were the monopoly of the Europeans.

3 In towns and cities housing was on a segregated basis geared to racial considerations, and this was equally true on most "mission stations".

4 The quality of European houses in the city and on the "mission station" was often superior, while that of the African was often inferior.

5 The differential salary scales based on the colour of a man's skin were accepted by both European government and missionary alike who felt that it was right and proper for the African worker to receive a lower salary than his European counterpart.

6 The usual racial arrogance and stand-offishness of the ruling whites also had their representatives among missionaries.

7 The ordinary Europeans practised social discrimination, and the missionaries found it difficult to do otherwise since they had to accept the prevalent social pattern the rejection of which would have invited their ostracization by Europeans in general.

In short, the European society hammered out an all-round

policy of racial discrimination, and the missionaries—the visible representatives of Christianity—also accepted this policy, but it should be borne in mind that in practice racial discrimination as practised by missionaries was much milder than by ordinary whites. The principle of racial discrimination was common to both missionaries and the ordinary whites; the difference was only in application. This state of affairs has given a strong feeling that Christianity is European imperialism masquerading in religious garbs. Hence in some African circles the acceptance of Christianity by Africans is interpreted as the acceptance of European imperialism, and the concentration of ecclesiastical power in European hands corresponding to the concentration of political and economic power in European hands has tended to substantiate this view.

The causes of the break-away of African Christians from European-controlled churches are many and varied, and what has been already said forms a good background. Dr Edgar Brookes says forthrightly: "Separatism has been the result, to a large extent, of the presence of the colour bar within the Christian Church." Dr B. G. M. Sundkler has also observed that the African has been driven out of the Missionary Church by the South African calvinism of no equality between Black and White in Church and State. Dr Hendrick Kraemar observes that non-Europeans break away from the missionary churches because they seek to be masters of the household of their own faith. It should also be noted that separatism arises out of a genuine desire to adapt the Christian message of the Church to the African people themselves.

The similarity between the reasons for the emergence of African independent churches and exclusively or predominantly African political parties is most striking. The colour bar has driven the African out of European churches and political parties. The African desire to be master of the household of his own faith has led him to break away from European churches just as his desire to be master of his own political affairs has led him to break away from European political parties. His desire to adapt the Christian message to his own particular religious needs has also led him to desire to adapt the government of the country to his own particular political needs. We may note here in broad outline:

1 That the move towards African emancipation from missionary authority is inspired by the same conditions and factors that inspire African nationalism.

2 That ecclesiastical paternalism tends to produce the same results as European political paternalism.

3 That missionary opposition to the emergence of African independent churches bears a striking resemblance to the general European opposition to the rise of African nationalist movements.

4 That African religious and political movements are, in most cases, complementary in the general African struggle to emancipate the African from foreign domination. (One hand washes the other.)

5 That the African Christian has learnt the close alliance between African Christianity and African nationalism from the close alliance between European Christianity and White supremacy.

6 That the enormous vitality generated through Christian religious experience has also been diverted to African nationalism, and the present African political vigour is also being diverted to African independent churches.

7 That the white churches and the colour-bar Missionary Churches have fanned a strong religious consciousness corresponding to the present upsurging political consciousness expressing itself in the present trends of African nationalism.

Perhaps a jet-like narration of the emergence of the African independent churches may give more substance to what we have so far said.

The movement towards missionary-independent churches goes back, in the Union of South Africa, to 1872. Nehemiah Tile—a Tembu with strong nationalistic sympathies—broke away from the Hermon congregation of the Paris Mission in Basutoland. In 1884 he set up the Tembu Church with Chief Ngangelizwe as its visible head. In 1885 the Native Independent Church, with Chief Kgantlapane as its visible head, was established in Bechuanaland. In 1889 the Lutheran Bapedi Church was formed. In 1895 the Ethiopian Church came into being. In 1932–33 the Bantu Methodist Church of South Africa also made its appearance.

As the African independent churches multiplied in South

Africa the question of church unity became a pressing one before these churches, and in an effort to solve this problem of lack of unity among these churches, the doctrine of "one United Native Church" was, in 1919, formally accepted at a representative conference of these churches. It should be noted that the appeal for Church Union was under the aegis of the African National Congress. Influential African intellectuals welcomed the move. In 1937, the Bantu Independent Churches Union of South Africa was formed.

It may be pointed out, in passing, that there is no clear line of demarcation between African religious consciousness as manifested in the emergence of African independent churches and African political consciousness as represented by existing African national organizations or purely African political parties. The two movements—nationalism and separatism—are the reverse sides of the same coin. The African political hand washes the African religious hand, and the religious the political.

But, of course, the general exodus from missionary-controlled churches was not only confined to the Union of South Africa but also to other parts of Africa. In Nyasaland Ethiopianism spread like a wild fire, and African independent churches, supported and encouraged by Joseph Booth, became champions of African political emancipation. These taught that the political, economic and social salvation of Africa would have to be undertaken by the African himself. There is therefore a sense in which it is true that the first organized arch enemy of European imperialism was the African independent church.

In Kenya the Kikuyus, in opposition to missionary churches, established their own churches which were nationalistic in outlook. In what was then the Belgian Congo, until June 30, 1960, but now the Republic of Congo, a similar movement occurred. As far back as 1921 politico-religious movements had already made their appearance on the scene. Simon Kibangu, for instance, had set himself up as the messiah, saviour and redeemer of his people. He intended saving his people from European control and Christianity. The rising that occurred in 1921 was a result of this movement, and this was repeated in 1940–1 by Kitiwala.

Before we close this section of our paper it is important to observe:

1 That African religious separation from European churches inevitably leads to African political withdrawal from European-dominated politics, and the reverse is equally true.

2 That the desire for religious self-determination has its counter-part in the desire for political self-determination.

3 That the religious fanaticism, zeal and vitality of the African all correspond to his uncompromising national demands for freedom and independence.

4 That the African's religious separatism is really his deep desire to assert the African religious personality which has its counterpart in his desire to assert his political personality in terms meaningful and helpful to himself.

In conclusion it should be noted that both African religious separatism and African nationalism are a new African awareness, a new self-evaluation, a new sense of destiny, a new approach to problems facing him, a new way of finding his place in the world, a new way of removing other-determination, and of establishing self-determination, in all important fields of human activity. . . .

43. African Nationalism: concept or confusion?

ROBERT I. ROTBERG *Journal of Modern African Studies* Vol. 4, No. 1, 1966 Cambridge University Press; pages 33–46

In common usage, African nationalism is descriptive shorthand for an assembly of separate and distinct phenomena, some of which have already taken on the protective colouring of popular understanding. Africans generally agree that they have experienced nationalism; they know the tree of nationalism when they see it and have tasted some, at least, of its fruits. For many of them, and for students of recent African events, its manifestations are obvious, although the quality of its spirit remains, like most spirits, capable only of inexact description. It is, in essence, pretty much what it is.

Sceptics and critics are, however, entitled to seek greater precision. Since Africa historically possessed few nations in the classical European cultural, linguistic, or religious sense, and since few now exist in such terms, how can we write and speak of nationalism? The mere expression of anti-colonial hostility clearly does not provide sufficient proof of its existence. In a tropical African setting, the descriptive usage of nationalism dates only from the late 1940s; for hostile critics it thus seems nonsensical to assign to nationalism a long African history roughly parallel to the period of colonial intervention. Yet that is one hypothesis, the testing of which depends to a large extent upon a definition of terms.

'Nation', 'nationality', and 'nationalism' are catch-words that have been used to describe a multitude of situations, human conditions, and states of mind. I need not here rehearse the relevant literature; we all know the different uses to which 'nationalism' has been put and the inability of the various definitions adequately to depict each of the particular situations.[1] Nationalism is a morass of misapplication; it describes much in general and little in particular. To add 'African' narrows the area of example but complicates the search for comparative generality. We cannot really approach the subject without knowing what it is and how it relates to similar experiences at other times and in other parts of the world.

'Nation' has historical associations. In pre-nineteenth-century western Europe, the growth of monarchial power, and the consequent establishment of centralised states, in turn brought about the creation of the nations from which nationality and nationalism flowed. Although the emergence of national cultures did not everywhere in Europe depend upon the prior establishment of political unity, such unity may almost be considered a necessary pre-condition. By the end of the seventeenth century, the monarchial quest for power had involved the bourgeoisie as well as the dynastic aristocracy; the monarchs had invoked and, in many cases, manufactured national sentiments. They had, largely in order to satisfy the designs of their own statecraft, subordinated feudal, ecclesiastical, communal, and numerous

---

[1] For an excellent study of the over-all problem, see Rupert Emerson, *From Empire to Nation: the rise to self-assertion of Asian and African peoples* (Cambridge, Mass., 1959).

other centres of control to the overriding needs of what came to be called a 'national design'.

Monarchs hardly conjured nations from nothing. As the power of the centralised state grew, it both fed upon and nurtured the parallel growth of linguistic and cultural unity. Monarchs conscripted, taxed, and educated their subjects. Such actions assisted the spread of an often already existing vernacular while encouraging a new appreciation of the national culture. And in writing in this way, I telescope the almost imperceptible changes that took decades to achieve and longer to notice. Nevertheless, by the middle of the eighteenth century, the nation was an accepted form: it referred generally to a definite territory that was inhabited by a people who possessed a distinctive common culture and language and who felt that they constituted a nation. The concept of nationality—that is, the state or quality of belonging to a nation—naturally followed and nationalism, if the word were used at all, continued to possess a very narrow connotation.

During the eighteenth century in Europe, populations increased, commercial and ideological intercourse intensified the relationships of hitherto isolated cities and provinces, means of communication and transport improved, and the institutional reponsibilities of the state correspondingly grew more complex and important. Individuals became less self-sufficient; they depended more and more upon the efforts of others, particularly of groups of fellow nationals, and on the nation itself as the embodiment of their effort. As they depended, so they developed loyalties. Nationality acquired greater status; governments conversely became, to a degree, of the people as well as by the king. 'The people' were generally propertied, and, especially in Western Europe, the bourgeoisie were the principal medium for the spread of nationalistic sentiments. They thought of themselves as nationals, although some still considered themselves equally Christians and, say, Burgundians.

But these events would have comparatively little meaning for our study of African nationalism if they had not been overtaken in Western Europe by a widespread consciousness among the literate, and sometimes among the masses, that the nation was a common enterprise that deserved to be run by all the nationals or their middle-class representatives. This flowed from the gradual erosion of parochial ties and the growth and acceptance of the idea (sceptics would call it the myth) of a national culture. Worship of the state became acceptable. Nationalism provided an ideology to which people (usually of the middle class) seeking an escape from the old oppressions of church or monarch, or even from foreign rule, could devote their efforts in the hope of obtaining liberty. It was the feeling of which revolutions were made.

Out of the passion of revolution and the blood of war, men espoused and spread the gospel of nationalism. This became the credo of an age when men throughout Europe and America sought to sunder the chains that deprived them of their freedom. Nationalism eclipsed previous political emotions; nationalists fought for the liberty of the oppressed everywhere. The new religion of nationhood easily gained converts. A new priesthood developed of the ambitious and the forward-looking. The fervour of the French and American revolutions stimulated others to seek the ecstasy of a nationalist religion. In this way the nation symbolised relief from oppression; the nation seemed to enshrine and to incorporate the idea of liberty. Yet the religion of nationalism had its component churches. In England, France, what became Germany, the United States, and Haiti, for example, the character and content of the devotion differed. Despite such variations, however, nationalism remained an answer to oppression, since a nation—which was far more than the sum of its individual citizens—by its very existence promised a better future to peoples possessing common cultural traits who lived within its by now well-defined borders. By extension, peoples everywhere deserved to enjoy the better future—the New Jerusalem. It is from such revolutionary roots that the notion of national self-determination stems.

The martial experience of the nineteenth century enriched the ethos of nationalism and gave birth to new nations at the same time as the older nation-states steadily made—of still somewhat disparate peoples—citizens who owed loyalties primarily to the national will. As Greeks, Germans, Italians, and others discovered their common cultural roots and rebelled and fought in order to recover their liberty, so Britons and Frenchmen (and Germans, Italians, and others) constructed the railways, roads, and canals that encouraged further unity. Telegraph and telephone lines followed. Common currencies were assumed; sometimes a customs union enhanced political attempts to achieve geographical or cultural unity. As men of ambition found their own elevation in the promotion of nationalism and national ends, so the pace of this natural process accelerated. By the end of the century, westerners assumed that nations and nationalism were the most complete embodiments of a natural human need. They could conceive of few other positive ways by which the lives of individuals might be organised.

Revolutionary nationalism diffused an ideology, and the actions of national governments unified relatively homogeneous peoples. On the basis of the European experience, states began to presuppose definite nationalities. Nationalism came to mean the consciousness on the part of individuals or groups of their membership of a nation and/or the desire to further the liberty or prosperity of a particular nation. And a 'nationalist', in the English language, generally wanted to further the interests of a particular established or submerged nation. (More narrowly, he wanted to see Ireland govern itself.)

Such definitions, abbreviated as they must be, suffice for much of Western Europe. But they blur our understanding of the older Latin American and more recent Middle Eastern and Asian revolutions, and, if we let ourselves become carried away by their seeming good sense, the definitions also obscure the meaning of the African experience. Pre-colonial tropical Africa had very few nations in the accepted sense, and even fewer that retained their national identity intact throughout the colonial interlude. The colonies themselves usually comprised two or more (often many more) tribal and political entities. In the ordinary sense of our definition, none of these colonies were nations. They were demonstrably not of one people. How then can we talk of the rise of African nationalism—as the self-assertion of African colonial peoples is usually described—and moreover intend that phrase to encompass a time span of four or five decades?

If we compare the African experience with that of one of the older non-European examples, many similarities are apparent. In India, Britain provided the first common, 'national', government. It defended the frontiers and gave the sub-continent its first common measure of internal security. The British Raj furthermore provided common communications, laws, and—although this is debatable—a common language. It unified India physically and, of perhaps greatest relevance, gave Indians common aspirations and a sense of a common destiny. (It is really unimportant, for our purposes, that colonial India became two independent nations; at least they both owe their existence as separate entities to the British experience). Britain created India of many kingdoms and principalities—we might call them proto-nations—in much the same way as, together with France, it destroyed the pan-Arabia that might have emerged from the Ottoman collapse and, in its place, substituted Iraq, Transjordan, etc.

By their very presence, the alien powers (and, conceptually, being alien is more important than western or European) made the indigenous 'nationals' more conscious than before that they were one people. They organised the states, propagated ideals that were of supposedly universal application, and, without necessarily meaning to, imposed the physical and ideological framework within which the ruled could strive against their rulers.

Without the partition and subsequent colonial rule of tropical Africa by the powers of Europe, there might have been no African nationalism. Were it not so often denied, there would be little point in stating the obvious—that the colonial powers alone created the bases of the present nations of independent Africa by arbitrarily dividing the continent into administrative entities and imposing thereupon imported legal, linguistic, and cultural concepts. This is not to say that the colonial powers completed the nation-building process; in most areas, the independent rulers must now strive to complete the unfinished national designs left to them by their previous rulers. But, in the sense of eighteenth- and nineteenth-century Europe, the colonial territories had become nations of intent; the process of unification indeed began with the conquest and continued with the 'detribalisation' of a territory like Malawi or the Congo (Léopoldville). Furthermore, for them the model of a nation existed as an absolute value.

During the colonial interlude, the populations resident within most of the various colonies admittedly possessed no common indigenous culture or language. But colonial domination gave them common experiences, a sense of common history, however brief, and, in the manner of India, a common language. They shared common grievances. They also lived within a single definite territory and, admittedly without enthusiasm, subjected themselves to the same laws and methods of administration. The Lozi of Zambia may have constituted a nation in some senses before the partition; afterwards they were in practice treated like any other member of the colonial community known as Northern Rhodesia. Although it is hard for students of European history to conceive it, the Lozi even began—in the manner of the Burgundian Christians who gradually came to think of themselves as above all French—to regard themselves as Northern Rhodesians and 'British protected persons' in addition to being Africans and Lozi from the district of, say, Senanga.[1] The Ganda during the colonial interlude may have envisaged a future apart from the greater Uganda; nearly everywhere else, however, I think Africans—or at least the Africans of influence who cared—sought to satisfy their aspirations within territorial boundaries. Because of the all-embracing nature of the colonial form of government, they very early accepted the idea that their fates were inextricably bound up with the new colonial nations into which they had been born. The sentiment of pan-Africanism is not new, but as the example of the National Congress of British West Africa shows, even feelings of regional unity have almost always been subordinate to 'nationalism'.

If we accept that, at some point during the colonial period, the alien-administered territories passed into the realm of partial nationhood without losing their dominated status, then the nature of African nationalism really holds no mysteries. In its passionate form, it stems in some senses directly from the French and American revolutionary experience, and draws even more upon the sentiments that were operative in, for example, Ireland and India. The role which was played in, say, Eastern European and Irish nationalism by a ruling caste with a national consciousness differing radically from that of its subjects was to some degree played in Africa—as is Asia—by men of a strikingly different colour, religion, and cultural background, who appeared in the garb of conquerors and masters, who

---

[1] Cf. Emerson, op. cit., pp. 110, 118, and 128.

destroyed traditional ways of life, and promised, or appeared to promise, to turn all Africans into black Europeans.[1]

Writing of Ireland, Shaw expressed the Irish sense of common grievance against the 'intolerable abomination' of English rule:

Like Democracy, national self-government is not for the good of the people: it is for the satisfaction of the people. One Antonine emperor, one St. Louis, one Richelieu, may be worth ten democracies in point of what is called good government; but there is no satisfaction for the people in them.[2]

These sentiments have often been unconsciously echoed by Africans. Much earlier, Loewe ben Bezalel, a sixteenth-century rabbi, articulated the axioms of self-determination, particularly if we read 'submerged group' for 'people' and 'creed' for 'God'. For him, it was clear 'that every people has a might of its own and ought not to be subject to any other people, that every people has its natural habitation and a right to live there, and it must be granted to every people to choose its own God according to its own ideas.'[3]

Africans, antagonised by the realities of colonial rule while educated in and aware of the ideals of the European national image, eventually asserted themselves with a patriotic fervour that made real the possibility of national self-determination.[4] But could they be patriots without a *patria*? Without a common culture, could they really achieve self-determination on a national basis? I submit that Africans not only could—they did. And the fact that the integrity of formerly colonial 'national' borders is everywhere so important is an indication that colonies in their latter stages were well on their way to becoming nations. Their inhabitants, led as in Europe by the ambitious, upwardly mobile, middle-class 'agitators', manned the proverbial barricades and dumped imaginary tea into the waters of disturbance. They manifested extreme anti-European attitudes, which were,

---

[1] E. H. Carr, in *Royal Institute of International Affairs Study Group Report on Nationalism* (London, 1939), p. 145.

[2] G. B. Shaw, 'Preface for Politicians', in *John Bull's Other Island* (New York, 1907), pp. xxxvi–xxxix.

[3] Quoted in Boyd C. Shafer, *Nationalism: myth and reality* (New York, 1955), p. 95.

[4] See Emerson, op. cit., pp. 19 and 27.

in the best tradition, anti-establishment. One could label their feelings racialism, xenophobia, anti-Europeanism, Africanism, or patriotism.[1] But none is satisfactory. Only by using 'nationalism' can we place the African revolution where it belongs—squarely in the mainstream of man's long struggle to enter the New Jerusalem of liberty and equality.

If we agree that the nationalism of Africans was similar in content to the earlier Asian and European nationalisms and, broadly speaking, that virtually from the time of their conquest the African colonies all were nations in embyro, then the nationalism of Africa need not be conceptually confined—as many wish—exclusively to the 'wind-of-change' era after World War II. We can demonstrate for most of the areas a series of stages that, certainly for me, constitute the gradual but nevertheless perceptible rise of different forms of national consciousness. We can discern the three stages that I call awakening, incipient action, and triumph.

I contend that, admittedly to a greater or lesser degree, nearly all of the ex-colonies of tropical Africa experienced a gradual growth in nationalist sentiment from the time of their annexation by aliens. Yet many would say that we should not confuse the gentle murmurs of early protest with the full-blown aggressive activities of the latter-day revolution. But the hesitant early manoeuvrings are just as much a part of the total process as the more obvious final phase; Africans possessed common grievances and shared the hope of common, libertarian aspirations. If we probe sufficiently deeply—as David Kimble has done for Ghana and James Coleman for Nigeria[2]—I think that almost everywhere in tropical Africa we can demonstrate a geometric continuity of African nationalism and isolate its different stages. With this generalisation in mind, let us discuss, for the sake of expository and analytical clarity, the illustrative example of Malawi.

By the time of the coming of the first European missionaries and settlers, the old area of Malawi had been disintegrated by

---

[1] Lord Hailey's 'Africanism' seems particularly lacking in descriptive utility. See his *An African Survey: Revised 1956* (London, 1957), pp. 251–2.

[2] David Kimble, *A Political History of Ghana: the rise of Gold Coast nationalism, 1850–1928* (Oxford, 1963); James S. Coleman, *Nigeria: background to nationalism* (Berkeley, 1960).

the efforts of African invaders from the south and Arab and African slave raiders from the east. When the Europeans thus conquered what they called Nyasaland, they found it a comparatively easy task. They met resistance, but of a piecemeal, tribal, rather than a concerted, national kind. British-armed and officered African soldiers ousted recalcitrant chiefs, pacified their peoples, and, over a period of about fifteen years, subordinated Nyasaland to British administrative and legal ideas. They taxed their subjects, encouraged Africans to make roads and missionaries to open schools and hospitals, and improved the existing methods of communications. They introduced new entrepreneurial and agricultural concepts, eventually constructed a railway and, in various ways, hastened the economic development of the Protectorate. Such initiatives—particularly the collection of taxes and the consequent need to speak English for the purposes of most wage-earning employment—brought together for the first time a disparate congeries of tribal peoples. Administrative regimentation hastened the process, and the spread of educational facilities, the employment of the peoples of the Protectorate in World War I, and the steady migration of labour from the rural to the urban and plantation areas of the Protectorate quickened it still faster. By about 1920 the Nyasa nation, an artificial creation like so many other African states, could be said to exist, however embryonically. The time spans might differ, but other colonies had similar experiences.

Already the tightening grip of the administrative noose, the introduction of 'modern' codes of behavioural expectation, the hard lot of the agricultural labouring class, the spread and intensification of a colour bar, and an obvious contempt for and an attempt to transform the traditional way of life, had turned reluctantly acquiescent subjects into discontented ones. There was what we might call a nationalist awakening in various parts of the Protectorate. The self-assertive message of the millenarian preacher Elliott Kenan Kamwana received a ready response from Africans. A few years later, after the Government of Nyasaland had decisively legislated chiefs—as a group—out of existence, members of the new middle class organised the first 'native association'. Both types of responses were subsequently to provide important outlets for the expression of nationalistic feeling. Both signified that Africans were not altogether content to remain the subjects of aliens. Both had national ends in mind, but neither their leadership nor their activities were, strictly speaking, national in scope.[1]

From the stage of awakening we move to the stage of incipient action. Usually, this corresponds to the period during which associations were especially active and millenarians found ready adherents. In Malawi, however, there was an intervening stage that shared many of the characteristics of both the stages of awakening and incipient action. John Chilembwe, an American-educated preacher, in 1914–15 launched a crusade in order to achieve for his fellow Nyasas the freedom that he thought they deserved. In concert with a number of chiefs and members of the emerging middle class, he viewed with dismay the way in which white employers treated their African plantation labour. He had his own difficulties with settlers and, despite his own independent financial position as the leader of the American-backed Providence Industrial Mission, Chilembwe must himself have shared the experience of racial discrimination with the mass of Africans. But what precipitated the overt expression of his dissatisfaction was the conscription of Nyasas during the opening weeks of World War I. He, like others, failed to see why Nyasas should participate in a war in which they had no stake, and from which—if Africans knew whites—Nyasas would receive little improvement in their own hard lot.

Chilembwe, at the behest of a number of other Nyasas, first adopted one of the standard means of protest—he drew up a petition in the form of an open letter to the national newspaper. In this famous letter, the admittedly westernised preacher aired national grievances and sought specifically national solutions. He wrote as a nationalist and already thought of Nyasaland as a nation and its inhabitants as fellow countrymen; but, significantly, he did not so regard the neighbouring British-protected persons of Northern Rhodesia, many of whom spoke the same language as his own people. He responded to the colonial situation in a nationalistic manner that Rabbi Bezalel, Shaw, and numerous Asians and Arabs would have applauded. In part, Chilembwe's letter read:

[1] For details and references concerning much of what follows, see Robert I. Rotberg, *The Rise of Nationalism in Central Africa: the making of Malawi and Zambia, 1873–1964* (Cambridge, Mass., 1965).

We understand that we have been invited to shed our innocent blood in this world's war which is now in progress throughout the wide world . . . . [But] will there be any good prospects for the natives after the end of the war? Shall we be recognised as anybody in the best interests of civilisation and Christianity after the great struggle is ended?

. . . we are imposed upon more than any other nationality under the sun. [We] . . . have been loyal since the commencement of this government. . . . At no time have we been ever known to betray any trust, national or otherwise, confided to us. . . . For our part we . . . have unreservedly stepped to the firing line in every conflict and played a patriot's part with the Spirit of true gallantry. But in time of peace everything [is] for Europeans only. . . . But in time of war it has been found that we are needed to share hardships and shed our blood in equality. It is even true that there is a spot of our blood in the cross of the Nyasaland Government.[1]

This letter was signed simply, 'John Chilembwe, on behalf of his countrymen'.

Because of the actions of the official censor, few of Chilembwe's countrymen saw the letter. Even if they had, it is hardly to be supposed that it would have evoked a national response. Predictably, the Government turned it aside, and Chilembwe and the members of his cabal decided to take more positive steps to air the grievances of their fellow countrymen. Early in 1915, without having made of their own conspiracy a national movement, they rose briefly and abortively against the Government of Nyasaland.[2] The African masses—never privy to the conspiracy—remained aloof. Afterwards, there was no overt upsurge of national feeling. The Government regarded the rebellion as an aberration. Its only immediate effect was to provide the administrators of the Protectorate with an excuse to regard every subsequent manifestation of discontent as the dangerous sedition of revolt. None the less, the Chilembwe rising marked an extreme example of the influence on Africans—on the middle classes if no other—of the sentiments that I have been calling nationalistic. Had the rising by some fluke succeeded—and we have already shown that the nationalist prerequisites of success

[1] Quoted, ibid., p. 82.

[2] Ibid., pp. 85–91. See also George Shepperson and Thomas Price, *Independent African: John Chilembwe and the Origins, Setting and Significance of the Nyasaland Native Rising of 1915* (Edinburgh, 1958), pp. 269–319.

were lacking—Chilembwe would simply, as later nationalists did, have taken over the existing governmental apparatus and adapted it to the needs of his fellow countrymen. We would probably not now question its nationalist character. Similarly, had the Thuku movement in Kenya somehow brought about the end of British rule in 1921, that too would unquestionably have found a place in the panorama of nationalism.[1] But both of these dramatic failures serve again to remind us that the rise of nationalism has had a long period of gestation.

During the years between the two world wars, politically-aroused Africans (at first only an articulate minority) almost everywhere occupied the stage of evolutionary nationalism that I have called incipient action. In a few areas, like the Gold Coast, Africans had long before begun to act politically in concert without embarking upon the third and final stage of their affair with colonialism. Elsewhere in Africa, civil servants and teachers formed associations for the first time, evangelists rebelled against European missionary supervision and established separatist sects, and millennially-minded preachers directed their quasi-political attacks against the colonial establishment.[2] Although collectively these themes—often overlooked in the literature of and about the period—may be regarded as but a modest prelude to the triumphant march of the 1940s and 1950s, they expressed the dominant sentiment of what I have called nationalism. Africans sought a redress of common grievances within a common territorial framework. Those who thus agitated—if that is the correct word—generally accepted the particular national structure of their aspirations and spoke and acted in terms of programmes of national action. Even though few were at this time demanding self-government or even equality of representation in their respective legislative assemblies, their efforts still justify the use of the collective term nationalism.

To return to Nyasaland, associational forms of endeavour were obscured by the more immediate events of World War I, the Chilembwe rising, and its aftermath. Immediately after the European armistice, however, civil servants, teachers,

[1] For the Thuku disturbance, see W. McGregor Ross, *Kenya From Within: A Short Political History* (London, 1927), pp. 225–35.
[2] Cf. Thomas Hodgkin, *Nationalism in Colonial Africa* (London, 1956), p. 114.

evangelists, and small businessmen, with some chiefs and head-men, continued the old, and organised a number of new, native associations. These groups met to talk political reform and they may, in an African context, be considered proto-parties. The associations provided convenient platforms for the airing and discussion of grievances, the training of leaders, and experimen-tation with different techniques of protest. Since the Government controlled all the usual methods of communication, and could and did prescribe within certain narrow limits the forms of overt protest that it considered legitimate, the associations attempted to accomplish their aims by petitioning the Governor, the Sec-retary of State for the Colonies, and the reigning British King, by passing innumerable resolutions in the hope that the Govern-ment would take notice, and by seeking interviews with the Governor or other administrative officials in person. But little was accomplished by such means, the Government often ignor-ing the very existence of the associations.

Along with separatist sects and millennial movements, rural and urban associations existed in almost every part of Nyasa-land. Some operated continually, some intermittently, others occasionally. The most important were the district and provin-cial associations that were composed of the indigenous leaders of the Protectorate. Certain members belonged at the same time to two or more associations, others belonged to several in turn. The membership of the various associations overlapped with that of the separatist sects and millennial movements; in certain cases the leaders were identical. I doubt if any of these associations could ever have counted members or adherents in as many as four figures. But no matter how parochial and ineffectual the associations appeared, their thoughts and their actions expressed more than tribal or individual interests. They talked in terms of the Nyasa nation (few then spoke of Malawi) and accepted the integrity of its colonially-derived borders.

To name only a few of the more prominent association lead-ers, Charles Chinula, George Mwase, Levi Mumba, James Sangala, and Isa Macdonald Lawrence, much as they desired governmental reforms, all expressed a loyalty to the abstract nation of Nyasaland that had much in common with the feelings of nationality accepted by the middle class in, say, eighteenth-century France. Both, when the time came to feel and express their nationalism, followed the lead of the more advanced bourgeoisie. It was distinctly in the interests of the nascent bourgeoisie to keep alive and promote the cause of nationalism; and, in Nyasaland, several among their number finally realised that they could never hope to redress grievances of national concern if the voice of African protest were to continue to be expressed by many scattered sounds rather than by one united chorus that could claim and, in time, achieve a national following.

Out of this sense of the national need emerged the Nyasaland African Congress, an organisation of associations and individuals that held its inaugural meeting in 1944. Sangala, its founder, professed national aims. The speeches and resolutions of the first few meetings reflected similar ends. 'In the past grievances and other vital matters affecting the country and people have been presented to the government and/or other authorities by local organisations who were interested only in their local worries. It is considered', the Congress decided, 'that the time is ripe now for the Africans in this country to strive for unity so as to obtain the greater development of the peoples and country of Nyasaland.'[1] But, in terms of methods and accomplishments, the Congress retained an aura reminiscent of its predecessor associations. Only the attempt by white settlers to gain an overwhelming control of the destinies of the indigenous inhabitants of Central Africa, by federating Nyasaland and the two Rhodesias, provided an issue that could arouse the most apathetic tribesman and give the Congress' national aspirations the mass appeal of a full-fledged movement of nationalism.

Without taking space here to discuss the unsuccessful campaign against the Federation and the political strategies of the time, suffice it to say that Nyasaland entered the stage of triumphant nationalism when chiefs and members of the Congress together devoted all their energies to destroying the edifice of Federation. At first, under leaders who had gained their experience during the politically-tentative days before World War II, the Congress proved unable to take advantage of the growing anti-government sentiment in the countryside. But, from about 1955, under a group of impressively tough-minded young men and, after 1958, under the over-all direction of Dr H. Kamazu Banda, the Congress opened branches and gained paid-up

[1] Rotberg, op. cit., p. 183.

adherents everywhere. They manoeuvred themselves by the end of 1958 into a sufficiently strong position to challenge the Governments of Nyasaland and the Federation openly, to defy their laws, and to precipitate a state of unrest that became a state of emergency and resulted in their own imprisonment. Nationalism in its most obvious form had achieved results of a kind that led, a few years later, to the achievement of self-government and, finally, to the independence of Malawi.

To generalise, with adjustments to the outline that I have sketched for Malawi, most of tropical Africa has exhibited this threefold time scale of nationalism.[1] Kenya, Zambia, Ghana, Nigeria, Senegal, Togo, the Congo (Brazzaville), and Gabon appear to confirm the paradigm. Depending upon how the terms are defined, Uganda and the Sudan fit. Tanzania, with a certain allowance for time lag, also meets the criteria that I have sketched. The Congo (Léopoldville) provides an example of extreme telescoping, and many other nations seem to fall in between. But we know comparatively little about tropical Africa in the years between the two world wars. A close examination of those years would, I think, substantiate my contention that the rise of African nationalism is no recent phenomenon, that in most parts of tropical Africa it possesses roots that reach deep into the oldest colonial soil, and that we can conveniently divide the tree of nationalism into the three branches of awakening, incipient action, and triumph.

I would be the last to say that the mere achievement of independence by a territory concludes the working of the ethos of nationalism within it. For only a few parts of independent Africa can we say that the process of nation-building has been completed. Almost everywhere, the new rulers, inheriting the problems that colonial administrations were either unwilling or not equipped to face, are involved in a difficult struggle to finish the process of unification that began almost at the beginning of the colonial era. Despite the overwhelming support given to the nationalist movement by Africans of all classes during the final phases of the struggle and the fervour that the movement aroused in the hearts of its supporters—who thus became the

[1] Crawford Young, in *Politics in the Congo: decolonization and independence* (Princeton, 1965), pp. 281–98, proposes a fivefold schema that unnecessarily includes overlapping categories.

relevant nationals—the present-day rulers have inherited only unconsolidated nations; as in early America, so in Africa there remain fissiparous social, economic, and psychological forces that must be overcome before we can say that the colonial nations have survived the shocks of independence.

To summarise, I see African nationalism in historical terms. For me, it has qualities reminiscent of the older nationalisms of Europe, Arabia, and Asia; despite the number of putative peoples and distinctive languages that exist within each territorial boundary, I maintain that the policies and practices of the colonial powers created national entities of their arbitrarily-contrived and assigned territories, and that the indigenous inhabitants not only came to accept their status as nationals, but that they began to think almost exclusively in terms of achieving their freedom from alien rule within the perimeters of their colonial existence. Within almost every territory the nationalist spirit found ready vessels. Its success owes much to the techniques and experiences of the older nationalisms; as hot wars loosened the grip of colonial control in Latin America, Eastern Europe, the Middle East, and Asia, so the cold war assisted the progress and made possible the success of the nationalist movements of tropical Africa.

44. Party politics and traditional structure: single-party rule

PHILIPE DECREANE *Table des Partis Politiques de l'Afrique* Centre d'Etude des Relations Extérieures, Paris May 1963; pages 21–6, 27–34 (In translation)

African political parties are short of trained officials, and so, pending the emergence of new *élites*, very often lean on the traditional chiefs: hereditary monarchs like Mogho Naba or Yatenga Naba in Upper Volta, elected sovereigns like the Obas of Yoruba country or the Akans chiefs of Ghana, canton chiefs in ex-French East Africa. When, in September 1962 at Korhogo, Gbong Couibaly the paramount chief of the Senufos died, the

President of the Ivory Republic recalled how precious the support of this provincial chief had been for the creating of national unity, first within the syndicate of African planters, and then within the democratic party of the Ivory Coast.

On the other hand it is sometimes the chiefs themselves who make use of the political parties: such is the case with the Northern People's Congress in North Nigeria within which the Sardauna of Sokoto and the Muslim emirs until recently occupied all the posts of responsibility.

An exceptional and no doubt extreme case is that of the Somali Republic where the old tribal clans seem to have been elevated into parties. Pan-Somali nationalism in general has been not so much an abandonment of clan interests in favour of a sort of super-nationalism, as a real adaptation of these interests to a new situation.

The problem of the relationship between the chiefs and the political parties is quite different in English-speaking Africa, where a system of indirect administration is the rule, and in French-speaking Africa. In the latter the chiefs have either been eliminated more quickly—in Guinea or Mali, for example—or else been better integrated into modern political life—in Upper Volta and Chad especially. None the less the chiefs have often resisted the new political institutions. In these cases this structure can be an element of balkanisation or a source of more or less permanent conflict with the modern political parties.

In certain territories syndicates of chiefs have set themselves up in competition with the parties proper. In 1958 in Chad, for example, the Group of Rural and Peasant Independents (G.I.R.P.), which comprised the majority of the hereditary chiefs of Chad, considered elevating itself into a syndicate with an affiliation to the French Trade Union *Force Ouvrière*. And it was the traditional chiefs who, by withdrawing their support from the Chad Progressive Party, and by abruptly leaving the government coalition, brought about, in December 1958, the overthrow of M. Gabriel Lisette. They were partly responsible, too, for the series of ministerial crises which followed the brief premiership of M. Gontchomé Sahoulba, himself paramount chief of the Mundang—a series which only ended when M. Tombalbaye became President of the Republic.

In Ghana a trial of strength has been taking place since 1957 between the traditional Ashanti authority and the Accra government. A few tribes are still more or less openly preaching secession, and it was with only numerous reservations that the Ashanti chiefs accepted the integration of the territories they controlled into the unitary state of Ghana. The Ghanaian Constitution had to make some concession to this political force: hence its express provision for the maintenance of a House of Chiefs in each of the six regions which make up the territory of the Republic. The retention of such Houses has been called a purely formal gesture, however, and this may well be the case.

The Katanga Constitution, on the other hand, expressly provides that 15 per cent of their National Assembly shall be constituted by 'members co-opted by the elected representatives and chosen from among the hereditary chiefs and notables'. There has even been set up alongside the Assembly a Grand Council of twenty members elected by the hereditary chiefs from among their number. This Council can give a preliminary hearing to the principal bills even including those dealing with such questions as the granting of mining concessions. If the Grand Council opposes a bill the Assembly must vote it at a joint session of the two Houses by a qualified majority of two-thirds of those present—the quorum being half the members of each House.

In Cameroon M. Ahidjo, the President of the Republic, established himself in power with the support of the great Islamised chieftains in the north of the country. But he then drew away from these first allies and it was because of subsequent rivalries between the chieftains that the revolutionary movement, the Union of the Populations of Cameroon, was able to gain a brief foothold in Bamileke country.

In Upper Volta in January 1962 M. Maurice Yameogo, the President of the Republic, issued very firm decrees forbidding henceforth 'all signs and exterior manifestations of the old hereditary hierarchies'. Thus the wearing of loin cloths or of hair styles denoting the rank of slave or chief was forbidden. Also forbidden were 'all types of subordination incompatible with the principles of the equality and dignity of all citizens'. The target in the first part of this text was the Moagha (the singular of Mossis) institution of the Sorones. Up till then, in fact, the hereditary chiefs of the Mossis had kept pages at their court

E1TCA

called Sorones who wore feminine garments and rings on their feet and arms and whose hair was plaited. The second part of the decree was aimed at another Moagha custom whereby a servant had to follow the high dignitaries of Moro and Yatenga, whenever they went out on horseback in public, to hold the tail of the animal—no matter how fast it went.

The aim of the President was to stress firmly that the only ally he would recognise in governing the country was the Volta Democratic Union, and that only party dignitaries and members of the government could benefit from the rules of protocol. Thus the decree of December 1961 concerning the order of organised bodies and authorities in public ceremonies placed the members of the political bureau of the party immediately after members of the National Assembly, even before the members of the Supreme Court and of the Economic and Social Council, while the secretary-general of the sub-section U.D.V.–R.D.A. took precedence over the military authorities. All these measures were the more necessary as there was in fact a time when Mogho Naba of Ugadugu tried to exercise influence on Volta affairs, leading the Volta government to reverse the decision they had taken in January 1959 to join the Federation of Mali. The fear of legal action or administrative sanctions in the affair of the Sorones was enough, even before the decree was adopted, forty-eight hours before the anniversary celebrations of the granting of independence, to make Mogho Naba remove his Sorones' bracelets.

A characteristic example of the refusal of certain traditional authorities to adapt to the modern forms of political life can be found in the King of Swani who was reprieved in December 1961 by the Ivory Coast Government and on his own request re-admitted into the 'national community'. King H. M. Amon Ndoffu III, the sovereign of a kingdom of 8,000 square kilometres, with a population of 45,000, had refused in the summer of 1959 to recognise the government of Abidjan, and claimed the right to establish direct relations with Paris by virtue of treaties drawn up during the Ancien Régime. This led to a political trial in Abidjan, and now to an amnesty, and the final result will no doubt eventually be the King's joining the government party.

It was to protect the Democratic Party of Guinea from such

open challenges that M. Sékou Touré, even before Guinea gained independence, took strong preventive measures. He abolished the chiefdoms, rendering powerless in particular the Peul Almamys of Fouta-Djallon, who seemed to him to be a main centre of resistance to the building up of the party.

In the same way, as early as 1959, the governments of Senegal and Sudan carried through important administrative reforms which led to the replacement of most of the chiefs of cantons.

The chiefs continue to have importance where they have become effective intermediaries between the leaders and the masses. Barthélémy Boganda until his death incarnated the Movement for the Social Evolution of Black Africa (M.E.S.A.N.); M. Houphouët-Boigny incarnates today the Democratic Party of the Ivory Coast (P.D.C.I.); in a lesser measure M. Kenyatta once incarnated the Kenya African Union (K.A.U.). All of these draw—or drew—a part of their authority from traditional structures. The old allegiance to the clan and its chief has been partly replaced by loyalty to the party and its leader. To become a leader in Black Africa a politician must in part be considered as sacrosanct—even if he has to be himself the artisan of this process, as happened with Dr Nkrumah in Ghana. In fact what the official Ghanaian press calls 'Nkrumahism'[1] is an extreme case of this personality cult and firmly establishes the semi-divinification of the head of state.

The notion of the sacred comes in again in the way some parties adapt themselves to the African cultural context. Doctrinal debates are held sometimes in traditional palavers and ritual is given a place in political activities. Dr Nkrumah, for example, made his dawn broadcast of 8 April 1961 on Radio Accra at five o'clock in the morning in order, as he said, 'to return to the great traditions of our ancestors' who took their important decisions at dawn. In the same spirit one should read the description by Richard Wright in his book *Black Power* of a meeting of the women's section of the Convention People's Party in a district in Accra. Wright notes a number of resemblances between this political meeting and a church service. The atmosphere is religious, and the fact that libations of maize

---

[1] The same phenomenon is found in other parts of the world. In Haiti, for example, where M. François Duvalier, the President of the Republic, himself refers to 'duvaliérisme' or 'personalism'.

wine in honour of the ancestors are drunk side by side with
hymns sung to Dr Nkrumah suggests that two cults are being
celebrated.

One should note also that some secret societies have lent support to the parties, as the Mau-Mau supported the Kenya
African Union. The age classes are among these, as are typically
African cultural associations like the Egbe Omo Ododuwa, the
association of the descendants of Ododuwa, the mythical ancestor of the Yoruba, which played a part in founding the Action
Group in Nigeria. Other examples are to be found among
societies of initiates—like the Komo of the Bambaras of Sudan—
and sects, such as the Mbouiti of the Mitzogos and Fangs of
Gabon, the Kibanguisme of the ex-Belgian Congo, and Matswan-
ism and lassysm in the ex-French Middle Congo. There are,
too, certain traditional groups which do not fit easily into the
normal classification of political science. Most of them have
been if not 'resuscitated' at least reactivated, like the Fokon
'olona of Merina country in Madagascar, but some have been
created from the ground and in recent political developments
have had decided influence on the life of the parties. Thus, in
Cameroon, in an attempt to counteract the dynamism of the
hereditary chiefs of the north—the lamimbes or paramount
chiefs, the louanes or canton chiefs—the peoples in the south of
the country have institutions which are to all intents a halfway
mark between the assembly, or traditional type of association,
and the modern political party: the Ngondo of the Douala, the
Kumze and Manjong of the Bamileke, the Kolo-Beti of the Beti,
the traditional assembly of the Bamun people. It should be
noted that some sects, after having played a great part in the
rise of a party, have then opposed that same party; an example
of this was the Matswanist sect which was used by M. Fulbert
Youlou, the President of the Republic of Congo-Brazzaville,
during the years 1955 to 1957, but which he then tried to dis-
band by force in 1959.

There are also leaders, of course, whose influence is wide precisely because they do not belong to a dominant tribe—Dr
Nkrumah in Ghana or Mr Tom Mboya in Kenya for example—
or because on the contrary they belong to the dynamic tribe but
try to govern in the interests of all.

The changes taking place in the conception of the chief explains to some extent the general evolution of the states of Black Africa towards a presidential system. One should not simplify the situation too much, however, for political, social and economic conditions vary considerably from one country to another, and so does the form of power.

But it is certain that, in spite of the charismatic nature of power in Africa, in spite of everything that can distinguish it from monarchial power as it existed for centuries in Europe, it is none the less personalised. Only a leader whose authority is sovereign can mobilise the masses and gather round him the support of public opinion. Although this leader has the title of president, he exercises in fact complete and total power, even if he does not hold all the attributes of it. All those surrounding him, ministers, members of parliament, civil servants, only partake of this power and receive their authority from him.

The authority of this political leader is sometimes in strict conformity with the ancestral tradition. At any rate the leader can only be established as a leader when he is accepted in this rank by his subjects. One important consequence of this in many cases is that he must come from the region over which he rules. This means that his area of influence is necessarily restricted, and it is beyond doubt that, however well known certain chiefs of state may be, their authority—in the strict sense of the term— does not go beyond the territorial or even tribal frontiers of their country. This phenomenon can be a complication in the achievement of pan-African aspirations both in the West and in the East of the Continent. . . .

The Single Party and Personal Power

There is a conflict between the character of political power in contemporary Africa and the idea of an opposition, such as this is known in Western parliamentary democracies. This is the origin of the one-party system. Opponents have to be disposed of one way or another, either by integrating them into the single party or by eliminating them. In most cases, in point of fact, they do join the party, without this being felt to be a betrayal of their principles, as it would in Europe.

Indeed, in so far as power belongs to the person exercising it, there must be unanimity round the person of the chief. As in most traditional societies the leader of the people is the holder of the 'regalia' or royal attributes. Thus in Rwanda the sign of the power of the Mwami is the Kalinga, the drum to which are attached the vital parts of killed enemies. Consequently M. Gitera, the leader of the Association for the Social Advancement of the Masses (A.P.R.O.S.O.M.A.), made the destruction of the sacred drum the first plank in his party's programme.

In African societies in transition there is usually a certain evolution in the attitude of the leader towards the various social groups. Before independence he tries, often without success, to gain the co-operation of all of them. The gaining of independence usually leads to a certain 'sacred union'. But, as the country moves into the post-colonial period, pressure groups emerge, provoking a more or less violent response on the part of the government.

Before independence the authoritarianism of the party is, in any case, tempered by the fact that it does not have the means to exercise control over all the social groups and pressure groups. Moreover both leaders and militants are engaged in the struggle against the colonial power. After independence the withdrawal of the colonial administration makes it necessary to find new targets for criticism. It is then that the party censors attack some social group or other. At Conakry for example, in December 1961, the Democratic Party of Guinea—never in any case particularly indulgent towards certain student elements—took the intellectuals as their target, preaching the need to transcend the division between people and intellectuals, and stressing that the degree of commitment to the party was much more important than the possession of a diploma.

It is a too hasty generalisation to think that the single party leads naturally to personal power. This is an error because the strength of the Democratic Party of Guinea, that of the Sudanese Union, or even of the Convention People's Party, has been due less to Sékou Touré, Modibo Keita or Kwame Nkrumah than to the political bureaux of these respective parties. The elected leader is, in fact, the representative of the whole people at the national level. Sometimes, as the spokesmen for a political doctrine and the guardian of that doctrine, he has to carry through the programme of the party. He safeguards cohesion and unity, and the validity of communal decisions. He has to be the servant of the party at all times. Thus Dr Nkrumah refused the life presidency of the Ghanaian Republic in October 1962, but even before that he had powers which appeared more autocratic in the official text than they actually were in daily political life. In spite of the outward appearances of 'Nkrumahism' and of public demonstrations of homage to the 'Osagyefo', the executive commission of the party for long played an important part in the elaboration of C.P.P. policies. The veritable deification of Dr Nkrumah, attacked in August 1961 by Dr Richard Rosavere, the Anglican bishop of Accra, did not prevent the secretary-general from being subordinated, to some extent, to the collegial structure of the party. Reconciling the different tendencies within the C.P.P. Dr Nkrumah for long behaved as a high-level arbitrator rather than as a real dictator. This became less true after the arrest, in August 1962, of Mr Tafia Adamafio, the Ghanaian Minister for Information and the power behind the left-wing of the C.P.P., and that of Mr Ako Adjei, the Minister for Foreign Affairs, the principal leader of the right-wing of the C.P.P. But perhaps it was precisely when he felt his position as an arbitrator becoming insecure that the president of the Ghanaian Republic decided to strike the factions at their head.

From the multi-party system or common front made imperative by conditions of colonial dependency—the F.R.A.I.N. of Portuguese overseas provinces, for example—it is an established fact that there is a more or less rapid evolution to a one-party system. The transition can take various forms: the fusion or integration of the parties opposed to the government party; the dissolution or outlawing of some, or all opposition parties; the arrest and trial of leading politicians on various charges, among them anti-national plot; or individual politicians can spontaneously join the ruling party.

Dahomey which was for long quoted as the very type of a well-balanced tri-party state went over, in November 1960, not without difficulty, to the single-party system, with the fusion of the various existing parties into the Dahomey Party of Unity (P.D.U.). And when the round table of Mauritian parties met in Nouakchott, in December 1961, all the old political groups in Mauritius united under the single label of Hisb Chaeb—the Party of the People.

In January 1962 M. François Tombalbaye, the President of the Chad Republic, nine months after having created a single party under the name of Union for the Progress of Chad (U.P.T.), outlawed all parties other than the government Chad Progressive Party (P.P.T.). In August M. Toura Gaba, the Chad Minister of Public Works, was arrested for plotting against the Head of State, then he was removed from his post as Mayor of Fort-Lamy, just as his two predecessors, M. Gabriel Lisette and M. Jean Baptiste, had been.

The example of Chad is not the only one. In recent months, in Western and Central Africa, there have been many accusations of undermining or plotting against the security of the state brought against politicians who did not see eye to eye with their governments.[1] In December 1960 M. Abel Goumba, the ex-Vice President of Ubangui-Chari, and leader of the Movement for the Democratic Evolution of Central Africa (M.E.D.A.C.), was arrested in Bangui, on the charge of conspiring with agents of foreign powers, and placed under house arrest. In May 1961 M. Justin Ahomadegbé, ex-President of the Dahomey Assembly, and Leader of the Dahomey Democratic Union, was arrested at Cotonou and appeared several weeks later before the high court at Porto-Novo. In October 1961 Dr Kwame Nkrumah had arrested under the Preventive Detention Act Mr Joe Appiah, the son-in-law of the late Sir Stafford Cripps, and several dozen personalities belonging to the United Party. In November 1961 the 'teachers' plot' was uncovered at Conakry, and this led to the elimination of those members of the Democratic Party of Guinea who were thought to be out of sympathy with the line of the national political bureau—Messrs Ray Autra and Keita Koumendian especially. In December the government of Lomé had Messrs Anani Santos and Firmin Apa-Abalo, the leaders of the Juvento, arrested. In February 1962 M. Doudou Gueye, the ex-leader of the Senegal Progressive

[1] In September 1962 the Tanganyika Parliament passed a law giving the government the necessary powers to arrest and detain without trial any person suspected of acting against the security of the state. On this occasion, despite his reputation for moderation, Mr Julius Nyerere, the leader of the government, and since then the President of the Republic, declared: 'I know that this law will be criticised abroad, but if we neglect our security we will make ourselves look foolish . . . I would rather be criticised now than laughed at later.'

Union, who had sought political asylum, in August 1960, at Bamako, was sentenced, in his absence, at a trial in Dakar. In April 1962 M. Fulbert Youlou had arrested, on a charge of plotting against the security of the state, M. Jacques Opangault, the ex-Vice President of the Middle Congo, and ex-Vice President of Congo-Brazzaville. . . . In July 1962 four leaders of the Cameroon opposition—Messrs Andre Marie Mbida, the former leader of the Cameroon government, Théodore Mayi Matip, Charles Okala and Bebey Eyidi—were sentenced to thirty months—then on appeal to two years—on a charge of 'Subversion and provoking hatred against the government'. In the course of the same month, after demonstrations had broken out, a few weeks earlier, at Bamako, protesting against the creation of a Mali national currency, M. Modibo Keita and his associates arrested two former secretaries of state of the French government: Messrs Fily Dabo Sissoko and Hammadoun Dicko; the two men were sentenced to death by a special tribunal in September, but had their sentence commuted to hard labour for life in October. Still in the same month, Nigeria—often quoted as one of the independent countries of Africa where the plurality of parties was most strongly entrenched—went through a crisis when the Federal Government decided to strike at the opposition party, Action Group, in its very electoral stronghold, the Western Region. And in October the Leopoldville government, often accused of being too indulgent towards party intrigues, decided to arrest M. Christophe Gbenye, the leader of the opposition.

Three successive conferences held at Antsirabé and Tananarive failed in the attempt to create a unified front of the Malgache parties. However, many individuals joined the Malgache Social Democrat Party, on their own account, and it now controls 99 out of the 107 seats in the Malgache National Assembly, and most of the 30 political formations which existed as late as 1960 have disappeared.

As for Ghana, whether due to a desire to keep up appearances or through some whim of the Osagyefo, a single party was set up in that country via a vote in parliament, in September 1962. All those who spoke in favour of the motion declared that the multi-party system inevitably gave rise to differences of opinion which ran counter to Ghanaian traditions. Despite what certain jurists may say, it does not seem that a revision of the Constitution will be necessary for this motion to be put into effect.

The distinctions drawn in African capitals between 'single party', 'unified party' or 'unified front of the parties', are a matter of dialectical subtlety. Thus at a political seminar in Abidjan, in 1962, the chairman of the first commission, 'political institutions and forces', made the remark that 'the Democratic Party of the Ivory Coast is not properly speaking a single party, but rather a party on its own'.

But it is the spirit which is the important thing here, not the letter. Before setting up a one-party system in the Central African Republic, in October 1962, M. David Dacko, the Head of State, and President of the Movement for the Social Evolution of Black Africa, gave warning of his move several weeks in advance, and explained the reasons for it. When he opened the second national conference of the M.E.S.A.N. at Bambari, in July 1962, he was heard to say: 'We will act as Senghor, Houphouët-Boigny, Ould Daddah, and Modibo Keita have acted in their respective countries and require the minority parties to join the ranks of the national majority party . . . I will recognise in the Central African Republic only one political movement: the M.E.S.A.N.' M. Michel Adama Tamboux, the President of the Central African National Assembly, explained this attitude further, in October 1962, when he said: 'The multi-party system as it exists is established democratic societies is a costly luxury which we cannot afford. . . . The political parties which want to remain in existence are mere picturesque survivals of a revolutionary past. True democracy for us is social democracy, which is expressed not in the quarrels of parties but in the concord of people.'

Thus it does seem, as M. Alfred Sauvy pointed out, that 'under-development is incompatible with Western democracy. Without a minimum of education the people can not be sovereign nor have a share in sovereignty'.

Indeed it has to be noted that in the political systems of the new independent states of Africa government by coalition is quite exceptional. In his *Autobiography* Dr Kwame Nkrumah expresses the opinion which is in fact shared by most leaders of contemporary Africa.

I must explain that, in a democratic society, if a political party is in the minority it ought to form itself into an opposition. If, on the contrary, the party is in the majority it is its prerogative to form the government, and for our part we would admit of no compromise on this point. A coalition government with the other political groups of the country, such as we know them, would be dangerous.

The multi-party system is thus either a short-term phenomenon, as it was in most African states after their independence, or an exception, as it was in the case of Senegal, or finally a pretence. Nigeria might be quoted to prove that it is a pretence, in so far as the multi-party system only works at the federal level in the Lagos Parliament, but disappears at the level of the local Parliaments in the three federated regions.

When he announced his intention of creating a single party in Congo-Brazzaville in July 1962, M. Fulbert Youlou, the President of the Republic, explained his decision in these terms:

The proliferation and spread of political parties works against a healthy democracy, which does not lie essentially in a mass of conflicting opinions, but in the possibility for each people to satisfy its most noble national ambitions while respecting the equality of all citizens, without distinction of birth, race or religion. It is all too certain that, in a state which is still building up its structures, the numerous associations which flourish in our cities can only work against the policies of national cohesion and national union which we have been pursuing so patiently.

But the clearest justification of the one-party system was no doubt given by M. Ernest Boka, the President of the High Court of the Ivory Coast, in his speech on "Education for Democracy" at the political seminar held in Abidjan. M. Boka said:

. . . we believe that the multi-party system can be identified with democracy only at a certain stage in human evolution—at the time when an industrial society begins to develop. In such a situation the parties express the divergent interests of the various social strata.

In states that have just gained independence these various factors are not present. There is not the same multiplicity of social classes as in the old countries. There are no historical memories creating barriers between certain groups of individuals. The whole future and development of these countries implies certain policies which their leaders must inevitably follow. All citizens share the same ideology, the same love for their newly acquired independence, the same desire for an improvement in the standard of living. They take part in the same struggle against ignorance, disease and poverty.

In countries where immense efforts have to be made in education and economic progress, and where there are no fundamental differences in outlook, there is no place for byzantine discussions on points of detail.

The opinion expressed by M. Boka is shared by most of the leaders of Black Africa. It is, at any rate, the official line of the leaders of the P.D.C.I. M. Samuel Kouamé, the secretary-general of the National Assembly of the Ivory Coast, put it in these terms:

... having a single party gives a special tone to elections and parliamentary work. The relationship between parliament and government, and between the members of parliament themselves, are not overshadowed by ideological rivalries which result from a multiplicity of parties and policies, and are all too often heedless of the real interests of the country.

The multi-party system is not the only short-lived phenomenon in contemporary political life in Africa. Inter-racial co-operation is another example. Nationalist leaders praise it when circumstances make it expedient to do so, especially during the gaining of independence. Thus Mr Jomo Kenyatta, even in 1960 and 1961, frequently evoked the rights of the 65,000 European settlers in Kenya. The case of the Ivory Coast, where the European minority takes an active part in local political life, continues to have seats in the various assemblies, and votes in large numbers, seems to be the exception which confirms the rule. It is to be noted, moreover, that the governments of French-speaking African Republics no longer have any non-African ministers except in very special cases. In 1957 there were 26 ministers of European extraction in African governments and in 1958 there were still 11. At the present time only two European ministers continue to bear office, in two states; M. Peytavin, the Minister of Public Works in the Republic of Senegal, comes from metropolitan France and M. Raphaël Saller, Minister of Finance in the Republic of Ivory Coast, is from the French West Indies.

The idea of inter-racial co-operation is given up in most cases even before gaining independence. Thus the British plan for a Federation of Capricorn never saw the light, and in Nyasaland and the Rhodesias both Africans and Europeans have already renounced all forms of co-operation. The South African Republic is a specific case which requires no further comment. In the territories of Central and East Africa, where the tension is particularly high between the various social groups, it is most common to find parties recruiting their members from the European population alone. Thus in Southern Rhodesia the Confederate Party of Mr Stanley Gurland proclaimed its faith in "the perpetual supremacy of the white race"; while the Dominion Party of Mr W. H. Harper advocated the creation of an independent white state after the secession of the territory from the rest of the Central African Federation. In Kenya, the Kenya coalition of Sir Ferdinand Cavendish-Bentick demanded the retention of the White Highlands—the upland region which is reserved for white settlers and includes some of the best land in Kenya—while the United Party of the late Group-Captain Briggs openly preached absolute segregation.

It is not impossible that the persistence of non-African influences has sometimes aggravated inter-racial tension. The clearest illustration is provided by the C.O.N.A.K.A.T. in Katanga, in part the heir of the ex-Katanga Union, within which certain Belgian influences had a preponderant place. And one wonders about the exact extent of the part played by the Portuguese authorities within parties like the Movement for the Defence of Angola Interests (M.I.D.A.).

The influence of Catholic missions must not be underestimated but it has to be approached with caution. In fact the changes which the Vatican made in its policies in Africa quite some time ago make it impossible to speak of it, in the strict sense, as a foreign influence. Also through its ecumenical vocation the Catholic church helps to remove tension between the races. For some extremist commentators, however, its influence is in no way different from that of the old colonial powers, and it has to be recognised that Catholic missions have played a direct part in certain African parties: for example, the Uganda Democratic Party (U.D.P.) of Mr Benedicto Kiwanuka, the Christian Social Democratic Party (C.S.D.P.) of Mr Chester Katsonga in Nyasaland, the Christian Democratic Party (P.D.C.) of M. Joseph Birola in Burundi. Again, the rivalry between missions may have had certain repercussions on the development of the parties, at least in the early days of African political awareness. This was the case in Madagascar, where the Jesuits of the province of Tananarive and the Protestant ministers tried to outbid each other in political influence, and so marked the direction taken by the Malgache nationalist movement.

There is constant evolution also in the field of methods, means and doctrine. The parties start to alternate violence and non-violence; instead of being simply anti-colonialist, themes and slogans concentrate on national reconstruction; once the armed struggle is over a doctrine of government begins to emerge.

Translated by Dr Keith Cameron

45. External factors in the development of African nationalism

GEORGE SHEPPERSON *Historians in Tropical Africa* University College, Salisbury, Rhodesia 1960; pages 317–20

At a time when nationalism is marching across Africa with giant strides, the relevance of the concept to African conditions has been questioned and various substitutes, such as "Africanism", "African consciousness", "tribalism" and "racialism", have been suggested. Those, however, who are critical of the term "nationalism" in the new Africa, are often unaware that it has frequently been called misleading in a European context as well, and has had to be assisted in this by a battery of supplementary adjectives. Miss Hannah Arendt, for example, who finds "racialism" as pronounced a characteristic of the European political scene as the critics of the term nationalism proclaim it to be in Africa, is compelled to invent for her study of European history the expression "tribal nationalism".

Indeed, that Africa is obliged to express its most pressing political problem in these vague European terms indicates the importance of external factors in the growth of African "nationalism". In one sense, of course, all nationalism is the product of a reaction against external forces. But in Africa, whose partition and introduction to the apparatus of the modern State came at

a time when Europe was throwing up chaotically those processes for which the terms "nationalism", "imperialism",
"racialism" and "socialism" are inadequate but necessary
labels, external factors have a peculiar force. It would be possible, certainly, to group them all in one great bracket of extern-
ality: the forcible imposition of the European-style State
system. Yet by breaking this down into a number of elements,
the special features of African nationalism, as well as those
which it shares with Europe, may be more readily appreciated.
Six external factors have struck me as particularly important. I
am sure that they could be expressed differently and that others
could be added. Nevertheless, I shall state them in the manner I
have found most useful in my own studies, add a few examples
from outside my special field of African interest, and then go on
to illustrate these factors with particular reference to that field,
Nyasaland, or as I shall sometimes call it, by the old name,
British Central Africa, because that brings to mind the fluidity
and artificiality of its frontiers.

The first of these factors is, quite simply, the character of the
culture of the occupying power: a factor which seems to be
proving remarkably persistent—especially in the diverse forces
of the French and English languages. A minor, amusing example comes from McGregor Ross's 1927 book on Kenya, in
which, paying tribute to the *Pax Britannica* and its improvement
of communications, he associated the British national passion,
sport, and the development of African nationalism:

Football teams now travel hundreds of miles by train and steamer to
play the teams of other tribes. In 1922 a Kikuyu firebrand (Harry
Thuku) . . . was addressing enthusiastic meetings, 5,000 strong, in
Kavirondo—where some few years earlier he would have been
swiftly clubbed. Our Administration officers are welding tribes into
a *nation* . . .

A second external factor is the agency in the growth of African
nationalism of a person, originally alien to the particular society,
who comes into it from outside, identifies himself enthusiastically with it and then *plus écossais que les écossais*, as it were, plays a
leading role in the development of its consciousness. The outstanding example is, undoubtedly, Edward Blyden, that remarkable
West Indian whose writings and speeches did so much to

lay the theoretical foundations for the concepts of "African personality" and *négritude*. What Blyden's work began was completed by another West Indian, George Padmore.

The third external factor, which seems to me to be of great importance, is a period of residence overseas. Almost all of the modern African political leaders have spent some formative part of their lives in Europe or America: an alien environment has strengthened their feeling of national consciousness which, before they went overseas, had sometimes been the prey of local and ethnic differences. An interesting early example is Orishatukeh Faduma, who was baptized in Sierra Leone as William Davis; adopted a Yoruba name in 1887 at a time when the "Africanizing" influence of Edward Blyden was growing; went to America; associated with a wide range of Negro American movements to which he contributed several influential papers and which increased his African consciousness; and returned to Africa late in 1914 as a leader of a "back-to-Africa" movement of coloured Americans. He was read by early Nigerian nationalists. This is clear from the use of Faduma's denunciation of Europe in a 1918 pamphlet by Patriarch J. G. Campbell, leader of the separatist "West African Episcopal Church":

The two gods of Europe are the idolatry of Domination and money before which great nations bow and crush weaker ones in the name of religion.

African political movements, however, can be influenced by periods of residence by Africans not necessarily overseas but in other States in Africa. This is a fourth external factor worth examining. Labour migration is an obvious example. But there are the movements from State to State of individuals which should not be overlooked. What, for example, would the South African political scene of the 1920s have been like without a Nyasa migrant, Clements Kadalie, and his Industrial and Commercial Workers' Union of Africa, the famous I.C.U.? And what was the role in the growth of nationalism in West Africa during the First World War of the Ivory Coast "prophet movement" led by William Wade Harris from Liberia? Certainly Casely Hayford of the Gold Coast saw in this wandering preacher, thrice imprisoned, a political figure of some importance.

This First World War character draws attention to a fifth

factor of enormous significance in the rise of African nationalism: the impact of two world wars. One must not, however,
exaggerate the significance of the 1939–45 War, the real importance of which was to accelerate dramatically a trend which
went back to 1885 when Bismarck said at the West African
Conference of Berlin that "The evils of war would assume a
specially fatal character if the natives were led to take sides in
disputes between the civilized powers." The coming of the 1939
War did not hit Africans with the same force as the 1914 War
which brought about a "deep and fundamental" change "in
the relations of the African people with the great unknown
world which suddenly fell upon them and insisted that they
must become a part of it, however unwilling and without
understanding they might be".

In one sense, of course, this War and its 1939 successor are
special instances of my third and fourth external factors.
Certainly, it was the Africans who served with European forces,
in Africa and overseas, who may be assumed to have felt the
influence of these two Wars the most. One must remember here
the effect of the 1914–18 War on French African nationalism
through the recruitment of black troops for service with the
French armies in Europe, the role of the Senegalese politician,
Blaise Diagne, in the recruiting drive and the part which he
played in the post-war Pan-African Conference in Paris.

But these two great external events affected also those Africans who stayed at home, not only by their economic consequences and through the new ideas which were brought back
by returning soldiers but also through the feelings about those
who did not come home. Mr F. D. Corfield notes appropriately
the effect of service in the 1914 War on the widening of Kikuyu
political horizons and claims that wilful misuse of post-War
gratuities embittered many Kikuyu ex-servicemen, who "refused to accept the fact that their mistakes had been of their own
making", against the Government. He does not, however,
mention the loss of Kikuyu and other African lives in the carrier
corps. For this, one must turn to Sir Philip Mitchell's testimony:

A large number died on service, a larger number than that service
justified, for, though there were exceptions, the feeding and care of
the porters and protection against excessive loads were seldom of an
adequate standard.

This became a grievance of the Kikuyu and other African people and passed into their political folklore.

Yet perhaps the most serious outcome of the First World War was its deflation of the white man's prestige. "It cannot be pretended," wrote Mr F. S. Joelson mordantly in 1920, "that it will ever be as high as it was before the war taught blacks to butcher the ruling whites". This was the main legacy of the 1914 War to emerging African nationalism, out of which the 1939 War made a dramatically increased but by no means new kind of political capital.

A sixth external factor is what may be termed foreign ideological influences. I am not here thinking of Christianity, not only because it has as long a history in Africa as in Europe but mainly because I feel that Christian influences should be construed initially in terms of the culture pattern of the first European country which introduced them to particular African regions: that is, in terms of my first external factor. The foreign ideological influences I am thinking of are those which have entered Africa relatively independently of this culture. Here one must include the nationalist movements, both in Europe and its empires, especially Indian and Irish nationalism. Marxism is a relative late-comer and its onslaught on Africa had to wait until after the Second World War. Before this, the attention of official Marxism in the colonial sphere was largely focussed on Asia.

A specially interesting foreign influence has been the role of American Negroes in the emergence of African nationalism. As President Nkrumah put it at the end of the first All-African People's Conference at Accra in 1958:

Many of them have made no small contribution to the cause of African freedom. Names which spring immediately to mind are those of Marcus Garvey and W. E. B. Du Bois. Long before many of us were even conscious of our own degradation, these men fought for African national and racial equality.

It may be worth noting here that, although the Conference at which these words were spoken endorsed "Pan-Africanism", paid a special tribute to its founder, the Negro American, Dr W. E. B. Du Bois, and saw itself in the line of descent from the five Pan-American Congresses in Europe and America from 1919 to 1945, it did not style itself "Pan-African" but called

itself an All-African People's Conference. Was the change for-
tuitous? Certainly, it served to mark a new epoch in which such
conferences were to be in Africa and under the direct control of
African peoples. The prefix "Pan-" calls to mind the European
and American "Pan-" movements of the late nineteenth and
early twentieth centuries. The first, premature Pan-African
Conference in London in 1900 clearly took over this prefix from
the Pan-Slav, Pan-German, Pan-Islamic and Pan-American
complex of its time. In 1892, Du Bois went to the University of
Berlin for two years for postgraduate work and travelled in
eastern and central Europe at a moment when all these "Pan-"
movements—and the rise of anti-Semitism in Germany—were
in rapid growth. The young Du Bois thus saw the Continent at
a time when the kaleidoscope of racialism and nationalism, out
of which emerged the Europe of the First World War which he
was to see again when he went to Paris in 1919 to organize the
Pan-African Conference, was being shaken so fiercely. Out of
these European experiences came some of the ideas and attitudes
which the father of Pan-Africanism handed on to the movement,
irregular, halting and often confused, but still a movement, that
led to the 1958 Conference in Accra. . . .

46. The nature of pan-Africanism

COLIN LEGUM *Friedrich-Ebert-Stiftung E. V.* Bonn 1963; pages
17–21

Elsewhere I have defined Pan-Africanism as a *movement of ideas
and emotions*; at times it achieves a synthesis; at times it remains
at the level of thesis and antithesis. In one sense Pan-Africanism
can be likened to socialism; in another sense it can be likened to
World Federalism, Atlantic Union or Federal Europe; each
allows for great scope of interpretation in its practical application. And yet, in its deepest sense, Pan-Africanism is different
from all these movements in that it is exclusive. For the purposes
of this paper we are concerned only with those of its ideas directed towards *suprastate political unification*. This aspect has been

likened by Nigeria's Governor-General, Dr Nnamde Azikiwe, to "an African Leviathan in the form of a political organisation or associations of states. . . ." In a different sense he sees it as "a miniature United Nations". Of its essential diversity he has said: "The African states can be as separate as fingers in domestic matters, but can be as united as a fist in matters of external and general concern."

Pan-Africanism is not easy to classify in terms of other Pan-movements: even an expert in this field like Professor Hans Kohn admits bafflement, yet as long ago as 1937 he forecast that "it bids fair to becoming a growing force and to constitute one of the major problems of the twentieth century". Professors Coleman and Apter, seeking to relate Pan-Africanism to similar movements, say:

It differs from so-called pure Pan-national movements—Pan-Germanism and Pan-Arabism, for example—in that the peoples being united do not have an identical language or nationality. Here it resembles more closely such super-national movements as Pan-Slavism and Pan-Turanism (Turkish unification). To the extent that it is directed towards the political emancipation and unification of all of Africa, irrespective of nationality, language, race or religion, it falls into the category of Pan-continentalism. Here it can be related to two types of continental solidarity movements distinguished by principle of unity and motive. Where the basic principle of unity is geographical contiguity and the motivating force is the desire to transcend parochialism and to achieve the power, security and economic benefits of large-scale political organization, it resembles Pan-Europeanism and Pan-Americanism. Where the principle of unity is common status (i.e. colonialism) and the motivating force is the desire to remove alien rule and all of the indignities and disabilities connected therewith, it resembles Pan-Asianism and Latin-Americanism.

Nationalism vs. Pan-Africanism?

At the outset the question was posed: "Will nationalism in Africa work in favour of, or against, Pan-Africanism?" At least it should, by now, be clear that in their origins these two forces are not antagonists: they stem not from different but from the same ideas and feelings—a desire to be free from alien rule, to create a new role for the African in Africa and for Africa in the world, and to build new states and societies in Africa. These aspirations are well summed up by President Nyerere:

Twentieth-century nationalism is the African and Asian expression of man's world-wide demand for equality, and the attainment of national independence is only the first, though an essential step. If it is to have any meaning for mankind our nationalism must go forward from that triumph; it must express itself in the struggle of the common man throughout the world for equality and justice.

Each of these two forces should therefore be seen to be intrinsically concerned with ideas of political unification, though at different levels.

Pan-Africanism is concerned with achieving large political units: these might either consist of regional federations of states, or the political unification of certain functions of a number of states: its ultimate aim is a *commonwealth* of African states. Nationalism is primarily concerned with the political unification of different ethnic groups within a single state. But in Africa this limited definition given to nationalism does not hold entirely: as we have seen from what has gone before, African nationalism is infused with political ideas about the 'oneness of Africans'; and about the interdependence of African states in achieving rapid economic and social progress, in defending themselves from external enemies, and in establishing an effective African presence in world affairs. This infusion of ideas comes from Pan-Africanism, which *preceded* modern African nationalism.

The test will be whether the ideas of Pan-Africanism are sufficiently strong to overcome the vested interests of national states. As has already been noted, there are tendencies within African nationalism which run counter to Pan-Africanism, e.g. traditionalism and economic nationalism. But while these counter-forces have grown stronger since independence, the dynamism of Pan-Africanism has grown stronger too. Before 1958—the year of the first Pan-Africanist conferences on Africa soil—few leaders of note were outspokenly in favour of Pan-Africanism. Indeed many of them derided it.

Today the leadership of Pan-Africanism includes many of those who have derided it. Either they have grown convinced of its importance because of their experiences since achieving independence, or they fear to be isolated by standing outside the movement. Either way, Pan-Africanism has proved itself to be a tremendously dynamic force. In another respect, too, it has shown its strength: it has overcome efforts to prescribe a doctrine for Pan-Africanism and to elevate it to an orthodoxy. The trend of Pan-Africanism is rather the other way—towards pragmatism and towards heterodoxy. Thus it never denies the objective of an eventual unification of the whole of Africa (ardently espoused by President Nkrumah); but its approach to it is empirical. At present, the majority view favours the idea of working towards closer unity through functional cooperation—seeking to coordinate their social, educational, economic and political policies, but without abrogating their separate sovereignties. Even President Nkrumah, who insists on the importance of ceding at least some of each state's sovereign powers to a central authority, does not think that sovereignty can be rubbed out immediately; nor is this, in fact, what he proposes in *Africa Must Unite*.

For the time being, therefore, Pan-Africanism postulates no direct threat to national sovereignty. The Organisation of African Unity provides for continental cooperation as between sovereign independent states. How effective will this be? The next stage in the development of Pan-Africanism will probably depend on the answer to this question.

The heterodoxy of Pan-Africanism is shown by its ability to attract and hold together the leaders of 32 independent African states. It can achieve agreement on a Charter despite the fundamental challenge to the ideas of the majority made by President Nkrumah; and it can provide a framework within which quarrelling groups like Ethiopia and Somalia, Morocco and Mauritania, the UAM and Ghana, can work together.

Its framework is undoubtedly weak; the loyalties of members of the OAU are dubious in many cases; the actual extent of effective cooperation is comparatively limited. But even when full allowance has been made for these important qualifications, what remains is that in 1963 African nationalism produced a Pan-Africanist organisation—the OAU—which seeks to regulate the affairs and promote the interests of the entire continent. To this extent it must be conceded that despite the obvious paradoxes between African nationalism and Pan-Africanism these two forces are still moving in the same direction, with each influencing the other and often strengthening it.

But what of the future? Will Pan-Africanism be able to maintain its thrust once the nation-states have had a chance to become stronger, when nationalism begins to freeze into nationality, when frontiers have become permanent, and sovereignty has become sovereignly important to the new power groups in each state? There are factors that undoubtedly make for growing tensions between African states and which will intensify their differences. Here one would note down:

frontier problems;
language-culture grouping tensions, especially if the francophone group orientates itself too closely to France and the European Economic Community;
economic nationalism;
sharpening differences over attitudes towards the speed and extent to which the OAU should be reformed;
leadership roles;
alliances with foreign powers; trends in international economic relationships; sincerity to non-alignment principles;
interference in each other's internal affairs;
conflicts over limits of regional federations.

As against this one would note down the following list of factors which could help to intensify the drives for greater unity:

the poorness, weakness and smallness of most African states; and their interdependence;
fear of reconquest; and of neo-colonialism;
economic forces, increasing intra-African trade, communications, etc.;
mutual desire to stay out of East-West conflicts; to make Africa's voice strong at the UN; to give greater reality to non-alignment; to maintain the collective security of Africa;
support for liberation struggles, and anti-colonialist feelings;
emergence of fresh ideas about achieving greater African unity; confidence of working together in OAU; greater knowledge of each other, and more understanding for each other's viewpoints;
the diminution of tensions over frontiers;
the spirit to be free, to be strong, to be respected, to be modern, to be equal, to be united.

47. Pan-Africanism: the Communists and the West

COLIN LEGUM *African Affairs* Vol. 63, No. 252, July 1964 Royal African Society, London; pages 189–92

. . . The sixth reality is the flood of international rivalry which plays on Africa's shores. Internationally, Africa is heavily courted by both the West and the East. And a new dimension in the courtship has been introduced by the split between Moscow and Peking. Considerations of cold war politics are bound never to be too far below the surface in decisions that are taken by any of the major powers in their relations with Africa. And so far as the Africans are concerned, although non-alignment is the aspiration of most of the African leaders, its practice is rather inconsistent.

The seventh reality is the irresistible rise of the single party state; because of its universality not only in Africa but in most of the newly independent countries—it seems that we must accept that their emergence meets a special need in the transition period after the ending of their dependency status. But whether the one party state can fulfil the wants as well as meet the needs of Africa is quite a different question.

These then are the realities which will determine the future shape of Africa. The objective conditions suggest that the continent needs a high degree of unity; that this is the only way in which the aspirations of African nationalism can be fulfilled; in other words, that Pan-Africanism is not just an ideal, but that it is the right answer to Africa's needs. To come to this conclusion, however, is not the same thing as concluding that this is in fact what will happen. One must take into account the negative factors operating against the consummation of unity.

Here one notices the fact that while the balkanisation of Africa is largely the result of historical processes and to a considerable extent of colonial policies as well, it is also a reflection of parochial nationalist aspirations. And one can say of Africa as Peter Calvocoressi has said of the Middle East: "There is a fission-fusion process at work. When fission is in the ascendant we get a host of small units whose quarrels may be dangerous; when fusion gains the day, the units are fewer, but they are also so large that they must be difficult to discipline." In Africa to-day we have both fission and fusion at work; and even as it is being balkanised the movement towards unification proceeds. Whether these states will prove amenable to the necessary disciplines still remains to be seen.

I now turn to the other aspect of my lecture which is the relationship between Pan-Africanism and Communism. The first thing that is to be said about Pan-Africanism is that this is much older than Communism in its modern form; that it has aspirations, desires and ends of its own. And the second point is that its confrontation with Communism is by no means new; it has been going on for forty years. What is new is the confrontation between Communism and Pan-Africanism inside Africa itself: this is the present phase which started only about five years ago.

Pan-Africanism is not, and never has been, a unified or a structured political movement. It is a movement of ideas and emotions: its recent political history has been a search for a viable political organisation. Its history can be broadly divided into four parts—and I am not going to spend a lot of time on this, but it does throw an important light on what we talked about. Those of you who have any real interest in Pan-Africanism might be interested in a book by that title, cost 22/6 and the fact that I am the author of it is not my only reason for mentioning it! The first is the period of its nascence from roughly the seventeenth century to the beginning of the twentieth century. The second period is the primary political stage—beginning with the first Pan-African conference in London in 1900—which was highlighted by the conflicting attitudes of the two giants of Pan-Africanist thinking—Marcus Garvey and W. E. B. DuBois. And those of you who are *Sunday Telegraph* readers who read the story about Nkrumah last week should not fail to notice that DuBois, who is presented as the great influence on Nkrumah's life, was not the leader of the "Back to Africa" movement, but in fact spent the whole of his life fighting Marcus Garvey who was. Thirdly, the period which might be called the period of synthesis, beginning with George Padmore's break with the Comintern in the middle 1930s, and with the start of his activities in London. This period reached its apogee in 1945 at the Manchester Pan-African Conference. Here one finds the first attempt at resolving basic conflicts within Pan-Africanist thinking, giving a greater coherent relationship between emotions and ideas, and establishing a sophisticated political framework for Pan-Africanism and especially its attachment to the idea of non-alignment.

And finally there is the fourth period which is also the first African continental period. It begins with the rooting of Pan-African ideas in Africa itself when the first Conference of Independent African States was convened by Dr Nkrumah in Accra in 1958, and reached its high point in the first African Summit Conference of African Heads of State in Addis Ababa in May 1963.

So far as the Communists are concerned, they took an active interest in the second period of Pan-Africanism, trying hard to win over either Garvey or DuBois, who had managed to get considerable mass following among the American Negroes; since the Communists could not get a hold on the Negroes in America or on the Africans in South Africa, they concentrated all their efforts to win over Pan-African leaders in these two countries, and they failed in both cases.

But the problems in Africa which faced the Communists in 1958—the moment when Pan-Africanism was set up in a proper form in the continent—are not difficult to understand. For almost forty years they had tried to ally these Negro movements, as I have just said, to the Communist International and failed. The analysis of the colonial liberation movement had led them widely astray. Having been guided by the Stalinist theory that the colonial revolution proceeds from the premise that the solution of the colonial problem and the liberation of the oppressed peoples from colonial slavery is impossible without a proletarian revolution and the overthrow of imperialism—they were almost wholly unprepared for the sudden disengagement by the Western colonial powers in Africa. Although they had always recognised the importance of the bourgeois nationalists as allied in the liberation struggle, the Communist theories did not allow for these forces to be capable of developing sufficient militancy to wrest independence without the cadres of what they called "the proletariat vanguard" to inspire them. The Communist International had forecast bitter struggles as the imperialists fought rearguard actions, as in Indo-China, during which time the revolutionary cadres would emerge to take over the leadership. But this did not happen in Africa.

It was only in 1955 that the Communists began to have serious doubts about the correctness of the diagnosis of colonial revolution. The Bandung conference, the successful challenge of the Neguib-Nasser officers' movement, and the relatively quick breakthrough by the CPP in the Gold Coast caused them to revise their theories. But by then it was already too late. They were confronted by a totally new and unforeseen situation—a whole string of "bourgeois nationalist" governments, nearly all of which had outlawed the Communists in their own countries as one of their earliest acts. These new governments were, in fact, much tougher and more competent than the colonial powers had been in this particular field. And one can understand the mournful reactions of a Communist theorist who surveyed the African scene and commented of it:

Anti-Communism, Communist-phobia, the suppression of Marxism-Leninism as a system of thought, the attempt to crush the Communist organisation—all this is not only a limitation of democracy in Africa. It is no less a limitation on national development, a weakening of the national cause, of the truest interests of the mass of the people, and an assistance to the imperialists. It is regrettable that some African leaders have picked up this tattered mantle of the dictators and imperialists.

So we see in Moscow, as in London, the Communists are not terribly happy with what has happened.

There are just a few points with which I wish to deal very briefly. One is the attitude or the mood of African nationalism which I believe is seriously misunderstood both in the Communist world and in the West. Modern African nationalism developed largely as a reaction to European nationalism, rooted in its ideas of European supremacy and of a world revolving around Western Europe. Its reaction therefore is not only against alien rule (anti-colonialism) but equally against race supremacy. For the African nationalist the ending of colonialism is the beginning not the end of a struggle—a point not sufficiently understood. How often does one hear the complaint: Now that colonialism is finished, what more do the Africans want? They want to abolish the status of inferiority—social, cultural, economic and political—cast upon Africa as a continent, and upon Africans as a people. African nationalism is a forceful assertion of the dignity of the individual African; it is a force struggling to establish real equality between Africa and the rest of the world, especially with its former alien rulers with whom it remains deeply entangled—and not altogether unwillingly so.

These aspirations give it two distinctive qualities. Externally, it operates as a force working for the total abolition of the old relationship as between superior and inferior—Europe and Africa—and as between European and African. Internally, it is a regenerating force seeking to destroy Africa's colonial mentality, and to uplift the African—economically, culturally and socially. It seeks to bring about a cultural Renaissance in Africa as well as an economic revolution. And an important aspect of African nationalism is its ambivalence towards Europe: the very nationalist leaders working actively to extrude Europe are at the same time willing to continue working with the former colonial powers and their allies. African nationalism does not reject Europe altogether; it seeks to create a new relationship based on true independence. There is a surprising lack of hatred and bitterness such as we have found as the result of the nationalism in Europe.

What I have really been trying to say throughout this talk comes down to this: that the majority of African leaders wish to be neither part of the West nor the East, that they will react against both, the strength of the reaction being determined by the pressures they feel placed upon them by one side or the other. Secondly, that African leaders see their interests not as an extension of the interests of Europe but as something totally separate. Thirdly, that whatever doubts Europeans might have about African capacity to defend their own interests against all comers, including the Communists, they themselves have no such doubt—and nothing causes greater resentment than the unfortunately frequent expressions of doubt about the Africans' capacity and ability to see who his real friends and enemies are. This is seen—and correctly seen—as a hangover from the old days when we regarded ourselves as superior in our wisdom over the Africans—and how many of us here in this hall today still do not hold this view to be true in our own hearts? Fourthly, that Africa is in for much worse troubles than anything we have yet seen. These are partly due to their inherited difficulties of balkanisation, economic and military weakness, to internal dissensions and to the forces of the cold war. These pressures make for revolutionary situations rather than for stability.

Finally, that the West should confine itself strictly to defending its own proper interests in Africa. These are confined only to three; economic interests; to the well-being of those white communities which still rest their dependance on the West rather than on the new African states; and to a proper concern that Africa should not turn in revulsion to the Communists. Such a revulsion might come—but if it does it will be principally against Western arrogance and lack of understanding of the true feelings and of the real economic and technical needs of Africa.

48. Non-alignment

MARGARET LEGUM *Non-Alignment* André Deutsch 1966; pages 56–61

There is nothing particularly moral about a policy of non-alignment. Nations which decide not to commit themselves to either side in the cold war make the decision in their own interests. Non-alignment is not a virtuous refusal to take part in 'power politics'; it is not based upon a rejection of modern weapons of war; it does not confer the ability to get above the battle and pass judgement with clean hands. Non-alignment is too often associated by its proponents with virtue in international affairs, by its detractors with a spurious self-righteousness and hence with 'double standards'. In short, the concept of non-alignment has nothing to do with morality or immorality; and nations which espouse it operate on the same principles of national self-interest as any state in NATO or the Warsaw Pact.

It is no coincidence that the nations of Africa and Asia have emerged into independence at the height of the world's hardening into two opposing blocs. Both had their origins in the second world war. Participation in that conflict gave the colonised nations the perspective to spur them to an irresistible nationalism; while the later development of the hydrogen bomb froze the then inherent conflict between Communism and the West into an uneasy war for influence. Western colonialism came to an end because it was no longer in the national interest of the Western nations to rule their colonies. The world had become smaller; it became more important to be on good terms with former subjects than to rule over them; it was necessary to take a longer view of the national interest. The process doubled the number of independent nations in five years.

The significance of these nations was highlighted by the existence of the United Nations Organisation, which became an important forum for the new struggle for ideological influence. The Assembly principle of one nation, one vote, gave the emergent nations of Africa and Asia a new sense of importance. How were they to use it? They were inevitably guided by a combination of calculation and emotion. Able at last to speak for themselves instead of being spoken for, they were strongly tempted to cock a snook at the former colonial power. Even more powerful, especially in Africa, was the positive desire to establish a uniqueness, to rediscover the dignity which goes with making a special contribution, not to be seen as an appendage of another more powerful continent. These emotions in themselves were enough to produce a spirit, if not a defined policy, of non-alignment.

But some cool calculations produced the same conclusions. Positive alignment with the former colonial power, and hence with the West, would have some advantages. These would include defence against attack, provided the assailant was a member of the Communist bloc; and possibly a certain amount of economic assistance when this could be afforded. But in exchange, as incomparably the weaker members of the Western bloc, the new nations would be required to toe an international line, and even perhaps adopt certain internal policies, without having very much influence in defining them. And there would be other disadvantages. There was always the danger that one's own commitment to the West would provoke a Communist initiative in a neighbouring state; so that one would find oneself at the front line of a battle between giants. If that happened there would be very little freedom of action, internal or international.

What, on the other hand, are the advantages of non-alignment? Clearly the first is the freedom to put the national interest before the interests of an alliance. In practice this means directing trade in the most profitable directions, accepting assistance from the most efficient sources, and casting a vote in the United Nations in accordance with the national interest. The overriding advantage of this kind of policy for small, weak nations is that they do not become too dependent upon any one benefactor or group of benefactors. This advantage depends very much, of course, on the existence of conflict between the richer nations; for in this situation—meaning at present the cold war—there is always someone to step in to fill a vacuum caused by the demise of an offended supplier. This is exactly what the Russians and the Czechs did in Guinea when the French tried to smash the economy after the 'no' vote in the 1958 referendum. And when the Americans refused to finance Egypt's High Dam, the Russians immediately stepped in with long-term credits. Moreover, the effect of these Communist initiatives was to heal the breach with the offended Western nations much quicker than it might otherwise have been.

For most of the emergent nations, therefore, non-alignment clearly pays off on balance. It is true that for some of the former French African colonies, which have always been more generously treated in terms of aid than the British African colonies, the advantages were not so clear. Even their recurrent budgets are subsidized by the French; and so complex has been their economic relationship with France that an enormous upheaval would have been required to cut loose and compete for attention among the other donor nations. Basically this is the explanation for their relative 'moderation', their *de facto* commitment to France. It is not that Africans in these countries are less nationalist than, say, Guineans; but the alternative for them is much less clearly advantageous than it is elsewhere. Once on a firmer economic footing, the attractions of non-alignment will claim them as well.

So much for the advantages for the new nations. What about the rest of the world? In the short run both sides in the cold war would rather have reliable allies than shifting relationships with non-aligned nations. But in the long run the world stands to gain by firm non-commitment by the emergent nations. First, the area of the cold war is limited, and with it the danger of international conflict. Second, there is an immense advantage in the existence of a body of nations which is not directly committed in cold war issues, and which can therefore be trusted, more or less, by both sides. The role of these nations has already been proved, notably in the Congo, and may even come to play a decisive role in disarmament. Finally, the existence of a sizeable group of countries which both sides have, *faute de mieux*, to woo, tends to produce compromise or at least a reluctance to appear intransigent. Again, this may well prove important in disarmament negotiations.

None of these advantages would follow, of course, if non-alignment simply meant negative neutralism—an opting out of world affairs. But its proponents do not so construe it. "We should remain constantly in touch with the two conflicting military camps, since non-alignment does not mean that we isolate ourselves from problems; it means we contribute positively to . . . understanding and the opening of channels for the passage of ideas . . ." (the former King of Morocco, Mohammed V). "This policy . . . must not be confused with *equilibrisme*, which takes up no fundamental position . . ." (President Nkrumah). "We say what we believe whether this pleases or displeases" (President Nasser).

Non-alignment is therefore a positive expression of a nations' own interests in international affairs. Whether or not it fits in with the wishes or designs of one side in the cold war is immaterial to the principle. At the end of 1961 the Soviet Ambassador was expelled from Guinea for attempting to incite a Marxist revolution against the government. Commenting on Western claims that this heralded a more Western orientation in Guinea, a M. Alpha Diallo, Director of Information said: "We do not fight colonialism to please Moscow, nor Communism to please London or Washington. We fight both in conformity with our principles."

Since principles, and indeed each government's conception of the national interest, vary from nation to nation, it is not surprising that the non-aligned nations speak with more than one voice. On issues of colonialism and racial discrimination, both of which they have all suffered to a lesser or greater degree, Africa and Asia are virtually solid. But on issues involving detailed decisions which do not directly concern them, the differences can be profound. Even on U.N. Congo policy, Africa was divided.

This is to be expected. Non-alignment is not a policy, it is an approach to policy-making. Nor is there any intention of creating a non-aligned bloc; that would be to undermine the basis of the approach, which is that each nation makes up its own mind on each issue according to its national interests. The effect was shown up very sharply over the India-China border fighting. Some countries, notably Ghana, the U.A.R. and Yugoslavia, called for negotiations between the two sides, the effect of which was support for China. Nigeria, Malaya, Burma and most of the other African countries expressed immediate sympathy for India. Both points of view were positively expressed: no nation considered the problem outside its field of interest.

On the Cuba crisis, most of the non-aligned nations considered both the United States and Russia at fault. Perhaps the most succinct expression of positive non-alignment came from President Sékou Touré of Guinea: "Having considered the Soviet government's statement which admits the existence of Soviet bases on Cuban soil, and taking into account the Cuban people's request for the evacuation of bases occupied by the United States forces on Cuban soil, the . . . government of Guinea reaffirms its position with regard to the immediate abolition of foreign bases."

We can expect that non-alignment will deepen its roots in the emergent nations of Africa, Asia, and ultimately, Latin America. It may even spread to other European countries, now satellites of the Soviet Union. For them, Yugoslavia has shown the way. We can expect too that opposition to non-alignment will come increasingly from the Communist rather than the Western bloc. Originally it was the West which took the line that non-alignment was no more than a cover for hostility, and the Communists who welcomed it as a means of prising loose the "imperialist" grip. But there is no place in Marxist-Leninist theory for non-alignment; and it is from the East that the governments of Africa and Asia will have to expect attempts to force them to abandon non-alignment. I do not expect they will succeed.

49. African states and the United Nations, 1958–1964

CATHERINE HOSKYNS *Journal of International Affairs* Vol. 40, No. 3, July 1964 Royal Institute of International Affairs; pages 466–80

In the Security Council this summer and in the General Assembly this autumn, the African states seem likely to mount the biggest campaign they have yet attempted with a view to getting some kind of United Nations action over the obdurate colonial and racial problems which still exist in Southern Africa. This seems an appropriate moment, therefore, to examine the way in which the African states are organised at the United Nations, to show how they have tackled other African issues which have come before the Organisation in the period 1958–64, and to discuss some of the criticisms which have been made, particularly in Britain and in the United States, against the whole trend of African activity in this context.

Since 1958 the African states have made it clear, in statement and practice, that they regard the United Nations as an indispensible element in the formulating and carrying out of their foreign policy. This is partly because the Charter of the United Nations, with its emphasis on equality, self-determination and economic development, appears to reflect some at least of the preoccupations of the African states; partly because the structure of the United Nations makes it possible for small states to exercise considerable influence; and partly because the bargaining position which the division of the world into two rival blocs has given to the uncommitted nations can be most effectively exploited through the United Nations and its organs.

The importance of the United Nations to Africa was first stated at the Conference of Independent African States held in Accra in April 1958. At this conference, the eight states which were then independent[1] declared their intention of projecting a 'distinctive African personality' into the field of foreign policy; affirmed 'their unswerving loyalty to and support of' the

---

[1] Ethiopia, Ghana, Libya, Liberia, Morocco, Tunisia, Sudan and the United Arab Republic (UAR).

Charter of the United Nations; and agreed that the permanent machinery of the conference should be established at the United Nations by the delegations of the participating countries. As a result, the African group (modelled on the Afro-Asian group to which the African states already belonged) was formally established in New York in May 1958. This group—which, as will be shown later, achieved considerable success in bringing about an accommodation between countries as different as Ghana and Ethiopia, and in projecting Africa's interests within the Afro-Asian group and in the United Nations as a whole—continued unchallenged and with a gradually increasing membership until September 1960.

At this point, differences over what policy should be followed with regard to Algeria and the Congo split the independent states, with the result that though neither the Conference of Independent African States itself nor the African group at the United Nations was ever formally disbanded, two mutually hostile sub-groups, the Casablanca bloc and the Brazzaville bloc (later the *Union Africaine et Malgache* (UAM)), were formed, each with its own organisation at the United Nations. During this period the African group continued to meet and some action was agreed on non-controversial topics. Its strength and effectiveness were sapped, however, by the existence of the other organisations and the most important questions were not discussed. But by the end of 1962 the main causes of the dispute had lessened, and with the revival, at Addis Ababa in May 1963, of the Conference of Independent African States, under the new name Organisation of African Unity (OAU), the Casablanca and the UAM blocs and their organisations at the United Nations were disbanded. This had the effect of restoring the authority of the African group and brought all the African states together once again in one organisation at the United Nations.

The structure of the African group has been described in some detail in a recent book by Thomas Hovet. Its two main organs are the co-ordinating body and the secretariat. The co-ordinating body consists of the leaders of the African delegations to the United Nations and their representatives. It meets at least once a month and the chairmanship rotates monthly among the delegations. The secretariat consists of representatives of four of the states elected for a two year period, and its purpose is to study the various questions at issue, to produce background papers and to make proposals to the co-ordinating body. African states are automatically admitted to the group on becoming members of the United Nations, and representatives of dependent countries are given observer status. Except on rare occasions, the group only discusses African issues, and its main aim is to formulate concrete proposals on African questions which can then be put up to the larger Afro-Asian group. Though great efforts are made to reach a consensus, no decision of the group is binding and each delegation retains the right to vote as it pleases. The organisation at the United Nations is used to prepare and plan the conferences of the Independent African States, and it also conducts a considerable amount of inter-African business which has no direct connection with the United Nations.

Subject to these vicissitudes, the African group has now existed at the United Nations for more than six years. These six years fall naturally into four periods: 1958–59 when the group was beginning to establish itself; 1960 widely known in the United Nations as 'Africa's year'; 1961 the year of maximum division; and 1962 to the present day, when the group's prime concern has been to bring pressure over the situation in Southern Africa. Each of these periods has its own character, and each marks a gradual increase in the influence and effectiveness of the African states.

One of the main purposes of the formation of the African group in 1958 was to establish a pressure group within the Afro-Asian bloc which would be prepared to lobby for more dynamic action on the various African and colonial issues which were due to be discussed. There seems to have been a fairly general feeling among the African states at this point that the Asians were too divided and too cautious to advocate the kind of policy needed, and that a more effective lobby was essential. This feeling was confirmed when India, together with a number of other Asian countries, supported the French proposal to give independence to the United Nations Trust Territory, the French Cameroons, in spite of the fact that the major nationalist party, the *Union des Populations du Cameroun* (UPC), was banned and had not contested the previous elections. Against the direct wish of India, the African states began actively to campaign for a United Nations resolution demanding that the ban should be lifted and that elections supervised by the United Nations should be held before independence. Although unsuccessful, the African initiative caused considerable comment and focused a new attention on the position of the UPC and the situation in the Cameroons as a whole.

The other main African issue of 1958–59 was the question of Algeria, and this quickly became the chief preoccupation of the group. Prompted by the New York representatives of the *Front de Libération Nationale* (FLN), who attended all meetings of the group, the African states sent diplomatic missions to a number of Latin American and Scandinavian countries in the summer of 1958 to lobby for a General Assembly resolution recognising the right of the Algerians to self-determination. A motion to this effect, first proposed by the African group and then taken up by the majority of the Asians, was finally rejected by one vote in the General Assembly on December 13. In 1959 a similar resolution was accepted paragraph by paragraph in the General Assembly, but defeated (after extensive lobbying by France and her allies) when voted on as a whole. These resolutions, and the debates which led up to them, though having no direct effect on the situation in Algeria, undoubtedly gave the FLN a platform and forced a whole number of states, which would not otherwise have been concerned, to consider the position of the FLN and the actions of France.

During 1958 and 1959 the African group lobbied actively about South-West and South Africa, and their pressure was in part responsible both for the rejection of the suggestion made by the United Nations Good Offices Committee that South-West Africa might be partitioned and for the fact that in 1958 a new group of countries, including the United States, began to vote for the annual resolution condemning South Africa, instead of abstaining.

By the end of 1959, therefore, the African group had established itself as a dynamic and cohesive element at the United Nations. Though not in a position to ensure the adoption of any controversial resolution, or to instigate effective action, its efforts served to publicise the situation in the various dependent territories and to push the Afro-Asian group as a whole into taking a more active stand. Even if the attitudes of countries such as Ethiopia and Ghana were still far apart, a fairly effective means of co-operation and consultation had been established.

The increasing activity of the African states (and the fact that there were likely to be between 20 and 25 new African members of the United Nations within the next few years) did not go unnoticed in the United Nations Secretariat, and in January 1960 Dag Hammarskjöld, the Secretary-General, made a six weeks' tour of Africa. He came back convinced that the United Nations must be responsive to African demands, and that the Organisation had a considerable role to play in insulating Africa from the effects of the cold war and in acting as a channel for economic aid. As a result, a fairly close relationship was established between him and the African group. At the same time the world Press suddenly became conscious of the rate at which the African states were moving towards independence, and at the turn of the year a number of articles were published designating 1960 as 'Africa's year' and speculating on the effects that this influx of new nations would have on the United Nations itself.

This preoccupation with African affairs was very soon justified by the disturbances in South Africa which culminated in the Sharpeville shooting. On March 25, 29 African and Asian states requested a meeting of the Security Council and, despite the protests of Britain, France and South Africa (but with the affirmative vote of the United States), a resolution was adopted on April 1 which called on South Africa to abandon apartheid and requested the Secretary-General to open consultations with the South African Government. This vote was regarded as a considerable triumph for the African states and as a defeat for those who maintained that apartheid was the concern of South Africa alone and that the United Nations had no right to discuss the situation, let alone pass resolutions on it. Rather surprisingly, the South African Government agreed that Mr Hammarskjöld should visit South Africa in July.

This activity on the South African question was almost immediately overshadowed, however, by the crisis in the Congo, and here for the first time the African states were able to translate their growing influence into concrete action. They showed immediately that they preferred that the United Nations should intervene rather than any individual country, and they displayed considerable diplomatic skill in persuading the Great Powers to agree. The African states then contributed the major part of the force which was set up by the Security Council. But the unanimity with which the operation in the Congo was begun did not last long, and differences over what action the United Nations should take with regard to Katanga, and in the dispute between Lumumba and Kasavubu, not only disrupted the close links between the African group and the Secretariat but also split the group itself. As a result, the more radical states[1] established the Casablanca bloc and the majority of the former French African colonies the Brazzaville bloc. These divisions were accentuated by differences of policy over Algeria, and an Afro-Asian resolution calling for a referendum in Algeria, supervised by the United Nations, was defeated in the General Assembly on December 19, 1960 because the Brazzaville states refused to support it.

This sudden concern about colonisation in general, and Africa in particular, led to a new development at the end of 1960. During his visit to the United Nations in September and October of that year, Mr Khrushchev had presented to the General Assembly a draft declaration on colonialism demanding immediate independence for all self-governing territories and the relinquishing by all states of bases in other countries. The idea of such a declaration was quickly picked up by the African states and, forgetting their other differences, they agreed to sponsor together a resolution setting out their own declaration on colonialism. This (though rejecting the Russian demand for immediate independence and making no mention of bases) stated unequivocally that all peoples had the right to self-determination and that immediate steps should be taken to transfer power to non-self-governing territories. In the General Assembly on December 14 the Russian draft was rejected and the African draft adopted by 90 votes to 0 with 9 abstentions. This resolution, and the unanimity with which it was adopted, were widely regarded as giving the United Nations much

[1] Ghana, Guinea, Libya, Mali, Morocco, United Arab Republic and the provisional government of Algeria (GPRA).

greater powers to discuss and to take action on questions of self-determination, which had hitherto been regarded as questions of domestic jurisdiction and outside the proper concern of the United Nations.

South Africa, the Congo and the general question of colonialism were in fact the main issues with which the United Nations had to deal in 1960, and the seriousness with which these problems were treated marked the emergence of the African states (in spite of their internal difficulties) as one of the most important elements in the Organisation. Though this was due largely to the sheer increase in numbers it was also due in some measure to the greater experience of the older members of the group and to their increased knowledge of the kind of complex diplomacy necessary at the United Nations.

If 1960 had been rightly designated at the United Nations as 'Africa's year', 1961 continued in the same vein. By February the African group was at its most divided, with the Casablanca and Brazzaville sub-groups in permanent operation and with a group of states which belonged to neither standing rather indecisively in between. Mainly because of pressure from the Casablanca states, the United Nations adopted in February a new resolution aimed at restricting foreign intervention in Katanga, and continuing pressure from these states (and from others which had large contingents in the Congo) eventually persuaded the United States to support further United Nations action in Katanga. By the end of the year this seemed likely to bring secession to an end.

Earlier in the year, the African states had brought before the Security Council and before the General Assembly both the situation in Angola and the dispute between France and Tunisia over Bizerta. Angola was discussed three times between March and April, and eventually a resolution was adopted in the Security Council by 9 votes to 0 with 2 abstentions which called upon Portugal 'to desist forthwith from repressive measures'. Though these discussions made very little difference to the situation in Angola, they served to highlight the extent of the revolt and the isolation of Portugal in the world community.

When the disputes between Tunisia and France over Bizerta flared up in July 1961, Tunisia's immediate reaction was to appeal to the Security Council. After several fruitless meetings, the Afro-Asians pressed for a special session of the General Assembly and this was finally held in August. At this session, a resolution demanding that France should withdraw her troops from around Bizerta and arrange for a total withdrawal from Tunisian territory was passed by 66 votes to o with 30 abstentions. The affirmative votes of eight of the Brazzaville group plus the Scandinavian countries caused France considerable embarrassment, and Press reports at the time suggested that as a result of this vote both Britain and the United States were in private urging France to negotiate.

At the end of 1961 a number of attempts were made to introduce into the General Assembly a resolution setting a definite time-limit by which all non-self-governing territories should be independent. A Soviet resolution suggesting 1962 was rejected as unrealistic; on the other hand, the date of 1970 suggested by Nigeria and Liberia seemed to the more radical African states to give too much leeway to the colonial Powers. In the end no time-limit was set, but a resolution was passed establishing a special United Nations committee to look into conditions in all the non-self-governing territories. This committee, known as the Committee of Seventeen, and consisting of representatives of the African, Asian and colonial Powers, plus the Soviet Union and the United States, was finally set up in January 1962.

From 1962 on, as the situation in both Algeria and the Congo began to ease, the differences between the various groups of African states grew less, and there was fairly general agreement on a campaign to press the United Nations into further action over South Africa, Southern Rhodesia and the Portuguese colonies.

At the beginning of the year, the African states became particularly concerned about the situation in Southern Rhodesia, and once the Committee of Seventeen had been established, a special United Nations sub-group was set up to decide whether a consideration of this situation came within the committee's terms of reference. In spite of a wealth of evidence to the contrary given by Britain, the committee decided that Southern Rhodesia was non-self-governing within the definition which the United Nations had established, and thenceforward the whole problem of Central Africa became the main preoccupation of the committee. After a delegation of its members had visited London, the question of Southern Rhodesia was brought before the General Assembly where the Africans tried in vain to extract a pledge from the British Government that independence would not be granted to Southern Rhodesia until a fully representative government was in power. Southern Rhodesia was again discussed in the General Assembly in October, and this time two resolutions were passed by big majorities; one urged the release of political prisoners and the lifting of the ban on the African political parties, and the other demanded that Britain suspend the constitution and call a conference to reconsider the whole matter.

What effect this sudden internationalisation of the Central African question had on the situation in Southern Rhodesia is extremely hard to assess. On the one hand, it almost certainly contributed to the overthrow of the more moderate Whitehead Government; on the other hand, the certainty that there would be both a Commonwealth and an international outcry if any concessions were made to the new Prime Minister, Winston Field, may well have stiffened the attitude of the British Government towards him. What is certain is that a great deal of publicity was given to a situation which had previously been very little examined outside Britain.

While the main effort of the African states in 1962 was directed towards the situation in Central Africa, renewed action was also taken against South Africa and Portugal. During 1961 attempts to introduce resolutions into the General Assembly urging states to impose sanctions unilaterally against South Africa had failed. But on November 6, 1962 a resolution to this effect was finally accepted, and at the same time a special United Nations committee was set up to consider the whole question of apartheid in South Africa. Though this resolution was a recommendation only and had no binding power, it was a striking indication of the direction in which international opinion was moving. At the same time, the International Court of Justice, against the pleadings of South Africa, found by eight votes to seven that the case being brought against South Africa by Ethiopia and Liberia over the whole status of South-West Africa did fall within its jurisdiction and could be heard. As for Portugal, a resolution was passed on December 14 calling on Portugal once again to abandon all repressive action and to open negotiations with a view to granting independence to her colonial territories.

In 1963 this action was intensified, particularly after the formation of the OAU which had the effect of co-ordinating more closely the foreign policies of the various African states. In the summer, after the Special Committee on Apartheid had recommended a number of possibilities, the question of what action to take over both South Africa and Portugal was brought before the Security Council by the African states. On July 31 a resolution was adopted on Portugal which more or less endorsed the General Assembly resolution adopted the year before. A week later a resolution was passed on South Africa which, although not mandatory, called on all states to cease immediately 'the sale and shipment of arms, ammunition of all types and military vehicles to South Africa'. Though Britain abstained on the resolution, the United States voted in favour, and during the course of the debate the United States delegation gave a guarantee that by the end of the year the sale of all types of arms to South Africa would be banned. In November, when the Security Council again considered South Africa, a fresh resolution was passed on the proposal of Norway extending the ban to equipment and materials for the manufacture and maintenance of arms and ammunition, and setting up a United Nations expert group to examine methods of resolving the race crisis in South Africa, and to consider the role the United Nations could play. This time all members of the Security Council voted for the resolution, though Britain and France made considerable reservations in doing so.

By the end of 1963, therefore, sustained African pressure had achieved, with certain qualifications, a Great Power agreement to ban the sale of arms to South Africa. But since the South Africans were by this time almost self-sufficient in arms, this was more a moral than a practical victory. At the same time, in the course of the debates the major Western Powers had made it clear that they did not think that at the present moment the situation in South Africa constituted a threat to the peace, and that they were therefore not willing to support a mandatory resolution advocating any kind of economic or military sanctions.

During the early part of 1964 the African states have been gathering strength to challenge this position, to attempt to prove that the situation in South Africa does constitute a threat to the peace and that the United Nations is therefore entitled to take stronger action. They have been helped in this by the papers presented at the Sanctions Conference held in London in April[1] (which represent the first serious discussion by experts of the practicability and the consequences of taking economic sanctions against South Africa), and by the report of the United Nations expert group published in the same month which recommends that the United Nations should take economic sanctions if all else fails. It is in the hope that these two events indicate a genuine shift in public opinion in the West, and that the case against South Africa will eventually be strengthened by an adverse judgment in the International Court over South-West Africa, that the African states are opening their campaign.

The extent of this African activity has not of course passed unnoticed, and at times criticism has been widespread both in Britain and the United States. In general, these criticisms have centred on three points; that in their dealings at the United Nations the African states are only interested in their own affairs and play no part in the general work of the Organisation; that they have a double standard regarding both the actions of the Afro-Africans and those of the rest of the world and the actions of the Soviet Union and the West; and that their actions are in fact distorting the purpose of the United Nations by forcing it into activity for which it was never intended.

For the first of these criticisms there was, particularly in the early days, considerable justification. In 1958 and 1959, when the African group was struggling to establish itself and the African states were trying desperately to arouse interest in African questions, they had no time to consider any other issue. At the same time, because there were so few of them, the African states felt that even if they had a point of view they had very little chance of influencing decisions taken on questions outside

---

[1] The International Conference on Sanctions against South Africa, convened by Ronald Segal and sponsored by the British Anti-Apartheid Movement. The papers and resolutions of the Conference have been published as a Penguin Special.

their direct sphere of influence. But since 1960, this criticism has been losing its force, and there have been indications that the African states, fortified by their increase in numbers, are beginning to feel that they do have a role to play at least in the big cold-war issues and in attempting to prevent a direct East-West confrontation.

The whole question of disarmament and testing is perhaps a good example of this. African interest in this subject was aroused in 1959 by the French decision to use the Sahara as a testing ground, and since then the African group has carried on an active campaign to get Africa declared a nuclear-free zone. But recently the concern of the African states has gone much wider than this, and they have taken an increasing interest in discussions on general disarmament and in efforts to find some common ground between the Soviet Union and the United States on this issue. By all accounts, the three African states at the Disarmament Commission—Ethiopia, Nigeria and the UAR—have taken their position very seriously, and there seems to have been some general discussion among the African states as to what line should be pursued. It was also noticeable that the resolutions at the May 1963 OAU conference dealt with the disarmament issue as a whole and not with its specifically African aspect. This same kind of concern was shown during the Cuba crisis in October 1962, when it was on a resolution presented by Ghana and the UAR that the Afro-Asian states appealed to U Thant to mediate between the United States and the Soviet Union.

The position at the moment would seem to be, therefore, that though the African states put their main effort into getting action on purely African questions, they are increasingly realising that their numbers now permit them to have a say in the more general issues which affect Africa and the other continents of the world. To date the action which they have taken on these issues has been by no means extreme, and has tended to support moderate and constructive solutions.

The accusation that the African states have a double standard, both as regards the Afro-Asian states and the rest of the world and *vis-à-vis* the Soviet Union and the West, is one that is frequently made, particularly in the American Press. On the first point, critics instance the case of Goa and point out that when Portugal brought the question of the Indian take-over of Goa before the Security Council, the African and Asian representatives refused to countenance any criticism of Indian actions, even though on the face of it these constituted a flagrant violation of the Charter. The African answer to this criticism is that by continuing to hold a colony on the Indian land-mass, and by refusing any attempt to negotiate, the Portuguese were in fact committing an aggression and India had the right to act the way she did. Though this argument has no legal standing in terms of the Charter, it has a certain logic and the case of Goa alone seems hardly sufficient to support a general charge of a double standard. On the other side, it should be remembered that the African states did not give unqualified support in the West Irian case to Indonesia (a state with which most of them had very close links and which had supported them on all important issues) but instead backed up the efforts being made to bring about negotiation and compromise and a solution through the United Nations. In general, therefore, it would seem that in this particular respect the African states are no better and no worse than any other group of states at the United Nations. The temptation in New York, as elsewhere, is for all states to apply quite different standards when judging their own actions or those of their allies, and if the African states fall short of the ideal so do most of the rest.

On the second point, there are persistent complaints in the Western Press that the African states go to extreme lengths to condemn every aspect of Western colonialism, but have nothing to say about the situation in Eastern Europe or about China's actions in Tibet and elsewhere. Though it is certainly true that the African states spend the vast proportion of their time in attacking the Western colonial Powers and that they are prepared to ally themselves with the Communist states in order to do so, the reasons for this attitude are surely obvious. In the first place, Western colonialism is something which they have experienced first-hand and which is of direct concern to them; most Africans have very little knowledge of how the Soviet Union has acted in Eastern Europe and feel in any case that it is not for them to take the initiative in such a question. Second, since their first concern is to get action over African questions, which in all cases involve the West, they cannot at the same time afford to alienate the Communist Powers whose support is vital. Third, whereas it is clear that pressure through the United Nations has some chance of getting action over the countries colonised by the West, it equally clearly has little chance of achieving action in Eastern Europe. That this is so is in fact a back-handed compliment to the West, and one which, in private at least, most African politicians will freely acknowledge.

The existence, even to this extent, of a double standard does not, however, prevent the African states from opposing the Soviet Union when they feel it necessary. Thus in 1960 they made it quite clear that they were not prepared to support the Soviet demand that Mr Hammarskjöld should be dismissed (even though they were very disturbed by his actions in the Congo) or the demand for a *troika* in the Secretariat (even though at a superficial level this would have given them more power). As a result, the Soviet Union was forced to climb down and the measures were defeated. Quite often when it appears that the African states are voting with the Soviet Union it is in fact the other way round, and the Soviet Union is following a lead given by the African states. In general too, a close look at the proceedings of the United Nations will show that in spite of the fact that most of the invective of the African states is reserved for the West, they are, in reality, in most cases much closer to the Western position than they are to any other, and much more influenced by Western tactics than they are by those of the Soviet bloc.

The third criticism, that the actions of the African states are distorting the United Nations itself, is much more difficult to discuss, if only because there are no fixed criteria by which to judge what the United Nations is or should be. The main complaint which people have in this context seems, however, to be that because Africa has come to independence in such a divided state, the African states have far more votes than either their financial or power position would warrant, and are therefore tempted to push through resolutions for which in the end they will not have to take the responsibility. It is clear, however, that those who drafted the Charter were well aware of this possibility, and that it was in order to guard against it that while all states

were given an equal voice and an equal vote in the General
Assembly, the Great Powers were given the veto in the Security
Council.[1] Thus, though the African states may by their numerical strength be able to get unwise recommendations through
the General Assembly, the Great Powers have an opportunity
to veto these before any really effective action can be taken.

But in the end criticisms of this kind usually boil down to
complaints that the African states, particularly over the Congo
question and in the current debate over Southern Africa, are
persistently forcing the United Nations into breaches of Article
2 (7) of the Charter, which prohibits the United Nations from
intervening in the domestic affairs of a country unless there is a
threat or breach of the peace or an aggression.

Though it is true that in baldly declaring that the secession of
Katanga must end, the final resolution passed by the Security
Council on the Congo situation did seem somewhat at odds
with the Charter, it is also true that this resolution was supported, or allowed to go through on an abstention, by the
United States and all other members of the Security Council.
If this resolution was therefore a 'distortion', those countries
which had the power to veto and did not use it were as responsible as the African states.

Over the issue of Southern Africa, there has certainly been an
increasing move to consider that questions of human rights and
self-determination do in fact merit more than talk at the United
Nations, and that persistent breaches of the human rights provisions in the Charter may in certain circumstances impose a
qualification on Article 2 (7). But as Dr Rosalyn Higgins points
out, this trend began long before the African states became
active, and it cannot therefore be wholly attributed to them.
The question now at issue at the United Nations is whether
South Africa's persistent breach of the human rights provisions
in the Charter, and her consistent refusal to obey any injunc-
tions of the Organisation, do in themselves constitute a threat to
the peace. If they do, the United Nations has every right to take
further action under the Charter; if they do not, then the
Organisation must be content for the moment with passing

[1] The fact that in 1950 the powers of the General Assembly were somewhat extended was not, of course, due to Afro-Asian pressure but to the
direct wish of the United States.

resolutions. Since the final decision on this will lie with the Western states in the Security Council, it can hardly be said (whichever way it goes) that the African states are distorting the processes of the United Nations. In this context it is perhaps worth pointing out that the Charter of the United Nations is not an entirely rigid document, and if the general trend in world opinion is towards a more flexible interpretation of Article 2 (7), then it is no distortion for the proceedings of the United Nations to reflect this change.

On all these questions it would seem, therefore, that the attitude of the African states at the United Nations is very similar to that of the other states, and that they are no more self-centred, prejudiced and irresponsible than the rest of the world community. Perhaps the main reason why they attract more criticism is because they use the United Nations more, but for that they can hardly be blamed.

This, then, is a brief account of the organisation and activity of the African states at the United Nations, and of the main criticisms which have been levelled against them. What conclusions can be drawn both about the past and for the future?

It is clear from what has been said that the United Nations plays a key role in the implementation of the foreign policy of the African states. It will be a long time before the OAU (even if its organisation grows in strength, and this is by no means certain) can put into the field even such a force as the United Nations mustered for the Congo operation, and until that time the United Nations is the only organisation which the African states can hope to persuade to act for them. At the same time, the occasional conferences of African and Asian states give nothing like the steady and regular platform for the views and preoccupations of the African leaders that is provided by the sessions of the United Nations and its various agencies. In addition, especially as the majority of African states cannot afford to set up embassies in all countries, the United Nations provides an extremely useful centre where they can keep in touch with each other and with the rest of the world. The African states have shown in practice that they will call on the United Nations when they feel themselves attacked by states outside Africa, as in the cases of the Congo and of Bizerta, and when they need to rally the rest of the world, as in the case of their current campaign against South Africa. It has yet to be shown whether they will call on the United Nations to mediate in intra-continental troubles, and the border dispute between Morocco and Algeria, where African rather than United Nations mediators were called in, suggests that they may not.[1]

The period since 1958 has seen the United Nations marked by an increasing preoccupation with African questions, and by a growth in African influence commensurate with the fact that at the beginning of 1964 there were 34 African members compared with the eight which were independent when the African group was first formed. Though the Congo operation is still the only case where one can point to direct United Nations action as a consequence of African pressure, there seems little doubt that African activity has led both to a concentration of international attention on the situation in the colonial territories and to the growing isolation of South Africa and Portugal in the world community. One of the most obvious of the achievements of the African states has undoubtedly been to accelerate discussion on and feeling over questions of human rights and self-determination, and the contrast between 1958, when a very mild resolution on Algeria was defeated in the General Assembly, and 1963, when the Security Council adopted unanimously a call for an arms boycott against South Africa, is striking. Perhaps the most important role of the African states in all this has been to act as a lobby within the Afro-Asian group and to push the Asians into more effective action.

Between 1958 and 1964 African activity has become steadily more effective and the influence of the African states has increased. The campaign this year will prove whether this influence has reached its maximum and will show whether the African states are yet strong enough to force the Western Powers into a position where they will endorse further action against South Africa. What happens seems likely to depend on a great number of arbitrary factors, such as the results of the elections in Britain and the United States, the extent to which China is prepared to become involved in Africa, and whether the United

---

[1] There is nothing, of course, in the Charter which insists that the UN should be asked to mediate on all occasions; indeed Art. 33 specifically recommends that regional organisations should be called in first.

Nations and the Great Powers are distracted by other disputes and conflicts. But what does happen may in the end prove decisive both for the position of Africa in the world and for the future of the United Nations itself.

50. The Charter of the Organization for African Unity

N. J. PADELFORD *International Organization* Vol. 18, No. 3, 1964
World Peace Foundation; pages 533–6

The instrument signed at Addis Ababa is a melange of the ideas and provisions found in the Charters of the United Nations, the Organization of American States, and the Monrovia Group. The Preamble reaffirms the principles of the United Nations and of the Universal Declaration of Human Rights. To promote the unity of the African states, eradicate colonialism, and provide a solid foundation for "peaceful and positive cooperation among states", the signatory powers agree to harmonize and coordinate their general policies in certain fields.

The membership of the Organization is to comprise each independent African state adhering to the Charter. All are to enjoy equal rights and duties. Among the principles to which the members agree to adhere are respect for the sovereignty and territorial integrity of each member, non-interference in the internal affairs of states, peaceful settlement of disputes, unreserved condemnation of political assassination and subversion, dedication to the total emancipation of the dependent African territories, and affirmation of a policy of non-alignment.

Four principal organs are provided for by the Charter. These are: (1) an Assembly of heads of state and government, (2) a Council of Ministers, (3) a General Secretariat, and (4) a Commission of Mediation, Conciliation, and Arbitration.

The Charter provides that "the supreme organ" of the Organization shall be the Assembly. This is to be composed of heads of all member states or governments, meeting at least once a year and in extraordinary session when approved by a majority. As in the UN, each state has one vote and resolutions require a two-thirds majority save for procedural matters. Among its functions, the Assembly is expected to harmonize policies and to review the acts of all other organs or agencies.

The Council of Ministers is to be composed of the foreign ministers or such other ministers as may be designated by the states. It is expected to meet at least twice each year and in special session when requested and approved by two-thirds of the members. It is responsible, among other things, for preparing the agenda for the annual Assembly, executing decisions of the latter, and coordinating intra-African cooperation under the guidance of the Assembly. This is a reversal of the roles envisioned in the scheme advanced by Mr Nkrumah. Resolutions are passed by a simple majority and there is no veto.

The Secretary-General is to be appointed as in the United Nations by the Assembly on recommendation of the Council of Ministers. Beyond indicating that he shall be "an administrative Secretary-General", the Charter does not spell out his powers or functions. In other words, these will be actions requested by the Assembly or Council and actions taken by the Secretary-General on his own which he may be able to persuade others to accept. At the present juncture when parties cannot agree upon a fully fledged Secretary-General and when experience is still lacking, it is premature to compare the role of this office with its counterparts in either the Organization of American States (OAS), the North Atlantic Treaty Organization (NATO), the Southeast Asia Treaty Organization (SEATO), or the UN. Basically, the design appears to have been drawn upon a more limited blueprint than the provisions of Chapter XV of the United Nations Charter. A comparison may possibly be made to the office of the Secretary-General of the League of Nations as conceived under the regime of Sir Eric Drummond—an international office of a high-level civil-servant type to carry out instructions rather than a guiding hand for the Organization as Secretary-General Dag Hammarskjöld came to visualize his role in the UN.

The member states pledge themselves to settle all disputes among themselves by peaceful means. To facilitate this a commission is to be formed under the direction and authorization of the Assembly. Provision is also made for other commissions as on economic and social affairs, education and cultural matters, health, sanitation and nutrition, defence, and scientific development and research. It is interesting to note that the parties did not provide for an African court of justice. This might tend to suggest that the concept of law is not advanced sufficiently to warrant the establishment of such an organ. It may be recalled, however, that neither the OAS nor most other regional arrangements, excepting the European Communities, have provided for such an institution. If a court of justice is deemed desirable in the future, this can of course be added through the amendment procedure provided that a majority of the member states are prepared to do so.

The budget is to be prepared by the Secretary-General and approved by the Council of Ministers and contributions are to be apportioned in accordance with the scale of the United Nations. Finally, provision was made for the instrument to enter into force when ratifications from two-thirds of the states had been deposited with the Government of Ethiopia, a step already achieved.

The Organization depends upon the willing cooperation of the member states. There are no sanctions to threaten them if they do not give this. There is no organ with disciplinary powers. No international force is provided for, to intervene in their territories if they do not fulfill the purposes of the Charter or comply with the resolutions of the Assembly or the Council of Ministers. The institutions are designed to promote cooperation, not to exact it; to urge collaboration, not to punish for its refusal.

The effectiveness of the Organization will obviously depend, as in the United Nations, on the measure of harmony that can be developed among the states. The only power implicit in the system is that of the opinion of the other states. This could become a force to compel recalcitrant or aggressive members to pause. As we shall see presently, this has already manifested itself in the criticism of the East African states for having invited British troops to help put down army mutinies, and in pressures upon the African and Malagasy Union (UAM) states to dissolve their political bloc.

There is a strong desire among the African states to keep their quarrels to themselves and not to allow situations to be used to advance the Cold War interests of outside nations. This may be an asset. But on the other hand the jealousies that still remain, as graphically illustrated in the complex attitudes associated with proposals to replace the UN force in the Congo with a purely African force, leave unresolved doubts as to what extent the African states can insulate the continent from the forces of world politics and keep their own disputes within limits.

One of the deep-seated apprehensions in Africa today is that some leader or combination of states will try to impose its will upon others in a new imperialism. This concern is expressed in the terms of Article 3 and again in the pledge exacted of members in Article 6 that they will carry out "scrupulously" the principles of non-interference and of respect for one another's territory.

One may be pardoned for raising a question about the ability of the OAU to hold its head above water financially in the light of the difficulties the UN has had. Payment of contributions is voluntary. There is no sanction comparable to Article 19 of the United Nations Charter providing for the loss of the right to vote if payments fall into arrears. If the bills do not become too onerous the Organization may have no trouble. But given the strong desires of some members for an active institution, there will be a tendency for the costs to creep up as they have elsewhere. So this will have to be watched with care.

Since the OAU is essentially a coordinating body, its principal organs will have to be supplemented by specific agencies in designated fields. It may perhaps be in these agencies that the foundation will be laid for an eventual further advance toward the politically powerful central organs which the Nkrumah plan envisioned but which the states were not ready to adopt in 1963. . . .

Maps

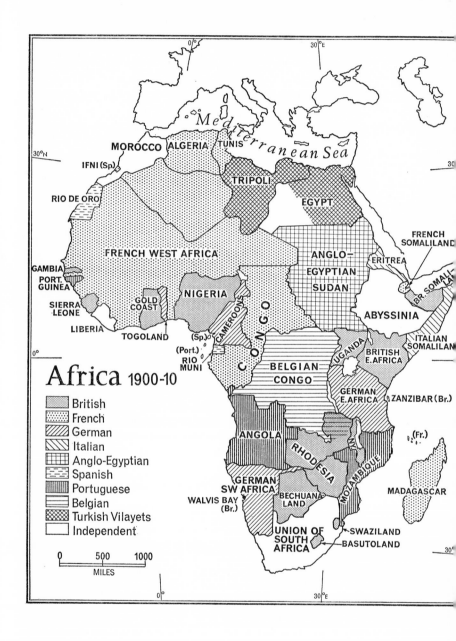

MOROCCO ALGERIA TUNIS

IFNI (Sp.)

RIO DE ORO

TRIPOLI

EGYPT

FRENCH SOMALILAND

FRENCH WEST AFRICA

ANGLO-
EGYPTIAN
SUDAN

ERITREA

BR. SOMALILAND

GAMBIA
PORT.
GUINEA

NIGERIA

SIERRA
LEONE

GOLD
COAST

LIBERIA

TOGOLAND

CAMEROONS

ABYSSINIA

ITALIAN
SOMALILAND

(Sp.)

(Port.)
RIO
MUNI

C O N G O

BELGIAN
CONGO

UGANDA

BRITISH
E. AFRICA

Africa 1900-10

British
French
German
Italian
Anglo-Egyptian
Spanish
Portuguese
Belgian
Turkish Vilayets
Independent

GERMAN
E. AFRICA

ZANZIBAR (Br.)

ANGOLA

RHODESIA

MOZAMBIQUE

(Fr.)

MADAGASCAR

GERMAN
SW AFRICA

WALVIS BAY
(Br.)

BECHUANA
LAND

0   500   1000

MILES

UNION OF
SOUTH
AFRICA

SWAZILAND

BASUTOLAND

Mediterranean Sea

30°N

0°

30°E

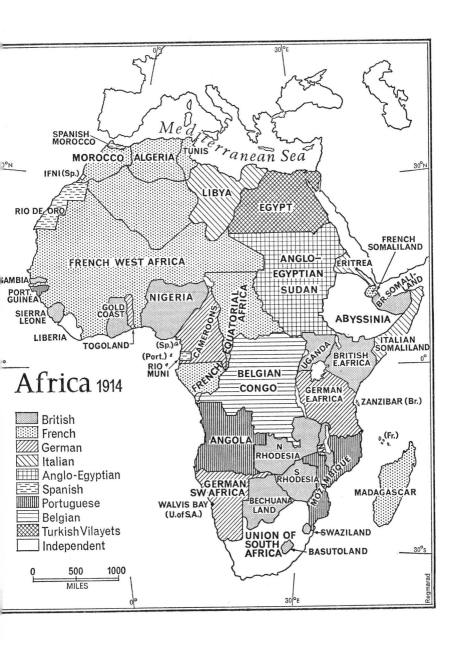

Africa 1914

SPANISH MOROCCO
IFNI (Sp.)
RIO DE ORO
MOROCCO
ALGERIA
TUNIS
LIBYA
EGYPT
Mediterranean Sea
FRENCH SOMALILAND
ERITREA
ANGLO-EGYPTIAN SUDAN
BR. SOMALI-LAND
FRENCH WEST AFRICA
GAMBIA
PORT. GUINEA
SIERRA LEONE
LIBERIA
GOLD COAST
NIGERIA
TOGOLAND
(Sp.)
(Port.)
RIO MUNI
CAMEROONS
FRENCH EQUATORIAL AFRICA
BELGIAN CONGO
FRENCH
ABYSSINIA
ITALIAN SOMALILAND
UGANDA
BRITISH E. AFRICA
GERMAN E. AFRICA
ZANZIBAR (Br.)
ANGOLA
N RHODESIA
S RHODESIA
MOZAMBIQUE
(Fr.)
MADAGASCAR
GERMAN SW AFRICA
WALVIS BAY (U. of S.A.)
BECHUANA LAND
SWAZILAND
UNION OF SOUTH AFRICA
BASUTOLAND

British
French
German
Italian
Anglo-Egyptian
Spanish
Portuguese
Belgian
Turkish Vilayets
Independent

0   500   1000
MILES

Regmarad

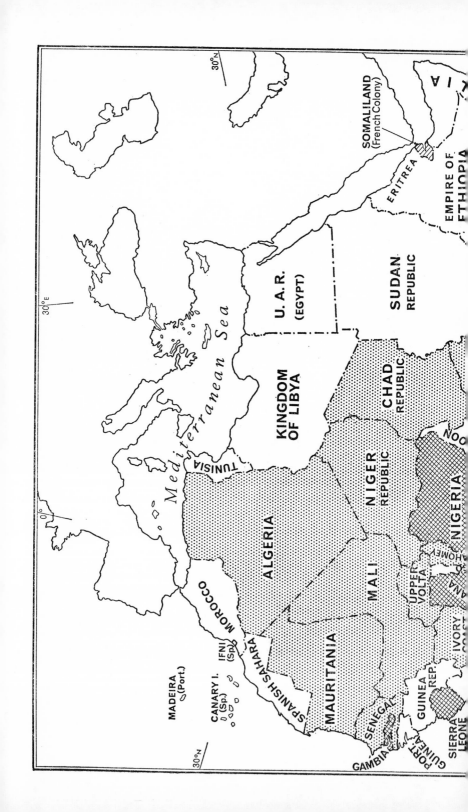

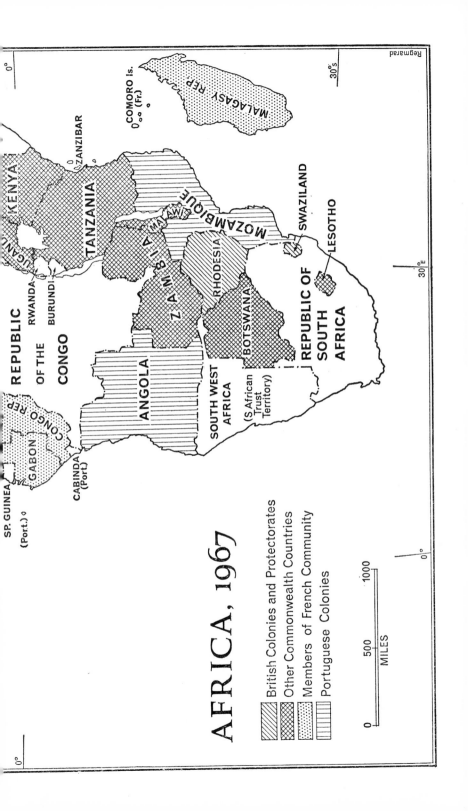

AFRICA, 1967

British Colonies and Protectorates
Other Commonwealth Countries
Members of French Community
Portuguese Colonies

0   500   1000
MILES

Select Bibliography

AJAYI, J. F. ADE 'Nineteenth Century Origins of Nigerian National-ism' *Journal of the Historical Society of Nigeria* Vol. II, 1961

APTER, DAVID E. *The Gold Coast in Transition* Princeton 1955

— *The Political Kingdom in Uganda* Princeton 1951

AWOLOWO, OBAFEMI *Awo : The Autobiography of Chief Obafemi Awolowo* Cambridge 1960

AZIKIWE, BENJAMIN NNAMDI *Zik: A Selection from the Speeches of Dr Nnamdi Azikiwe* Cambridge 1961

BARBOUR, NEVILLE *A Survey of Northwest Africa* London 1959

BELLO, AHMADU *My Life* Cambridge 1962

BENNETT, GEORGE *Kenya, A Political History: The Colonial Period* London 1963

BOURRET, F. M. *Ghana: The Road to Independence, 1919–1957* London 1960

CARTER, GWENDOLINE M. *The Politics of Inequality* London 1958

— *African One-Party States* Pall Mall 1962

DECREANE, PHILIPE *Table des Partis Politiques de l'Afrique* Paris 1963

DELF, GEORGE *Asians in East Africa* Oxford 1963

DESCHAMPS, HUBERT JULES *Les Méthodes et Doctrines Coloniales de la France* Paris 1953

DOXEY, G. V. *Industrial Colour Bar in South Africa* Oxford 1961

DRYSDALE, JOHN G. S. *The Somali Dispute* London 1964

GANN, LEWIS H. *The History of Northern Rhodesia: The Early Days to 1953* London 1964

GRAY, RICHARD *The Two Nations: Aspects of the Development of Race Relations in the Rhodesias and Nyasaland* London 1960

GUERNIER, EUGÈNE LEONARD (ed.) *Afrique équatoriale française* Paris 1950

HAHN, LORNA *North Africa: Nationalism to Nationhood* Public Affairs Press 1960

HANCOCK, W. KEITH *Survey of British Commonwealth Affairs; II: Problems of Economic Policy, 1918–1939* London 1942

HILLIARD, F. H. *A Short History of Education in British West Africa* London 1957

HODGKIN, THOMAS L. *Nationalism in Colonial Africa* London 1956
— *African Political Parties* London 1961
INGHAM, KENNETH *The Making of Modern Uganda* London 1958
— *The History of East Africa* London 1962
KERKEN, GEORGE S. VAN DER *La Politique coloniale Belge* Anvers 1943
KIMBLE, DAVID *A Political History of Ghana: The Rise of Gold Coast Colonialism, 1850–1928* Oxford 1963
LE CORNEC, JACQUES *Historie politique du Tchad, 1900–1962* Paris 1963
LEGUM, COLIN *Pan-Africanism: A Short Political Guide* London 1962
LEWIS, MARTIN D. 'One Hundred Million Frenchmen: The "Assimilation" Theory in French Colonial Policy' *Comparative Studies in Society and History* Vol. IV, 1962, pp. 129–53
LEYS, COLIN *European Politics in Southern Rhodesia* Oxford 1959
LOCKHART, J. G. and WOODHOUSE, C. M. *Rhodes* London 1963
LOW, D. ANTHONY 'Lion Rampant' *Journal of Commonwealth Political Studies* Vol. II, 1964, pp. 235–52
— and CRAWFORD PRATT, R. *Uganda and British Overrule, 1900–1955* London 1960
LUMUMBA, PHILIP *Congo, My Country* London 1962
MARLOWE, JOHN *Arab Nationalism and British Imperialism* New York 1961
MASON, PHILIP *The Birth of a Dilemma: The Conquest and Settlement of Rhodesia* London 1958
MBOYA, TOM *Freedom and After* London 1963
NASSER, GAMAL ABDUL *Egypt's Revolution: A Philosophy of the Revolution* Cairo 1958
NKRUMAH, KWAME *Ghana: An Autobiography* Edinburgh 1957
PERHAM, MARGERY *The Government of Ethiopia* London 1948
PICKLES, DAVID *Algeria and France* London 1963
ROBERTS, MARGARET *Mandate in Trust* London 1961
ROBINSON, KENNETH 'Political Development in French West Africa' *Africa in the Modern World* (ed. C. Stillman) Chicago 1955, pp. 140–81
ROUX, EDWARD *Time Longer than Rope* Wisconsin 1964
SENGLOR, LÉOPOLD SÉDAR *Nation et Voie Africaine du Socialisme* Paris 1961
SHEPPERSON, GEORGE A. and PRICE, THOMAS *Independent African: John Chilembwe and the Origins, Settings and Significance of the Nyasaland Native Rising of 1916* Edinburgh 1958

SHEPPERSON, GEORGE 'Negro American Influences in African Nationalism' *Journal of African History* Vol. 1, 1960

SITHOLE, NDABANINGI *African Nationalism* London 1957

STEER, GEORGE L. *Caesar in Abyssinia* London 1936

TATZ, C. M. *Shadow and Substance in South Africa* Natal 1962

THOMPSON, VIRGINIA and ADLOFF, RICHARD *The Emerging States of French Equatorial West Africa* Stansford 1960

WHEELOCK, KEITH *Nasser's New Egypt* London 1960

WILSON, CHARLES M. *Liberia* New York 1947

ZIÉGLÉ, HENRI *Afrique équatoriale française* Paris 1952

ZOLBERG, ARISTIDE R. *One-Party Government in the Ivory Coast* Princeton 1964

Chronological Table

The following list of dates is intended only as a guide and is not exhaustive. In order to facilitate an understanding of comparative trans-continental developments the following events have been listed in chronological order rather than by country or region.

1900 (22 April)	Rabah defeated and killed by three converging French forces
1900 (8 September)	France establishes military territory of countries and protectorates in western and equitorial Africa of Chad
1902	Portugal occupies Gorongosa district in Moçambique
1902	Ashanti becomes a British Crown Colony
1902	Lugard completes conquest of Hausaland
1903	Tunis—Habib Bourguiba born
1903	Unsuccessful revolt (against Portuguese) of Mutu ya Kirela, Chief of Bailundu, in Angola
1904	Benjamin Nnamdi Azikiwe born
1904	Anglo-French 'Entente'—frontier revisions
1904	Portuguese defeat Cuanhama warriors at battle of Roçados in Angola
1905	French agreement on Algerian border with Mali and Niger
1905–1907	Maji-Maji rebellion in East Africa
1906	French occupation of Wadai
1906	Railway link with Northern Rhodesia as far as Broken Hill
1907	Negotiations officially begin on Belgian annexation of Congo
1908	Italian-Ethiopian Convention for frontier settlement

1908	Leopold gives up claim to *Fondation de la Couronne*; Belgium assumes control of Congo Independent State (Colonial Charter)
1909	Obafemi Awolowo born
1909	Death of Leopold II
1910	Control of Chad taken over by Federation Equatoriale Afrique
1911 (3 October)	Italian attack on Tripoli
1911	South Africa—Native Labour Regulation Act (Mines and Works Act)
1911	North-eastern and North-western provinces united to form Northern Rhodesia
1911–1912	Italian occupation of Cyrenaica
1912 (October)	Treaty of Ouchy (Sultan of Tripoli and Italy)
1912	Abubakr Tafawa Balewa born
1912	Abolition of Moroccan slave trade
1912	Portuguese defeat Mataka (Yao), thus completing subjugation of Moçambique
1913	South Africa—Native Land Act
1913	British government recognizes Belgian annexation of the Congo
1913–1914	French occupation of Tibesti
1914	British and French occupy Togo and attack Germans in Cameroon
1915	Malagasy—Secret Society formed in Malagasy (V.V.S.)
1915	Chilembwe uprising in Nyasaland
1917	Fu'ād follows brother Husayn as Sultan of Egypt
1918	South Africa given mandate over South West Africa
1918	Togo and Cameroon become mandates of the League of Nations
1919	Sa'id Zughlūl of Egypt rebuffed by Britain and sent to Malta

1919	Muhammed Ali (Egypt) sets up council to manage transactions between Treasury and European merchants
1921 (July)	Italy appoints Giuseppe Volpi Governor of Tripolitania
1922 (27 October)	Europeans in Southern Rhodesia choose responsible government rather than admission to Union of South Africa (by 8771 votes to 5989)
1922	Restructured legislature in Nigeria (four elected African representatives)
1922	Fu'ād of Egypt proclaimed *malik* (king)
1923 (12 September)	Southern Rhodesia formally annexed to British crown
1923	H. S. H. Macaulay forms Nigerian National Democratic Party
1923	Tunis—French citizenship offered to 'qualified' Tunisians
1924 (July)	Treaty of London, ceding Jubaland to Italy (implemented 1925)
1924	Restructured legislature in Sierra Leone (three elected African representatives)
1925	South Africa—Wage Act
1925	Restructured legislature in Gold Coast (three elected African representatives)
1925	Enstoolment of Prempeh II of the Asantahene at Kumasi
1925–1926	Société Amicale des Originaires de l'Afrique Equatoriale Française formed in Paris by André Matswa
1926	Association of North African Muslim Students formed
1926	Mohammed Ghazi starts first free school of nationalists in Fès, in Morocco
1926	British Native Authorities Ordinance gives indirect rule to Tanganyika
1926	South African Mines and Works Amendment Act

1926	A. Chester Beatty reconstitutes Selection Trust in South Africa
1926–1939	Open warfare in French Morocco
1927	Moroccan Students Union and Supporters of Truth collaborate in new organization, the Moroccan League
1928	Rhodesian Anglo-American Company incorporated
1928	Ras Tafari uncrowned ruler of Ethiopia
1928	Italian–Ethiopian Treaty of Friendship (reaffirmed 1934)
1928	In Egypt, Muhammed Ali sets up a larger council on same principle as 1919
1929	Joseph K. K. B. Danquah and Casely Hayford form Gold Coast Youth Conference
1929	Committee of National Action formed by Moroccan League
1930	Moroccan Committee of National Action enacts *dahir*
1930	Northern Rhodesia gets indirect rule
1930	Land Apportionment Act in Southern Rhodesia prohibits Africans from living in white settler areas
1930	Ras Tafari crowned Haile Selassie I of Ethiopia
1931	Tunis Congress (North African Muslim Students)
1932	Algiers Congress (Association of North African Muslim Students)
1932	Tunis—*L'Action Tunisienne* inaugurated by Bourguiba
1932	Rabat Congress of North African Muslim Students forbidden, instead held in Paris
1932	Movement of Moroccan Scouts founded
1933	Morocco—Chekib Arslan and Mohammed Hassan Ouazzani start French-language newspaper in Fès—*L'Action du Peuple*

1933		Nyasaland gets indirect rule
1934	(March)	New party in Tunis, the Neo-Destour, formed
1934		Ethiopian groups attack Italian consulate at Gondar
1934		Moroccan King visits Fès
1934		Allal Al-Fassi received by King Mohammed V
1934	(5 December)	Walwal incident in Ethiopia
1934		Plan of Reforms presented to Moroccan King by nationalists
1935	(October)	Italian invasion of Abyssinia
1936		Anglo-Egyptian treaty: withdrawal of British troops from Canal Zone
1936		Formation of Nigerian Youth Movement
1936–1937		General Noguès grants amnesty to Moroccan political parties
1936		Morocco Congress formed (Association of North African Muslim Students)
1936		Algeria—failure to provide for easier access of Moslem élite to citizenship
1937		South Africa—Industrial Conciliation Act
1938		Twenty thousand Italians settle in Tripoli and Cyrenaica
1941		British defeat Italians in Ethiopia
1941		British (General Wavell) capture Benghazi
1943	(23 January)	Britain occupies Tripoli city, Italians ousted from North Africa
1943		Somaliland—Somali Youth League (S.Y.L.) founded
1944		National Council of Nigeria and the Cameroons under leadership of Nnamdi Azikiwe
1944		Brazzaville conference
1945	(May)	Algeria—Sétif revolt
1945		French union of West Africa created by decree
1946		Northern Rhodesia—Formation of African Representative Council

1946	Loi Lamire Guèye passed (all subjects in French West Africa become citizens without renunciating the right to have personal affairs regulated by customary law)
1946	Foundation of Rassemblement démocratique africain (R.D.A.) in Bamako
1946	Breakaway of Bloc démocratique Sénégalais (B.D.S.) from the S.F.I.O. (French Socialist Party) in Senegal
1946	New constitution in Nigeria
1947 (29 March)	Revolt against France in Malagasy led by sections of M.D.R.M.
1947	Algerian Statute passed
1947	United Gold Coast Convention (U.G.C.C.) founded in Accra (Dr Nkrumah appointed secretary)
1947 (18 March)	Franco-Algerian cease-fire agreement signed
1948	Malagasy—Mouvement Démocratique de la Renovation Malgache (M.D.R.M.) and Parti des Déshérités de Madagascar (P.A.D.E.S.M.) formed
1948	Dr D. F. Malan forms National Party Government, in coalition with Afrikaner Party (Mr N. C. Havenga)
1948	Northern Rhodesia—Formation of Northern Rhodesian African Congress, Godwin A. M. Lewanika elected first President
1949	South Africa—Prohibition of Mixed Marriages Act
1949	Kwame Nkrumah founds Convention People's Party in Ghana
1949	Four African members added to Governor's Executive Council (the Director of Medical Services was already an African) in Nigeria
1950	South African Immorality Act, 1927, Amendment Act

1950	South Africa—Population Registration Act
1950	Somalia becomes Trust Territory
1951 (December)	Libya becomes independent under Sayyed Mohammed Idriss el Senussi
1951	Somaliland—Somaliland National League (S.N.L.) assumes modern form
1951	Action Group gains large majority of seats in Western Nigerian House of Assembly
1952–1959	Mau Mau rebellion in Kenya
1952	Nigeria—MacPherson constitution in operation. First Parliament meets
1952 (25 July)	Egypt—Naguib in Alexandria and Nasser in Cairo assume control. King Farouk leaves Egypt
1953	South Africa—Native Labour (Settlement of Disputes) Act
1953 (February)	Nigeria—Nationalist Independent Party (N.I.P.) formed, led by Professor Eyo Ita
1953 (21 May)	Nigeria—Constitution withdrawn
1953 (18 June)	Egypt proclaims Republic with Mohammed Naguib as President and Prime Minister, Nasser as deputy Prime Minister
1953 (23 July)	Revolution in Egypt
1953	Sudan—Azhari's Egyptian-supported National Unionist Party win clear majority. Azhari becomes Prime Minister (1954)
1953	South Africa—National majority increased to twenty-nine
1953	Federation of Rhodesia and Nyasaland comes into being
1954	Southern Rhodesia—Native Industrial Workers Unions Bill, also Industrial Conciliation Bill
1954 (January)	Nigeria—Basis of Federation established
1954–1955	Start of Algerian revolution

1954	Tanganyika—Julius Nyerere and Oscar Kambona form Tanganyika National African Union
1954	Nigeria—National Council win election (72 out of 97 seats)
1954	Nigeria—Dr Azikiwe Premier of Eastern Region
1954 (October)	Ibrahim Shelhi, Controller of the Royal Libyan Household, assassinated. General divestment of royal titles
1954 (29 November)	Somaliland—Anglo-Ethiopian agreement returning the Haud and other reserve areas
1954	Gold Coast obtains self-government
1955	Uganda—Progressive Party formed by E. M. K. Mulira
1955	Togo—Semi-autonomous government granted
1955	Ethiopia—Constitution promulgated
1955	Somaliland—National United Front (N.U.F.) formed
1956 (1 January)	Sudan becomes a Republic
1956	Loi-cadre passed permitting establishment of semi-autonomous governments in A.O.F.
1956	Uganda—Democratic (Catholic) Party formed by Matias Mugwanya
1956	Parti Social Démocrate (P.S.D.) founded in Malagasy by Philibert Tsiranana
1956	Madagascar Congress and Independence Party (A.K.F.M.) founded
1956	South Africa—Industrial Conciliation Act amended
1956 (May)	Unification of British Togoland with Ghana following plebiscite
1956	South Africa—Bantu Education Act. Transkei Constitution Act
1957	Ghana becomes independent
1957 (January)	Creation of Union générale des travailleurs d'Afrique noire (U.G.T.A.N.)

1957 (August)	Nigeria—Alhaji Abubakar Tafawa Balewa appointed first Prime Minister
1957	Nigerian House of Representatives demand independence by 1959
1958	Uganda—first elections to Legislative Council
1958	Uganda People's Union formed
1958	South Africa—Nationalist Party majority increased to twenty-nine
1958 (April)	Conference of Independent African States in Accra
1958 (April)	French Togo elections bring to power Sylvanus Olympio
1958 (August)	South Africa—Dr H. F. Verwoerd succeeds Mr J. G. Strydom as Prime Minister
1958 (August)	Nigeria—Report of the Minorities Commission under chairmanship of Sir Henry Willink
1958	Togo—C.U.T. (Comité de l'Unité Togolaise) assumes power
1958	Referendum in French Africa. Only Guinea, under Sékou Touré, votes 'no' to French link
1958	Sudan—General Ibrahim 'Abbud seizes the government
1959	South Africa—Promotion of Bantu Self-Government Act
1959	Nigeria—Federal elections, Balewa reappointed Prime Minister, leading coalition government
1959 (May)	Ivory Coast. Sanwi independence movement established under Chief Amon Ndoufou III
1959	Foundation of Ivory Coast Republic
1959	Revolt in the Congo
1960 (March)	Uganda People's Congress formed (union of U.P.U. and Obote's wing of the Congress)
1960	Federation of Mali formed
1960 (June)	Somalia becomes independent

1960 (August)	Break-up of Federation of Mali
1960 (1 October)	Nigeria becomes independent
1960	Conference on Kenya in London (Lancaster House)
1960	Malagasy becomes independent—Tsiranana first President
1960	Mauritania becomes independent
1961 (29–30 May)	South Africa—African strike
1961	Jomo Kenyatta released from prison in Kenya
1961	Sierra Leone becomes independent
1961	Tanganyika becomes independent
1962	Ethiopia—Constitution promulgated
1962	Uganda becomes independent
1963 (January)	Assassination of Olympio in Togo
1963 (May)	African summit meeting at Addis Ababa
1963 (October)	Niamey Convention
1963 (October)	Dahomey—Parti dahoméen de l'unité (under Hubert Maga) overthrown by military coup under Col. Christopher Soglo
1963	Kenya becomes independent
1963	Break-up of Federation of Rhodesias and Nyasaland
1963	Northern Rhodesia becomes independent state of Zambia. Kenneth Kaunda first Prime Minister and President
1963	Nyasaland becomes independent state of Malawi. Hastings Banda first Prime Minister
1964 (July)	Second O.A.U. summit meeting at Cairo
1964 (October)	Maghreb reconciliation meeting at Tunis
1964	Zanzibar mergers with Tanganyika to form Tanzania, under President Nyerere
1965 (11 November)	Rhodesia—Unilateral Declaration of Independence
1 January 1966	In Central African Republic President Dacko is overthrown

15 January 1966	In Nigeria the army seizes power. Assassination of the Federal Prime Minister and the Premiers of the Northern and Western Regions
24 February 1966	In Ghana the army, under General Ankra, dismisses President Nkrumah
23 May 1966	In Uganda, Dr Obote charges the Kabaka of Buganda with treason; Palace occupied and over 1,000 people killed
6 July 1966	Malawi becomes a Republic within the Commonwealth; Dr Hastings Banda the first President
18 July 1966	International Court ruling on South West Africa
29 July 1966	Mutiny of Nigerian army. General Ironsi replaced by Colonel Gowon as head of Government
6 September 1966	Assassination in Parliament of Dr Verwoerd, Prime Minister of South Africa
30 September 1966	Bechuanaland becomes the Republic of Botswana within the Commonwealth; Sir Seretse Khama the first President
4 October 1966	Basutoland becomes the Kingdom of Lesotho ruled by King Moshoeshoe
29 November 1966	Republic proclaimed in Burundi; King Mtare overthrown
28 December 1966	In Lesotho King Moshoeshoe placed under house arrest

Index

K1cta